Politics in Mexico

D0647516

Politics in Mexico

The Democratic Consolidation

Fifth Edition

RODERIC AI CAMP

New York   Oxford
OXFORD UNIVERSITY PRESS
2007

Oxford University Press, Inc., publishes works that further Oxford University's
objective of excellence in research, scholarship, and education

Oxford   New York
Auckland   Cape Town   Dar es Salaam   Hong Kong   Karachi
Kuala Lumpur   Madrid   Melbourne   Mexico City   Nairobi
New Delhi   Shanghai   Taipei   Toronto

With offices in
Argentina   Austria   Brazil   Chile   Czech Republic   France   Greece
Guatemala   Hungary   Italy   Japan   Poland   Portugal   Singapore
South Korea   Switzerland   Thailand   Turkey   Ukraine   Vietnam

Published by Oxford University Press, Inc.
198 Madison Avenue, New York, New York, 10016
http://www.oup.com

Library of Congress Cataloging-in-Publication Data

Camp, Roderic Ai.
    Politics in Mexico : the democratic consolidation / Roderic Ai Camp.—5th ed.
        p. cm.
    Includes bibliographical references and index.
    ISBN-13: 978-0-19-531332-1 (pbk. : alk. paper)
    ISBN 0-19-531332-1 (pbk. : alk. paper)
        1. Mexico—Politics and government. I. Title.

JL1281.C35 2006
306.20972—dc21

                                                              2006045330

Printing number: 9 8 7 6 5 4 3 2 1

Printed in the United States of America
on acid-free paper

To Donald T. Butler,
master teacher and mentor

Contents

Acknowledgments

Anyone who has been in the business of teaching eventually writes a mental textbook, constantly revised and presented orally in a series of lectures. As teachers, however, we often dream of writing just the right book for our special interest or course. Such a book naturally incorporates our own biases and objectives. It also builds on the knowledge and experiences of dozens of other teachers. While still a teenager, I thought of being a teacher and, perhaps unusually, a college professor. Teachers throughout my life, at all levels of my education, influenced this choice. They also affected the way in which I teach, my interpersonal relationship with students, and my philosophy of learning and life. To these varied influences, I offer heartfelt thanks and hope that this work, in some small way, repays their contributions to me personally and professionally and to generations of other students.

Among those special teachers, I want to mention Thelma Roberts and Helen Weishaupt, who devoted their lives to the betterment of young children, instilling worthy values and beliefs and setting admirable personal examples, and to Mrs. Lloyd, for numerous afternoon conversations at Cambridge School. I wish to thank Ralph Corder and Don Fallis, who encouraged my natural interest in history toward a more specific interest in social studies. Sharon Williams and Richard W. Gully, my toughest high school teachers, introduced me to serious research and to the joys of investigating intellectual issues; and Inez Fallis, through four years of Spanish, prompted my continued interest in Mexico. Robert V. Edwards and Katharine Blair stressed the importance of communication, orally and in writing, helping me understand essential ingredients in the process of instruction. My most challenging professor, Dr. Bergel, during a high school program at Chapman College, opened my eyes to Western civilization and to the intellectual feast that broad interdisciplinary teaching could offer.

For his humanity, advice, and skill with the English language, I remain indebted to George Landon. As a mentor in the classroom and a model researcher, Mario Rodríguez led me to the Library of Congress and to the joys of archival research. On my arrival in Arizona, Paul Kelso took me under his wing, contributing vastly to my knowledge of Mexico and the out-of-doors, sharing a rewarding social life with his wife, Ruth. I learned more about Latin America and teaching in the demanding classrooms of George A. Brubaker and Edward J. Williams. Both convinced me of the importance of clarity, teaching writing as well as substance. Finally, Charles O. Jones and Clifton Wilson set examples in their seminars of what I hoped to achieve as an instructor.

Indirectly, I owe thanks to hundreds of students who have graced my classrooms and responded enthusiastically, sometimes less so, to my interpretations of Mexican politics. I am equally indebted to Bill Beezley, David Dent, Oscar Martínez, Steve Mumme, Kenneth Greene, and Edward J. Williams, devoted teachers and scholars, who offered many helpful suggestions for this book.

Politics in Mexico

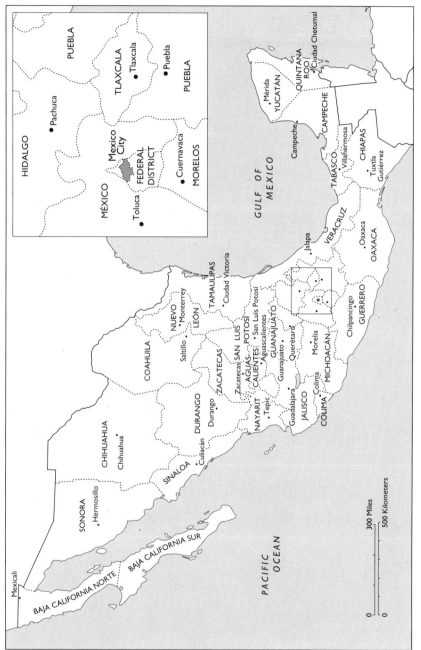

Mexico General Political Map, States and Capitals

1

Mexico in Comparative Context

> The contours of political development in modern Mexico often appear clearer and more pronounced when viewed as the products of tension among three key ideological traditions—namely, corporatism, pluralism, and Marxism. For its advocates, corporatism offers a humanistic alternative to both interest group liberalism identified with the United States and other western democracies, and communism as practiced in China, Cuba, North Korea, or the former Soviet union.
>
> GEORGE W. GRAYSON, *Mexico: From Corporatism to Pluralism?*

An exploration of a society's politics is, by nature, all-encompassing. Political behavior and political processes are a reflection of a culture's evolution, involving history, geography, values, ethnicity, religion, internal and external relationships, and much more. As social scientists, we often pursue topics of current political interest, ignoring the medley of influences from the past.

Naturally, each person tends to examine another culture's characteristics, political or otherwise, from his or her own society's perspective. This is not only a product of ethnocentrism, thinking of one's society as superior to the next person's, for which we Americans are often criticized, but also a question of familiarity. Although we often are woefully ignorant of our own society's political processes and institutions, being more familiar with the mythology than actual practice, we become accustomed to our way of doing things in our own country.[1]

I will attempt to explain Mexican politics, building on this natural proclivity to relate most comfortably to our own political customs, by drawing on implied as well as explicit comparisons with the United States. This comparison is further enhanced by the fact that Mexico and the United States have been joined together in a free-trade agreement since January 1994. We also are products of a more comprehensive western European civilization, into which other traditions are gradually making significant inroads. Some

1

critics suggest that we have relied too exclusively on Western traditions in our education; nevertheless they are unquestionably the primary source of our political values. Thus our familiarity with political processes, if it extends at all beyond United States boundaries, is typically that of the western European nations and England.[2] For recent immigrants, of course, that heritage is different. Again, where possible, comparisons will be made with some of these political systems in order to place the Mexican experience in a larger context. Finally, Mexico is a Third World country, a category into which most countries fall, and hence its characteristics deserve to be compared with characteristics we might encounter elsewhere in the Third World.

WHY COMPARE POLITICAL CULTURES?

The comparison of political systems is an exciting enterprise. One reason that the study of politics in different societies and time periods has intrigued inquiring minds for generations is the central question, Which political system is best? Identifying the "best" political system, other than its merely being the one with which you are most familiar and consequently comfortable, is, of course, a subjective task. It depends largely on what you want out of your political system. The demands made on a political system and its ability to respond efficiently and appropriately to them are one way of measuring its effectiveness.

Throughout the twentieth century, perhaps the major issue attracting the social scientist, the statesperson, and the average, educated citizen is which political system contributes most positively to economic growth and societal development. From an ideological perspective, much of international politics since World War II has focused primarily on that issue. As Peter Klarén concluded,

> U.S. policymakers searched for arguments to counter Soviet claims that Marxism represented a better alternative for development in the Third World than did Western capitalism. At the same time U.S. scholars began to study in earnest the causes of underdevelopment. In particular scholars asked why the West had developed and why most of the rest of the world had not.[3]

The two political systems most heavily analyzed since 1945 have been democratic capitalism and Soviet-style socialism. Each has its pluses and minuses, depending on individual values and perspectives. Given recent events in eastern Europe and the breakup of the Soviet state, socialism is in decline. Nevertheless, socialism as a model is not yet dead, nor is it likely to be in the future. Administrators of the socialist model, rather than the weaknesses inherent in the ideology, can always be blamed for its failures. Furthermore, it is human nature to want alternative choices in every facet of life. Politics is just one facet, even if somewhat all-encompassing. The history of humankind reveals a continual competition between alternative political models.

In short, whether one chooses democratic capitalism, a fresh version of socialism, or some other hybrid ideological alternative, societies and citizens will continue to search for the most viable political processes to bring about economic and social benefits. Because most of the earth's peoples are economically underprivileged, they want immediate results. Often, politicians from less fortunate nations seek a solution through emulating wealthier (First World) nations. Mexico's leaders and its populace are no exception to this general pattern.

One of the major issues facing Mexico's leaders is the nature of its capitalist model, and the degree to which Mexico should pursue a strategy of economic development patterned after that of the United States. Since 1988 they have sought to alter many traditional relationships between government and the private sector, increasing the influence of the private sector in an attempt to reverse Mexico's economic crisis and stimulate economic growth. In fact, Mexico received international notice in the 1990s for the level and pace of change under President Carlos Salinas de Gortari.[4]

In public statements and political rhetoric, Salinas called for economic and political modernization. He explicitly incorporated political with economic change, even implying a linkage.[5] Thus, he advocated economic liberalization, which he defined as increased control of the economy by the private sector, more extensive foreign investment, and internationalization of the Mexican economy through expanded trade and formal commercial relationships with the United States and Canada. Simultaneously, Salinas advocated political liberalization, which he defined as including more citizen participation in elections, greater electoral competition, and integrity in the voting process—all features associated with the United States and European liberal political traditions. In reality, he did little to implement democratic change, preferring instead to retain power in the hands of the presidency.

Salinas's successor, Ernesto Zedillo, who took office on December 1, 1994, inherited a political system in transition and an economic situation that shortly turned into a major financial and political crisis. A combination of economic decisions and an unsettled political context led to capital flight and a significant decline in investor confidence in the Mexican economy. Accordingly, Mexico began pursuing a severe austerity program, exceeding even those in the 1980s during a time of severe recession. By 1997, however, Mexican economic indicators showed strong growth, even if those results were not translated into improved income levels for most Mexicans. Investor confidence in Mexico returned. Zedillo continued to pursue an economic liberalization strategy and increase the pace of political reforms compared to his predecessor. Strong doubts about neoliberal economic policies remain from various quarters, however, generating some nationalistic, anti–United States sentiments. Nevertheless, when he left office in 2000, President Zedillo transferred a healthy economy to his successor, the first president in decades to do so. More importantly, he succeeded in creating a competitive electoral arena, administered by autonomous institutional actors, which witnessed the landmark election of Vicente Fox, the first opposition party candidate to defeat the Institutional Revolutionary Party (PRI) in a presidential race.

Vicente Fox, a former businessman, and representative of the National Action Party, formed a bipartisan cabinet and aggressively pursued a neoliberal economic model, including closer trade ties with the United States. His actions as president legitimized democratic practices and the rule of law. Mexicans voted for Fox because he represented change, and most importantly, they wanted increased personal security from crime and improvement in their standard of living.[6] The failures of the Fox administration however, have contributed to an increased level of frustration with, and a lack of confidence in, the democratic process. It remains to be seen in the presidential contest of 2006 just how Mexican voters will express their concerns through the candidates and parties they support, how existing parties may react, and what new parties or movements might emerge.

It is hotly debated among social scientists whether a society's political model determines its economic success or whether its economic model produces its political characteristics. Whether capitalism affects the behavior of a political model or whether a political model is essential to successful capitalism leads to the classic chicken-and-egg argument. It may well be a moot point because the processes are interrelated in terms of not only institutional patterns but cultural patterns as well.[7]

The comparative study of politics reveals, to some extent, a more important consideration. If the average Mexican is asked to choose between more political freedom or greater economic growth, as it affects him or her personally, the typical choice is the latter.[8] This is true in other Third World countries too. People with inadequate incomes are much more likely to worry about bread-and-butter than about more political freedom. A country's political model becomes paramount, however, when its citizens draw a connection between economic growth (as related to improving their own standard of living) and the political system. If they believe the political system, and not just the leadership itself, is largely responsible for economic development, it will have important repercussions on their political attitudes and their political behavior. If Mexicans draw such a connection, it will change the nature of their demands on the political leadership and system, and the level and intensity of their participation.[9]

The comparative study of societies provides a framework by which we can measure the advantages and disadvantages of political models as they affect economic growth. Of course, economic growth itself is not the only differentiating consequence. Some political leaders are equally concerned, in some cases more concerned, with social justice. Social justice may be interpreted in numerous ways. One way is to think of it as a means of redistributing wealth. For example, we often assume that economic growth—the percentage by which a society's economic productivity expands in a given time period—automatically conveys equal benefits to each member of the society. More attention is paid to the level of growth than to its beneficiaries. It is frequently the case that the lowest-income groups benefit least from economic growth. This has been true in the United States, but is even more noticeable in Third World and Latin American countries. In Latin American countries, a fourth of national income goes to only 5 percent of the population, and 40 percent goes to the richest 10 percent. "Only two out of ten individuals think distribution is just or very just, while the remaining eight say it is unjust or very unjust."[10] There are periods, of course, when economic growth produces greater equality in income distribution.[11] Per capita income figures (national income divided by total population) can be deceiving

---

Social justice: a concept focusing on each citizen's quality of life and the equal treatment of all citizens.

---

because they are averages. In Mexico, for example, even during the remarkable sustained growth of the 1950s and 1960s, the real purchasing power (ability to buy goods and services) of the working classes actually declined.[12] Higher-income groups increased their proportion of national income from the 1970s through the 1990s, decades of economic crisis, while that of the lower-income groups fell.[13] This pattern has been further exacerbated since early 1995. Although the percentage of Mexicans who are not poor has remained at approximately 57 percent of the population from 1984 to 1999, the number of Mexicans who have fallen into the category of extreme poverty has nearly doubled, from 16 percent in 1992 to 28 percent in 1999.[14] The importance of social justice to Mexicans, defined as redistribution of wealth, is illustrated by the fact that one-fourth of Mexicans surveyed in 1998 consider it to be the second most important task of democracy.[15]

Another way of interpreting social justice is on the basis of social equality. This does not mean that all people are equal in ability but that each person should be treated equally under the law. Social justice also implies a leveling of differences in opportunities to succeed, giving each person equal access to society's resources. Accordingly, its allocation of resources can be a measure of a political system.

The degree to which a political system protects the rights of all citizens is another criterion by which political models can be compared. In Mexico, where human rights abuses are a serious problem, the evidence is unequivocal that the poor are much more likely to be the victims than are members of the middle and upper classes. This is why the arrest of Raúl Salinas, brother of the former president, as the alleged mastermind of a political assassination, was such a dramatic departure from past practices. This also helps to explain why only a fifth of all Mexicans have any confidence in their court system.[16] The same can be said about many societies, but there are sharp differences in degree between highly industrialized nations and Third World nations.[17]

From a comparative perspective, then, we may want to test the abilities of political systems to reduce both economic and social inequalities. It is logical to believe that among the political models in which the population has a significant voice in making decisions, the people across the board obtain a larger share of the societal resources. On the other hand, it is possible to argue, as in the case of Cuba, that an authoritarian model can impose more widespread, immediate equality in the distribution of resources, even in the absence of economic growth, while reducing the standard of living for formerly favored groups.

Regarding social justice and its relationship to various political models, leaders also are concerned with the distribution of wealth and resources *among* nations, not just within an individual nation. The choice of a political model, therefore, often involves international considerations. Such considerations are particularly important to countries that achieved independence in the twentieth century, especially after 1945. These countries want to achieve not only economic but also political and cultural independence. Mexico, like most of Latin America, achieved political independence in the early nineteenth century, but it found itself in the shadow of an extremely powerful neighbor. Its proximity to the United States eventually led to its losing half of its territory and many natural resources.

A third means to compare political models is their ability to remake a citizenry, to alter political, social, and economic attitudes. A problem faced by most nations, especially in their infancy, is building a sense of nationalism. A sense of nationalism is difficult to erase, even after years of domination by another power, as in the case of the Soviet Union and the Baltic republics, but it is equally difficult to establish, especially in societies incorporating diverse cultural, ethnic, and religious heritages.[18] The political process can be used to mold citizens, to bring about a strong sense of national unity, while lessening or dampening local and regional loyalties. The acceptability of a political model, its very legitimacy among the citizenry, is a measure of its effectiveness in developing national sensibilities. Mexico, which had an abiding sense of regionalism, struggled for many decades to achieve a strong sense of national unity and pride.[19] In fact, a recent analysis by the Inter-American Development Bank argues that while Latin America ranks low in an index of ethnolinguistic fragmentation (level of ethnic and linguistic differences) compared with Africa, East Asia, and Asia, it is geographically (based on ecozones) the most fragmented region in the world. As the Bank argues, culture usually differs widely in different ecozones, and therefore geographic fragmentation is an important dimension of social conflict.[20] On the other hand, Mexico did not have sharp religious and ethnic differences, characteristic of other cultures such as India, to overcome.

Many scholars have suggested that the single most important issue governing relationships among nations in the twenty-first century will be that of the haves versus the have nots.[21] In fact, Mexico's linkage to the United States and Canada in a free-trade agreement highlights this point. One of the arguments against such an agreement was the impossibility of eliminating trade barriers between a nation whose per capita wage is one-seventh of the per capita wage of the other nation.[22] One of the arguments for such an agreement was that it could temper this disparity. More importantly, it might reduce the increasing numbers of Mexicans seeking work in the United States, which is why President Fox has proposed a guest worker program to address the controversial issue of immigration reform.

The dichotomy between rich and poor nations is likely to produce immense tensions in the future; yet the problems that both sets of nations face are remarkably similar. As the 1990 *World Values Survey* illustrates, an extraordinary movement in the coincidence of some national beliefs is afoot, for example, in the realm of ecology. This survey, which covers forty countries, discovered that from 1981 to 1990 an enormous change in concern about environmental issues occurred in poor as well as rich nations. Other problems that most countries share—regardless of their standard of living or political system—include availability of natural resources, notably energy; production of foodstuffs, especially grains; level of inflation; size of national debt; access to social services, including health care; inadequate housing; and maldistribution of wealth.[23]

Another reason that examining political systems from a comparative perspective is useful is personal. As a student of other cultures you can learn more about your own political system by reexamining attitudes and practices long taken for granted. In the same way a student of foreign languages comes to appreciate more clearly the syntax and structure of his or her native tongue and the incursions of other languages into its constructions and meanings, so too does the student of political systems gain. Comparisons not only enhance your knowledge of the political system in which you live, but are likely to increase your appreciation of particular features.

Examining a culture's politics implicitly delves into its values and attitudes. As we move quickly into an increasingly interdependent world, knowledge of other cultures is essential to being well educated. Comparative knowledge, however, allows us to test our values against those of other cultures. How do ours measure up? Do other sets of beliefs have applicability in our society? Are they more or less appropriate to our society? Why? For example, one of the reasons for the considerable misunderstanding between the United States and Mexico is a differing view of the meaning of political democracy. Many Mexicans attach features to the word *democracy* that are not attached to its definition in the United States.[24] For example, most Americans conceptualize democracy as liberty. Mexicans, however, reflect no consensus, giving equal weight to equality and, to a somewhat lesser extent, progress and respect. Problems arise when people do not realize they are using a different vocabulary when discussing the same issue.

Another reason for comparing political cultures is to dispel the notion that Western industrialized nations have all the solutions. It is natural to think of the exchange of ideas favoring the most technologically developed nations, including Japan, Germany, and the United States. But solutions do not rely on technologies alone; in fact, most rely on human skills. In other words, how do people do things? This is true whether we are analyzing politics or increasing sales in the marketplace. Technologies can improve the efficiency, quality, and output of goods and services, yet their application raises critical questions revolving around values, attitudes, and interpersonal relationships. For example, the Japanese have a management philosophy governing employee and employer relations. It has nothing to do with technology. Many observers believe, however, that the philosophy in operation produces better human relationships and higher economic productivity. Accordingly, it is touted as an alternative model in the workplace. The broader the scope of human understanding, the greater the potential for identifying and solving human-made problems.

Finally, as a student new to the study of other cultures, you may be least interested in the long-term contributions such knowledge can make for its own sake. Yet your ability to explain differences and similarities between and among political systems and, more important, their consequences is essential to the growth of political knowledge. Although not always the case, it is generally true that the more you know about something and the more you understand its behavior, the more you can explain its behavior. This type of knowledge allows social scientists to create new theories of politics and political behavior, some of which can be applied to their own political system as well as to other cultures. It also allows—keeping in mind the limitations of human behavior—some level of prediction. In other words, given certain types of institutions and specific political conditions, social scientists can predict that political behavior is likely to follow certain patterns.

SOME INTERPRETATIONS OF THE MEXICAN SYSTEM

We suggested earlier that social scientists set for themselves the task of formulating some broad questions about the nature of a political system and its political processes. A variety of acceptable approaches can be used to examine political systems individually or comparatively. Some approaches focus on relationships among political institutions and the functions each institution performs. Other approaches give greater weight to societal values and attitudes and the consequences these have for political behavior and the institutional features characterizing a political system. Still other approaches, especially in the last third of the twentieth century, place greater emphasis on economic relationships and the influence of social or income groups on political decisions. Taking this last approach a step further, many analysts of Third World countries, including Mexico, concentrate on international economic influences and their effect on domestic political structures.

Choosing any one approach to explain the nature of political behavior has advantages in describing a political system. In my own experience, however, I have never become convinced that one approach offers an adequate explanation. I believe that an examination of political processes or functions entails the fewest prejudices and that by pursuing how and where these functions occur, one uncovers the contributions of other approaches.[25] An eclectic approach to politics, incorporating culture, history, structures, geography, and external relations, provides the most adequate and accurate vision of contemporary political behavior. Such an eclectic approach, combining the advantages of each, will be used in this book.

In the past, the study of Mexican politics provoked continual debate about which features have had the greatest impact on political behavior and, more commonly, to what degree Mexico was an authoritarian model.[26] Today, however, the debate has shifted to analyzing Mexico as an example of democratic and neoliberal, capitalist transformation. The fundamental political questions in this new era are: To what degree has Mexico achieved a democratic political system? Has it gone beyond an electoral democracy? Has it shed many of its semi-authoritarian features? Has it improved the distribution of economic and social benefits? And perhaps most important of all, are democratic beliefs and practices sufficiently entrenched that Mexico will remain a democracy in the future?

For the last seven decades, Mexican politics could best be described as semi-authoritarian—a hybrid of political liberalism and authoritarianism that gave it a special quality or flavor—well documented institutionally in its 1917 constitution, currently in effect. This is also the reason why President Fox asked the Mexican congress in 2001 to reexamine the entire document to consider removing and revising terminology that no longer represents the current state of political affairs. Prior to July 2000, Mexico's political model also was characterized by corporatism, a formal relationship between selected groups or institutions and the government or state, and by *presidencialismo,* the concept that most political power lies in the hands of the president and all that is good or bad in government policy stems from the president.

Corporatism: a formal relationship between selected groups or institutions and the government or state.

Today, Mexico can be fairly labeled a democracy, if democracy is defined narrowly as a competitive political system, in which two or more parties compete in an open and fair electoral process and exchange control over national political leadership. Mexico dramatically achieved this form of democracy with the electoral victory of Vicente Fox in July 2000. Mexico has moved toward a more difficult and influential stage in this process since 2001, one deeply embedded in institutional and structural conditions inherited from the past.

As theorists of Latin American democracy have noted, to move beyond the first step of electoral democracy, countries need also to accomplish other significant goals, including legitimizing the legal system, maintaining civilian supremacy over the military, protecting human rights, and achieving social justice.[27]

Mexico presently is in the throes of a wholesale upheaval in its traditional political practices. Thus, if we are highlighting its most important features, these features, by necessity, are also in transition. In the recent past, Mexico featured a unique, semi-authoritarian system, unique because it allowed for much greater access to the decision-making process and, more importantly, its decision makers changed frequently. Under this system, its leadership remained largely in the hands of the executive branch, especially the president, who was limited to a six-year term. The presidency retains this important structural limitation, an individual can serve only one term in the presidency.

The strength of the presidency specifically, and the executive branch generally, continued well into the 1990s, resulting in a weak legislative and ineffectual judicial branch. Increasing electoral competition at the national level brought opposition party influence into the legislative branch, and by 1997, the Chamber of Deputies, Mexico's lower house, was in the hands of opposition parties. By 1998, a majority of Mexicans believed that congress was more important than the president for a functioning democracy. Nevertheless, the presidency remains the dominant political institution in Mexico, symbolically and practically.

As Mexico moves into the twenty-first century, federalism and decentralization replace semi-authoritarianism as a dominant feature of the political landscape.[28] Beginning under President Zedillo, the presidency

---

Federalism: a political concept that describes rights and obligations shared by national versus state and local governments.

---

experienced a gradual reduction of its power, both intentionally and unintentionally. President Fox accentuated that pattern during his administration, stressing the importance of other national institutions, notably the Supreme Court.[29] For example, he referred a serious dispute over state versus federal designations of the Federal Electoral Institute's representatives in Yucatán to the courts, rather than intervening directly in what was essentially a partisan, political matter, an approach that previous presidents likely would have pursued.

Decentralization has affected Mexico in two ways. First, at the state level, the PRI, which dominated Mexican national politics from 1929 to 2000, still retains approximately half (56 percent) of the governorships. Given the fact that the federal government exercises a dominant position in the revenue-collection process, it maintains potential fiscal control over the states. Some governors, who are jockeying for control over the PRI's national future, sought to oppose the Fox administration at every turn, creating various conflicts between state and national authorities.

Decentralization has another, even more complex face. As Mexico takes on participatory structural features in the political arena, it has generated alterations within institutions and organizations. For example, because of its loss of the presidency, various factions within the PRI are now struggling for control over the party. These factions represent different visions of the party's platform and internal structure. The National Action Party (PAN) is not immune to these same changes, largely because President Fox was an outsider who did not represent the interests of PAN's traditional leadership. If the PAN wishes to capitalize on Fox's personal victory, and increase its grass-roots strength, it too will have to undergo significant changes.

Similar changes are also occurring among other established institutions, such as the Chamber of Deputies and the Supreme Court. Both institutions are expanding their influence and changing their established roles, which have internal consequences and affect their relationship to other institutions, as well.

A second structural feature of a democratic Mexico is the rise of new political actors, or the altered influence of previously important actors. Established institutions, such as the Catholic Church and the armed forces, are expanding their roles and filling a vacuum in the political space created by the departure of PRI from the presidency, and by the democratization of the 1990s. Their new relationship to the state is complemented by the rise of civic and human rights organizations, some of which are likely to fill the role traditionally played by interest groups in other democratic societies.

The growing importance of nongovernmental organizations, autonomous interest groups, and independent institutions, such as the Catholic Church, has altered, but not yet entirely eliminated, another traditional feature of Mexican politics prior to 2000, *corporatism*. Corporatism in this political context refers to how groups in society relate to the government or, more broadly, the state; the process through which they channel their demands to the government; and how the government responds to their demands.[30] Perhaps no characteristic of the Mexican political model has undergone more change in the 1990s than corporatism. In the United States, any introductory course in U.S. politics devotes some time to interest groups and how they present their demands to the political system. Mexico, which inherited the concept of corporatism from Spain, instituted in the 1930s a corporate relationship between the state and various important interest or social groups, primarily under the presidency of General Lázaro Cárdenas (1934–1940). This means that the government took the initiative to strengthen various groups, creating umbrella organizations to house them and through which their demands could be presented. The government placed itself in an advantageous position by representing various interest groups, especially those most likely to support opposing points of view. The state attempted, and succeeded over a period of years, in acting as the official arbiter of these interests. It generally managed to make various groups loyal to it in return for representing their interests.

The essence of the corporatist relationship is political reciprocity. In return for official recognition and official association with the government or government-controlled organizations, these groups can expect some consideration of their interests on the part of the state. They can also expect the state to protect them from their natural political enemies. For example, labor unions hope the state will favor their interests over the interests of powerful businesses.[31] Businesses, however, were never part of the formal corporatist system.

The political victory of the National Action Party in the presidential race of 2000, however, breaks down the linkages that make corporatism possible. The most important of these relationships was the ability of the Institutional Revolutionary Party to use the state to provide economic rewards to favored individuals and groups, especially by appointing them to political posts. During PRI's long reign, essentially no separation existed between the state and the political party. Although President Zedillo himself altered this pattern somewhat in the last few years of his administration, Fox's government has provided clearer evidence of the separation.

Corporatist elements remain, however, especially in those states and municipalities where the PRI has retained control, thus providing at the state and local level a similar continuity it once guaranteed at the national level. The competitive nature of politics, and the increasing inroads of economic development, continue to erode the existing patterns.

The final structural feature of the Mexican model is the presence and level of influence exercised by international capital and, since the 1980s, international financial agencies. As was the case among so many of its fellow Latin American nations, the impact of foreign investment on macroeconomic policy, and on the lives of ordinary Mexican citizens, became paramount in the 1980s, and again to an even greater degree in 1995, when Mexico suffered its worst recession since the worldwide depression of the 1930s. The dependence of Mexico on outside capital and on foreign trade has exercised an important effect on policy making, if not to the same degree on how decisions are taken.[32] It has even been clearly demonstrated that links between international financial agencies and Mexican governmental institutions contributed importantly to the dramatic, economic ideological shift in the 1980s and 1990s.[33] Fox has committed his government to increased economic ties with the United States and Canada, and appointed a chief cabinet officer with two decades of experience at the

World Bank. Mexico also has specifically increased its trade ties with the United States, making it more sensitive to the vagaries of the U.S. economy. Such influences raise significant issues of national sovereignty and autonomy.

The structural features of Mexico's political model—electoral democracy, incipient federalism, the rise of autonomous actors, and the influence of international capital—are complemented by a dual political heritage incorporated into the political culture. The political culture is dominated by democratic attitudes, but strong strains of authoritarian beliefs remain ingrained among many Mexicans. It is contradictory: modern and traditional. Mexico, as the late Nobel Prize winner Octavio Paz argued, is built from two different populations, rural versus urban and traditional versus modern.[34] It bears the burden of many historical experiences, precolonial, colonial, independence, and revolutionary. These experiences produced a political culture that admires essential democratic values, such as citizen participation, yet many remain attracted to an authoritarian model. In a comparative study of Chile, Costa Rica, and Mexico conducted shortly before the electoral victory of Vicente Fox, Mexico's preference for democracy remained low, as suggested in Table 1-1.[35] Undoubtedly more Mexicans prefer democracy to authoritarianism since Fox's victory, but these figures suggest both how recent and how potentially tenuous are Mexicans' beliefs, and those of other Latin American citizens, who have only recently undergone a democratic transformation. In 2004, a United Nations survey found that only 43 percent of Latin Americans fully support democracy.[36]

Place and historical experience have also contributed to another feature of mass political culture: a psychology of dependence.[37] The proximity of the United States, which shares a border with Mexico nearly two thousand miles long, and the extreme disparities between the two in economic wealth and size tend to foster an inferiority complex in many Mexicans, whether they

Table 1-1 Preference for Democracy in Latin America

Country	Support for Democracy Minus Support for Authoritarianism (response in percentages)
Costa Rica	65
Chile	5
Mexico	4

Note: In Mexico, 50 percent preferred democracy, 26 percent either, and 20 percent authoritarian. In Costa Rica, the figures were 80 percent, 9 percent, and 6 percent, respectively. In Chile, the responses were 50 percent, 28 percent, and 17 percent.
Source: Roderic Ai Camp. "Democracy Through Mexican Lenses," *The Washington Quarterly,* 22(3) (Summer, 1999), 240.

operate in the worlds of business, academia, technology, or politics. The economic, cultural, and artistic penetration of the United States into Mexico carries with it other values foreign to its domestic political heritage. Psychologically and culturally, Mexicans must cope with these influences, most of which are indirect, often invisible. A strong sense of Mexican nationalism, especially in relation to its political model, is expressed in part as a defensive mechanism against United States influences. Underlying this defensive mechanism, however, are fundamental beliefs about many issues, including democracy, which are distinctly Mexican.

MEXICO'S SIGNIFICANCE IN A COMPARATIVE CONTEXT

From a comparative perspective, Mexico provides many valuable insights into politics and political behavior. The feature of Mexico that has most intrigued students of comparative politics in the past is the stability of its political system.[38] Although challenged seriously by military and civilian factions in 1923, 1927, and 1929, its political structure and leadership prevailed for most of this century, at least since 1930—an accomplishment unmatched by any other Third World country. Even among industrialized nations like Italy, Germany, and Japan, such longevity is remarkable. The phenomenon leads to such questions as, What enabled the stability? What made the Mexican model unique? Was it the structure of the model? Was it the political culture? Did it have something to do with the country's proximity to another leader of political continuity? Or with the values and behavior of the people?

We know from other studies of political stability that a degree of political legitimacy accompanies even a modicum of support for a political model. Social scientists are interested in political legitimacy and political stability each for its own sake, but they assume, with considerable evidence, that some relationship exists between economic development and political stability. It is misleading to think that the characteristics of one system can be successfully transferred to another; still, it is useful to ascertain which may be more or less relevant to accomplishing specific, political goals.

Mexico also has attracted considerable international interest because it was a one party–dominant system encountering only limited opposition from 1929 through 1988, the year in which a splinter group from the official party, supported by long-standing parties and groups on the left, ran a highly successful campaign. Mexico's system is unusual in that the antecedent of the PRI, the National Revolutionary Party (Partido Nacional Revolucionario, the PNR), did not bring the political leadership to power. Rather, the leadership established the party as a vehicle to *remain* in power; the PRI was founded and controlled by the government bureaucracy. This had long-term effects on the nature of the party itself, and on its importance to policy making.[39] In this sense, the PRI was unlike the Communist Party in the Soviet Union, whose death in 1991 spelled the end of Communist leadership in the successor states. The PRI, because it did not produce Mexico's leadership, as do the Democratic and Republican parties in the United States, was much more tangential to political power. As the Mexican model continued to evolve along democratic lines, the party's function, and consequently its importance, grew significantly. Although it lost its first presidential race in 2000 and suffered sharp divisions among its leadership, the party continues to thrive at the local level, winning back state governorships and municipalities from PAN and the Democratic Revolutionary Party (PRD).

A third reason that Mexico's political system intrigues outside observers has been its ability to subordinate military authorities to civilian control. Mexico, like most other Latin American countries, endured a century when violence became an accepted tool of the political game. Such acceptance makes it extremely difficult, if not impossible, to eliminate the military's large and often decisive political role. Witness many Latin American countries;[40] one has only to look at Argentina and Chile during the 1970s and 1980s. No country south of Mexico has achieved its extended *civilian* supremacy. Rather, in many Latin American countries where civilian leadership is once again in ascendancy, their dominance is tenuous at best. This is precisely why theorists of Latin American democracy have included civilian supremacy over the armed forces as a component of a functional democracy.

Mexico, therefore, is a unique case study in Third World civil-military relations. What produced civilian supremacy there? Is the condition found elsewhere? A confluence of circumstances and policies gradually succeeded in putting civilian control incrementally in place. Some involved the special characteristics of the system itself, including the creation of a national political party. Some are historical, the most important of which is the Mexican Revolution of 1910, which led to the development of a popular army whose generals governed Mexico in the 1920s and 1930s, and who themselves initiated the concept of civilian control.[41] As pluralization increases, many of the features that sustained the relationship prior to 2000 are disappearing. It remains to be seen whether those changes will alter the traditional pattern.

A fourth reason for studying Mexico is the singular relationship it has developed with the dominant religious institution, the Catholic Church. Throughout much of Latin America, the Catholic Church has been one of the important corporate actors. For significant historical reasons in the nineteenth and twentieth centuries, Mexico's leadership suppressed and then isolated itself from the Catholic hierarchy and even in some cases the Catholic religion.[42] The Catholic Church has often played a political role in Latin American societies and currently has the potential to exercise considerable political and social influence. A study of church–state relations in Mexico offers a unique perspective on how the church was removed from the corporatist structure and the implications of this autonomy for a politically influential institution. It is readily apparent that the church performed a significant task in bringing electoral democracy to Mexico. It is equally apparent that it has become a vocal critic of selected government policies.[43]

A fifth reason for examining Mexico in a comparative political context is the opportunity to view the impact of the United States, a First World country, on a Third World country. No comparable geographic relationship obtains anywhere else in the world: Two countries that share a long border exhibit great disparities in wealth. Mexico provides not only a test case for those who view Latin America as dependent on external economic forces but also an unparalleled opportunity to look at the possible *political* and *cultural* influences and consequences of a major power.[44] A recent survey of citizens in Mexico and the United States, which explored a series of political and social attitudes, suggests the importance of cross-national influences along the border.[45]

The relationship is not one way, but instead is asymmetrical.[46] The United States exercises or can exercise more influence over Mexico than vice versa. This does not mean that Mexico is the passive partner. It, too, exercises influence, and in many respects its influence is growing. Because of European civilization's influence on our culture, we have long studied the political models of England and the Continent. Our obsession with the Soviet Union exaggerated our focus on Europe. As Latino and other immigrant cohorts grow larger in the United States, our knowledge of the Mexican culture will become far more relevant to understanding *contemporary political behavior* in the United States than anything we might learn from contemporary Europe.

A sixth reason to explore the Mexican political model is its experiences since 1989 with economic liberalization. One of the issues that has fascinated social scientists for many years, but especially since the downfall of the Soviet Union and the emergence of new economic and political models in eastern Europe, is the linkage between economic and political liberalization. What does the Mexican case suggest about its strategy of concentrating on opening its markets, which then may create conditions favorable to political development? Indeed, is there a causal linkage between economic and political liberalization? If so, what lessons can be offered by the Mexican transition?[47]

A seventh reason Mexico may offer some useful comparisons is the transition taking place between national and local political authorities. Long dominated by a national executive branch in both the decision-making process and the allocation of resources, Mexico has witnessed, since the first opposition-party victory at the state level in 1989, an increasing pattern of decentralization and deconcentration of political control at the state and local level, as the National Action Party and the Democratic Revolutionary Party won more elections.[48] Now that Mexico has evolved into a three-party system on the national level, and the National Action Party controls the executive branch, how is it responding to PRI- and PRD-controlled local and state governments? How are these patterns affecting the process of governance, as distinct from electoral competition? The potential implications of such change from the bottom up offer many insights into structural political relationships in Mexico and the rise of federalism.

Finally, most scholars believe that Mexico's path along a political transition to democracy differed from many other countries in the 1980s and 1990s. For example, Steve Morris has argued in his cogent analysis of recent political scholarship that Mexico's democratic reforms occurred over a lengthy period. The incumbent party permitted, indeed sometimes initiated, institutional changes in the electoral process. These processes in turn encouraged opposition parties to mobilize their supporters. Second, political parties played a crucial role in the Mexican transformation. These parties operated within the electoral context created by a one-party monopoly. Although that electoral system generated peculiar characteristics within the opposition parties' structures, making them less flexible than would be the case in a typical competitive electoral arena, the parties were able to survive and successfully initiate and accomplish system reforms, allowing them ultimately to defeat the governing party. Third, Mexico's transformation occurred from the bottom up, in which state and local forces provided a firm grass-roots base for national political change. The growth of opposition-party control at the municipal level trained a new generation of leadership, altered voter behavior and partisan support, and increased demands for the decentralization of power.[49]

Mexico presently is shifting from a transition to democracy to a complex process of consolidation or deepening of democratic patterns of behavior, including fresh institutional relationships among the branches of government. This consolidation process raises questions about the accountability of leadership, the legitimacy of democracy in meeting citizen expectations, and their respect for opposing parties and actors.

Definitions of consolidation and democratic deepening abound. In the Mexican context, the clearest presentation of these two terms has been offered by Steven Barracca. Barracca suggests that consolidation refers exclusively to "a low probability of democratic breakdown. More specifically, I suggest that a democratic regime can be considered consolidated when a political system is free of factors that can be demonstrated to *clearly* and *directly* lead to a return to non-democratic rule."[50] Most definitions of this term are much broader and more ambiguous. Widely offered criteria for testing the broader definitions of democratic consolidation include such variables as the level of socioeconomic equality; the behavior, structure, and role of institutions; the routine practice of democratic politics; and the citizenry's view of the democracy as legitimate. Many of these characteristics have been criticized by students of recently democratically transformed societies, including Russia, as being far too demanding.[51]

The deepening of democracy in Mexico involves numerous tasks. These include establishment of the rule of law, strengthening of the federal judiciary, campaign finance reform, expansion of other actors, decentralization of decision-making, and increased accountability across institutions. The degree to which Mexico has implemented these changes, and the difficulties it has encountered, can be compared with the experiences of other countries engaged in similar reforms.

CONCLUSION

To summarize, then, approaching politics from a comparative perspective offers many rewards. It allows us to test political models against one another; it enables us to learn more about ourselves and our own political culture; it offers a means for examining the relationship between political and economic development and the distribution of wealth; and it identifies the common interests of rich and poor nations and what they do to solve their problems.

Scholars have interpreted Mexico's political system in different ways. This book argues that the system is democratic, but is in consolidation; is dominated by a declining presidency, with legislative and judicial branches growing in influence; is built on a contradictory political culture that includes liberal and authoritarian qualities; is characterized by international economic features embedded in its domestic structures; is affected psychologically and politically by its proximity to the United States; and reflects the growing significance of new actors, including NGOs and state and local governments. Mexico offers unique opportunities for comparative study because of its political continuity and stability, historic one party–dominant system, civil-military relations, unique separation of church and state, peaceful democratic transition, and nearness to a powerful, wealthy neighbor.

In the next chapter, the importance for Mexico of time, place, and historical roots is examined in greater detail and contrasted with the experiences of other countries. Among these elements are its Spanish heritage, the role of the state, nineteenth-century liberalism and positivism, the revolution, and U.S.-Mexican relations.

NOTES

1. Gabriel Almond and Sidney Verba, *The Civic Culture* (Boston: Little, Brown, 1965), 59.

2. Compare, for example, the number of academic course offerings and textbooks available on Europe and European countries with those representing other, especially Third World, regions and societies.

3. Peter Klarén, "Lost Promise: Explaining Latin American Underdevelopment," in *Promise of Development: Theories of Change in Latin America,* ed. Peter Klarén and Thomas J. Bossert (Boulder, Colo.: Westview Press, 1986), 8.

4. See for example, the glowing statement in the *Washington Post,* that Salinas "has proved to be as radical in his own way as the revolutionaries who galloped over Mexico at the beginning of the century." May 17, 1991.

5. For Salinas's views in English, see the interview "A New Hope for the Hemisphere," *New Perspective Quarterly* 8 (Winter 1991): 8.

6. Roderic Ai Camp, "Citizen Attitudes Toward Democracy and Vicente Fox's Victory in 2000," in *Mexico's Pivotal Democratic Election,* Chappell Lawson and Jorge Domínguez, eds. (Stanford: Stanford University Press, 2004), 25–46.

7. The clearest presentation of this argument, in brief form, can be found in Gabriel Almond, "Capitalism and Democracy," *PS* 24 (September 1991): 467–73.

8. In the World Values Survey (a collaborative survey of forty countries in 1981 and again in 1990, available in data format from the University of Michigan, Ann Arbor. Ronald Inglehart, Institute for Social Research, directed the North American project), 1990, data from Mexico show that approximately 60 percent of the population chose economic growth as most important, compared with approximately 25 percent who selected increased political participation. Similar results have been repeated in every major survey taken through 2000.

9. On a presidential level, most Mexicans have not yet made the connection, or if they have, it is not significant to their voting. See Jorge Domínguez and James

McCann, "Whither the PRI? Explaining Voter Defection from Mexico's Ruling Party in the 1988 Presidential Elections," paper presented at the Western Political Science Association meeting, March 1991, 23–24. They follow up this argument in "Shaping Mexico's Electoral Arena: The Construction of Partisan Cleavages in the 1988 and 1991 National Elections," *American Political Science Review* 89 (March 1995): 39–40, and in their *Democratizing Mexico: Public Opinion and Electoral Choices* (Baltimore: The Johns Hopkins University Press, 1996).

10. "Latin American Economies: A Disappointing Performance," *Latin American Economic Policies,* 9 (Fourth Quarter 1999), 2.

11. It has been argued, as a general rule, that as countries achieve advanced industrial economies, greater economic equality will be achieved. See Samuel P. Huntington, *Political Order in Changing Societies* (New Haven, Conn.: Yale University Press, 1968), 57. Also see Dan LaBotz's statement that real minimum wages for Mexicans declined 44 percent between 1977 and 1988, in *Mask of Democracy: Labor Suppression in Mexico Today* (Boston: South End Press, 1992), 19.

12. Roger D. Hansen, *The Politics of Mexican Development* (Baltimore: Johns Hopkins University Press, 1971), especially "Trends in Mexican Income Distribution," 72ff.

13. Sidney Weintraub, *A Marriage of Convenience: Relations Between Mexico and the United States* (New York: Oxford University Press, 1990), 36; and Wayne Cornelius, "Foreword," in *The Politics of Economic Restructuring: State-Society Relations and Regime Change in Mexico,* ed. Mario Lorena Cook, Kevin J. Middlebrook and Juan Molinar Horcasitas (La Jolla, Calif.: Center for U.S.–Mexican Studies, UCSD, 1994), xiv–xv.

14. "Población, pobreza y marginación," *Este País* (April 1999), 15.

15. "Democracy Through Latin American Lenses," Grant, Hewlett Foundation, principal investigator, Roderic Ai Camp, June, 1998.

16. "Democracy Through U.S. and Mexican lenses," Grant, Hewlett Foundation, principal investigator, Roderic Ai Camp, September, 2000.

17. Of course, this is true worldwide. Unfortunately, the problems *seem* less severe when these groups are the primary victims. Americas Watch, *Implausible Deniability, State Responsibility for Rural Violence in Mexico* (New York: Human Rights Watch, 1997), 15–18.

18. Karl W. Deutsch, *Nationalism and Social Communication: An Inquiry into the Foundations of Nationality,* 2d ed. (Cambridge: MIT Press, 1966), 156ff.

19. Frederick Turner, *The Dynamics of Mexican Nationalism* (Chapel Hill: University of North Carolina Press, 1968).

20. Within the region, Mexico ranks about in the middle. "The Dangers of Diversity," *Latin American Economic Policies,* 10 (First Quarter 2000), 6.

21. The classic argument for this was presented by Barbara Ward, *The Rich Nations and the Poor Nations* (London: Hamilton, 1962).

22. Jeff Faux, "No: The Biggest Export Will Be U.S. Jobs," *Washington Post Weekly Edition,* May 13–19, 1991, 8.

23. For empirical evidence of these patterns from 1990–1993, see Ronald Inglehart, Miguel Basáñez, and Alejandro Moreno, *Human Values and Beliefs: A*

Cross-Cultural Sourcebook (Ann Arbor: University of Michigan Press, 1999). For an update from 1999 to 2002, see Ronald Inglehart et al., *Human Beliefs and Values: A Cross-Cultural Sourcebook* (Mexico: Siglo XXI, 2004).

24. See one commissioner's statement that this is a source of bilateral problems in the blue-ribbon Report of the Bilateral Commission on the Future of United States-Mexican Relations, *The Challenge of Interdependence* (Lanham, Md.: University Press of America, 1989), 237; these findings are reinforced empirically in Roderic Ai Camp, ed., *Citizen Views of Democracy in Latin America* (Pittsburgh: University of Pittsburgh Press, 2001).

25. Some of these issues have been examined by Diane E. Davis, *Urban Leviathan: Mexico City in the Twentieth Century* (Philadelphia: Temple University Press, 1994); and Viviane Brachet-Márquez, "Explaining Sociopolitical Change in Latin America: The Case of Mexico," *Latin American Research Review* 27 (1992): 91–122.

26. For example, Susan K. Purcell, "Decision-Making in an Authoritarian Regime: Theoretical Implications from a Mexican Case Study," *World Politics 26* (October 1973): 28–54.

27. Terry Lynn Karl, "Dilemmas of Democratization in Latin America," *Comparative Politics* 23 (October 1990): 1–21.

28. Peter M. Ward and Victoria E. Rodríguez, "New Federalism, Intragovernmental Relations and Co-governance in Mexico," *Journal of Latin American Studies* 31 (1999): 673–710.

29. Kevin Sullivan and Mary Jordan, "Mexican Supreme Court Refuses to Take Back Seat," *Washington Post,* September 10, 2000, A31.

30. Ruth Spalding, "State Power and its Limits: Corporatism in Mexico," *Comparative Political Studies* 14 (July 1981): 139–61.

31. An excellent analysis of this relationship can be found in Ruth Berins Collier, *The Contradictory Alliance: State-Labor Relations and Regime Change in Mexico* (Berkeley: University of California International and Area Studies, 1992).

32. For reactions to the intervention of the International Monetary Fund, see Rick Wills, "The IMF's Economic Role Causes Controversy," *El Financiero International Edition,* October 6, 1997, 8. Fifty-six percent of Mexicans believe that U.S. influence over Mexico is excessive. "Mexico's Economic Situation Survey," *El Norte/Reforma* poll of 1,100 urban Mexicans with a ±3 percent margin of error, 1995. See *Dallas Morning News,* November 5, 1995, 3.

33. Roderic Ai Camp, *Mexico's Mandarins: Crafting a Power Elite for the Twenty-first Century* (Berkeley: University of California Press, 2002); and Sarah Babb, *Global Experts: Economists in Mexico, from Nationalism to Neoliberalism* (Princeton: Princeton University Press, 2001).

34. Octavio Paz, *The Other Mexico: A Critique of the Pyramid* (New York: Grove Press, 1972), 45. Paz noted the existence of "one fundamental characteristic of the contemporary situation: the existence of two Mexicos, one modern and the other underdeveloped. This duality is the result of the Revolution and the development that followed it: thus, it is the source of many hopes and, at the same time, of future threats."

35. Roderic Ai Camp, "Democracy through Mexican Lenses," *The Washington Quarterly,* 22, no. 3 (Summer 1999), 240.

36. "Latin America Losing Faith in Democracy," *Los Angeles Times,* April 22, 2004, A3.

37. See Octavio Paz's classic, *The Labyrinth of Solitude: Life and Thought in Mexico* (New York: Grove Press, 1961).

38. For an overview of these issues, see Kevin Middlebrook's review essay "Dilemmas of Change in Mexican Politics," *World Politics* 41 (October 1988): 120–41.

39. See Dale Story, *The Mexican Ruling Party, Stability and Authority* (New York: Praeger, 1986), 9ff; John J. Bailey, *Governing Mexico: The Statecraft of Crisis Management* (New York: St. Martin's Press, 1988).

40. This is nicely explained in Gary Wynia, *The Politics of Latin American Development,* 3d ed. (Cambridge: Cambridge University Press, 1990), 28ff.

41. For greater detail about the causes, see Roderic Ai Camp, *Generals in the Palacio: The Military in Modern Mexico* (New York: Oxford University Press, 1992).

42. Karl Schmitt, "Church and State in Mexico: A Corporatist Relationship," *Americas* 40 (January 1984): 349–76.

43. For evidence of this change, see Vikram K. Chand, *Mexico's Political Awakening* (Notre Dame: University of Notre Dame Press, 2001); and Roderic Ai Camp, *Crossing Swords: Politics and Religion in Mexico* (New York: Oxford University Press, 1997).

44. For some examples of noneconomic variables, see Clark W. Reynolds and Carlos Tello, *U.S.–Mexico Relations: Economic and Social Aspects* (Stanford, Calif.: Stanford University Press, 1983).

45. Rodolfo de la Garza, "National Origin vs. Socialization: Are Hispanics More 'Democratic' Than Mexicans?" Paper presented at the Conference on Democracy and Political Learning in Mexico and the United States," University of Texas, Austin, Texas, 2001.

46. For various insights into this, from the points of view of an American and Mexican, see Robert A. Pastor and Jorge G. Castañeda, *Limits to Friendship: The United States and Mexico* (New York: Vintage Press, 1989).

47. For an extensive discussion of the Mexican case, see Riordan Roett, ed., *Political & Economic Liberalization in Mexico, at a Critical Juncture* (Boulder, Colo.: Lynne Rienner, 1993), 17–94. The most imaginative comparative analysis is Juan D. Lindau and Timothy Cheek, eds., *Market Economics & Political Change: Comparing China and Mexico* (Lanham: Rowman and Littlefield, 1998).

48. See especially "The Politics of Public Administration," in *Opposition Government in Mexico,* ed. Victoria Rodríguez and Peter M. Ward (Albuquerque: University of New Mexico Press, 1995). The editors also provide an excellent case study in their *Policymaking, Politics, and Urban Governance in Chihuahua* (Austin: LBJ School of Public Affairs, University of Texas, 1992).

49. Stephen D. Morris, "Mexico's Long Awaited Surprise," *Latin American Research Review* 40 (2005): 418–21.

50. Steven Barracca, "Democratic Consolidation and Deepening in Mexico: A Conceptual and Empirical Analysis," paper presented at the Latin American Studies Association, March 2003, 3.

51. See, for example, Stephen E. Hanson, "Defining Democratic Consolidation," in *Postcommunism and the Theory of Democracy*, ed. Richard D. Anderson, Jr., et al. (Princeton, N.J.: Princeton University Press, 2001), 126–51.

2

Political–Historical Roots: The Impact of Time and Place

> The political life of all those states which during the early years of the last century arose upon the ruins of the Spanish Empire on the American mainland presents two common features. In all those states, constitutions of the most liberal and democratic character have been promulgated; in all, there have from time to time arisen dictators whose absolute power has been either frankly proclaimed or thinly veiled under constitutional forms. So frequently has such personal rule been established in many of the states that in them there has appeared to be an almost perpetual and complete contradiction between theory and practice, between nominal and the actual systems of government.
>
> CECIL JANE, *Liberty and Despotism in Spanish America*

Understanding politics is not just knowing who gets what, where, when, and how, as Harold D. Lasswell declared in a classic statement years ago, but also understanding the origins of why people behave the way they do. Each culture is a product of its own heritage, traditions emerging from historical experiences. Many aspects of the U.S. political system can be traced to our English colonial experiences, our independence movement, our western frontier expansion, and our immigrant origins. Mexico has had a somewhat similar set of experiences, but the sources of the experiences and their specific characteristics were quite different.

THE SPANISH HERITAGE

Mexico's political heritage, unlike that of the United States, draws on two important cultural foundations: European and indigenous. Although large numbers of Indians were never absorbed into the conquering culture in New Spain, a vast integration process took place in most of central Mexico. Conversely, British settlers encountered numerous Native Americans in their colonization of North America, but they rarely intermarried with them and thus the two cultures never blended. Racially, African blacks played an important role in some regions; politically, this was a limited role because of the small numbers brought to New Spain, the colonial Spanish viceroyalty that extended from Central America to what is now the United States Midwest and Pacific Northwest.

Mexico's racial heritage, unlike that of the United States, has a mixed or *mestizo* quality. In the initial absence of Spanish women, the original Spanish conquerors sought native mistresses or wives. In fact, cohabiting with female royalty from the various indigenous cultures was seen as an effective means of joining the two sets of leaders, firmly establishing Spanish ascendancy throughout the colony. The Indian–Spanish offspring of these unions at first were considered socially inferior to Spaniards fresh from Spain and the Spanish born in the New World. Frank Tannenbaum describes the complex social ladder:

> With the mixture of races in Mexico added to by the bringing in of Negroes in sufficient numbers to leave their mark upon the population in certain parts of the country, we have the basis of the social structure that characterized Mexico throughout the colonial period and in some degree continues to this day. The Spaniard—that is, the born European—was at the top in politics, in the Church, and in prestige. The *criollo,* his American-born child, stood at a lower level. He inherited most of the wealth, but was denied any important role in political administration. The *mestizo* and the dozen different *castas* that resulted from the mixtures of European, Indian, and Negro in their various degrees and kinds were still lower.[1]

In the late nineteenth century, mestizos reached a new level of social ascendancy through their numbers and control over the political system.

Early Mexican political history involved social conflicts based on racial heritage. Moreover, large indigenous groups were suppressed, exploited, and politically ignored. The prejudice with which Indians were treated by the Spanish and mestizo populations, and the mistreatment of the mestizo by the Spanish contributed further to the sharp class distinctions that have plagued Mexico.[2] Social prejudice was transferred to economic status as well, with those lowest on the racial scale ending up at the bottom of the economic scale. The degree of social inequality ultimately contributed to the independence movement, as the New World–born Spanish (*criollos*) came to resent their second-class status relative to the Old World-born Spanish (*peninsulares*). It contributed even more significantly to the Mexican Revolution of 1910, in which thousands of downtrodden mestizo peasants and workers and some Indians joined a broad social movement for greater social justice.

All societies have some type of social structure. Most large societies develop hierarchical social groups, but from one society to another the level of deference exacted or given varies. In the United States, where political rhetoric, beginning with independence, focused on greater social equality, class distinctions were fewer and less distinct.[3] In Mexico, in spite of its revolution, the distinctions remain much sharper, affecting various aspects of cultural and political behavior. For example, a major study of U.S. intellectuals found that 40 percent of the younger generation were from working-class backgrounds. By contrast, in Mexico, fewer than 5 percent fell into this social category.[4] In the political and economic realms, lower-income groups are rarely represented in influential, leadership roles. Only among Catholic clergy and the military do such individuals exist in larger numbers.[5] In addition, lower-income groups have limited protection from abuses by governmental authorities and rarely receive equal treatment under the law. In the United States differences exist in the legal treatment of rich and poor, but they are fewer, and the gap between them is much smaller than in Mexico.

The Spanish also left Mexico with a significant religious heritage: Catholicism. Religion played a critical role in the pre-Conquest Mexican indigenous culture and was very much integrated into the native political processes. In both the Aztec and Maya empires, for example, religion was integral to political leadership. The Spanish were no less religious. Beginning with the Conquest itself, the pope reached some agreements with the Spanish crown. In these agreements, known collectively as the *patronato real* (royal patronate), the Catholic Church gave up certain rights it exercised in Europe for a privileged role in the Conquest generally and in New Spain specifically. In return for being allowed to send two priests or friars with every land or sea expedition, and being given the *sole* opportunity to proselytize millions of Indians, the church gave up its control over the building of facilities in the New World, the appointing of higher clergy, the collecting of tithes, and other activities. In other words, Catholicism obtained a monopoly in the Spanish New World.[6]

The contractual relationship between the Catholic Church and the Spanish authorities in the colonial period established two fundamental principles: the concept of an official religion, that is, only one religion recognized and permitted by civil authorities; and the *integration* of church and state. In the United States, of course, a fundamental principle of our political evolution is the *separation* of church and state. Moreover, many of the settlers who came to the English colonies came in search of religious freedom, not religious monopoly. As Samuel Ramos suggested,

It was our [Mexico's] fate to be conquered by a Catholic theocracy which was struggling to isolate its people from the current of modern ideas that emanated from the Renaissance. Scarcely had the American colonies been organized when they were isolated against all possible heresy. Ports were closed and trade with all countries except Spain was disapproved. The only civilizing agent of the New World was the Catholic Church, which by virtue of its pedagogical monopoly shaped the American societies in a medieval pattern of life. Education, and the direction of social life as well, were placed in the hands of the Church, whose power was similar to that of a state within a state.[7]

The consequences of Mexico's religious heritage have been numerous. It is important to remember that Catholicism was not just a religion in the spiritual sense of the word, but extended deeply into the political culture, given the influence of the church over education and social organizations, such as hospitals and charitable foundations, and its lack of religious competition.

One of the consequences is structural. In the first chapter, corporatism was identified as one of the traditional features of the political system. Corporatism extends back to the colonial period, when certain groups obtained special privileges from civil authorities, giving them preferred relationships with the state. Among these groups were clergy, military officers, and merchants. The most notable privileges received by the clergy were special legal *fueros*, or legal rights, allowing them to try their members in separate courts, where they were not subject to civil laws.[8] The Spanish established the precedent for favored treatment of specific groups. Once groups are thus singled out, they will fight very hard to retain their advantages. Much of nineteenth-century politics in Mexico became a battle between the church and its conservative allies on just this issue.

The monopoly of the church in New Spain was very jealously protected. No immigrants professing other beliefs were allowed in before Mexican independence. The church also took on another task for the state: ferreting out religious and political dissenters by establishing the Inquisition in the New World. The primary function of this institution was to identify and punish religious heretics, those persons who threatened religious beliefs as taught by church authorities, but in practice the Inquisition controlled publishing, assembled a book index that censored intellectual ideas from abroad, and fielded special customs inspectors.[9] These activities were not entirely successful, but in general the church and the civil authorities were intolerant of any other religious and secular thought. The Inquisition has been described in this fashion:

> The belief that heretics were traitors and traitors were heretics led to the conviction that dissenters were social revolutionaries trying to subvert the politi-

cal and religious stability of the community. These tenets were not later developments in the history of the Spanish Inquisition; they were inherent in the rationale of the institution from the fifteenth century onward and were apparent in the Holy Office's dealings with Jews, Protestants, and other heretics during the sixteenth century. The use of the Inquisition by the later eighteenth-century Bourbon kings of Spain as an instrument of regalism was not a departure from tradition. Particularly in the viceroyalty of New Spain during the late eighteenth century the Inquisition trials show how the Crown sought to promote political and religious orthodoxy.[10]

The heritage of intolerance plagued Mexico during much of its post-independence political history. It has been argued that because culturally there had been little experience with other points of view and in promoting respect for them, accommodation was not perceived as desirable. Some analysts suggest that the Catholic religion's continuation as a dominant presence in spite of religious freedom and the existence of other faiths, encourages the persistence of intolerance. The applicability of that view in recent years requires reexamination in light of the Church's proactive posture on democratization.

To carry out the conquest of New Spain, the Spanish relied on armed expeditions and missionaries. Typically, once an area was made "safe" by an exploratory expedition, a permanent settlement around a mission and a *presidio,* or fort, was established. Some of the settlements were sited along a route known as the *camino real* (king's highway), which today is the old California Highway 1. The original mission towns are now among the most important cities in the Southwest: San Francisco (Saint Francis), San Diego (Saint James), Santa Barbara (Saint Barbara), Albuquerque, Tucson, and Santa Fe.

Originally, the authorities used Spanish armed forces; in the colonial period, American-born Spaniards began filling officer ranks as the government came to rely more heavily on the colonial militia. The armed forces were called on from time to time to protect the coast from French and British attacks, but the army was used primarily to suppress Indian rebellions and to keep internal order. It patrolled the highways to keep them free of bandits. Basically, then, it functioned as police, not as defenders against external enemies.

The military, like the clergy, received special *fueros* in New Spain. It too had its own courts for civil and criminal cases, but unlike the clergy, military officers were immune to civil prosecution.[11] Their favored status inevitably led to legal conflicts. Some historians have argued that one of the reasons for the disintegration of civil authority at the time of independence was declining respect caused by its inability to control military cases.

As in the case of the church, granting the military special privileges—which were passed on to the colonial militia before independence—created another powerful interest group. Their professional heirs in the nineteenth century wanted to retain the privileges. Furthermore, the close ties between military and civil authorities, and the unclear lines of subordination led to the blurring of distinctions in civil-military relations.[12]

In the nineteenth and early twentieth centuries, these patterns in civil-military relations and civil-church relations had a great impact on Mexico's political development. They complemented the corporatist heritage by establishing groups that saw their own interests, not those of society, as primary. These groups competed for political ascendancy, reinforcing the already-present social inequality by creating a hierarchy of interests and prestige.

To the legacies of corporatism, social inequality, special interests, and intolerance can be added the Spanish bureaucratic tradition. Critics tend to focus on the inefficiencies of the Spanish bureaucracy and the differences between legal theory and the application of administrative criteria.[13] In part, problems can be attributed to the distance between the mother country and the colonies, as well as to the distance between Mexico City, the seat of the viceroyalty of New Spain, established in 1535, and its far-flung settlements in Yucatán, Chiapas, and what is today the southwestern United States. A more important feature of Spanish religious and civil structures was their strongly hierarchical nature and centralization. Low-level bureaucrats lacked authority. Decisions were made only at the top of the hierarchy, with delay, inefficiency, and corruption as the outcome.[14]

The hierarchical structure of the Spanish state in the New World is no better illustrated than through the viceroy himself. The viceroy (*virrey*) was in effect the vice-king, a personal appointee of and substitute for the king of Spain. He had two sources of power: He was the supreme civil authority and also the commander in chief of the military. In addition, he was the vice-patron of the Catholic Church, responsible for the mission policies in the colonization process. Remember, this individual, along with a second viceroy in Lima, Peru, governed all of Spanish-speaking Latin America and the southwestern United States.

Upon its independence, the viceregal structure left Mexico with two political tendencies. First, the individual viceroys became extremely important, some serving for many years, completely at the whim of the crown. This shifted considerable political legitimacy away from Spanish institutions to a single person. The personalization of power tended to devalue the institutionalization of political structures, thereby enhancing the importance of political personalities. It also left Mexico with an integrated civil and religious/cultural tradition, complemented by an equally blended, hierarchical indigenous tradition of executive authority. Justo Sierra, a Mexican historian, described the viceroy's power and the church-state relationship:

> The Viceroy was the king. His business was to hold the land—that is, to conserve the king's dominion, New Spain, at all costs. The way to conserve it was to pacify it; hence the close collaboration with the Church. In view of the privileges granted by the Pope to the Spanish king in America, it could be said that the Church in America was under the Spanish king: this was called the Royal Patronate. But the ascendancy that the Church had acquired in Spanish America, because it consolidated, through conversions, the work of the Conquest, made it actually a partner in the government.[15]

Spanish political authority was top-heavy, placing most of the power in the hands of an executive institution. The viceroy's decision-making authority had few restrictions. In many respects, the viceroy's self-developed political aura was equivalent to the *presidencialismo* described earlier. The Spanish did create an *audiencia,* a sort of quasi legislative–judicial body that acted as a board of appeals for grievances against the viceroy and could channel complaints directly to the crown, bypassing the viceroy. Also, the crown appointed its own inspectors, often secret, who traveled to New Spain to hear charges against a viceroy's abuse of authority. These *visitadores* were empowered to conduct thorough investigations and report to the crown.

The minor restrictions on viceregal powers did not mean there was a separation of powers, an independent judiciary, a legislative body, or decentralization. Some participation at the local level existed, but Mexico had no legislative heritage comparable to that found in the British colonies' colonial assemblies. Thus, it is not surprising that although Mexico quickly established a legislative body after independence, it functioned effectively for only brief periods in the 1860s and 1870s and again in the 1920s, remaining ineffectual and subordinate throughout most of the twentieth century until the 1990s.

Finally, another important Spanish political heritage is the role of the state in society. The strong authoritarian institutions in New Spain and the size of the Spanish colonial bureaucracy established the state as the preeminent institution.[16] The only other institution whose influence came close was the Catholic Church. Educated male Spaniards born in the New World essentially had three career choices: the colonial bureaucracy, the clergy (which appealed to only a minority), and the military. New Spain's private sector was weak, underdeveloped, and closed. The crown permitted little commercial activity among the colonies or with other countries. The monopolistic relationship between Spain and the colonies kept the latter

from developing their full economic potential. Michael Meyer and William
Sherman characterized Spain's policies as

> protectionist in the extreme, which meant that the economy in New Spain was
> very much restricted by limitations imposed by the imperial system. Thus the
> natural growth of industry and commerce was significantly impeded, because
> manufacturers and merchants in Spain were protected from the competition
> of those in the colony. In accord with the classic pattern, the Spanish Indies
> were to supply Spain with raw products, which could be made into finished
> goods in the mother country and sold back to the colonists at a profit. As a
> consequence, the character of the colonial economy in Mexico was essentially
> extractive.[17]

A long-term political consequence of a strong state and a weak private
sector was the overarching prestige of the state, to the disadvantage of the private sector. Economically, then, the state was in the driver's seat, not because
it controlled most economic resources, but because it provided the most
important positions available in the colonial world. The same mentality
developed in the twentieth century in other colonial settings. For example,
Indians came to believe that the British civil service was the preeminent institution in India and that government employment would grant them great
prestige.[18] In the same way, positions in the Mexican state bureaucracy were
seen by many educated Mexicans as the ultimate employment, and so the
competition for places was keen. One cultural theorist, Glen Dealy, argues
that "public power like economic wealth is rooted in rational accumulation.
Capitalism measures excellence in terms of accumulated wealth; *caudillaje*
[Latin American culture] measures one's virtue in terms of accumulated public power."[19] This way of life did not end with the decline of the Spanish
empire and Spain's departure from Mexico. Figures from the last third of the
nineteenth century demonstrate that the government employed a large percentage of educated, professional men, suggesting again the limited opportunities in the private sector.

The Mexican state's importance can be explained by not only economic underdevelopment, but also by the status of the state in the New
World. In other words, it was natural for Mexicans to expect the state to play
an influential role. Not liking state intervention in their lives, similar to the
feeling of most people in the United States,[20] Mexicans nevertheless came
to depend on the state as a problem solver, in part because there was no institutional infrastructure at the local level or the same self-reliant thinking.

Spain bequeathed to Mexico an individualistic, cultural mind-set.
North Americans, although characterized by self-initiative and independence, exhibited a strong sense of community. That is, throughout the western expansion, U.S. settlers saw surviving together as in the interest of the

group as well as in the interest of its members. Mexicans, on the other hand, exhibited a strong sense of self. This, combined with the sharper social-class divisions and social inequality, led to a preeminence of individual or familial preservation, unassociated with the protection of larger groups. The lack of communal ties reinforced the primacy of personal ties. It was a familiar phenomenon elsewhere in Latin America as well. In the political realm, it generally translates into *whom* you know rather than *what* you know. This statement is an almost universal truism, but whom you know gains in importance where access to authority is limited.[21]

Finally, the structural arrangements of the Spanish colonial empire and the distances between the colonies and the mother country and between the colonies themselves made for considerable dissatisfaction with the rules imposed. The Spanish settlers, and later their mestizo descendants, increasingly disobeyed orders from overseas. Sometimes they could justifiably assert that a law no longer applied to the situation at hand. At other times they would flout a law they found inconvenient. The inefficiencies inherent in the transatlantic management of possessions in two continents, built-in social inequalities, and the gap between Old World theory and New World reality meant the marginalization of Spain's laws in the Western Hemisphere. A lack of respect for the law and the importance of personal and familial interests were fundamental factors in Mexico's political evolution from the 1830s through the end of the twentieth century.

NINETEENTH-CENTURY POLITICAL HERITAGE

Shortly after its independence Mexico experimented briefly with a monarchical system, but the rapid demise of the three-hundred-year-old colonial structure left a political void. The only legitimate authority, the crown, and its colonial representative, the viceroy, disappeared. Intense political conflict ensured as various groups sought to legitimize their political philosophies. The battle for political supremacy affected the goals of the antagonists and influenced the process by which Mexicans settled political disputes. By the 1840s, Mexico had fluctuated between a political model advocating federalism, the decentralization of power similar to that practiced in the United States, and centralism, the allocation of more decision-making authority to the national government.

As was true of many Latin American countries, Mexico was caught between the idea of rejecting its centralized, authoritarian Spanish heritage and the idea of adopting the reformist U.S. model. The obstinacy of their proponents kept political affairs in constant flux. Violence was a frequent means for settling political disagreements, which enhanced the presence and importance of the army as an arbiter of political conflicts, and consumed much of the government budget that might otherwise have been spent more productively.

By the mid-nineteenth century two mainstreams of political thought confronted Mexicans: conservatism and liberalism. Mexican liberalism was a mixture of borrowed and native ideas that largely rejected Spanish authoritarianism and tradition and instead drew on Enlightenment ideas from France, England, and the United States. Some of its elements included such basic U.S. tenets as guarantees of political liberty and the sovereignty of the general will. Among its principles were greater citizen participation in government, free-speech guarantees, and a strong legislative branch. Liberals complemented these principles with a concept known as Jeffersonian

---

Mexican liberalism: an amalgam of basic concepts of political liberty and nineteenth-century laissez-faire economic principles.

---

agrarian democracy. Jefferson had advocated encouraging large numbers of small landholders in the United States. His rationale was that people with property constitute a stable citizenry; having something to lose, they would vigorously defend the democratic political process. The liberals also believed in classic economic liberalism, the philosophy pervading England and the United States during the same period. Economic liberalism of this period referred to the encouragement of individual initiative and the protection of individual property rights.[22]

Mexican conservatives held to an alternative set of political principles. Whereas an examination of Liberal ideas reveals that most of them were borrowed from leading thinkers and political systems foreign to Mexico's experience, the Conservatives praised the reform-minded Bourbon administration of the Spanish colonies prior to independence and emphasized a strong central executive. They argued for a strong executive because it would follow naturally after centuries of authoritarian colonial rule, and because the postindependence violence in the 1830s, 1840s, and 1850s seemed to be part of a larger struggle between anarchy and civilization in Latin America. Without forceful leadership, Mexico would succumb to disorder and remain underdeveloped economically.[23]

The conservatives favored policies promoting industrialization, stressing light manufacturing rather than expansion of the small-landholder class. Mexico desperately needed capital, much of which had fled after independence and during the chaotic political period that followed. Both conservatives and liberals looked approvingly on foreign investment and encouraged policies that would attract outside capital, particularly to mining and struggling industries such as textiles.[24]

Neither the conservatives nor the liberals gave much attention to the plight of the Indians. Because the thinkers in both camps generally were *criollos* of middle- and upper-middle-class background, their primary concerns were the maintenance of social order and the interests of their classes. Although the conservatives essentially ignored the Indians, the liberals sought to apply their philosophy of economic individualism to the Indian system of communal property holding, believing it to be an obstacle to development.

Liberals and conservatives clashed most violently on the role of the Catholic Church. The liberals believed, and correctly so, that the church, as an integral ally of the Spanish state, conveyed support for the hierarchical, authoritarian, political structure.[25] Essentially, it was the church's control of education and nearly all aspects of cultural life that permitted its influence. The conservatives, on the other hand, saw the church as an important force and worked toward an alliance with it.

Because the liberals viewed the church as a staunch opponent and as the conservatives' political and economic supporter, they wanted to reduce or eliminate altogether its influence. They introduced the Ley Lerdo (Lerdo law) on June 1, 1856, essentially forcing the church to sell off its large landholdings, which at that time accounted for a sizable portion of all Mexican real estate. But the law did not have its intended consequences. The church traded land for capital, thereby preserving a source of economic influence and at the same time enlarging the already substantial estates of the buyers.[26] The liberals also attacked the church's special privileges, which had been left inviolate by the 1824 constitution immediately after independence. They eliminated its legal *fueros* and placed cemeteries under the jurisdiction of public authorities.[27]

From this brief overview, we can see that each side had something useful to offer. Yet their unwillingness to compromise and the intensity with which they held their opinions led to a polity in constant disarray. The battles between conservatives and liberals culminated in the War of the Reform (1858–1861), in which the victorious liberals imposed, by force, their political views on the defeated conservatives. These views are well represented in the constitution of 1857, a landmark political document that influenced its revolutionary successor, the constitution of 1917.

The issue of church versus state, or the supremacy of state over church, was a crucial element of the conservative–liberal battles and a focus of nineteenth-century politics. The leading liberals of the day saw the classroom as the chief means of social transformation, and the church's control in that arena as undesirable, and so decided to establish secular institutions. To implement this concept, President Benito Juárez appointed in 1867 a committee under Gabino Barreda, an educator who set down some basic principles for public education in the last third of the nineteenth century. The liberals hoped to replace church-controlled schools with free, mandatory public education, but their program was never fully implemented. Most important, they introduced a preparatory educational program, a sort of advanced high school to train future leaders in secular and liberal ideas.

By 1869 the liberals succeeded in defeating the conservatives' forces. Their unwillingness to compromise and their introduction of even more radical reforms—particularly those associated with suppressing the Catholic Church, and incorporated into the 1857 constitution—impelled the conservatives and their church allies to take the unusual step of seeking help from abroad. This ultimately led to the French intervention of 1862–1867, and an attempt to enthrone a foreign monarch, Austrian archduke Ferdinand Maximilian. The liberals were nearly defeated during this interlude, but under Benito Juárez's leadership they ultimately won and executed the archduke.

The liberals reigned from 1867 to 1876. This brief period is important because it gave Mexicans a taste of a functioning, liberal political model. The legislative branch of government exercised some actual power. The successors to Benito Juárez lacked the political skills and authority to sustain the government, and their experiment came to an end with the successful revolt of Porfirio Díaz, a leading military figure in the liberal battles against the French.[28]

Díaz's ambition and his overthrow of Juárez's collaborators introduced a new generation of liberals to leadership positions. These men, most of whom were combat veterans of the liberal–conservative conflicts and the French intervention, were *moderate* liberals, distinct from the radical orthodox liberals of the Juárez generation. Díaz and the moderate liberals paved the way for the introduction of a new political philosophy into Mexico: positivism. As described by historian Charles Hale,

> Scientific or positive politics involved the argument that the country's problems should be approached and its policies formed scientifically. Its principal characteristics were an attack on doctrinaire [radical] liberalism, or "metaphysical politics," an apology for strong government to counter endemic revolutions and anarchy, and a call for constitutional reform. It drew upon a current of European, particularly French, theories dating back to Henri de Saint-Simon and Auguste Comte in the 1820s, theories that under the name of positivism had become quite generalized in European thought by 1878. Apart

from the theoretical origins of their doctrine, the exponents of scientific politics in Mexico found inspiration in the concrete experience of the contemporary conservative republics of France and Spain and in their leaders.[29]

The motto for many positivists in Mexico and elsewhere in Latin America was liberty and progress through peace and order. The key to Mexican positivism, as it was implemented by successive administrations under Profirio Díaz, who ruled Mexico from 1877 to 1880 and 1884 to 1911, was order. After years of political instability, violence, and civil war, these men saw peace as a critical necessity for progress. Their explanation for the disruptive preceding decades centered on the notion that too much of Mexico's political thinking had been based on irrational or "unscientific" ideas influenced by the spiritual teachings of the church and that alternative political ideas were counterproductive. As Díaz himself suggested, "all citizens of a republic should receive the same training, so that their ideas and methods may be harmonized and the national identity intensified."[30]

Building on the philosophy of their orthodox liberal predecessors, the Díaz administrations came to believe that the most effective means for conveying rational positivist thought, or this new form of moderate liberalism, was public education. Education therefore became the essential instrument for homogenizing Mexican political values. It would turn out a new generation of political, intellectual, and economic leaders who would guide Mexico along the path of material progress and political development. Preeminent among the public institutions was the National Preparatory School in Mexico City, which enrolled children of regional and national notables. Its matriculation lists read like a roll of future national leaders.[31]

The acceptance of positivist ideas by the moderate liberals ultimately led to the dominance of order over liberty and progress. Indeed, it can be argued that after decades of civil conflict, positivism became a vehicle for reintroducing conservative ideas among Mexico's liberal leadership. Díaz increasingly used the state's power to maintain political order, allowing economic development to occur without government interference. His government encouraged the expansion of mining and made generous concessions to foreigners to obtain investment.

The Porfiriato, as the period of Díaz's rule is known in Mexico, had significant consequences that led to the country's major social upheaval of the twentieth century, the Mexico Revolution of 1910, and numerous political and social legacies. Díaz attacked two important social issues: the relationship between church and state and the role of Indians in the society.

Ironically, the Catholic Church regained considerable influence during the liberal era. Even Benito Juárez realized after Maximilian's defeat that pursuit of radical antichurch policies would only generate further resistance and disorder. Díaz pursued a pragmatic policy of reconciliation in the 1870s, separating church and state, but permitting the church to strengthen its religious role as long as it remained aloof from secular and political affairs.[32] Thus, the two parties achieved a modus vivendi, although the state remained in the stronger position, and the 1857 constitution retained repressive, antichurch provisions.

Díaz's attitude toward the Indians was also significant because it reflected a broader attitude toward social inequality. He and his collaborators, as did the original liberals, saw the Indians as obstacles to Mexican development. They applied the provisions of the law forcing the sale of church property to the communal property held by Indian villages, accelerating the pace of sales begun by the orthodox liberals in the 1860s. But the positivists were not satisfied with this economic measure. Many of them accepted the notion, popular throughout Latin America at the time, that Indians were a cultural and social burden and were racially inferior.[33] To overcome this racial barrier, they proposed introducing European immigration, in the hope of wiping out the indigenous culture and providing a superior economic example for the mestizo farmer.

To ensure that immigration would take place, the Mexican government passed a series of colonization laws in the 1880s that granted generous concessions to foreigners who would survey public lands. By 1889 foreigners had surveyed almost eighty million acres and had acquired large portions of the surveyed acreage at bargain-basement prices. For the most part, however, these people were not typical settlers; rather, they, like the Mexicans who purchased church and Indian lands, were large landholders. Two million acres of communal Indian lands went to them and to corporations. Hence, the colonization laws not only increased the concentration of land in the hands of wealthy Mexicans and foreigners, but antagonized small mestizo and Indian farmers, who became a force during the Mexican Revolution.

Díaz implemented policies that improved the country economically, but the primary beneficiaries were the wealthy at home and abroad. The laboring classes, generally mestizo in origin, benefited little from the politics of peace. Díaz focused on a small group of supporters and ignored the plight of most of his compatriots. Even middle-class mestizos, who rose to the top of the ladder politically by 1900, were limited in their abilities to share in the economic goods of the Díaz era. As two recent historians of Mexico suggested,

> The structure of Mexican society during the Porfiriato consisted of a number
> of levels that must be noted in order to understand the social dynamics of the

era. Large holders of commercialized agriculture land constituted the top of the pyramid. Land provided the economic core as well as status. From this base large landholders diversified into manufacturing, mining, or other profitable activities. An elite, allied with national and regional political groups, with business and personal connections to foreign capitalists and investors, formed an interlocking socioeconomic and political directorate. They used their political, economic, and social influence to reinforce their position. Economic concessions, contracts, and other forms of political patronage fell to this group. They negotiated among themselves for a share of the political power and economic fruits of modernization.[34]

To understand Mexican politics in the twentieth century, in the postrevolutionary era, it is even more important to explore the political heritage left by Díaz and his cronies. In the first place, although church and state were separate and the lines were more firmly drawn between secular and religious activities, Díaz maintained fuzzier relationships between the state and two other important elements, the army and the private sector.

In effect, Díaz established the pattern for civil–military relations that characterized Mexico until the 1940s. Because he himself was a veteran of so many civil conflicts, it was only natural that he recruited many of his important collaborators, on both the national and state level, from among fellow officers.[35] Military men occupied many prominent positions. Although the presence of career officers in the top echelon declined across Díaz's tenure as they were replaced by younger civilian lawyers, no clear relationship of subordination between civil and military authorities was established (see Table 2-1). Díaz left a legacy of shared power and interlocking leadership.[36]

The unclear lines between military and civilian political power were duplicated between politicians and the business elite. It is the nature of a capitalist system to have an exchange of leaders between the economic and political spheres, as in the United States, but such linkages in an authoritarian political structure, where access to power and decision making is closed, can produce potentially significant consequences. Díaz, who had control over most of the important national political offices, used appointments to reward supporters or as a means to co-opt opponents. At no time since 1884 has any administration had stronger elite economic representation in political office than under Díaz. Approximately a fifth of all national politicians from 1884 to 1911, with the peak in 1897, were businessmen. For most of the twentieth century they made up fewer than 10 percent of Mexico's public figures.[37] Giving these positions, especially at the provincial level, to members of prominent families, further closed paths of upward social mobility to less-favored groups, especially the mestizo middle class.[38]

Table 2-1 Career Military Officers in National Politics

Presidential Administration	Military Officers (%)	Presidential Administration	Military Officers (%)
Díaz		Portes Gil	14
1884–1889	54	Ortiz Rubio	41
1889–1893	46	Rodríguez	33
1893–1897	32	Cárdenas	27
1897–1901	16	Avila Camacho	19
1901–1905	11	Alemán	8
1905–1910	9	Ruiz Cortines	14
1910–1911	35	López Mateos	15
De la Barra	27	Díaz Ordaz	7
Madero	26	Echeverría	11
Huerta	61	López Portillo	6
Carranza	49	De la Madrid	4
Obregón	40	Salinas	6
Calles	30	Zedillo	2

By the time Díaz began his third term as president in 1888, he had succeeded in controlling national elections, although he had not created a national electoral machine similar to that of the Partido Nacional Revolucionario (PNR), established in 1929, and its successors. He continued to hold elections to renew the loyalty of the people to his leadership and to allow him to reward his faithful supporters with sinecures as federal deputies (congressmen) and senators. His control was so extensive that occasionally he chose the same person for more than one elective office.

Building on the original conservative philosophy and the colonial heritage, Díaz reversed the tenuous decentralization trend begun under President Juárez. He accomplished this structurally by decreasing the powers of the legislative and judicial branches, making them subordinate to the executive branch and to the presidency specifically. He also strengthened the presidency as distinct from the executive branch.

Díaz went beyond aggrandization of political authority in the executive branch and the presidency by strengthening the federal government or state generally. He did this by expanding the federal bureaucracy. Between 1876 and 1910 the government payroll grew some 900 percent. In 1876 only 16 percent of the middle class worked for the government; by 1910 the figure was 70 percent.[39] As in the colonial period, the private sector was not incorporating new generations of educated Mexicans; rather, their careers were being pursued within the public sector, notably the federal executive. Díaz provided the twentieth century with a dominant state, an apparatus that most successful Mexicans would want to control because it was essential to their economic future.

Because Díaz held the presidency for some thirty years, a personality cult developed around his leadership. His collaborators conveyed the message that progress, as they defined it, was guaranteed by his presence. His indispensability enhanced his political maneuverability. On the other hand, Díaz put in place a political system that was underdeveloped institutionally. In concentrating on his personality, political institutions failed to acquire legitimacy. Even the stability of the political system itself was at stake because continuity was not guaranteed by the acceptability of its institutions, but by an individual person, Díaz.

The Porfiriato also reinforced the paternalism handed down from the political and social culture of the precolonial and colonial periods. Díaz's concessions to favored people, providing them with substantial economic rewards, encouraged dependence on his personal largesse and the government generally. This technique, which he used generously to pacify opponents and reward friends, produced corruption at all levels of political life. It encouraged the belief that political office was a reward to be taken advantage of by the officeholder rather than a public responsibility. The political cultures of many other countries are similarly characterized to a greater or lesser degree.

Against his most recalcitrant foes, Díaz was willing to use less ingratiating techniques. Toward the end of his regime, press censorship became widespread. As a whole, he favored a controlled, complimentary press to counter criticism from independent sources. If threats or imprisonment were not sufficient to deter his opponents, he resorted to more severe measures. Typically, lower social groups were the victims of violent suppression. A notorious example of this policy was the treatment of the Yaqui Indians in northwestern Mexico, who rebelled after influential members of the Díaz administration began seizing their lands. The Yaquis were subjected to brutalities and were forced into what were in effect concentration camps, and many were deported to Yucatán, where most perished in forced labor on the henequen plantations in the hot tropical climate.[40]

As Mexico emerged from the first decade of the twentieth century, it acquired a political model that drew on Spanish authoritarian and paternal heritages. Like the viceroys before him, but without reporting to any other authority, Díaz exercised extraordinary power. He built up a larger state apparatus as a means of retaining power, and although he strengthened the role of the state in society, he did not legitimize its institutions. While he did succeed in building some economic infrastructure in Mexico, he failed to meet social needs and maltreated certain groups, thereby continuing and intensifying the social inequalities existing under his colonial predecessors. His favoritism toward foreigners caused resentment and contributed to the rise of nationalism after 1911. The lack of separation between civilian and military leadership left Mexicans unclear about the principle of civilian supremacy and autonomy, an issue that would confront his successors. Finally, although the moderate liberals/converted positivists replaced orthodox liberals and, in many cases, substituted conservative principles for their original political ideas, the excluded liberal followers who remained faithful to the cause rose up once again after 1910.[41]

THE REVOLUTIONARY HERITAGE:
SOCIAL VIOLENCE AND REFORM

It can never be forgotten that contemporary Mexico is the product of a violent revolution that lasted, on and off, from 1910 through 1920. The decimation of its population—more than a million people during the decade—alone would have left an indelible stamp on Mexican life. The revolution touched all social classes, and although it did not affect all locales with the same intensity, it brought together the residents of villages and cities to a degree never achieved before or since. In the same way that World War II altered life in the United States, the revolution brought profound changes to Mexican society.

The causes of the revolution have been thoroughly examined by historians. They are numerous, and their roots can be found in the failures of the Porfiriato. Among the most important to have been singled out are foreign economic penetration, class struggle, land ownership, economic depression, local autonomy, the clash between modernity and tradition, the breakdown of the Porfirian system, the weakness of the transition process, the lack of opportunity for upward political and social mobility, and the aging of the leadership.[42] Historians do not agree on the primary causes nor on whether the 1910 revolution was a "real" revolution, that is, whether it radically changed the social structure.[43]

In my own view, the revolution introduced significant changes, although it did not alter social structures to the degree one expects of a major social revolution on a par with the Cuban, Soviet, or Chinese revolutions.[44] Nevertheless, to understand Mexican political developments in the twentieth century, it is necessary to explore the ideology of the revolution and the political structures that emerged in the immediate postrevolutionary era.

Ideologically, one of the best ways to understand the diverse social forces for change is to trace the constitutional provisions of 1917 to the precursors and revolutionary figures. Among the most important precursors, Ricardo Flores Magón and his brothers offered ideas leading up to the revolution and revived the legitimacy of orthodox liberalism by establishing liberal clubs throughout Mexico.[45] This provided a basis for middle-class participation in and support for revolutionary principles. Flores Magón and his adherents published a newspaper in exile in the United States, *La Regeneración,* banned in Mexico. Many prominent political figures in the revolution, including General Alvaro Obregón, cited its influence on their attitudes. Perhaps more than in any other area, Flores Magón offered arguments in support of workers' rights, establishing such principles as minimum wage and maximum hours in strike documents and Liberal Party platforms.[46] He also advocated the distribution of land, the return of communal (*ejido*) properties to the Indians, and the requirement that agricultural land be productive.

Politically, the most prominent figure in the pre- and revolutionary eras was Francisco I. Madero, son of wealthy Coahuilan landowners in northern Mexico, who believed in mild social reforms and the basic principles of political liberty. He founded the Anti-Reelectionist Party to oppose Porfirio Díaz. A product of his class, he did not believe in structural change but did believe in equal opportunity for all.[47] His *Presidential Succession of 1910,* the Anti-Reelectionist Party platform, and his revolutionary 1910 Plan of San Luis Potosí advocated three important political items: no reelection, electoral reform (effective suffrage), and revision of the constitution of 1857. The most important of Madero's social and economic ideas concerned public education; he believed, as did the orthodox liberals, that education was the key to a modern Mexico.

More radical social ideas were offered by such revolutionaries as Pascual Orozco, who later turned against Madero; Francisco Villa; and Emiliano Zapata. Orozco, who expressed many popular social and economic views, some complementary to those of Flores Magón, also called for municipal autonomy from federal control in response to Díaz's centralization of political authority. Villa, from the northern state of Chihuahua, did not offer a true ideology or program, but the policies he implemented in the regions under his control reflected his radical social philosophy. In Chihuahua, for example, he nationalized large landholders' properties outright and, because of his own illiteracy (he learned to read only late in life), instituted a widespread primary school program. Zapata, who came from the rugged state of Morelos just south of Mexico City, fought largely over the issue of land. His ideology, expressed by his collaborators, appeared in his famous Plan de Ayala.[48]

With the exception of Madero, these men offered few specific political principles. Consequently, the political ideology of the revolution, with the possible exception of effective suffrage and no reelection, emerged piecemeal, either in the constitutional debates at Querétaro, before the writing of the 1917 constitution, or from actual experience.

One of the most important of these themes was Mexicanization, a broad form of nationalism. Simply stated, Mexico comes first, outsiders second. In the economic realm, it can be seen in placing Mexicans instead of foreigners in management positions, even if the investment is foreign in origin. An even more important expression of economic nationalism occurred in regard to resources: the formalization of Mexican control. With few exceptions, at least 51 percent of any enterprise had to be in the hands of Mexicans. But after 1988, desperate for foreign investment, the government loosened up many restrictions in most economic sectors.

Mexicanization spread to cultural and psychological realms. On a cultural level, the revolution gave birth to extraordinary productivity in art, music, and literature, in which methodology was often as important as the content. In the visual fields, the Mexicans revived the mural, an art form that could be viewed by large numbers of Mexicans rather than remain on the walls of private residences or inaccessible museums.[49] Political cartoons during and after the revolution blossomed. In literature, the social protest novel—the novel of the revolution—came to the fore. Often cynical or

---

Mexicanization: a revolutionary principle stressing the importance of Mexicans and Mexico, enhancing their influence and prestige.

---

highly critical, these works castigated not only the failures of the Porfiriato, but the apparent failures of the revolutionaries too.[50] Musicians paid attention to the indigenous heritage, even composing the classical *Indian Symphony,* whose roots lie in the native culture. Ballads and popular songs flourished throughout Mexico as each region made its contributions.[51]

Mexicanization also affected a line of intellectual thought known as *lo mexicano,* which was concerned with national or cultural identity, and pride in Mexican heritage. Henry Schmidt, one of the most insightful students of the Mexican cultural rebirth, assessed its impact:

> The 1910 Revolution generated an unprecedented expansion of knowledge in Mexico. At the same time as it lessened the tensions of an unresponsive political system, it ushered in a new age of creation. If the post-Revolutionary political development cannot always be viewed favorably, the efforts to reorient thought toward a greater awareness of national conditions at least merit

commendation. Thus the 1920's is known as the period of "reconstruction" and "renaissance," when the country, having undergone its most profound dislocation since the Conquest, attempted to consolidate the gains its people had struggled for since the waning of the Porfiratio.[52]

Another important theme of the revolution was social justice. Economically, although not expressed specifically in the constitution, this included a fairer distribution of national income. Socially, and called for by nearly all revolutionary and intellectual thinkers, it involved expanded public education. Madero wanted to improve access. Many others promoted education as an indirect means to enhance economic opportunity, particularly for the Indians, whose integration into the mainstream mestizo culture could thereby be accomplished. A leading intellectual, José Vasconcelos, who made significant contributions to Mexican education, praised a coming "Cosmic race," suggesting that a racial mix would produce a superior, not inferior, culture.[53]

The revolution did not react adversely to a strong state. Instead, building on the administrative infrastructure created under the Porfiriato, postrevolutionary regimes contributed to its continued expansion. Yet unlike Díaz, the revolution heralded a *larger state role,* giving the state responsibilities not expected of a government before 1910. According to Héctor Aguilar Camín and Lorenzo Meyer, the construction of a new state incorporated "the first bold attempts at developing the state as an instrument of economic, educational, and cultural action and regulation."[54] For example, as a consequence of Mexicanization, the state gained control over subsoil resources and eventually became the administrator of extractive enterprises. The phenomenal growth in the value of the nation's oil in the 1970s cast the state in an even more important role. When the state nationalized foreign petroleum companies in 1938, it established national and international precedents elsewhere.[55] In later periods, the state came to control such industries as fertilizers, telephones, electricity, airlines, steel, and copper. In the mid-1980s the trend gradually began to be reversed.

The revolution stimulated the political liberalism that had lain dormant under the ideology of positivism during the last twenty years of the Porfiriato. Freedom of the press was revived during the revolution. The media underwent a regression in the 1920s, and although censorship continued to raise its head, the conditions under which the media operated were much improved. The most important principle of political liberalism—increased participation in governance expressed through effective suffrage—was given substance in Madero's election in 1911, probably Mexico's freest, but never returned to that level until 1997.[56]

The political mythology of the revolution, "Effective Suffrage, No Reelection," was stamped on official government documents until the 1970s.

Effective suffrage remains an ideal, but is close to being achieved in practice. On the other hand, no reelection, with but a few exceptions in the 1920s and 1930s, has become the rule. When General Alvaro Obregón tried to circumvent it in 1928 by forcing the congress to amend the constitution to allow him to run again after a four-year hiatus, he was elected but then assassinated before taking office. No president since has tried the maneuver. No elected executive, including mayors and governors, repeats officeholding, consecutively or otherwise. Legislators may repeat terms, but not consecutively, a concept introduced in the 1930s.

The revolution also had an extraordinary influence on Mexico's political leadership after 1920. Half the national political leaders born between 1870 and 1900 had participated in this violent event. Among those who held national office for the first time, 47 percent had fought on the side of the revolutionaries, 9 percent in opposition to these forces, and 2 percent on both sides. Presidents Alvaro Obregón (1920–1924) and Plutarco Elías Calles (1924–1928), as well as Díaz, recruited many of their wartime cronies. Through 1940, the presidents who succeeded them were, with one exception, generals who had fought in these battles, often under these two predecessors. As the data in Table 2-2 illustrate, veterans continued to dominate Mexican administrations from 1914 through 1934. As might be expected, the 1910 revolution introduced a different type of politician as well, one whose social origins were quite distinct from those of his noncombatant contemporary. In effect, the revolution reintroduced the importance of working-class origins among Mexico's leadership, since 72 percent of the public figures who were combat veterans were from working-class families, compared with only 34 percent who had middle- and upper-class back-grounds.

Another revolutionary outcome was the changed relationship between church and state. Once again, the seeds of orthodox liberalism appeared in the constitutional debates. Many of the revolutionaries eyed the church with

Table 2-2 Revolutionary Experiences of National Politicians

Presidential Administration	Experience (%)				
	Revolutionary	Antirevolutionary	Both	None	Total
Madero, 1911–1913	28	4	4	64	100
Huerta, 1913–1914	5	48	8	39	100
Convention, 1914–1915	77	0	0	23	100
Carranza, 1914–1920	71	0	0	29	100
Obregón, 1920–1924	61	1	1	37	100
Calles, 1924–1928	56	1	1	42	100
Portes Gil, 1928–1930	58	0	0	42	100
Ortiz Rubio, 1930–1932	54	0	0	46	100
Rodríguez, 1932–1934	56	0	0	44	100

severe distrust and reinstituted many of the most restrictive provisions advocated by the early liberals. Until 1992 these provisions could be found, unchanged, in the constitution. They include removing religion from primary education (Article 3), taking away the church's right to own real property (Article 27), and secularizing certain religious activities and restricting the clergy's potential political actions (Article 130). No clergy of any faith were permitted in their capacity as ministers to criticize Mexican laws or even to vote.

The breakup of large landholdings is also a primary economic and social product of revolutionary ideology. As part of the redistribution of land in Mexico after 1915, the government made the Indian *ejido* concept (village-owned lands) its own, distributing land to thousands of rural villages to be held in common for legal residents, who obtained use rights, not legal title, to it.[57] In effect, the government institutionalized the indigenous land system that the liberals and positivists had attempted to destroy. This structure remained unchanged until 1992.

The revolution also introduced a change in attitude toward labor. For the first time, strikes were legalized, and the right to collective bargaining was sanctioned. Provisions regarding hours and wages, at least for organized labor, were introduced. The 1917 constitution was the first to mention the concept of social security, although it was not implemented until 1943. Organized labor helped General Obregón defeat president Venustiano Carranza in the last armed confrontation of the revolutionary decade.

Finally, although this list is incomplete, the revolution gave greater emphasis to a sense of constitutionalism. In a political sense, constitutionalism provides legitimacy for a set of ideas expressed formally in the national document. It is not only a reference point for the goals of Mexican society after 1920, as a consequence of the revolution, but it also identifies the basic outline of political concepts and processes. The constitution of 1917 itself took on a certain level of prestige. Although many of its more radical social, economic, and political provisions are observed more in abeyance than reality, its contents and its prestige together influenced the values of successive generations.[58]

THE POLITICS OF PLACE:
INTERFACE WITH THE UNITED STATES

The proximity of the United States has exercised an enormous influence on Mexico. As I argue, "The United States constitutes a crucial variable in the very definition of Mexico's modern political culture."[59] Beginning with independence, the political leaders who sought solutions emphasizing federalism, and later the decentralizing principles of liberalism, borrowed many of their concepts from U.S. political thinkers and documents. In fact, the intellectual ideas provoked by U.S. independence from England provided a fertile literature from which independence precursors could also borrow.

The destiny of the two countries became intertwined politically in more direct ways as a consequence of the annexation of Texas, a northern province of New Spain. Immediately after Mexico won independence, large numbers of Americans began to settle in Texas, quickly outnumbering the Mexicans there. The differences within Texas between Mexicans and Americans and between Texas and the Mexican government led to armed conflict. The Mexican army under General Antonio López de Santa Anna lay siege to the Alamo in February 1836, but was routed from Texas later that year. Texas remained independent of Mexico until 1845, when the United States, by a joint congressional resolution, annexed it. This provoked another conflict, one with even more serious repercussions.[60]

Desirous of more territory, President James Polk used several incidents as a pretext for war. In 1846, U.S. troops drove deep into Mexico's heartland and, in addition to occupying outlying regions of the former Spanish empire in New Mexico and California, seized the port of Veracruz and Mexico City. In the Treaty of Guadalupe Hidalgo, signed on February 2, 1848, Mexico ceded more than half its territory to the United States. Seven years later, the Mexican government, again under Santa Anna, sold the United States a strip of land (in what is now southern Arizona and southern New Mexico), known as the Gadsden Purchase, although this time it was not done under duress.

The war left a justifiably bitter taste in the mouths of many Mexicans. As has been suggested, "The terms of the Treaty of Guadalupe Hidalgo are among the harshest imposed by a winner upon a loser in the history of the world."[61] More than any single issue, the terms established a relationship of distrust between the two nations. Physical incursion from the north took place twice more. Voices in the United States always seemed to call for annexations. Even as late as the first decade of the twentieth century, California legislators publicly advocated acquiring Baja California.

During the Mexican Revolution the United States repeatedly and directly or indirectly intervened in Mexican affairs. The intense personal prejudices or interests of its emissaries often determined U.S. foreign policy decisions. Henry Lane Wilson, ambassador during the Madero administration (1911–1913), played a role in its overthrow and in the failure to ensure the safety of Madero and his vice-president, who were murdered by counterrevolutionaries led by Felix Díaz and Victoriano Huerta. Huerta established himself in power, and the violent phase of the revolution began in earnest. President Woodrow Wilson removed the U.S. ambassador and sent personal

emissaries to evaluate Huerta. He decided to channel funds to the Constitutionalists, revolutionaries who had remained loyal to Madero and to constitutional government. But after a minor incident involving U.S. sailors in the
port of Tampico, Wilson used it as a pretext to order the occupation of the
port of Veracruz, resulting in the deaths of numerous Mexicans.[62]

Wilson's high-handedness produced a widespread nationalistic response in Mexico that nearly brought Wilson's intention—to oust Huerta
from the presidency—to naught. Mexicans alive at the time of the occupation recall discontinuing classes in English, switching back to Mexican cig-
arettes, and throwing away their Texas-style hats in symbolic protest. Young
men as far away as Guadalajara, in western Mexico, readily joined volun-
teer companies to go fight the Americans.[63] But Huerta fell, and the North
Americans did not invade and, indeed, soon left Veracruz.

After the Constitutionalists' victory under Carranza, rebel chieftains
began to bicker among themselves. They divided into two major camps:
one led by Francisco Villa and Emiliano Zapata and the other by Álvaro
Obregón and Carranza. After several major battles, Obregón defeated Villa's
forces. In March 1916, after remnants of Villa's forces moved north and
attacked Columbus, New Mexico, Wilson ordered a punitive expedition
under General John "Black Jack" Pershing against Villa. The U.S. forces
battled the Constitutionalists, never caught Villa, and remained in Mexico
until 1917.[64]

From this necessarily brief selection of historical examples, it is clear
that Mexicans have reason to distrust the United States and to have created
an extremely strong sense of nationalism, especially directed toward its
northern neighbor. The economic, political, and cultural exchanges between
the two countries, especially since the 1920s, have given rise to issues common to Mexico's relations in all parts of the world, as well as others peculiar to relations between Mexico and the United States. The geographic
proximity of two such culturally and economically different societies has
had numerous consequences for domestic politics and their respective
national security agendas. These issues will be examined in a broader perspective in a later chapter. For now, I just want to emphasize that Mexico's
nearness to the United States has noticeably affected its political and economic history and development.

CONCLUSION

Throughout its recent history, Mexico, as both a colony and an independent
nation, established patterns that have contributed heavily to the development

of its political model. Some of the more important remnants from the Spanish colonial period are the conflicts of social class, exacerbated by sharp social divisions. Catholicism, introduced as the official religion of the Spanish conquerors, has been equally significant. Its monopoly encouraged a cultural intolerance of other ideas or values and enabled a symbiotic, profitable relationship between the state and the church. The Spanish also fostered a strong sense of special interests, granting privileges to other selected groups, including the military, and ultimately contributing to a particularized civil–military relationship. These elements led to corporatism, an official relationship between important occupational groups or institutions and the state. The Spanish, through their own political structure, especially the viceroy, imposed three hundred years of authoritarian, centralized administration. Great powers accrued to the executive, to the neglect of other government branches. Restrictive economic policies discouraged the growth of a strong colonial economy, thus shoring up the role of the state versus that of an incipient private sector. The state's power and prestige attracted New Spain's most ambitious citizens.

Many features of the colonial period were further enhanced after independence. The conflicts between the liberals and conservatives, driven by an intolerance of counterviews, produced ongoing civil war and anarchy. Although Mexico experimented briefly with a more decentralized form of government, authoritarian qualities were back in the saddle by the end of the nineteenth century. The presidency replaced the viceroyship in wielding power, and President Díaz expanded the size and importance of the executive branch, thereby continuing to enhance the state's image. Díaz introduced political stability and some economic development, yet he perpetuated the social inequalities inherited from the Spanish period. He also made sure that the military would have a large voice in the political system, leaving unresolved the matter of military subordination to civilian authority. The Spanish paternal traditions remained.

The revolution reactively introduced changes but in many respects retained some of the basic features from the previous two periods. One important innovation was Mexicanization, an outgrowth largely of Mexico's exploitation by foreigners and especially its proximity to the United States. Mexicanization strengthened Mexican values and culture as well as political nationalism. The revolution altered Mexicans' political rhetoric and social goals of legitimizing the needs and interests of lower-income groups and Indians. Yet instead of reducing the role of the state, it made the state into an even more comprehensive institution. The revolution also revived important principles of orthodox liberalism, including political liberties, suppression of the church's secular role, and decentralization of authority, but a decade of civil violence and the need for effective leadership in the face of successive rebellions in the 1920s discouraged implementation of a federal, democratic system. Instead, the revolution left Mexico with a heritage of strong, authoritarian leadership, and military supremacy. Even so, it established the importance of constitutionalism, even if many of the constitution's liberal provisions were never enforced. The legitimacy of its concepts provided the basis for political liberalization under Presidents Salinas and Zedillo (1988–2000).

Finally, Mexico's long, troublesome relationship with the United States has implications for its political evolution and the functioning of its model. The level of the United States's economic influence in Mexico, and the United States seizure of more than half of Mexico's national territory, prompted Mexican nationalism and anti-Americanism. Mexico has had to labor under the shadow of its internationally powerful neighbor, a psychological as well as a practical, political burden. Historical experience and geographic proximity influenced many domestic policy decisions and perhaps subtly encouraged a strong, even authoritarian regime that could prevent the kind of instability and political squabbling that had left Mexico open to territorial depredation.

NOTES

1. Frank Tannenbam, *Mexico: The Struggle for Peace and Bread* (New York: Knopf, 1964), 36.

2. For an extensive discussion of racial relations in Mexico and elsewhere in Latin America, see Magnus Morner's classic study *Race Mixture in the History of Latin America* (Boston: Little, Brown, 1967).

3. Interestingly, this is even true when comparing the United States with its colonizer, England. See Richard Rose, *Politics in England,* 5th ed. (Boston: Little, Brown, 1989), 69.

4. Charles Kadushin, *American Intellectual Elite* (Boston: Little, Brown, 1974), 26.

5. Roderic Ai Camp, *Mexico's Mandarins: Crafting a Power Elite for the Twenty-first Century* (Berkeley: University of California Press, 2002).

6. For background, see Robert Ricard, *The Spiritual Conquest of Mexico* (Berkeley and Los Angeles: University of California Press, 1966).

7. Samuel Ramos, *Profile of Man and Culture in Mexico* (Austin: University of Texas Press, 1962), 27.

8. Nancy Farris, *Crown and Clergy in Colonial Mexico, 1759–1821* (London: University of London Press, 1968).

9. For a fascinating account of the importance of imported books in the colonies, see Irving A. Leonard, *Books of the Brave* (Cambridge, Mass.: Harvard University Press, 1949).

10. Richard Greenleaf, "Historiography of the Mexican Inquisition," in *Cultural Encounters: The Impact of the Inquisition in Spain and the New World*, ed. Mary Elizabeth Perry and Anne J. Cruz (Berkeley and Los Angeles: University of California Press, 1991), 256–57.

11. Lyle McAlister, *The "Fuero Militar" in New Spain, 1764–1800* (Gainesville: University of Florida Press, 1967).

12. Edwin Lieuwen, *Mexican Militarism* (Albuquerque: University of New Mexico Press, 1968).

13. Henry Bamford Parkes, *A History of Mexico* (Boston: Houghton Mifflin, 1966), 87. For an excellent discussion of some of the consequences of the Spanish bureaucratic system, see Colin M. MacLachlan, *Spain's Empire in the New World* (Berkeley and Los Angeles: University of California Press, 1991), 34ff.

14. For background, see Charles Gibson, *Spain in America* (New York: Harper & Row, 1967); Clarence Haring, *The Spanish Empire in America* (New York: Oxford University Press, 1947); Lillian Fisher, *Viceregal Administration in the Spanish American Colonies* (Berkeley and Los Angeles: University of California Press, 1926).

15. Justo Sierra, *The Political Evolution of the Mexican People* (Austin: University of Texas Press, 1969), 107.

16. *La formación del estado mexicano* (Mexico City: Porrúa, 1984); Juan Felipe Leal, "El estado y el bloque en el poder en México," *Revista Mexicana de Ciencias Políticas y Sociales* 35 (October-December 1989): 12ff.

17. Michael Meyer and William Sherman, *The Course of Mexican History* (New York: Oxford University Press, 1991), 168.

18. Edward A. Shils, *The Intellectual Between Tradition and Modernity: The Indian Situation* (The Hague: Mouton, 1961).

19. Glen Dealy, *The Public Man: An Interpretation of Latin American and Other Catholic Cultures* (Amherst: University of Massachusetts Press, 1977), 8.

20. In his examination of the heartland, William Least Heat Moon reported that rural Kansas still strongly opposes any project representing federal government intervention. See his *PrairyErth* (New York: Houghton Mifflin, 1991).

21. For an excellent discussion of this in contemporary Mexico, see Larissa Lomnitz, "Horizontal and Vertical Relations and the Social Structure of Urban Mexico," *Latin American Research Review* 17 (1982): 52.

22. For the views of a leading theoretician, and the larger context of liberalism in Mexico, see Charles A. Hale's *Mexican Liberalism in the Age of Mora, 1821–1853* (New Haven, Conn.: Yale University Press, 1968).

23. For many interesting interpretations of the origins of authoritarianism, see John H. Coatsworth, "Los orígenes del autoritarismo moderno en México," *Foro Internacional* 16 (October-December 1975): 205–32; and Lorenzo Meyer, "The Origins of Mexico's Authoritarian State, Political Control in the Old and New Regimes," in *Authoritarianism in Mexico*, eds. Luis Reyna and Richard Weinert (Philadelphia: ISHI, 1977), 3–22.

24. For examples, see David M. Pletcher, *Rails, Mines, and Progress: Seven American Promoters in Mexico, 1867–1911* (Ithaca, N.Y.: Cornell University Press, 1958).

25. For the long-term consequences of this relationship, see Karl Schmitt, "Church and State in Mexico: A Corporatist Relationship," *Americas* 40 (January 1984): 349–76.

26. Robert J. Knowlton, "Some Practical Effects of Clerical Opposition to the Mexican Reform," *Hispanic American Historical Review* 45 (1965): 246–56, provides concrete examples.

27. Jan Bazant, *Alienation of Church Wealth in Mexico: Social and Economic Aspects of the Liberal Revolution, 1856–1857* (Cambridge: Cambridge University Press, 1971).

28. The conflicts and ideologies are described insightfully by Paul Vanderwood, "Betterment for Whom? The Reform Period: 1855–1875," in *The Oxford History of Mexico*, eds. Michael C. Meyer and William H. Beezley (New York: Oxford University Press, 2000), 371–396.

29. Charles A. Hale, *The Transformation of Liberalism in Late Nineteenth Century Mexico* (Princeton, N.J.: Princeton University Press, 1989), 27.

30. Robert M. Buffington and William E. French, "The Culture of Modernity," in *The Oxford History of Mexico,* eds. Michael C. Meyer and William Beezley (New York: Oxford University Press, 2000), 401.

31. *Inscripciones,* Universidad Nacional Autónomo de Mexico, Escuela Nacional Preparatoria, official registration records.

32. Karl Schmitt, "The Díaz Conciliation Policy on State and Local Levels, 1867–1911," *Hispanic American Historical Review* 40 (1960): 513–32.

33. Martin S. Stabb, "Indigenism and Racism in Mexican Thought, 1857–1911," *Journal of Inter-American Studies and World Affairs* 1 (1959): 405–23.

34. Colin MacLachlan and William H. Beezley, *El Gran Pueblo: A History of Greater Mexico* (Englewood Cliffs, N.J.: Prentice Hall, 1994), 131.

35. For evidence of this, see the officer promotion lists from various battles in the published records of the Secretaría de Guerra y Marina, *Escalafón general de ejército* (Mexico City, 1902, 1911, 1914). For his collaborators, see Roderic Ai Camp, *Mexican Political Biographies, 1884–1934* (Austin: University of Texas Press, 1994).

36. For background and the long-term consequences of this relationship, see Roderic Ai Camp, *Generals in the Palacio: The Military in Modern Mexico* (New York: Oxford University Press, 1992).

37. Roderic Ai Camp, *Political Recruitment Across Two Centuries: Mexico 1884–1991* (Austin: University of Texas Press, 1995), 132.

38. For excellent case studies of these interlocking economic-political families, see Mark Wasserman, *Persistent Oligarchs: The Political Economy of Chihuahua, Mexico* (Durham, N.C.: Duke University Press, 1993); and Gilbert Joseph and Allen Wells, "Yucatán: Elite Politics and Rural Insurgency," in *Provinces of the Revolution: Essays on Regional Mexican History, 1910–1929,* eds. Thomas Benjamin and Mark Wasserman (Albuquerque: University of New Mexico Press, 1990).

39. See Francisco Bulnes, *El verdadero Díaz y la Revolución* (Mexico City: Editorial Hispano-Mexicana, 1920), 42. This latter figure is probably exaggerated but indicates the bureaucracy's importance.

40. For a firsthand view of some of these methods, see John Kenneth Turner's muckraking, autobiographical account in *Barbarous Mexico* (Austin: University of Texas Press, 1969); or Evelyn Hu-Dehart, "Development and Rural Rebellion: Pacification of the Yaquis in the Late Porfiriato," *Hispanic American Historical Review* 54 (1974): 72–93.

41. A nice comparison between the nineteenth and twentieth centuries can be found in Aldo Flores-Quiroga, "Legitimacy, Sequencing, and Credibility," in *The Divine Charter, Constitutionalism and Liberalism in Nineteenth-Century Mexico*, ed. Jaime Rodríguez (Lanham, Md.: Rowman & Littlefield, 2005), 339–50.

42. This latter variable has been strongly emphasized. However, more careful empirical examination suggests the following conclusion: "Future analysis of continuity and turnover in Mexico and elsewhere needs to examine the interrelationship between generational and individual political mobility to determine which, if either, is a more useful variable of political upheaval. I am suggesting that *intra-generational* mobility, measured by access to political office for the first time, may be far more significant in explaining political stability and instability than *generational* access to power, measured by age cohort alone." See my *Political Recruitment Across Two Centuries*, 45.

43. An excellent but brief discussion of these arguments can be found in Paul J. Vanderwood, "Explaining the Mexican Revolution," in *The Revolutionary Process in Mexico: Essays on Political and Social Change, 1880–1940*, ed. Jaime E. Rodríguez (Los Angeles: UCLA Latin American Center, 1990), 97–114.

44. Support for this view can be found in John Womack Jr., "The Mexican Revolution, 1910–1920," in vol. 5 of *The Cambridge History of Latin America*, ed. Leslie Bethell (Cambridge: Cambridge University Press, 1986), 74–153.

45. For background on Flores Magón and other precursors, see James Cockcroft's excellent *Intellectual Precursors of the Mexican Revolution, 1900–1913* (Austin: University of Texas Press, 1968).

46. These can be found in Jesús Silva Herzog, *Breve historia de la revolución mexicana, los antecedentes y la etapa maderista* (Mexico City: Fondo de Cultura Económica, 1960), annexes.

47. Stanley R. Ross, *Francisco I. Madero: Apostle of Mexican Democracy* (New York: Columbia University Press, 1955).

48. See John Womack Jr., *Zapata and the Mexican Revolution* (New York: Knopf, 1968); Michael Meyer, *Mexican Rebel: Pascual Orozco and the Mexican Revolution, 1910–1915* (Lincoln: University of Nebraska Press, 1967).

49. Jean Charlot, *The Mexican Mural Renaissance, 1920–1925* (New Haven, Conn.: Yale University Press, 1967), provides an overview of this movement. For its influence on United States culture, see Helen Delpar, *The Enormous Vogue of Things Mexican: Cultural Relations Between the United States and Mexico, 1920–1935* (Tuscaloosa: University of Alabama Press, 1992).

50. See John Brushwood's, *Mexico in Its Novel: A Nation's Search for Identity* (Austin: University of Texas Press, 1966), 173ff.

51. For wonderfully revealing examples of popular appraisals of various revolutionary figures, see Merle E. Simmons, *The Mexican Corrido as a Source for Interpretive Study of Modern Mexico, 1879–1950* (Bloomington: Indiana University Press, 1957).

52. Henry C. Schmidt, *The Roots of Lo Mexicano: Self and Society in Mexican Thought, 1900–1934* (Austin: University of Texas Press, 1978), 97.

53. José Vasconcelos, *La raza cósmica: Misión de la raza iberoamericana* (Paris: Agencia Mundial de Librerías, 1925).

54. Héctor Aguilar Camín and Lorenzo Meyer, *In the Shadow of the Mexican Revolution: Contemporary Mexican History, 1910–1989* (Austin: University of Texas Press, 1993), 78.

55. Paul Sigmund, *Multinationals in Latin America: The Politics of Nationalization* (Madison: University of Wisconsin Press, 1980), 81.

56. The August 1994 presidential elections could be said to have been the most successful in the level of participation and the degree of integrity on election day until the July, 2000 contest. However, the larger electoral setting in which these elections occurred left much to be desired, especially since the conditions were favorable to the government party. An excellent discussion of this can be found in "Mexico's Electoral Aftermath and Political Future," *Memoria* of the papers presented at a binational conference, University of Texas, Austin, September 2–3, 1994 (Austin: Mexican Center, Institute of Latin American Studies, 1994).

57. For an account of these developments, see Eyler N. Simpson's classic, *The Ejido: Mexico's Way Out* (Chapel Hill: University of North Carolina Press, 1937); Nathan Whetten, *Rural Mexico* (Chicago: University of Chicago Press, 1948), the most comprehensive picture of land-tenure conditions; Paul Lamartine Yates, *Mexico's Agricultural Dilemma* (Tucson: University of Arizona Press, 1981). In 1992, the Mexican government introduced radical reforms in the *ejido* land structure. See Claire Poole, "Land and Life," *Forbes,* April 29, 1991, 45–46, and *El Financiero International,* March 30, 1992, 11.

58. The best discussion of this consequence can be found in Frank Brandenburg, *The Making of Modern Mexico* (Englewood Cliffs, N.J.: Prentice-Hall, 1964), 10–11. For the state's role in evolving a revolutionary myth, see Thomas Benjamin, *La Revolución: Mexicós Great Revolution as Memory, Myth and History* (Austin: University of Texas Press, 2000).

59. John H. Coatsworth and Carlos Rico, eds., *Images of Mexico in the United States* (La Jolla, Calif.: Center for U.S.-Mexican Studies, UCSD, 1989), 10.

60. For background, see Karl M. Schmitt, *Mexico and the United States, 1821–1973: Conflict and Coexistence* (New York: Wiley, 1974), 51ff.

61. Josefina Váquez Zoraida and Lorenzo Meyer, *The United States and Mexico* (Chicago: University of Chicago Press, 1985), 49.

62. Robert E. Quirk, *An Affair of Honor: Woodrow Wilson and the Occupation of Veracruz* (New York: Norton, 1962), 95ff.

63. Interview with Ernesto Robles Levi, Mexico City, May 21, 1985.

64. For a firsthand account of this experience by a U.S. officer on the expedition, see Colonel Frank Tompkins, *Chasing Villa* (Harrisburg, Pa.: Military Service Publishing Company, 1934).

3

Contemporary Political Culture:
What Mexicans Believe

What is problematic about the content of the emerging world culture is its political character. Although the movement toward technology and rationality of organization appears with great uniformity throughout the world, the direction of political change is less clear. But one aspect of this new world political culture is discernible: *it will be a political culture of participation* [italics added]. If there is a political revolution going on throughout the world, it is what might be called the participation explosion. In all the new nations of the world the belief that the ordinary man is politically relevant—that he ought to be an involved participant in the political system—is wide-spread. Large groups of people who have been outside of politics are demanding entrance into the political system. And the political elites are rare who do not profess commitment to this goal.

GABRIEL ALMOND AND SIDNEY VERBA, *The Civic Culture*

The political culture of any society is partially a product of its general culture. Culture incorporates all the influences—historical, religious, ethnic, political—that affect a society's values and attitudes. The political culture is a microcosm of the larger culture, focusing specifically on those values and attitudes having to do with a person's *political* views and behavior.[1]

In the Mexican society, as in many societies, the intensity with which someone holds certain beliefs is related to religion, level of education, income, age, gender, place of residence, and other variables. Their consequences will be examined in the following chapter and are important to understand. Equally important for comparative purposes is to evaluate the beliefs that may influence Mexico's politics and Mexican attitudes toward the political and economic system.

LEGITIMACY: SUPPORT FOR THE POLITICAL SYSTEM

One of the most significant explanations for a political system's stability is its legitimacy in the eyes of the society. Of course, any political model consists of a variety of institutions, some of which have been accorded greater respect than others. Level of respect permits a comparison of citizen trust toward political and other types of institutions.

When Mexicans evaluate their institutions, it is apparent that those most closely associated with the state are held in lowest regard (see Table 3-1). Only three institutions are widely esteemed: family, church, and schools.[2] The selection of family is not surprising because a culture with strong values generally ranks family and tradition highly. Of course, if loyalty to family is excessive, it makes transferring loyalty to governmental institutions difficult. It could be argued that this might be the case in Mexico, since Mexicans express some serious reservations about the trustworthiness of *governmen-*

Table 3-1 Legitimacy of the State in the United States and Mexico: Confidence of Citizens in Institutions

Institution	Percentage of Respondents Giving Positive Evaluation					
	United States 1990	United States 2000	Mexico 1988	Mexico 1998	Mexico 2000	Mexico 2003
Family	—	99	84	92	92	—
Church	85	86	62	77	75	57
Schools	82	—	60	64	—	62
Television[a]	—	58	37	36	38	—
Law/courts	—	80	32	31	22	26
Army	86	90	32	45	49	47
Newspaper/media	69	53	25	29	24	48
Business	84	—	22	52	41	—
Congress	83	—	16	28	21	24
Unions	52	—	14	24	25	—
Political parties	—	56	—	29	20	26
Police	88	87	12	33	23	27

Sources: Este País, August 1991, 5; Laurence Parisot, "Attitudes About the Media: A Five-Country Comparison," *Public Opinion* 10 (1988): Table 1; Marta Lagos, "Actitudes económicas y democracia en Latinoamérica," *Este País* (January 1997): Table 16; "Democracy Through Latin American Lenses," Grant, Hewlett Foundation, Principal investigator, Roderic A; Camp, June, 1998; "Democracy Through U.S. and Mexican Lenses," Grant, Hewlett Foundation, principal investigator, Roderic A; Camp, September, 2000; World Values Survey, 2000; "Confianza en las instituciones," *Este País* (January 2003): 45–47.
[a]For the United States in 1990 and Mexico 2003, included under newspapers.

tal institutions and institutions as a whole. The same pattern is found in Japan, where the level of trust in institutions is lower than in Mexico.[3] A more persuasive explanation might be that Mexicans became disenchanted with their governmental institutions during the decades of a one-party system.

The figures in Table 3-1 permit us to view the evolution of Mexican attitudes toward institutions over the last two decades, beginning in 1988, which marks the initiation of significant, national, electoral competition. What is remarkable about these figures is that for the most part they remain stable, even after the Fox victory in July 2000. For example, one might have expected increased citizen confidence in political parties, in the legal system, and even in the media, given the fact that each contributed to some degree to the fair presidential election in 2000.

The confidence Mexicans have in the church and schools is significant. In the first place, as suggested in the previous chapter, both the liberal tradition and the revolution encouraged anti-church sentiment. Nevertheless, although we will discover that Mexicans developed sentiments supporting the separation of church and state, secular criticism has not done away with respect or sympathies for the Catholic Church, particularly in a society in which at least 85 percent of the members are Catholic. Regard for the church as an institution may be a partial reaction to state suppression, especially before the 1992 constitutional reforms.

The fact that support for the church has increased from 1988 to the late 1990s suggests, however, that it has earned Mexicans' respect. Even the lower figure for 2003 in Table 3-1 is an anomaly since a 2004 study, which used a different ranking system, placed the Catholic Church at the top of the list.[4] On a political and social level, the church has been the most pro-active, traditional autonomous actor in favor of democracy. It openly favored free and fair elections, it maintained a constant barrage of criticism against fraud, and it encouraged its parishioners to vote, arguing that it was a Christian responsibility. It is noteworthy that Americans also give high marks to the church as an institution, indicating both their respect and, implicitly, the importance of religion and religious beliefs in the U.S. culture.

Mexican attitudes toward education, borne out in survey after survey, are usually quite positive. The significance of this for the legitimacy of the political system is perhaps more important for Mexico than for the United States, where schools are also viewed positively. The school system in Mexico is largely public, although Catholic schools do play an important role. Unlike in the United States, however, public schools until the 1990s were operated by the federal government, and so the teachers were its employees. Today, financial control is in the hands of state governments. Schools may not be perceived as doing so, but they could serve as a positive, indirect means of reinforcing the state's legitimacy—especially because texts in elementary schools are selected by the government. Most important, Mexicans' satisfaction with the school system is one of the few consistent pluses for the government.

In comparing Mexican figures with those from the United States, several patterns immediately stand out. Americans give equally high marks to family, church, and schools, suggesting their importance across cultures. Americans also give extremely high marks to governmental institutions, or agencies representing national and local governments, including the courts, the armed forces, and the police. Mexicans' confidence in other institutions is low. What one notices immediately when comparing it with that of Americans is the generally significantly lower levels of support. The weaker positive responses are not necessarily an indication of extreme frustration with the Mexican system; rather, Mexicans are likely to have lower expectations of their institutions, given their institutions' past performances, than Americans have. Nevertheless, the fact that police, political parties, the courts, and congress tail off in the rankings indicates a lack of confidence in as well as alienation from these institutions.

Attitudes toward the police are an important indication of basic trust in government. On the local level, police are the most likely representatives of government to come in contact with the citizenry. Therefore, a good opinion of the police is generally seen as an important grassroots indicator of trust in government. A sense of personal security is often a variable in one's evaluation of government performance. In the United States among formal institutions, the police achieved the highest level of confidence in 1990, and second highest in 2000; in state and local surveys throughout Mexico, the police consistently rank lowest. Explanations usually include the perception that they are dishonest, often involved in criminal activities, and abuse their authority, especially among lower-income and rural groups. Given the rapid increase in crime in the 1990s and 2000s and the widespread involvement of police as criminals, confidence remains low. One out of five residents in the capital in 2002 reported being a victim of crime, the same percentage as in 1998.[5] More importantly, only a small minority of citizens believed the government could actually reduce the level of crime, and their numbers have declined.[6] By 2002, 47 percent of Mexicans asserted that they lived in an unsafe state.[7] In 2004, fed up with the level of crime, 250,000 citizens staged a silent march in the capital. Nevertheless, a year later, nationwide 14 percent of all Mexican households reported a family member was a victim of crime.[8]

The connection between services and specific institutions in society is shown in Table 3-2. When Mexicans are asked about the quality of specific government services, they point most often to education and health care.

Table 3-2 Legitimacy of the Mexican State: The
Case of Public Services

Service	Percentage of Respondents with Favorable Image
Schools	67
Medical	55
Trash disposal and sanitation	41
Telephone	40
Security	32
Police	24

Source: Este País, August 1991, 4.

Generally speaking, they are most concerned on the local level, with education, health care, transportation, and sanitation. Agencies associated with the government render services that win widespread approval, thus contributing to the legitimacy of the government. In contrast, in the case of the police and the security apparatus, they offer services that the average Mexican views as inadequate.

Mexican attitudes toward institutions may be explained in part by the unpredictable economic, political, and social conditions of Mexican life in the 1980s and 1990s. Mexicans faced a number of political crises in the last year of the Salinas administration, beginning with the uprising of indigenous groups in Chiapas in January 1994, followed by the assassination of the PRI's presidential candidate, Luis Donaldo Colosio in March. The assassination of Colosio, an unprecedented event in recent Mexican politics, began to initiate some doubts about both their personal economic future and their governmental institutions. Then, a few months after Ernesto Zedillo took office in December 1994, their confidence as a whole began to erode dramatically with the economic devaluation and harsh austerity policies—combined with an untested cabinet and president. By the end of 1995, 80 percent described their economic situation as worse than the previous year, and only 15 percent thought economic recovery would occur in a year's time.

By the time Zedillo left office in November 2000, he had been able to restore considerable confidence in the presidency and in the government.[9] For the first time in recent history, he was able to provide for a presidential transition without a devaluation and economic crisis. Although his party lost the presidency, Zedillo was able to give his successor a stable economic situation on which to build citizen trust in institutions. Fox's personal popularity ratings remained high throughout his presidency. His performance ratings, however, declined by his second year in office and have remained disappointing. Mexicans expressed a much more favorable opinion of society in general than they did of specific institutions, governmental or otherwise, indicating a much higher level of trust in societal responses to problems. Scholars cite the 1985 earthquake in Mexico City as an example.[10] Criticism abounded of government efforts to save persons trapped in the rubble, in contrast, neighborhood volunteers' efforts were looked upon as exemplary. The same pattern was repeated in 1992 in the aftermath of a devastating explosion in Guadalajara's storm sewers.

The government's inadequacies after the quake produced a groundswell of popular movements that together pressed demands on the government. One analyst had this to say about their cooperation:

> In the aftermath of the disastrous Mexico City earthquake in 1985, a coalition of urban organizations successfully forced the Mexican government and the World Bank to alter housing relief plans, accelerate the process of reconstruction, and reverse several fundamental urban policies. The coalition achieved this by uniting scores of neighborhood organizations. Hundreds of thousands of earthquake victims joined other urban poor to wrest concessions through deft media manipulation and political bartering.[11]

During the last two decades, there has been a remarkable change in Mexican attitudes toward fellow citizens, rather than toward institutions. In 1981, only 18 percent of Mexicans expressed confidence in their fellow citizens. By 1990, that figure grew dramatically to 33 percent of respondents with positive views of other Mexicans. By the end of the decade, it declined once again to 1981 levels. Even after the Fox election, citizen confidence in other Mexicans remained low (Table 3-3). By 2003, it reached an all-time low of only 10 percent. The fluctuations in confidence levels suggest that citizen responses to such questions, even in the United States, are determined by immediate conditions, and not necessarily by long-term impressions. In the Mexican case, personal insecurity may have played a significant role, since unemployment rates were found to have a significant impact on crime, and

Table 3-3 Confidence in People in Mexico and the United States

Country	1981	1990	1999	2000	2003	2005
Mexico	18	33	21	18	10	19
United States	45	50	36	30	30	—

Source: World Values Survey, 1990; World Values Survey, 2000; and "Democracy Through U.S. and Mexican Lenses," Grant, Hewlett Foundation, September 2000; Alejandro Moreno, *Nuestros Valores* (Mexico: Banamex, 2005), 145; "Voluntary Work Survey," courtesy of Miguel Basáñez, 497 respondents, October 2005.

Mexicans faced a major economic crisis from 1995 to 1998. Personal insecurity has become pronounced since 2000. In terms of political behavior, trust in people is an important measure of the potential for democratic political institutions. Mexicans have demonstrated their interest in democratizing their political institutions, sharing in the wave of democratization occurring elsewhere. To survive, democratic institutions rely on the high levels of personal trust necessary to effect compromise and operate within the rules of the political game. On an individual level Mexico has not produced a consistent direction in the last decade.

PARTICIPATION: ACTIVATING THE ELECTORATE

One of the most important variables that might explain citizen attitudes toward politics and their trust in institutions and fellow citizens is citizens' level of political interest and participation. At least since the early 1960s, interest in political affairs in urban Mexico has been much lower than in the United States and England. In the early 1990s, a survey of forty-three countries revealed that only 52 percent expressed some or much interest in politics. In 1995, shortly after the presidential election with the highest voter turnout ever, only 32 percent expressed a similar interest, well below the world average.

Mexicans' lack of interest in politics continued well into the 2000 presidential race. As the Mexico Panel Survey discovered in February 2000, only 28 percent expressed some or much interest in politics. In fact, an equally low percentage were specifically following the presidential race. By May, however, the figure increased to 36 percent, and less than a month before the election, 44 percent of Mexicans expressed an interest in politics. Two months after Vicente Fox's electoral victory, marking the most radical change in Mexican politics since the 1920s, only 38 percent continued that same degree of interest.

These figures demonstrate that ordinarily, most Mexicans share little interest in politics. Their interest does increase when the stakes are higher and they have an opportunity to affect the outcome of a major national election. Accomplishing such a result does not, as these data suggest, sustain citizen interest in politics. It is even possible that as the time since the Fox victory lengthens, political interest will return to the original, preelection levels.

Why has Mexican interest remained so low, despite the dramatic changes in the political system? It has been shown that certain characteristics can accentuate citizen interest in politics. Among these are increased education, male gender, higher income, and "post-materialist beliefs," which are attitudes emphasizing self-expression and quality of life. Such attitudes are not only critical in explaining stronger levels of interest in politics, but in much higher levels of support for democracy.[12]

Among Mexicans, a citizen's ideological affinity also explains a stronger interest in politics. Nearly two-thirds of Mexicans who considered themselves to be on the ideological left expressed an interest in politics, nearly twice that of all other Mexicans. These Mexicans have typically supported political parties, including the Party of the Democratic Revolution (PRD), which laid the groundwork for the democratic, electoral transformation. Many of them were persecuted for their political views. To have been a PRD partisan in the early 1990s required a strong, committed interest in politics.[13]

People generally move from an interest in politics to political activism when they believe they can affect outcomes in the system. One way to test peoples' attitudes toward outcomes is to examine *political efficacy*. This measures the degree to which a person believes he or she can participate in politics and the responsiveness of the system to their involvement. When Americans were asked whether or not they have a say in what government does, somewhere between 33 and 41 percent, from 1980 to 1988, replied that they do.[14] A similar but more specific question was posed to Mexicans:

Political efficacy: the belief in one's ability to participate in or influence political affairs.

When asked whether they could do something about election fraud prior to 2000, 56 percent thought not (see Table 3-4). It is not surprising that more than half of all Mexicans believe they cannot affect the outcome of government policy; they have lived under a semi-authoritarian political model in which control over decision making was concentrated at the top all their adult lives. After all, if a third of all Americans described themselves as ineffectual politically in a system where honest elections are the norm and competition is regularized, the higher Mexican response should be expected. After the election of Vicente Fox, when many voters for the first time discovered that their votes could radically change the outcome of a national election, citizen efficacy, as measured by the question "can voting make things better in the future," appeared quite high, with two-thirds of Mexicans agreeing with that statement.

Most citizens in political systems where elections occur become involved through voting. Therefore, their ability to affect the outcome of

Table 3-4 Political Efficacy of Mexicans

Response to Statement "Can do nothing about electoral fraud"	Percentage of Respondents
Definitely true	8.9
True	47.3
False	31.5
Definitely false	4.0
Not sure	5.6
No answer	2.7

Source: Los Angeles Times poll, August 1989.

government policy is influenced by their perception of the integrity of the voting process.[15] Mexico has had a long history of voter fraud in the twentieth century. Before 1988 the accusations of wrongdoing were based solely on observation and political commentary,[16] but shortly before the presidential elections that year Mexicans were asked for the first time in a nationwide poll if their vote would be respected (see Table 3-5). More than half of those interviewed thought their votes would not be counted honestly. Only a fourth believed in the integrity of the electoral process, and an equal number were unsure.

The question was repeated shortly before the off-year elections in August 1991, when many governors, half the senate, and all congresspersons were elected. Although the "don't knows" remained the same, those who viewed the elections as honest increased by 83 percent. Despite intense election battles and evidence of election fraud since 1989, the government successfully allayed the doubts of some Mexicans in the 1991 elections. By the spring of 1994, after several political crises had led to a number of structural reforms in the electoral process, including the presence of international observers, Mexicans again were asked if they thought the forthcoming presidential elections would be fair. Their response, which had fluctuated considerably throughout 1994, remained fairly consistent with the 1991 responses. By 2000, shortly before the presidential election, 30 percent of Mexicans believed their vote would not be counted honestly, almost exactly the same as the responses in 1991 and 1994. On the other hand, a huge decline occured among those citizens with no opinion, producing a dramatic increase among those Mexicans who believed the election would be honest.

Citizen efficacy can be altered significantly if citizens view the consequences of participation as accurately reflecting their involvement. In the case of elections, of course, it would reflect an accurate count of their votes. The Vicente Fox electoral victory produced such a dramatic change. The percentage of Mexicans who thought the elections were clean after Fox's

Table 3-5 Mexicans' Views of Elections

Responses to Question "Will Your Vote Be Respected?"	Percentage of Respondents									
	1988 Elections	Percentage of Change	1991 Elections	Percentage of Change	1994 Elections	Percentage of Change	2000 Elections	Percentage of Change	2005
Yes	23	83+	42	12–	37	81+	67	12+	75
No	53	40–	32	6+	34	12–	30	23–	23
Don't know	24	8+	26	12+	29	90–	3	33–	2

Source: Este País, August 1991, 6; *Este País,* weekly poll, urban voters only, May 25, 1994. In a much larger poll, conducted by Alianza Cívica, of 9,507 voters in twenty locations, 47 percent believed that the elections might be fraudulent. "The Mexico 2000 Panel Survey," NSF Grant, Principal investigator, Chappell Lawson; *Reforma,* 1,515 respondents, November 2005. The question in the 2005 survey was: In our country, can people vote freely?

Table 3-6 Organizational Membership in Mexico and the
United States

Organizational Affiliation	Mexico	United States
	Percentage of Respondents	
Religious	36	71
Sports	25	43
Parent/Teacher	16	40
Union	10	28
Neighborhood	10	51
Political	7	27

Source: "Democracy Through U.S. and Mexican Lenses," Grant, Hewlett
Foundation, September 2000.

victory increased to 75 percent. However, those Mexicans who were most
convinced of the election's integrity were supporters of the National Action
Party, Fox's party.[17] Those Mexicans who were least persuaded by a large
margin were, not surprisingly, supporters of PRI, the incumbent party that
lost the election. These figures are important for another reason. They indicate the fragility of beliefs among some Mexicans toward the integrity of
electoral structures and institutions, determined not just by their actual performance, but by the success of their specific candidate.

People's proclivity to participate in the electoral process is affected to
some extent not only by confidence in their political efficacy or by the
integrity of the institutions and the process itself, but also by their level of
activism in general. Mexicans' involvement in organizations is not high (see
Table 3-6). Among the most important organizations are religious and sports
organizations followed by parent-teacher groups. Most Mexicans belong to
no organization. With the exception of unions, membership is voluntary,
which is a measure of level of interest in involvement. Mexicans who belong
to organizations typically belong to voluntary groups. Only 2 percent of Mexicans in the late 1980s belonged to political parties or political organizations,
suggesting a relatively low level of interest in politics when the democratic
transformation began.[18] By 2000, 7 percent of Mexicans had worked for a
political party or a candidate. Compared with the United States, Mexican participation in neighborhood groups and political organizations remains low,
fewer than four to five times less involvement than their northern neighbors.
Nevertheless, the small absolute numbers of Mexicans politically involved
has increased threefold since 1989, suggesting that a democratic opening has
increased such participation and, in return, their participation has encouraged
electoral competition.

Table 3-7 Dispositions Toward Political Action in Mexico and the United States

Action	Mexico					United States			
	1981	1990	1996	1998	2000	1981	1990	1995	2000
Signed a petition	8	31	28	13	6	61	70	70	38
Joined a boycott	1	6	9	1	7	14	17	18	19
Attended lawful demonstration	8	20	10	11	8	12	15	15	17
Joined an unofficial strike	2	7	6	2	2	3	4	4	10
Occupied a building	1	5	4	2	0	2	2	2	12

Source: World Values Surveys, 1981, 1990, 1996–97; "Democracy Through Latin American Lenses," Hewlett Grant, June 1998; "Democracy Through U.S. and Mexican Lenses," Hewlett Grant, September 2000.

If we move higher up the ladder of political participation, from membership in an organization to some type of action, it is possible to obtain a good sense of citizens' attitudes toward political involvement and of their level of commitment to direct political participation. One way to measure such participation is to ask citizens about their attitudes toward modes of political action. In other words, to test receptivity to greater political involvement, people are asked whether or not they favor such highly visible and committed activities as boycotting, legal demonstrations, illegal demonstrations, and occupation of buildings or factories.

Traditionally, as scholars have suggested, Americans have been more likely than their Mexican counterparts to participate in orthodox activities, such as signing a petition or joining a boycott.[19] In 1981, for example, nearly two-thirds of Americans but fewer than one in twelve Mexicans claimed to have signed a petition (Table 3-7). In both Mexico and the United States, an increase in most forms of activity occurred in the 1980s, but especially in Mexico. In the Mexican case, however, it appears to have reached a peak in the mid-1990s after the implementation of a much stronger electoral law in 1996, the victory of the opposition parties in the national congress in 1997, and an economic recovery from a terrible recession in 1995. With the exception of participating in boycotts, Mexican involvement in these types of political actions declined in 2000, possibly because they viewed democratic institutions as legitimate, and therefore this form of participation unnecessary. Nevertheless, the fact that 250,000 Mexicans living in the capital participated in a march in 2004 to protest against inadequate government protections from crime suggests that more Mexicans, when a policy issue affects them personally, will go beyond voting as a direct form of political participation.

What explains the dramatic increase in Mexican political actions in the 1980s and early 1990s? It is apparent that the greater competitiveness of the national political system in Mexico, beginning with the local elections in 1985 and culminating in the national congressional elections in 1997, affected the nature of political activism. During the twelve-year period, public opposition to electoral fraud reached new highs.[20] It was given legitimacy in the media through announcements and advertisements by intellectuals and leading clergy. In fact, the clergy threatened after northern elections in 1986, if a recount did not take place, to cease celebrating masses, something that had not happened since the 1920s.[21] The claims of fraud attracted international attention, and the U.S. media helped legitimize the claims of the domestic opposition.

Another provocative explanation was offered in recent research on Mexican political stability. Linda Stevenson and Mitchell Seligson presented the hypothesis that "over the past sixty years, negative memories of the Mexican Revolution of 1910 have sparked fear of a return to the violence of that period, which in turn inhibited the willingness of Mexicans engaged in anti-system political actions."[22] They believe that this collective memory has faded with the passage of time and that the surviving generation of the revolution has passed from the scene, thus eliminating an important source of inhibitions toward high-risk political actions, which they predicted would increase after 1994. The uprising of the Chiapan Indians in early 1994 sparked sympathy movements throughout Mexico, and in early 1995, within weeks of imposing austerity measures, thousands of Mexicans, including numerous middle-class professionals, demonstrated in front of federal agencies their anger toward government policies.[23]

One of the most imaginative Mexican leaders of this new set of political techniques is "Superbarrio," a masked version of superman who is a wrestler. Sheldon Annis described him as "a colorful good guy sworn to oppose the bureaucracy, greedy landlords, and political hacks. Dressed in yellow tights, red cape, and mask emblazoned with 'SB,' Superbarrio led tens of thousands of people in street protests over renters' rights, housing codes, construction credit, and low-cost housing."[24] Collectively, among the most interesting and active organizations among the growing number of urban movements which emerged from the changing electoral process in the 1990s, and performed a crucial role in the 1994 and 1997 elections, was Acción Democrática (AD), an umbrella organization of civic organizations designed to observe and publicly certify elections. Although not engaging in partisan politics, AD provided national coordination to dozens of civic groups, developing stronger linkages among various social organizations, and demonstrating the potential for exercising policy influence, national and interna-

Table 3-8 Party Sympathy in Mexico

Party	Percentage of Respondents			
	1991	1994	2000	2005
No party	56	43	28	—
Institutional Revolutionary Party (PRI)	28	23	30	21
National Action Party (PAN)	6	19	32	26
Democratic Revolutionary Party (PRD)	6	12	10	19
Other	4	3	1	—

Source: Este País, August 1991, 3; *Este País,* June 1, 1994, 3; "Democracy Through U.S. and Mexican Lenses," Grant, Hewlett Foundation, September 2000; *Reforma,* February 28, 2005, 8A.

tionally, to its thousands of affiliated members. Organizations like AD, through their involvement in the day to day process of participatory politics, expand the potential pool of Mexican activists.[25]

Most Mexicans, as do most Americans, however, participate politically through voting. Most Mexicans, on the other hand, have not supported a political party. In fact, approximately two-fifths of all Mexicans in the 1990s are what Americans label independent or uncommitted. In the United States in 2000, only 12 percent of all Americans considered themselves independent or uncommitted; 52 percent, Democrats; and 32 percent, Republicans. The higher percentage of Americans affiliated with a party is a consequence of a higher level of knowledge about the two major parties, which have operated during the entire century, and the fact that both parties have controlled both branches of government.[24] Among Mexicans, 44 percent sympathized with specific parties in 1991, 57 percent did in 1994, 73 percent did in 2000, and 66 percent did in 2005. Party identification increased dramatically in Mexico in the 1990s as its importance became apparent to the Mexican voter. Parties other than the PRI not only were winning state and local offices, but took control of the national legislative branch in 1997. Vicente Fox's victory in July 2000, as the candidate of PAN, reinforced the importance of partisan support (see Table 3-8).

The distribution of Mexican partisan support can be explained, in part, by the ideological preferences of the average citizen. In the past, most analysts viewed the PAN as representing the right, the PRI as the center-right, and the PRD as the left. Today, however, Mexicans themselves view the PRI as representing the right, the PAN as center-right, and the PRD as the left. This probably can be explained by the fact that PRI's strong resistance to democratization, and therefore its support for the status quo, shifted its image in the 1990s to a more conservative position.

Table 3-9 Political Ideology in Mexico and the
United States

Ideology	Mexicans	Mexican Americans	Americans
		(percentages)	
Left	19	15 ⅄	13
Center	39	46	56
Right	42	39	31

Source: "Democracy Through U.S. and Mexican Lenses," Grant,
Hewlett Foundation, September 2000.

When Mexicans and Americans are asked to identify their own ideological preferences, the responses are revealing (Table 3-9). Both countries'
citizens are similar in that they view themselves on the center-right of the
political spectrum. Unless their ideological preferences changed dramatically, it is unlikely that Mexican or American voters would support a party
on the left. What does not show up in these summary figures, however, is
that there is a much larger percentage of Mexicans on the extreme left, and
to a lesser degree the extreme right, suggesting the existence of a broader
ideological spectrum in Mexico. On the other hand, Mexicans are gradually
moving toward the center, the ideological position shared by the majority of
Americans.

Citizens tend to vote for political parties that they believe subscribe to
their views, but ideology is often not an important determinant of why people vote for a candidate. In fact, the candidate's ideology or program has
been shown to have less significance than other variables in explaining Mexicans' reasons for voting, even in presidential races.[27] This pattern was replicated in the 2000 presidential election (see Table 3-10). In a post-election
poll conducted by *Reforma,* the data make it clear that change was the fundamental variable in determining voter preferences. Apparently, "change"
broadly referred to a change in party control of the executive branch, a
change in the political model in the direction of greater pluralism, and possibly a change in the type of leadership. More than two-fifths of Mexican
voters gave change as their primary reason for voting. Only a fifth indicated
the candidate's proposals as significant in their choice. Of the citizens who
gave change as their reason for voting, the vast majority voted for Fox. "The
fact that so many Mexican voters identified with change, and that democracy permitted them to make this choice, produced the Fox victory. Mexicans were not voting for Fox, they were not voting for PAN, they were not
voting for substantive policy issues; they were voting for change, conceptu-

Table 3-10 Why Mexican Voters Cast Their Ballots for President in 2000

Reasons for Voting	Candidate (percentages)				
	Fox	Labastida	Cárdenas	Others	Total
Change	66	15	18	1	43
His proposals	37	42	17	4	22
The candidate	28	50	18	4	9
By custom	12	82	5	1	7
Other	34	43	22	2	6
Party loyalty	8	79	12	1	5
Least bad	37	40	20	3	4
Obligation	31	56	13	0	2
Don't know	27	55	14	3	2

Source: Roderic Ai Camp, "Citizen Attitudes Toward Democracy and Vicente Fox's Victory in 2000," in *Mexico's Pivotal Democratic Election*, ed. Jorge I. Dominguez and Chappell Lawson (Stanford, Calif: Stanford University Press, 2004), 33.

alized pragmatically as an alteration in power, replacing incumbent politicians and the party they represented with something different."[28]

DEMOCRACY: WHAT DOES IT MEAN?

We have explored Mexican attitudes toward legitimacy and participation, attitudes that may affect their political behavior and their views of democracy. Mexico formally achieved an electoral democracy on December 1, 2000, when Vicente Fox took office. But what is the extent of Mexican beliefs in democracy? How do Mexicans conceptualize democracy? Are Mexicans deeply committed to attitudes that will sustain democracy in the next decades? Some observers remain skeptical about Mexican support for democracy either because democratic practices are not the norm within other settings, including interpersonal relationships, social and economic organizations, and even the family.[29]

Recent research does make clear that Latin Americans generally, and Mexicans specifically, conceptualize democracy differently from each other, and from Americans (Table 3-11). Their differing interpretations of the meaning of democracy also have dramatic consequences for what citizens expect from democracy. Americans, not surprisingly, define democracy primarily in terms of liberty. Costa Ricans, who are typically viewed by analysts of the region as the most democratic country, also define democracy in

Table 3-11 Citizen Views of Democracy in Latin America and the United States

	Chile	Costa Rica	Mexico		United States	
			(Figures in Percentages)			
How Defined	1998	1998	1998	2000	1999	2000
Liberty/freedom	25	54	21	25	68	64
Equality	18	6	21	26	5	8
Voting/elections	10	3	12	11	2	4
Form of government	12	6	14	9	2	2
Well-being/progress	8	7	14	7	1	1
Respect/lawfulness	10	3	13	8	1	4
Don't Know/No Answer	8	13	3	—	12	—
Other	8	7	2	14	9	12

Question: In one word, could you tell me what democracy means to you?

Note: N = 3,396, Latin American columns, N = 1659, United States column.

Source: "Democracy Through Latin American Lenses," Grant, Hewlett Foundation, June 1998; *Wall Street Journal,* Hewlett Foundation Poll, April 1999. "Democracy Through U.S. and Mexican Lenses," Grant, Hewlett Foundation, September 2000.

similar terms. What is also distinctive about the American and Costa Rican response to defining democracy is that both countries' citizens share a high level of consensus on its meaning.

Mexicans, similar to Chileans, who have only recently restored an electoral democracy, share more disparate views about democracy. In the first place, an equal number of Mexicans, about one-fifth of the respondents, give equality and liberty the same importance in defining democracy. Mexicans' views of democracy include four additional interpretations, each receiving about the same level of support: voting/elections, form of government, welfare/progress, and respect/rule of law. The fact that Mexicans define democracy in numerous ways suggests a lack of consensus about democracy. This lack of consensus potentially creates problems in developing citizen unity about the legitimacy of a political model and in agreeing on the rules of political behavior.

The preferences that Mexican citizens give to equality and liberty are inherently interesting. In fact, when Mexicans were asked to choose between equality and liberty in defining democracy, more than two-fifths chose equality compared to one-third who chose liberty. The American response was the reverse. Half of all Americans chose liberty followed by a third who believed democracy had more to do with equality. These differences in defining democracy are not surprising given the comparatively higher levels of social and economic inequality in Mexico compared with the United States. Mexicans, consequently, view democracy as a political model that can ameliorate the levels of inequality.

The manner in which Mexicans conceptualize democracy affects their expectations about governmental performance. In spite of the fact that sufficient democratic practices exist in Mexico to have permitted the election of Vicente Fox who, as suggested, represented an alternative symbolizing change, Mexicans are not satisfied with the level of democracy in their country. When citizens were asked: How democratic would you say this country is? the majority described it as having little or no democracy. Only 46 percent of Mexicans considered Mexico to be somewhat or very democratic. Nearly double that number in the United States, 85 percent, described their country in these democratic terms. In 2005, only 59 percent of Mexicans rated democracy as preferable to other kinds of government, and only a fourth were satisfied with democracy.

CONCLUSION

Attitudes and beliefs, as do other institutional and structural factors, play a significant role in the evolution of a political system and the behavior of its citizens. Political attitudes, as a component of general cultural beliefs and values, are most important. In particular, two sets of beliefs, legitimacy and participation, are central to the interrelationship between societal values and political behavior.

Mexicans have high levels of respect for and trust in certain institutions, especially churches and schools, but Mexicans have very low levels of respect for political institutions of any sort and the persons associated with them, such as bureaucrats and police. Their appraisals reflect a general lack of trust in government. This may be explained by their belief that most government agencies, and their representatives, are corrupt. Indeed, they believe corruption is the single most important obstacle to achieving democracy in Mexico. Mexicans are unusual, compared with Americans, for the low levels of respect they give to most societal institutions. This is likely to change as their own involvement in and respect for civic and social organizations grow, and if the democratic government of Vicente Fox fulfills some of their expectations.

Although governmental institutions receive lower levels of support, and therefore have less legitimacy in Mexico than in the United States, the universal decline in governmental legitimacy in most nations during the 1980s was less sharp in Mexico. It is likely that Mexicans reached an even lower level of support for institutions in the mid-1980s and, through the efforts of President Salinas, who personally achieved high levels of popularity in the early 1990s, recovered from that level, thus considerably reducing the overall decline in government legitimacy before 1994. Serious political and economic events throughout 1994 and the first half of 1995 reversed this pattern, destroying gains in legitimacy and bringing perceptions of the presidency and governmental institutions to new lows. Since 1998, however, the pattern remains contradictory. The police and congress improved their levels of trust since the late 1980s, but they remain among those institutions with the lowest rankings. What is surprising as of 2005 is the low levels of respect for political parties and courts, two institutions that will be crucial to democracy's success.

Mexicans also expressed less trust than did Americans or Canadians in their fellow human beings. Their confidence in others rose dramatically during the 1980s, but was still substantially below that found in the United States in the 1990s. Mexicans' low levels of trust in one another, even after Fox's victory, may create an obstacle to implementing democratic institutions.

Other changes have also taken place in how Mexicans view their political efficacy. Many remain cynical about the election process and consequently their ability to influence government policy or leadership, but a considerable shift occurred between 1988 and 1994 in the number of Mexicans who see the integrity of the process positively. More Mexicans view the election process as an accurate measure of their demands, and the principal reason for not participating relates to lack of interest.

Not many Mexicans are highly active in voluntary social organizations. Even fewer are involved in political parties or organizations. In fact, 85 percent reported no membership in any kind of organized group in 2001. Most of those who are politically involved are members of party organizations. Of some surprise is Mexicans' increasing tolerance of informal channels of political participation. They favored, to a much greater degree than in the 1980s, direct and unorthodox political actions on par with the level of support found in the United States for selective activities, but their actual involvement in such actions tapered off in the mid-1990s. As the legitimacy of the government increases, support for the most extreme alternatives is likely to decrease in the next decade.

The average Mexican, however, is not in favor of radical social and economic change but prefers a peaceful, incremental approach. For example, poll after poll demonstrated public sympathy for the goals of the Zapatista National Liberation Army (EZLN), but few agreed with its original methods, specifically violence. In a 1996 poll in the newspaper *Reforma*, two-thirds of urban Mexicans surveyed did not favor the use of violence to achieve political change.[30] In fact, as suggested earlier, most Mexicans consider themselves moderate or conservative ideologically.

Mexico is also part of a universal cultural shift described by Ronald Inglehart, Neil Nevitte, and Miguel Basáñez:

> [A] change from a world in which most people are absorbed in the tasks of sheer survival, to a world in which concern for the quality of life is becoming increasingly important. As we might expect, the peoples of Canada and the United States are well ahead of the Mexican public on this dimension, but during the 1980s, all three publics showed substantial shifts toward increasing emphasis on Postmaterialist concerns.[31]

A recent examination of post-materialist values and politics found in forty-eight societies, including Mexico, showed a clear relationship between those who profess these values and their support for democracy.

Finally, most Mexicans favor a democratic political model. The majority of citizens believe that they have a functioning democracy, but are not yet satisfied with its performance. Many Mexicans hope that democracy will improve their economic and social situation. The crucial question for the first decade of the twenty-first century remains, however, whether a fledgling democracy can fulfill citizen expectations, increase confidence in governmental or political institutions, and encourage participation in civic and social organizations, while solving serious economic and social problems, the most widespread of which is poverty.

NOTES

1. For a more comprehensive definition, see Walter A. Rosenbaum, *Political Culture* (New York: Praeger, 1975), 3–11.

2. In a comparative survey of Canada, Mexico, and the United States, Ronald Inglehart, Neil Nevitte, and Miguel Basáñez found that Mexico demonstrated greater levels of "strong" confidence in *nongovernmental* institutions. See *Convergencia en norte américa, comercio, política y cultura* (Mexico City: Siglo XXI, 1994), Figure 4-3.

3. Ibid., Figure 4-2. Many Mexican capitalists have also found it difficult to transfer loyalty to modern corporate forms in business, thus maintaining extensive family control. See Larissa Lomnitz and Marisol Pérez-Lizaur, *A Mexican Elite Family, 1820–1980: Kinship, Class, and Culture* (Princeton, N.J.: Princeton University Press, 1987).

4. See Jorge Buendía, Alejandro Moreno, and Mitchell Seligson, *La cultura política de la democracia en México, 2004, México en tiempos de competencia electoral* (Mexico: OPAL, 2004), 21. Family was not included in this questionnaire, but

the top institutions were Catholic Church, armed forces, National Human Rights Commission, and the media.
5. "Seguridad pública," *Reforma*, May 22, 2002.
6. *Este País*, 41, January 2000, random survey of 1567 residents of the Federal District, +/–2.5 percent margin of error, December 4–5, 1999. Victimization rates in Mexico were higher than any other country in Latin America except Guatemala, El Salvador, and Venezuela, from 1996–1998. See Alejandro Gaviria and Carmen Pagés, "Patterns of Crime Victimization in Latin America," Unpublished paper, Inter-American Development Bank, November, 1999. A World Bank study in 1999 reported that two in five residents of the capital had been a victim of crime in the previous twelve months, more than ten times the official crime rate, and that three-quarters of all Mexico City households had a family member who had been a crime victim during the previous year. *Los Angeles Times*, June 29, 2001, A3.
7. Isabel Vázquez, "Socio-Political Indicators: Public Insecurity," *Review of the Economic Situation of Mexico*, February 2003, 82.
8. "La violencia en México, *Consulta Mitofsky*, 2005; Mary Anastasia O'Grady, "Mexicans Vent Their Anger over Rampant Crime," *Wall Street Journal*, July 2, 2004, A1; and Chris Kraul, "Hundreds of Thousands March in Mexico Against Violent Crimes," *Los Angeles Times*, June 28, 2004, A4.
9. Roderic Ai Camp, ed., *Citizen Views of Democracy in Latin America* (Pittsburgh: University of Pittsburgh Press, 2001), CD-ROM, national survey of 1,200 Mexicans, +/–3.0 margin of error, June 1998.
10. Carlos B. Gil, *Hope and Frustration: Interviews with Leaders of Mexico's Political Opposition* (Wilmington, Del.: Scholarly Resources, 1992), 48–57.
11. Sheldon Annis, "Giving Voice to the Poor," *Foreign Policy*, no. 84 (Fall 1991): 100.
12. Alejandro Moreno, "Democracy and Mass Belief Systems in Latin America," in *Citizen Views of Democracy in Latin America*, ed. Roderic Ai Camp (Pittsburgh: University of Pittsburgh Press, 2001), 37.
13. Roderic Ai Camp, "Learning Democracy in Mexico and the United States," *Mexican Studies* 19, no. 1 (Winter 2003), 3–28.
14. William H. Flanigan and Nancy H. Zingale, *Political Behavior of the American Electorate*, 7th ed. (Washington, D.C.: Congressional Quarterly, 1991), 180.
15. James McCann and Jorge Domínguez, "Mexicans React to Electoral Fraud and Political Corruption: An Assessment of Public Opinion and Voting Behavior," *Electoral Studies*, 17, no. 4 (1998), 499.
16. For a brief discussion of polls and elections, see Juan Carlos Gamboa, "Media, Public Opinion Polls, and the 1994 Mexican Presidential Election," *Polling for Democracy; Public Opinion and Political Liberalization in Mexico*, ed. Roderic Ai Camp (Wilmington, Del.: Scholarly Resources, 1996), 17–19.
17. "Socio-Political Pulse of the Population," National sample of 2,400 Mexicans, +/–4 percent margin of error, September 2000, *Review of the Economic Situation of Mexico*, October 2000, 429.

18. Alberto Alvarez Gutiérrez, "Cómo se sienten los mexicanos?" in *Cómo somos los mexicanos,* eds. Alberto Hernández Medina, and Luis Narro Rodríguez (Mexico City: CREA, 1987), 81, 87. Specifically, in order of response, Mexicans' organization memberships were religious groups, 17.6 percent; unions, 10.3 percent; charities, 7.8 percent; educational or artistic organizations, 4.1 percent; youth groups, 3.4 percent; professional associations, 2.9 percent; ecology organizations, 2.6 percent; parties or political groups, 1.9 percent; consumer advocacy groups, 1.7 percent; human rights organizations, 1.5 percent.

19. Frederick C. Turner and Carlos A. Elordi, "Mexico and the United States, Two Distinct Political Cultures?" in *Citizen Views of Democracy in Latin America,* ed. Roderic Ai Camp (Pittsburgh: Pittsburgh University Press, 2001), 172.

20. For background on this period, see Judith Gentleman, ed., *Mexican Politics in Transition* (Boulder, Colo.: Westview Press, 1987); Arturo Alvarado Mendoza, ed., *Electoral Patterns and Perspectives in Mexico* (La Jolla, Calif.: Center for U.S.–Mexican Studies, UCSD, 1987).

21. Javier Conteras Orozco, *Chihuahua, trampa del sistema* (Mexico City: Edamex, 1987); Jaime Pérez Mendoza, "Por peteción de Bartlett, el Vaticano ordenó que hubiera misas en Chihuahua," *Proceso,* August 4, 1986, 6–13.

22. Linda Stevenson and Mitchell Seligson, "Fading Memories of the Revolution: Is Stability Eroding in Mexico?" in *Polling for Democracy: Public Opinion and Political Liberalization in Mexico,* ed. Roderic Ai Camp (Wilmington, Del.: Scholarly Resources, 1996), 59–80.

23. See the numerous examples cited in Carmina Danini, "Chiapas Uprising Apparently Inspires Demands Elsewhere," *Fort Worth Star-Telegram,* February 18, 1994, 3G.

24. Annis, "Giving Voice to the Poor," 101.

25. For examples of activities and member groups among one of Mexico's leading civic umbrella organizations, see the bulletin of the Movimiento Ciudadano por la Democracia (MCD), *Movimiento democrático,* March 1994, 15.

26. Flanigan and Zingale, *Political Behavior of the American Electorate,* 52.

27. Jorge I. Domínguez and James A. McCann, "Shaping Mexico's Electoral Arena: The Construction of Partisan Cleavages in the 1988 and 1991 National Elections," *American Political Science Review* 89 (March 1995): 46; and James A. McCann, "The Mexican Electorate in a North American Context: Assessing Patterns of Political Engagement," in *Polling for Democracy: Public Opinion and Political Liberalization in Mexico,* ed. Roderic A. Camp (Wilmington, Del.: Scholarly Resources, 1996), 81–106; James McCann and Chappell Lawson, "An Electorate Adrift? Public Opinion and the Quality of Democracy in Mexico," *Latin American Research Review* 38, no. 3 (October 2003), 60–81.

28. Roderic Ai Camp, "Citizen Attitudes Toward Democracy and Vicente Fox's Victory in 2000," in *Mexico's Pivotal Democratic Election,* ed. Jorge I. Domíñguez and Chappell Lawson (Stanford, Calif.: Stanford University Press, 2004), 34.

29. Luis Rubio, "Economic Reform and Political Liberalization," in *The Politics of Economic Liberalization in Mexico,* ed. Riodan Roett (Boulder, Colo.: Lynne Rienner, 1993), 19–20.

30. *Dallas Morning News,* September 8, 1996, 1A.

31. Inglehart, Nevitte, and Basáñez, *Convergencia en Norte América,* chap. 7, 3.

4

Political Attitudes and Their Origins: Partisanship, Alienation, and Tolerance

> Support for democracy is seen as a cultural matter. . . . support for democracy is also a matter of information, cognition, and belief systems. The way people think about democracy is based on cognitive and informational skills and resources. The concept of democracy varies depending on society's belief systems, and mass belief systems depend on individual characteristics such as education, informational background, cognitive skills, degrees of political "sophistication," and so on.
>
> ALEJANDRO MORENO, *Democracy and Mass Belief Systems in Latin America*

Many experiences have a bearing on the formation of beliefs in general, and political beliefs specifically. Attitudes are general orientations toward basic aspects of life: abstract principles that guide behavior.[1] Children, for example, are affected by the attitudes and values of their parents, and most chil-

---

Attitudes: general orientations toward basic aspects of life, abstract principles that guide behavior.

---

dren carry the consequences with them for years.[2] Other persons have reported the influence of education and the specific role of teachers and professors.[3] Experiences other than those within the family and in school contribute to the formative years of many citizens, especially when the experiences are broad and deep, permeating the environment of an entire nation. The Great Depression, for example, tremendously affected Americans, their political and social values, and their voting behavior.[4] Undoubtedly, although we have no surveys to prove it empirically, the revolution exerted a similar influence in Mexico.[5] In the mid-1990s, Mexicans identified liberty and justice most strongly with the Revolution.[6] A small exploratory study of workers in three cities in 1978 revealed surprisingly strong memories of the revolution among third-generation Mexicans. The size of the sample makes it impossible to generalize about the data, nevertheless 45 percent reported family participation in the event, and 25 percent reported lost property or injury of a family member. Family involvement was associated with fears of renewed violence and has helped discourage political protests in the present period.[7] Some individuals, generally as young adults, consciously or unconsciously take on the attitudes of their peers or of their working environment.

Surprisingly (in the last two decades), social scientists have largely ignored how citizens learn their political attitudes.[8] In Mexico, for example, no broad studies of this phenomenon exist. Fortunately, the Hewlett Foundation survey in September 2000, for the first time explored this issue in considerable detail. In the previous chapter we noted that Mexicans and Americans both expressed considerable confidence and trust in religion, school, and the family. Therefore, one might expect these institutions to play significant roles in influencing citizen beliefs generally, and political attitudes specifically.

Interestingly, when citizens from both countries were asked to identify which sources influenced the formation of their political attitudes, a correlation did not necessarily emerge between institutions receiving strong levels of trust and their perceived impact on individual beliefs (Table 4-1). For example, among Americans, religion is a significant source of political attitudes. Mexicans, who ranked religion at the very top of trusted institutions,

Table 4-1 Sources of Political Socialization in Mexico and the United States

Source of Political Socialization	Group (percentages)	
	Americans	Mexicans
Religion	69	26
Family	77	48
School	78	40
Television	59	40
Friends	71	28
Work	58	32

Note: Question: For each of the following . . . please tell me how strongly each one has influenced your way of thinking with respect to politics. "Democracy Through U.S. and Mexican Lenses," Grant, Hewlett Foundation, September 2000.

rank it at the bottom of sources of political beliefs. In fact, nearly half of all Mexicans considered religion to play no role whatsoever in molding their political attitudes. On one hand, this is not a surprising finding, given the fact that the role of Catholicism outside of its narrow spiritual boundaries was denigrated by post-revolutionary governments. On the other hand, since the Catholic Church was a vocal and pro-active actor in laying the ground-work for electoral democracy since the late 1980s, it is surprising how few Mexicans attribute any influence to that institution.

Another highly ranked institution among Americans and Mexicans both is school. The general literature has always considered schools a pri-mary source of attitudes and values. Again, as Table 4-1 reveals, schools are the number one source of American political values. Although not as impor-tant to Mexicans comparatively speaking, schools tie for second as an important source of political beliefs.

The third and the single most revered institution among both Mexicans and Americans is the family. Family produces the strongest correlation between trust and socialization, ranking at the top as the source of Mexican political attitudes and essentially tied with schools as Americans' primary source of political attitudes. What is remarkable, however, is that given the importance of family in the Mexican culture, only half of all Mexicans attribute their political beliefs to that institution. In fact, a third of all Mexi-cans say the family plays no role in determining their political attitudes. A strong explanation for this divergence might be that only half as many Mex-ican compared with American families actually discuss politics at home.[9]

Studies from other countries suggest a number of variables that affect the political attitudes and values of ordinary citizens. They typically include race, ethnicity, socioeconomic background, level of education, occupation, region, and religion. Mexico has an Indian population, but Indians account for only approximately 8 percent of the population, depending on the defi-nition of *Indian*. Indians, however, are a minor political and economic pres-ence and hence have not been treated as a separate group in national politi-cal surveys. The typical Mexican thinks of himself or herself as, and is, mestizo, thereby minimizing race or ethnicity as a significant variable in voting behavior. According to Miguel Basáñez and Pablo Páras, some evi-dence now exists to suggest that ethnicity in Mexico does affect political beliefs, including Mexicans' receptivity to democracy.[10]

As elections become more competitive and, more important, if Indians in certain states or regions were to organize themselves politically, ethnicity may become a more significant variable. The consequences of this on a national level can be seen as a result of the Zapatista National Liberation Army's (EZLN) uprising in Chiapas in January 1994, which affected the larger political context through 1995, and again in 2000–2001. This is particularly the case because the EZLN has demanded indigenous autonomy in its negotiations with the Mexican government, rejecting a government bill in 2001.

Because of sharp social-class divisions, Mexican values are likely to be influenced by income level. Furthermore, the origins of Mexico's leaders, particularly political and economic, set them apart from the ordinary citizen. Consequently, it is important to ascertain differences between mass and elite political opinion. And because political knowledge has much to do with education, and disparities in schooling are substantial in Mexico, education is a way of distinguishing one Mexican from another and is strongly related to social class and occupation.[11] Historically, as suggested in Chapter 2, regionalism played an important role in national politics. It declined in prominence by the 1960s, yet it continues to exert an influence over some values, in the same way that it does in the United States. As different political movements strengthen their representation at the local and state levels, dominating specific regions politically, and as regional–ethnic groups such as the Zapatistas focus on local social and economic issues, geography will reassert its influence. As suggested earlier, Mexico ranks high among geographically fragmented countries in the world, and those divisions have been found to have cultural consequences. Religion is often still another determinant of political behavior and in many societies, plays a role in the formation of social and political values, especially when religious diversity is present. In Mexico, however, the predominance of Catholicism has obviated sharp religious differences. Most of the disharmony historically related to religion can be described as a battle between secularism and religion, not among religions. Nonetheless, the rise of evangelical Protestantism throughout Latin America since the 1960s, although not yet as greatly felt in Mexico, and the presence of a small proportion of nonbelievers and atheists, render religious beliefs deserving of consideration, too.

INCOME AND POLITICS

The confidence people have in a political system and in their ability to influence the outcome of political decisions—level of political efficacy—depends on many things. One is income level. People who have achieved economic success not only perceive the system as fairer and more beneficial to their own interests but also believe they can change aspects of it that they dislike. When Gabriel Almond and Sidney Verba published the first results of their multicountry study in the 1960s, they declared that Mexicans had a much lower sense of political efficacy than did Americans or the English but was equivalent to that of the Germans.[12] In the late 1960s Rafael Segovia replicated the research on political efficacy among school-children and found that Mexican children were characterized by low levels of political efficacy. He also found that the parents' socioeconomic background had something to do with those levels; as the parents' income increased, so did the children's political efficacy and confidence in the system.[13]

In 1989, in a national survey, half of Mexican respondents with high incomes believed they could do something about electoral fraud. By contrast, only one in four low-income respondents agreed with that statement.[14] Regardless of income, only slightly more than a third of all Mexicans thought they could alter this particular problem in their country. During this same period, over half of all Americans thought they could affect government policies.[15] In 2000, after President Fox was elected, Mexican responses to a different question measuring political efficacy reflect a dramatic increase. When asked if their vote would make a difference in improving conditions in the future, two-thirds believed that was true. As democratic influences affected the outcome of elections, and parties other than PRI began winning state and local elections and congressional seats in large numbers in the 1990s, Mexicans became convinced that their votes could affect governmental leadership and, therefore, policy outcomes. Income levels, as we suggested, significantly affect perceptions of efficacy, with only six out of ten Mexicans in lower income brackets believing they can change conditions by voting, compared with nearly 80 percent of wealthier Mexicans (Table 4-2).

Another explanation for why Mexicans increased their political efficacy in the 1980s and 1990s is related to their increased participation in civic organizations. As Ann Craig and Wayne Cornelius argue, even low-income

Table 4-2 Mexicans' Political Efficacy, by Socioeconomic Status

Response to the Statement "Voting can make things better in future"	Income Level			
	Low (%)	Middle (%)	High (%)	All Respondents (%)
Can make a difference	61	74	77	66
Will not make a difference	32	23	23	29
Don't know/No answer	7	3	0	5

Question: Some people say that the way a person votes could make things better in the future. Others say that regardless of how people vote, they will not make things better in the future. With which statement are you most in agreement?
Source: "Democracy Through U.S. and Mexican Lenses," Grant, Hewlett Foundation, September 2000.

84

Table 4-3 Mexicans' Risk-taking, by Socioeconomic Status

Response to Statement "Nothing ventured, nothing gained"	Low (%)	Middle (%)	High (%)	All Respondents (%)
	Income Level			
Agree	58	67	78	62
Disagree	39	30	21	35
Don't know/No answer	3	3	1	3

Source: "Democracy Through U.S. and Mexican Lenses," September 2000.

people who become active in nongovernmental organizations and make demands on the system collectively develop a stronger sense of efficacy.[16] The growing numbers of such groups and their greater involvement has raised the level of participation.[17] Over time, an increase in middle- and higher-income groups would also contribute to an increased level of political efficacy, but a redistribution of the population among income groups in Mexico was not significant in the 1990s.

A variable as important as political efficacy in the 1990s, and perhaps the most influential in bringing about the defeat of PRI in the 2000 presidential race, is the willingness of individual Mexicans to risk a political change. Survey researchers have long asked citizens questions about their level of political risk-taking. In Mexico, naturally, as suggested in the previous chapter, this is a particularly significant issue among a citizenry that had not witnessed a change in partisan control over the executive branch for seventy years.[18] When Mexicans were asked if they agreed with the statement "nothing ventured, nothing gained," or "stick to the devil you know," nearly two-thirds expressed a general philosophical position favoring risk and change. In the United States, the figure was over 80 percent. Again, however, if we break those responses down by income levels, they reveal an even greater difference than is the case for income differences and political efficacy. As the data in Table 4-3 illustrate, Mexicans with high incomes are much more willing to risk change. In fact, high-income Mexicans differ very little from the average response among all Americans, illustrating the importance of income in leveling cultural differences on certain political attitudes between two groups of citizens. Nearly twice as many poorer Mexicans as higher-income groups opted for the status quo statement "stick with the devil you know."

Analysts of Americans' voting behavior have always been attentive to variables affecting political sympathies for the Republicans and Democrats. Their studies suggest that among the most important of these variables is

Table 4-4 Mexicans' Partisan Sympathies, by Socioeconomic Status

Sympathy for Party	Low (%) 1989	Low (%) 2000	Middle (%) 1989	Middle (%) 2000	High (%) 1989	High (%) 2000	All Respondents (%) 1989	All Respondents (%) 2000
PAN	12	28	13	40	21	35	13	31
PRI	26	32	38	21	44	19	31	29
PRD	17	9	16	10	5	15	16	10
Other	3	0	3	1	3	3	3	1
None	32	27	23	25	21	25	28	27
Don't know/No answer	10	4	7	3	6	3	9	2

Source: Los Angeles Times poll, August 1989; "Democracy Through U.S. and Mexican Lenses," September 2000.

personal income. This was also true in the case of Mexicans. Over the last decade, some dramatic changes in partisan sympathy have taken place on the basis of income. Traditionally, the PRI obtained its strongest support among higher income groups, illustrated in the data for 1989 in Table 4-4. In fact, 44 percent of Mexicans in the upper income brackets expressed a preference for PRI in 1989. By 2000, however, that figure had changed dramatically, falling by more than half to only 19 percent of adult citizens. Among middle-income groups, the same pattern, with almost the same percentage of change, took place. Only among lower-income groups did PRI retain considerable support during the 1990s. The PAN, which won the presidency in 2000, attracted most of those middle- and upper-income voters who abandoned the PRI. For example, middle-income voters increased their support for PAN in just eleven years by more than 200 percent. PAN also was able to more than double its support among lower-income groups. The PRD, which was the second-strongest party in 1989, lost more than a third of its partisan supporters by 2000. The only party that increased its partisan support from 1989 to 2000 was PAN. However since many voters may have temporarily altered their partisan preferences to oust the PRI from the presidency, it remains to be seen if these trends persist.[19]

The consequences of the changing face of partisan sympathies over the last decade can be seen in data reporting actual voter intentions shortly before the 2000 presidential race. When Mexicans were asked who they intended to vote for in May 2000, 40 percent of Mexico's poorest citizens planned to vote for Francisco Labastida, the PRI candidate. As voter income increased, voter support for Labastida declined. Only 26 percent of the wealthiest Mexicans supported Labastida. Fox, on the other hand, received the support of one-third of Mexico's poor, slightly less than Labastida; but the four other income categories supported him by large margins. In fact, more than half of the voters in the highest three of five income categories reported they would vote for Fox. Cuauhtémoc Cárdenas, the PRD's candidate, garnered only a fifth of the poorest voters, and his supporters declined as income levels increased.

EDUCATION AND POLITICS

A variable closely related to income in determining political preferences is education. Access to education, especially in a country like Mexico where opportunities are fewer than in the United States, is strongly related to parental income; the higher the income, the more likely a person will attend and *complete* higher education. For example, of the students at the National University in the early 1990s, more than 90 percent were from families with incomes in the upper 15 percent.[20] Many Mexicans attend public universities, which charge minimal fees, but most low-income students do not complete their degree requirements. Students with higher education obtain the necessary credentials to pursue the most prestigious professions, just as they do elsewhere, and thus on the whole earn more.

With education come knowledge, social prestige, economic success, and greater self-confidence. Consequently, when Mexicans were asked whether they could change conditions by voting, 75 percent of those with higher education believed they could (Table 4-5). In contrast, only slightly more than half who had received a primary education believed they could alter political conditions. In the United States, education affects responses in the same direction, although anyone with a secondary education or higher

Table 4-5 Mexicans' Political Efficacy, by Level of Education

Response to the Statement that "Voting can make things better in future"	Educational Level			
	Primary (%)	Secondary (%)	Preparatory (%)	University (%)
Can make a difference	58	66	76	75
Will not make a difference	33	31	23	24
Don't know/No answer	9	3	1	2

Source: "Democracy Through U.S. and Mexican Lenses," September 2000.

Table 4-6 Mexicans' Risk-taking, by level of Education

Response to Statement "Nothing ventured, nothing gained"	Level of Education				All
	Primary	Secondary	Preparatory	University	
Agree	50	57	79	76	62
Disagree	46	41	20	21	35
Don't know/No answer	4	2	1	3	3

Source: "Democracy Through U.S. and Mexican Lenses," September 2000.

believes in the efficacy of voting.[21] If efficacy is taken to the next logical step, participation measured in terms of voting, a strong relationship exists between higher education and actual voter turnout. For example, 46 percent of the population has a primary education, but those with a primary education accounted for only 36 percent of the ballots cast in 1994. Mexicans with college degrees (only 8 percent of the population) accounted for twice as many (16 percent) of the actual voters.[22] This larger turnout among educated voters helped Vicente Fox in 2000.

Education not only affects citizen confidence and knowledge about the political system but also determines to some extent citizens' acceptance of certain attitudes. One of the most influential Mexican political attitudes in the 1990s was, as we have witnessed, the willingness of the average voter to risk change. Education, as is the case with political efficacy, does play a significant role; indeed, it has more influence on risk-taking than on efficacy among Mexicans. As recent survey data illustrate (Table 4-6), only a third of all Mexicans preferred the status quo over the possibility that risking something new might alter their lives for the better. Among Mexicans with only an elementary school education, 25 percent fewer were willing to take such a chance. The better educated voters, who opted for change in large numbers, also voted more frequently for Vicente Fox, whose electoral alliance, in the minds of most voters, represented change.

In the United States, education as a single variable does not have a dramatic effect,[23] but because Mexico also is characterized by sharper class divisions, the relationship is stronger. Even in the United States, citizens with only a sixth grade education differ from the rest of the population on measures of political efficacy and risk-taking.

Educational achievement played an important role in determining partisan preferences in Mexico during the 1990s. The evolution of this pattern is clearly illustrated in the data comparing partisan responses in 1989,

Table 4-7 Mexicans' Party Preference, by Level of Education

| | Education Level | | | | | | | | | |
Preferred Party	Primary (%)		Secondary (%)		Preparatory (%)		University (%)		All Respondents (%)	
	1989	2000	1989	2000	1989	2000	1989	2000	1989	2000
PRI	27	39	34	24	33	18	38	19	31	29
PAN	10	25	13	33	14	40	24	36	13	31
PRD	15	9	17	8	17	9	12	15	16	10
Other	3	0	4	0	3	2	2	1	3	1
None	35	24	24	32	24	27	18	27	28	27
Don't know/ No answer	11	3	7	2	9	3	6	2	9	2

Source: Los Angeles Times poll, August 1989; "Democracy Through U.S. and Mexican Lenses," September 2000.

shortly after the benchmark Mexican election, in which viable national options became a reality, and 2000, following Vicente Fox's victory (see Table 4-7). Since the late 1990s, voters consider the PRI to be the far-right party, the PAN center right, and the PRD center left. The comparative data between 1989 and 2000 support several significant trends. PRI, which has traditionally done well among less-educated voters, retains its appeal among that group. PAN, which has done poorly among such voters, increases its support dramatically, by 150 percent. The PRD, which relied heavily on these voters in the 1988 election, lost their support. The second trend revealed that among Mexican voters, educational level determines the dramatic decline in support for PRI. About the same percentage of voters preferred PRI in 2000 as in 1989, but only half as many college-educated voters expressed that same preference in 2000 as in 1989, a significant decline. PAN, on the other hand, more than doubled its partisan support among all citizens. Whereas PRI led in all educational categories in 1989, PAN replaced it among the three most well-educated groups, increasing its support 150 to 200 percent among secondary and preparatory educated voters.

Just three years later, in the 2003 congressional elections, frustrated with the failures of the Fox administration to pass and implement major reforms, voters sympathetic to PAN in 2000 began to shift their support back to PRI and PRD. Whereas PAN continued to dominate among high school– and college-educated voters, its margin over PRI declined dramatically, in the case of secondary students, to only 1 percent. Among professional people and business owners, PRI outpolled PAN.

RELIGION AND POLITICS

Students of the Catholic heritage in Mexico identify it as an important contributor to values within the family and within the culture generally. When ranking the role of God in their lives, Mexicans and Americans give it equal importance; only one in four Canadians consider God important.[24] Religion's potential for influencing the formation of societal norms is enhanced by the fact that most Mexicans consider themselves religious (see Table 4-8), and 85 percent declare they received a religious education in their homes.[25] Although it is true that the number of Mexicans who attend church services has fallen since the turn of the century, the number who attend regularly is higher than is typically believed. Throughout the 1990s, 44 percent of all Catholics went to church weekly or more often, and 20 percent monthly.[26] In 1994, three-quarters of all Mexicans described themselves as practicing Catholics.

Given the overwhelming dominance of Catholicism, it would be useful to measure its effect on political attitudes according to the intensity of belief. For example, when Gabriel Almond and Sidney Verba completed their classic study, which largely ignored religion, they discovered that the more religious a person was, regardless of faith, the more intolerant of others' political beliefs he or she would be.[27] I will offer some observations regarding the variable of intensity, but for comparative purposes, it is helpful to identify the potential influence of religion on some of the major political attitudes discussed.

How does religion affect political efficacy? Table 4-9 presents responses according to religious belief. Because Catholics account for the overwhelm-

Table 4-8 Mexicans' Religious Affiliations

| | Percentage of All Respondents | |
Affiliation	1989	2000
Catholic	92	85
Protestant	5	4
Other	1	4
None	1.7	6
No answer	.3	1

Source: Los Angeles Times poll, August 1989; "Democracy Through U.S. and Mexican Lenses," September 2000; Roberto Blancarte, "Religionesy creencias en México," *Este País* (April 2002), 49, uses the following figures: 88 percent Catholic, 7.27 percent Protestant, and 3.52 percent none.

Table 4-9 Mexicans' Political Efficacy, by Religion

Response to Statement "Voting can make things better in the future"	Religion (percentages)			
	Catholic	Protestant*	None	All Respondents
Can make a difference	67	70	61	66
Will not make a difference	28	23	32	29
Don't know/No answer	5	7	6	5

*Figures were used for evangelical Protestants, the largest Protestant faith in Mexico.
Source: "Democracy Through Mexican Lenses," September 2000.

ing majority of Mexicans, their views and that of the average Mexican are likely to correspond closely. Essentially, in terms of political attitudes, religion is not a very significant variable. Differences between Catholic and Protestant responses are relatively minor. The only religious belief that produces some variation in citizen responses is among those who profess no religious beliefs. Atheists tend to be more cynical than their religious peers and are less convinced that participation will change political conditions.

The contribution of religion to Mexican attitudes is embedded in the general culture. Scholars have argued that the Catholic Church might function as an *indirect* agent of socialization (even though Mexicans suggested earlier that the Church is not an important source of their political beliefs). Analysts also have suggested that Catholicism may have encouraged deference, obedience, and respect for hierarchy in laity interactions with secular authorities because those are the norms it has conveyed in its own interactions.[28] Such patterns are obviously changing, and whatever impact the Church may have had in the past, its openly critical posture implicitly in favor of political change is also reflected among practicing Catholics. Most Catholics are in favor of taking a chance on change. What is noteworthy, however, is that a significantly higher percentage of Protestants and atheists favor change (Table 4-10). It is possible, therefore, that the common view of

Table 4-10 Mexicans' Risk-taking, by Religion

Response to Statement "Nothing ventured, nothing gained"	Religion (percentages)			
	Catholic	Protestant	None	All Respondents
Agree	61	75	75	62
Disagree	37	21	22	35
Don't know/No answer	2	4	3	3

Source: "Mexican Democracy Through U.S. and Mexican Lenses," September 2000.

Table 4-11 Religious Partisanship in Mexico

Response to Question "Do you sympathize with any political party? Which one?"	Religious Beliefs		
	Intense Catholic (%)	Moderate Catholic (%)	General Population (%)
National Action Party	18.2	9.5	11.4
Democratic Revolutionary Party	2.0	6.5	6.3
Institutional Revolutionary Party	9.2	25.1	24.8

Source: Miguel Basáñez, *Encuesta nacional de opinión pública, iglesia–estado,* 1990.

the Church conveying traditional attitudes has left an important residue among a certain portion of the laity to an extent not found among non-Catholics, regardless of beliefs.

What has most intrigued students of Mexican politics and religion is an assumed relationship between Catholicism and party affiliation. The reason for this assumption is that the National Action Party adopted many of the ideas of the European and Latin American Christian Democratic movements. Moreover, prominent early leaders of the party were known to be active Catholics.[29] Contrary to a common belief, being Catholic has little or nothing to do with party sympathy in Mexico. In fact, as I pointed out in a more comprehensive examination of the issue, all the survey data from the 1980s and 1990s indicate that the only relationship between PAN and Catholicism is between the party and a tiny group of Catholics, 3.4 percent, who attend church daily (see Table 4-11). This group does differ from the rest of the population in its intensity of support for the PAN. Because they are so small in number, they exert little influence on partisanship and electoral outcomes.

Religious and party preferences are revealing, even if a tie between the PAN and Catholicism does not exist.[30] Indeed, it is the Protestants and the nonreligious who deviate from the norm. Both in 1989 and 2000, Protestants gave the least support to the PAN (Table 4-12). In fact, although PAN increased its support among Protestants in the last decade, it lost ground among this group compared with Mexicans professing other religious preferences. Nearly a third of all Mexicans preferred PAN by 2000, but that was the case among only one out of ten Protestants. In fact, by 2003, PRI regained a slight edge over PAN among Catholics. On the other hand, PAN improved its support among non-Catholic Christians. PRI, on the other hand, improved its support among Protestants, the group most likely to support that party on the basis of their religious beliefs. Half again as many Mexican Protestants as Mexicans preferred the PRI. This preference among

Table 4-12 Mexicans' Partisan Sympathies, by Religion

	Catholic		Protestant		None		All Respondents	
Sympathy for Party	1989	2000	1989	2000	1989	2000	1989	2000
PAN	13	32	8	12	10	29	13	31
PRI	32	29	27	44	21	19	31	29
PRD	15	10	20	11	21	13	16	10
No Party	28	25	35	29	28	37	28	27
Other	3	1	1	4	5	0	3	1
Don't know/No answer	9	3	9	0	15	2	9	2

Source: Los Angeles Times poll, August 1989; "Democracy Through U.S. and Mexican Lenses," September 2000.

Protestants is also explained by the fact that most of their adherents live in rural communities, the strongest regional supporters of PRI. The most interesting group, religiously speaking, based on partisan preferences, are nonbelievers. They always have shown a higher level of support for the PRD, a pattern continuing into the twenty-first century. But in 2000, the nonreligious were also the group most likely to express no party preference, thus making up a larger percentage of independent voters.

Protestants illustrate differing political sympathies, indicating they may be a more heterogeneous group in terms of background characteristics. Protestants are much more diverse, however, in religious composition. From 1992 to 1994, the Secretariat of Government registered 2,010 religious associations in response to newly introduced constitutional reforms. Of those, only 21 percent were Catholic, and 77 percent were evangelical Protestant. The evangelicals could be subdivided as follows: independent groups, 48 percent; Baptists, 29 percent; Pentecostals, 21 percent; and traditional Protestants (such as Methodists), 2 percent.[31] This level of diversity is very important to differences in partisanship, because as recent research from the United States reveals, churches do have distinctive political orientations, and the extent of theological traditionalism prevailing in a congregation moves individual members toward more conservative positions on social issues and makes them more likely to identify themselves as political conservatives.[32] In short, substantial differences in religious-political orientations, if they exist, are most likely to occur within each individual religious community.

The impact of religion on Mexican partisan politics continues to be moderated by the small numbers of non-Catholics. If Protestantism's growth were to mirror that found in Central America, where numbers have risen extraordinarily in the past two decades, religion might become a significant variable in Mexican voting behavior.[33] Recent research among Mexican evangelicals suggests that "a nascent Evangelical social and political movement is underway. . . . The evidence is fairly clear and seems to be mounting that a once reserved and almost invisible religious minority is now emerging and demanding a seat at the table."[34]

As I stated elsewhere, and recent survey data confirm, many Mexicans are interested in redefining the church's role in society. Their redefinition has serious, long-term implications for the role of the church as both an institution and a religion in Mexicans' political life. Fewer than half of all Mexicans define the church's task as religious, whereas more than half viewed its primary activities as political, social, moral, economic, or something else. This suggests that large numbers of Mexicans do not view church activities in a narrow and traditional sense, and this same group is most critical of the church's response to social and economic needs.[35] In the 1990s, large numbers of Mexicans believed that the Catholic Church should become involved in social work, health, and education, and more than two-thirds believed that the government should take the church into account on important social issues.[36]

GENDER AND POLITICS

One of the influences on values about which we have the least understanding is the role of gender in Mexico. A number of studies of Latin America examine political behavior from a female viewpoint. Research on the political behavior of women in the United States have rarely discovered sharp differences with men, but they typically note that women are not as interested in politics, have less knowledge of politics, and are somewhat more alienated from the political system than are men. In fact, one study concludes that a high level of alienation was associated with the rise of feminism and the recognition of their exclusionary treatment by the system.[37] Almond and Verba found the same pattern for Mexican women in the 1960s but with differences that were much more extreme.[38] For example, when asked if they discussed politics, 29 percent of Mexican women said yes, compared with 55 percent of Mexican men. In the United States, although fewer women than men discussed politics, the gap was relatively small: 70 versus 83 percent. Gender differences continue to remain marginally stronger in Mexico.

Differences in political attitudes and behavior attributable to gender can be explained by roles assigned to Mexican women.[39] Although many women today obtain an advanced education and a large percentage are in the

Table 4-13 Educational Discrepancies Among the Economically Active Population, by Gender*

	Women	Men
Level of Education	(percentages)	
Uneducated	9.2	9.1
1 to 3 years of grade school	10.6	13.5
4 to 5 years of grade school	6.4	7.4
Completed grade school	21.2	21.8
1 to 2 years of junior high school	4.1	6.1
Completed junior high school	13.5	16.1
Subprofessional	13.9	3.9
1 to 3 years of preparatory school	6.9	9.1
Mid-level professional	1.7	1.2
High-level professional	12.6	11.8

Notes: *Only 35 percent of women over twelve years old were economically active, compared with 78 percent of men.
Source: Review of the Economic Situation of Mexico, October 1998, 398.

workforce, opportunities for women are fewer than for men (see Table 4-13). In part this is due to education, since women over the age of fifteen accounted for 63 percent of illiterate Mexicans.[40] Women who do enter the workforce have educational achievements that, on the whole, are equivalent to that of men. It is the two-thirds of women who do not participate in the economically active workforce who have fewer educational attainments. This fact helps explain why women who do household work continued to provide substantial support for PRI. Moreover, the most detailed study of their attitudes implies that most women are not yet committed to liberation and to a change in their traditional roles.[41]

Given these and other conditions that have restricted women's roles in society and hence in politics, it is natural that they might feel more powerless to change the political system. However, a remarkable change in political efficacy seems to have occurred since the 1960s. When Fagen and Tuohy carried out a study of Jalapa, Veracruz, in the 1970s, they found extreme differences between men and women, regardless of social class. Typically, only half as many women as men reported high levels of political efficacy.[42] By 1989 almost no statistical difference existed between men and women on this issue, a pattern persisting to the present (see Table 4-14). This finding is similar to recent U.S. data on women and men.[43]

As Mexicans make the transition from a more authoritarian political culture to one characterized by democratic characteristics, it is desirable to understand women's potential role. Given the traditional literature on women, it might be expected that more women than men would be unwilling

Table 4-14 Mexicans' Political Efficacy, by Gender

Response to Statement "Voting can make things better in the future"	Gender (percentages)		
	Male	Female	All Respondents
Agree	68	64	66
Disagree	27	31	29
Don't know/No answer	5	5	5

Source: "Democracy Through U.S. and Mexican Lenses," September 2000.

to risk political change. The data on the issue of risk-taking identify a more definitive difference between men and women in Mexico, and bear out gender-related tendencies found elsewhere. Twenty-five percent more women than men were inclined to stick with the status quo than to risk change (see Table 4-15). This also explains, in part, another more significant pattern. Where women differ most from men politically in Mexico is on political activism. Few Mexicans have actually participated in some type of political protest, but only half as many women as men have done so.[44]

These data could convey the false impression that women are not politically active. In fact, recent research shows that women in urban areas are the backbone of the social and civic organizations that have flourished in Mexico in recent years. As one researcher commented, "Independent organizations are giving women a political experience which is profoundly affecting their lives, leading them to question the power relations which limit them at societal level, as well as within their personal, familial relations."[45]

This active feminist presence emerged in earnest in the 1970s, especially in Mexico City. By the 1980s, a network of women's organizations existed throughout Mexico, linking together NGOs, unions, and urban poor and middle-class organizations. As was true elsewhere in the region, socioeconomic differences among women created tensions in generating a common agenda.[46] The expansion of women into different employment opportu-

Table 4-15 Mexicans' Risk-taking, by Gender

Response to Statement "Nothing ventured, nothing gained"	Gender (percentages)		
	Male	Female	All Respondents
Agree	67	57	62
Disagree	30	40	35
Don't know/No answer	3	3	3

Source: "Democracy Through U.S. and Mexican Lenses," September 2000.

nities, and the changing political landscape in the 1990s, encouraged the growth of women's organizations and increased the breadth and influence of a feminine political agenda. Sex crimes became the most important issue contributing to unification of a feminist agenda.

More recently, as the democratic transition in electoral politics became a reality, women fought successfully for affirmative action quotas among party candidates for political office. Members of the PRD were the first to achieve this goal, persuading the party to require 20 percent of its candidates to be women in 1990. A year later they increased that level of representation to 30 percent of the party's candidates, and the same percentage among the party's national executive committee. PAN has refused to pass such a mandate, but the PRI accepted the same percentage levels among its national congressional candidates in 1996.[47] In the fall, 2001, however PRI increased the percentage of female candidates to 40 percent, the highest level of any party. Some state party committees have also begun replicating these patterns for legislative candidates. More importantly, in 2002, the Mexican congress passed its own quota law requiring that no more than 70 percent of the candidates for single-member districts (accounting for 300 of the 500 seats in the lower house of congress) can be of the same gender. According to Lisa Baldez, who examined this issue in detail, the Federal Electoral Institute has imposed strict compliance requirements, and the Supreme Court confirmed its legality. It went into effect in the 2003 congressional elections, and as a result, women members of congress rose from 16 to 23 percent.[48]

Studies of European countries have generally found women to be somewhat ideologically more conservative than men.[49] This is not the case for Mexican women today, but more of them are uncommitted or support centrist views than men do, and fewer identify with leftist political ideologies.[50] Typically, women everywhere are less interested than men in politics and hence participate less; this also is true of Mexican women.[51] Ideological differences between men and women can be translated into sympathy for political parties. Some observers allege, for example, that women are more sympathetic to PAN, the center-right party, than are men. This is not the case. In fact, in a 1991 national survey, PAN received stronger support from men than women. However, women did favor PAN's presidential candidate in 2000 by a ten-point margin,[52] but in 2003, PRI recaptured their support by three points.

However, a new study demonstrates that there are some significant differences in political attitudes between men and women, and these cross national boundaries, including Mexicans, Mexican-Americans, and Americans. One of the most interesting differences is that women and men have different expectations from democracy. Among Mexicans, men were more likely than women to see democracy as liberty, voting/elections, and type of government. These conceptualizations incorporate the three most traditional definitions of democracy, two of which, voting/elections and type of government, can be viewed as a *procedural* conceptualization, that is, defining democracy by its process. Mexican women, on the other hand, are more likely than men to view democracy as improving one's quality of life and standard of living, viewing government in productive economic and social terms. Gender does make a difference in the specific way in which a person defines expectations from democracy. Women in general are more likely than men to view democracy as a means of achieving equality, as improving the culture of law, and as producing progress.[53]

REGION AND POLITICS

Many years ago Lesley Byrd Simpson wrote the classic *Many Mexicos*. *Many* in the title referred in large part to regionalism's influence on Mexican values. As Mexico developed and communications improved, regional differences declined, but they did not disappear. Economically speaking, the north is highly developed. It is characterized by heavy in-migration, dynamic change, industrialization, and of course, its proximity to and economic and cultural linkages with the United States. The south, on the other hand, is the least developed economically. It is rural; has a large Indian population, mainly in Oaxaca and Chiapas; and is the most isolated from the cultural mainstream. The center, which includes the Federal District, has been the traditional source of political leadership, religious infrastructure, industrialization, and intellectual activity.[54]

Regional differences can be translated into political behavior. In the first place, interest in politics varies among individual citizens on the basis of many variables, and region may be prominent among them. Northern and Mexico City residents are most interested in politics, measured by its importance to their daily lives. Furthermore, their level of sophistication produces an interest in politics that leads to greater political competition. As the data in Table 4-16 show, a majority of Mexicans, typically three out of four, discuss politics. But among those who *discuss it frequently,* nearly twice as many do so in the north and in Mexico City as in the south. It is impossible to determine whether Mexicans' interest in politics has increased electoral competitiveness in both regions or whether electoral competitiveness has exaggerated their interest. It is fair to conclude, however, that interest and activity are interrelated.[55]

Table 4-16 Mexicans' Interest in Politics, by Region

	Region			
Response to Statement "How often politics are discussed"	North (%)	Center (%)	South (%)	Mexico City (%)
Frequently	19	13	11	18
Occasionally	53	58	63	54
Never	25	26	24	27
Don't know	3	3	2	1

Source: World Values Survey, 1990, courtesy of Miguel Basáñez.

Regional patterns also exist when measuring citizen political efficacy. The data in Table 4-17 suggest a complex pattern, not easily explained, but the regional differences are sharp. Clearly Mexicans from the center, which in terms of population would be dominated by the Federal District and the state of México, believe going to the polls has actually changed conditions for the better. This idea may be due to citizen satisfaction with two consecutive elected governors from the PRD since 1997. What is interesting about these responses to political efficacy from the west and the north is that both have witnessed selective PAN victories at the state and local levels, yet their residents remain cynical about voting producing change. It may be that while some Mexicans in these regions brought the PAN into power as an alternative to PRI, their level of expectation toward change was not actually met. Non-PRI parties will have to govern in other states in the region before clearer and more pronounced patterns of regional efficacy can be determined.

Place of residence can also affect other attitudes, including religious beliefs, which in turn, as was shown earlier, may have some effect on political preferences. Regional differences do not affect all politically related attitudes equally. In many circumstances, region is not an influential variable. On the issue of risk-taking, citizens in the north and west are more likely to stick with the status quo. Many residents from these two regions

Table 4-17 Mexicans' Political Efficacy, by Region

Response to Statement "Voting can make things better in the future"	Region (percentages)					All Respondents
	North	South	Center	East	West	
Agree	57	62	75	73	50	66
Disagree	39	29	22	24	40	29
Don't know/No answer	4	9	3	2	10	5

Source: "Democracy Through U.S. and Mexican Lenses," September 2000.

Table 4-18 Mexicans' Risk-taking, by Region

Response to Statement "Nothing ventured, nothing gained"	Region (percentages)					All Respondents
	North	South	Center	East	West	
Agree	57	62	75	73	50	62
Disagree	39	29	22	24	40	35
Don't know/No answer	4	9	3	2	10	3

Source: "Democracy Through U.S. and Mexican Lenses," September 2000.

have been supportive of the PAN. Their candidate won the national election prior to the date of the survey data reported in Table 4-18. Therefore, they may believe that what they already are experiencing represents change, and consequently they are supportive of the political status quo. This pattern is especially true in the northern states, where citizens are equally divided in supporting change versus maintaining the status quo at a time when nearly two-thirds of Mexicans nationally supported change. Mexicans from the east are the most willing to support change, which may be attributable to the fact that they have been among the least affected by electoral competition, having little experience with non-PRI governance.

The most significant consequence of region as one of the variables analyzed in this section is partisan political preferences. Traditionally, the opposition, primarily the PAN, has done well in Mexico's most dynamic regions—those showing the highest levels of economic growth. The PAN's greatest number of sympathizers, based on those economic figures, have been the north and the Federal District, including the Mexico City metropolitan area, which is found in the center region (Table 4-19). In 2003, with PRI's strong showing and the decline of support for PAN, PRI took the lead in the North, performing more strongly in that region than any party in any region. PRI also outperformed PAN among urban voters, who previously

Table 4-19 Mexicans' Partisan Sympathies, by Region

Sympathy for Party	Region (percentages)					All Respondents
	North	South	Center	East	West	
PAN	33	22	38	28	24	31
PRI	32	34	22	31	36	29
PRD	6	12	14	6	4	10
No Party	27	28	22	32	32	27
Other	0	3	2	1	0	1
Don't know/No answer	2	2	2	3	4	3

Source: "Democracy Through U.S. and Mexican Lenses," September 2000.

supported PAN in 2000. The PAN has always done poorly in the south, Mexico's least developed and most indigenous region; consequently, the lack of partisan supporters there is not surprising. PRI, on the other hand, has relied heavily on the south and the west for support. Of the three leading parties, its partisans are the most evenly distributed by region. Their significant weakness, regionally, is in the Federal District and state of México, the country's most populous entities, and the most industrialized. PRI's regional weakness in the center is explained by PRD's strength.[56] The PRD, in 1989, counted numerous adherents in Mexico City and in several central states, notably Morelos and Michoacán. It demonstrated its strength again in these states in 1997, reaching its apex nationally, and decisively won control of Mexico City in the capital's first mayoralty race in seventy years, repeating that victory in 2000.

Higher levels of political interest, activism, and sophistication are associated with higher levels of economic development, education, and urbanization. In turn, these qualities are most likely to promote the development of alternative political views, sympathy for political parties not in power, and opposition to closed decision-making. One of the most strongly held beliefs among all Mexicans is that decision making is inaccessible and that local and state policymaking should be more autonomous and less under the thumb of the national authorities. Increasing federalism, giving greater decision-making authority and fiscal resources to state and local governments, is likely to reinforce rather than moderate regional differences. Whether the changing allocations in power will affect attitudes on specific, local issues, or whether it will influence broader political attitudes, remain to be seen.

AGE AND POLITICS

Age often determines important variations in values and, more important, indicates changes in the offing as generations reach political maturity.[57] In their significant comprehensive study, Inglehart, Nevitte, and Basáñez found that thirty-four issues had been characterized by intergenerational change in the past decade.[58] Inglehart and others had discovered in earlier studies that economic conditions during a person's preadult years were the most significant determinant of adult values. Changing economic conditions, then, are likely to alter values from one generation to the next. For example, in the first *World Values Survey*, Inglehart learned that attitudes toward authoritarian values changed for each age cohort, moving in the direction of greater freedom and autonomy. The pattern peaked in all countries in the cohort aged twenty-five to thirty-four years old and began to reverse among the next generation.

Another consequence of generational change appears in party identification. As Inglehart reports, studies of western Europe and in the United States demonstrate that older citizens identified more strongly with political parties but that in recent decades younger voters are less likely to identify with a specific party. Although better educated than their elders and more interested in politics, younger Mexicans, like people elsewhere, no longer exhibit strong party loyalty. This phenomenon makes it difficult to predict future partisan sympathies and gives the independent or uncommitted voter considerable power to determine electoral outcomes. These voters were crucial to the outcome of Fox's victory.

Younger Mexicans, when the PRI was in power, were much more likely to be attracted to opposition parties. Specifically, in the 1990s, voters under age twenty-four showed a marked preference for the National Action Party. Before the 1994 presidential election, 19 percent of the potential voters said they would cast their ballots for the PAN, but 29 percent of the eighteen-to-twenty-four age group, a difference of 65 percent, claimed they would vote for the PAN. When the elections were held in August, 32 percent of this age group supported the PAN, and among all occupational groups, the PAN did better among students (5 percent of the voting population) than any other group, with 41 percent voting for their candidate.

Younger voters persisted in a similar pattern in 2000, providing a significant portion of Fox's supporters. After Fox won the election, 31 percent of Mexicans claimed to be partisan sympathizers of PAN. But among those individuals from age 18–24, 39 percent expressed a preference for PAN. In contrast, PRI, which had nearly the same percentage of sympathizers nationally, obtained support from only 20 percent of this age cohort, half of that received by PAN. The next age cohort, 25–39, follows a similar pattern favoring PAN, but the differences are not as dramatic. There is no question that Mexicans under the age of 39, who have witnessed the dramatic changes in Mexico since 1988 as young adults, determined the outcome of the 2000 presidential race. One of the reasons why their partisan preferences favored PAN, and why they were translated into actual votes for Fox, is the attitude of younger Mexicans toward risk-taking. As one might expect, this group, seven out of ten Mexicans, most favored a change. Over half of all Mexicans over 60 opposed change, yet those older Mexicans were PRI's strongest partisans among any age group. Twice as many older Mexicans sympathized with PRI compared with PAN.

Nevertheless, younger voters, like any other group we have analyzed in this chapter, may shift partisan preferences given certain conditions. Again, disappointed with the performance of the Fox administration, many of those younger voters—and students—cast their ballots for PRI candidates in the 2003 elections. While PAN continued to maintain a lead among both groups, especially students, it lost considerable ground to PRI, edging PRI among the 18–29 age group by only three percentage points.

CONCLUSION

The foregoing brief analysis of just a few variables in the making of political attitudes demonstrates their complexities. Many Mexicans have gained confidence in their ability to change the political system, but large numbers, nearly a third, believe themselves powerless. Those expressing the least confidence in their ability are the uneducated, and the poor. Nevertheless, the civic attention focused on the 1994 presidential elections and the unprecedented turnout of nearly four-fifths of Mexican voters indicate that numerous citizens took their responsibilities seriously and that even many first-time voters believed that they might make a difference. Turnout was lower in the 2000 elections, but voters further strengthened opposition representation nationally, and first-time voters played a crucial role.

Mexican political attitudes are undergoing change, and support for change itself is strong among them. Younger people are contributing most to this alteration, as are those who are more highly educated, who come from affluent backgrounds, and who live in the most dynamic regions. Mexicans are religious, but their Catholicism does not impinge on their political behavior, their support for change, or their partisanship. Many of the trends in political attitudes as well as attitudes in general that are apparent in Mexico appear in other countries as well, including the United States.

NOTES

1. Joseph A. Kahl, *The Measurement of Modernism: A Study of Values in Brazil and Mexico* (Austin: University of Texas Press, 1974), 8.

2. K. L. Tedin, "The Influence of Parents on the Political Attitudes of Adolescents," *American Political Science Review* 68 (December 1974): 1592.

3. Alex Edelstein, "Since Bennington: Evidence of Change in Student Political Behavior," in *Learning about Politics,* ed. Roberta Sigel (New York: Random House, 1970), 397.

4. Richard Centers, "Children of the New Deal: Social Stratification and Adolescent Attitudes," in *Class, Status and Power,* ed. Richard Bendix and Seymour Martin Lipset (New York: Free Press, 1953), 361.

5. For example, see such memoirs as Ramón Beteta, *Jarano* (Austin: University of Texas Press, 1970); and Andrés Iduarte, *Niño, Child of the Mexican Revolution* (New York: Praeger, 1971).

6. Ulises Beltrán, *Los mexicanos de los noventa* (Mexico: UNAM, 1996), 137.

7. See Linda Stevenson and Mitchell Seligson, "Fading Memories of the Revolution: Is Stability Eroding in Mexico?" in *Polling for Democracy: Public Opinion and Political Liberalization in Mexico,* ed. Roderic Ai Camp (Wilmington, Del.: Scholarly Resources, 1996), 61–80.

8. Harry Eckstein, "Culture as a Foundation Concept for the Social Sciences," *Journal of Theoretical Politics,* 8, no. 4 (October 1966), 485.

9. Roderic Ai Camp, "Learning Democracy in Mexico and the United States," *Mexican Studies* 19, no. 1 (Winter 2003): 3–28.

10. Miguel Basáñez and Pablo Páras, "Color and Democracy in Latin America," in *Citizen Views of Democracy in Latin America,* ed. Roderic Ai Camp (Pittsburgh: Pittsburgh University Press, 2001), 151. The authors note that this preference exists independent of the level of education.

11. The most important variable determining the level of education that a child obtains in Mexico is the socioeconomic status of the father, according to Kahl, *The Measurement of Modernism,* 71.

12. Gabriel Almond and Sidney Verba, *The Civic Culture: Political Attitudes and Democracy in Five Nations* (Boston: Little, Brown, 1965), 142.

13. Rafael Segovia, *La politización del niño mexicano* (Mexico City: El Colegio de Mexico, 1975), 130.

14. *Los Angeles Times* poll, August 1989.

15. Michael M. Gant and Norman R. Luttbeg, *American Electoral Behavior, 1952–1988* (Itasca, N.Y.: Peacock Publishers, 1991), 140.

16. Ann Craig and Wayne Cornelius, "Political Culture in Mexico, Continuities and Revisionist Interpretations," in *The Civic Culture Revisited,* ed. Gabriel Almond and Sidney Verba (Boston: Little, Brown, 1980), 369.

17. For evidence of these ongoing changes and their linkage to politics, see Joe Foweraker and Ann L. Craig, eds., *Popular Movements and Political Change in Mexico* (Boulder, Colo.: Lynne Rienner, 1990).

18. In Mexico, this was typically referred to as the "fear vote." The PRI leadership, aware of the fact that many Mexicans might be overly cautious about change, built up the image of the two major opposition parties as representing a risky choice in comparison to retaining PRI control over the executive branch. Vicente Fox raised this issue publicly early in his campaign. Shortly before the July election, in a poll conducted by the *Mund* polling service, 72 percent of respondents admitted they would support a radical change if it would produce reform of the system. That was up from only 50 percent in December 1999. See "Fox alerta sobre el peligro del 'voto del miedo'," *Diario de Yucatán,* December 13, 1999, *www.yucatan.com.mx;* and "Los

antiprístas se inclinan por Fox," *Diairo de Yucatán,* June 23, 2000, www.yucatan. com.mx.

19. For another way of viewing this pattern of partisan support, see Irina Alberro, "Political Competition and Empowerment of the Poor," paper presented at the Midwest Political Science Association Meeting, Chicago, Illinois, Spring 2004.

20. Ramon Eduardo Ruiz, *Triumphs and Tragedy: A History of the Mexican People* (New York: Norton, 1992), 469.

21. Gant and Luttbeg, *American Electoral Behavior,* 141, indicates that in 1988, only 25 percent of college-educated Americans reported little political efficacy, compared with 57 percent of those with less than a high school diploma.

22. Rafael Giménez-Valdés, "Las encuestas en México durante el proceso electoral federal de 1994," Paper presented at The National Latin American Studies Association, Washington, D.C., 1995.

23. William Flanigan and Nancy Zingale, *Political Behavior of the American Electorate,* 7th ed. (Washington, D.C.: Congressional Quarterly Press, 1991), 68.

24. Ronald Inglehart, Neil Nevitte, and Miguel Basáñez, *Convergencia en Norte América, comercio, política y cultura* (Mexico City: Siglo XXI, 1994). Figure 3–20. Forty-six percent of citizens in the United States and 40 percent in Mexico consider God important in their lives.

25. *World Values Survey,* 1990.

26. Miguel Basáñez, *Encuesta nacional de opinión pública, iglesia y estado* (1990), 14; "Democracy Through U.S. and Mexican Lenses," September 2000.

27. Almond and Verba, *Civic Culture,* 101.

28. Charles L. Davis, "Religion and Partisan Loyalty: The Case of Catholic Workers in Mexico," *Western Political Quarterly* 45 (March 1992): 227.

29. See Donald Mabry, *Mexico's Acción Nacional: A Catholic Alternative to Revolution* (Syracuse, N.Y.: Syracuse University Press, 1973), for the well-documented ideological influence. For the stereotypical allegation, without foundation, see Carlos Martínez Assad, "State Elections in Mexico," in *Electoral Patterns and Perspectives in Mexico,* ed. Arturo Alvarado (La Jolla, Calif.: Center for U.S.-Mexican Studies, UCSD, 1987), 36.

30. See Roderic A. Camp, "The Cross in the Polling Booth: Religion, Politics, and the Laity in Mexico," *Latin American Research Review* 29 (1994): 89–90. Charles Davis, in an analysis of survey data of Catholic workers in 1979/80, had similar findings. See his "Religion and Partisan Loyalty," 279.

31. Rubén Ruíz Guerra, "Las verdades de las cifras," *Este País,* May 1994, 17.

32. Kenneth D. Wald, Dennis E. Owen, and Samuel D. Hill Jr., "Churches as Political Communities," *American Political Science Review* 82 (June 1988): 543–44.

33. For figures on this phenomenal growth, see David Stoll, *Is Latin America Turning Protestant? The Politics of Evangelical Growth* (Berkeley and Los Angeles: University of California Press, 1990).

34. Paul J. Bonicelli, "Testing the Waters or Opening the Floodgates? Evangelicals, Politics and the 'New' Mexico," *Journal of Church and State* 39 (winter 1997); 107–30.

35. Camp, "The Cross in the Polling Booth," 92–93.

36. "Estado, élites y clerecía," a survey of 458 public, private, and social leaders, October-November 1993, 4.2 percent margin of error, reported in *Este País,* May 1994, 23–29.

37. Robert S. Gilmour and Robert B. Lamp, *Political Alienation in Contemporary America* (New York: St. Martin's Press, 1975), 55.

38. The best study using these data for Mexico is William J. Blough, "Political Attitudes of Mexican Women: Support for the Political System Among a Newly Enfranchised Group," *Journal of Inter-American Studies and World Affairs* 14 (May 1972): 201–24.

39. Almond and Verba, *Civic Culture,* 327.

40. Alicia Inés Martínez, "Políticas hacia la mujer en el México moderno," paper presented at the Latin American Studies Association, Atlanta, March 1994, 36.

41. Enrique Alduncin, *Los valores de los mexicanos, México: Entre la tradición y la modernidad* (Mexico City: Banamex, 1986), 189.

42. Richard Fagen and William Tuohy, *Politics and Privilege in a Mexican City* (Stanford: Stanford University Press, 1972), 117.

43. Forty percent of men and 43 percent of women asserted a lack of political efficacy in 1988. Gant and Luttberg, *American Electoral Behavior,* 141.

44. *World Values Survey,* 1990, courtesy of Miguel Basáñez.

45. Nikki Craske, "Women's Political Participation in *Colonias Populares* in Guadalajara, Mexico," in *Viva: Women and Popular Protest in Latin America,* eds. Sarah A. Radcliffe and Sallie Westwood (London: Routledge, 1993), 112.

46. Marta Lamas et al., "Building Bridges: The Growth of Popular Feminism in Mexico," in *The Challenge of Local Feminisms: Women's Movements in Global Perspective,* eds. Amrita Basu and Elizabeth McGrovy (Boulder: Westview, 1995), 340–41.

47. Linda Stevenson, "Gender Politics in the Mexican Democratization Process: Sex Crimes, Affirmative Action for Women, and the 1997 Elections," Paper presented at the David Rockefeller Center for Latin American Studies, Harvard University, Cambridge, 1997.

48. Lisa Baldez, "Elected Bodies: The Gender Quota Law For Legislative Candidates in Mexico," *Legislative Studies Quarterly* 29 (May 2004): 231–58; and María del Carmen and Alanis Figueroa, "Women and Politics," *Voices of Mexico* 56 (July–September 2001): 7–11.

49. For perceptions of this during the revolutionary era, see Sandra McGee Deutsch, "Gender and Sociopolitical Change in Twentieth-Century Latin America," *Hispanic American Historical Review* 71 (May 1991): 270–71.

50. *World Values Survey,* 1990, courtesy of Miguel Basáñez.

51. Ivan Zavala, "Valores políticos," in *Cómo somos los mexicanos,* eds. Alberto Hernández Medina and Luis Narro Rodríguez (Mexico City: CREA, 1987), 97.

52. Alduncin y Asociados and *El Universal,* presidential 2000 poll, 1,700 respondents nationally, +/–2.5 percent margin of error, May 9–18, 2000. Women

were much more important in the presidential campaign itself, and according to one source, Fox's support among some women was based on sex appeal. See Ginger Thompson's statement that Fox's penchant for blue jeans and cowboy boots made "him just plain sexy" to many women. "Women Become the Darlings of the Candidates in Mexico," *The New York Times,* June 30, 2000.

53. Roderic Ai Camp and Keith Yanner, "Democracy Across Cultures, Does Gender Make a Difference?" in *Citizenship in Latin America*, ed. Joseph S. Tulchin and Meg Ruthenburg (Boulder, Colo.: Lynne Rienner, 2006).

54. The most comprehensive historical and theoretical exploration of this issue in Mexico can be found in Eric Van Young, ed., *Mexico's Regions, Comparative History and Development* (La Jolla, Calif.: Center for U.S.-Mexican Studies, UCSD, 1992).

55. See Roderic Ai Camp, "Province Versus the Center, Democratizing Mexico's Political Culture," in *Assessing Democracy in Latin America: A Tribute to Russell H. Fitzgibbon*, ed. Philip Kelly (Boulder: Westview Press, 1998), 76–92.

56. For some analysis of regional trends in the 1997 elections, see Joseph Klesner, who has long argued the importance of regionalism, in "Democratic Transition? The 1997 Mexican Elections," *PS* 30 (December 1997): 703–11.

57. Russell J. Dalton, *Citizen Politics in Western Democracies: Public Opinion and Political Parties in the United States, Great Britain, West Germany, and France* (Chatham, N.J.: Chatham House, 1988), 85ff.

58. Inglehart, Nevitte, and Basáñez, *Convergencia en Norte América,* chap. 1, 12.

5

Rising to the Top: The Recruitment of Political Leadership

> One of the most critical sets of questions about any political system concerns the composition of its leadership: Who governs? Who has access to power, and what are the social conditions of rule? Such issues have direct bearing on the representativeness of political leadership, a continuing concern of democratic theorists, and on the extent to which those in power emerge from the ranks of "the people"—or from an exclusive oligarchy. These themes also relate to the role of the political system within society at large, and to the ways in which careers in public life offer meaningful opportunities for vertical (usually upward) social mobility.
>
> PETER H. SMITH, *Labyrinths of Power*

Most citizens in a society where elections are typical participate by voting. A small number become involved in a political demonstration or join a party or organization to influence public policy actively. An even smaller number seek political office and the power to make decisions.

The structure of a political system, the relationships between institutions and citizens, and the relationships among various political institutions affect how a person arrives at a leadership post. The process by which people reach such posts is known as political recruitment.[1] An examination of

---

Political recruitment: the collective process by which persons reach political offices.

---

political recruitment from a comparative perspective is revealing for what it tells us about leadership characteristics and, equally important, what it illustrates about a society's political process.

All political systems and all organizations are governed by rules that prescribe acceptable behavior. The rules of political behavior are both formal and informal. The formal rules are set forth in law and in a constitution. The informal rules often explain more completely the realities of the process, or how the system functions in practice as distinct from theory. The political process melds the two sets of rules, and over time each influences the other to the extent that they often become inextricably intertwined.

THE FORMAL RULES

Formally, the Mexican political system has some of the same characteristics of the U.S. system. It is republican, having three branches of government—executive, legislative, judicial—and federal, allocating certain powers and responsibilities to state and local governments and others to the national government. In practice, the Mexican system has been dominated by the executive branch, which has not shared power with another branch from the 1920s until the 1990s, and allocates few powers to state and local governments. While this pattern was the norm for nearly seventy years, political transformations are changing the structural balance of power nationally and between the federal and state governments, altering well-established recruitment patterns.

In a competitive, parliamentary system, such as that found in Britain, the legislative branch is the essential channel for a successful, national political career. The legislative branch is the seat of decision-making power and the most important institutional source of political recruitment. In the United States, decision-making power is divided among three branches of government, although in the legislative policy process both the executive branch and Congress play equally decisive roles. Not only is the structure in the United States different, measured by the actual exercise of political authority, but two parties have alternated in power.

The significance of these characteristics for recruitment is that they affect how candidates for office are chosen. The degree to which the average citizen participates effectively in the political process determines, to some extent, his or her voice in leadership selection. Of course, it is not just a choice between candidates representing one political organization or party versus another, but how specific persons initially become candidates. The possible paths followed by potential political leaders in Mexico contrasts, although undergoing significant change the last few years, with approaches in the United States. The approaches between the two countries, beginning in 2000, began to take on more similarities. Fox's presidential victory brought an end to the dominance of a single political organization, the PRI and its antecedents, and a single leadership group within Mexico's political system. The change of parties in power have reinforced structural changes that impact on Mexico's traditional recruitment patterns.

When individual people in a small group exercise power over a long period of time, they tend to develop their own criteria for selecting their successors.[2] Moreover, they personally exercise the greatest influence over the

---

Sponsored selection: political recruitment dominated by incumbent officeholders.

---

selection process. Students of political recruitment call this *incumbent,* or *sponsored, selection.*[3]

In the formal structure, given the monopoly exercised by the PRI historically, one would expect the party itself to be crucial to the identification and recruitment of future political leaders. Until 1994, its role has been minimal. The reason is that the PRI was not created nor has it functioned as an orthodox political party, that is, to capture power. The PRI, as suggested earlier, was formed to help *keep* a leadership group in power. Yet even a tight leadership group that exercises power in an authoritarian fashion must devise channels for political recruitment. Not to do so would eventually deprive it of the fresh replacements necessary to its continued existence.

In Mexico, until the mid-1990s, most decision-making positions were obtained through sponsored selection, whether the position was appointive or elective. Beginning in 1994, however, two structural conditions began to change that ultimately affected the recruitment process. First, the incumbent party began to experiment with a more open form of selecting its candidates, especially those nominees for state governors and ultimately for president in 1999. Instead of the president of Mexico making that decision, typically the pattern in the past, President Zedillo began to withdraw from that process. In 1999, the PRI, for the first time, held an open presidential primary, in which several leading politicians competed intensely for the party's nomination, eventually won by Francisco Labastida.[4] The National Action Party, which for some time had engaged in a closed primary in which party delegates voted for their presidential candidate, selected a party outsider, Vicente Fox, as their choice.

The second major structural change is that the electoral process itself became increasingly competitive in the 1990s. This is illustrated by the data in Table 5-1. As the data indicate, all opposition parties combined governed

Table 5-1 Growth of Party Competition in Mexico

	Year						
	1988	1990	1992	1995	1996	1997	2001
Percentage of Mexicans governed at the state or local level by parties other than PRI	3	10	14	24	38	50	61

Source: "Notable avance de la oposición en una década," *Diario de Yucatán,* November 22, 1999, www.yucatan.com.mx, and "Consolidating a Three Party System," *Review of the Economic Situation of Mexico,* December 2001, 539–40.

only 3 percent of the population at the state or local level in 1988. In just two years time, after the strong showing by Cuauhtémoc Cárdenas in the 1988 presidential race, the figure tripled to over 10 percent of the population. By 1995, nearly a fourth of Mexico's citizens had leadership from the PRD and PAN, and by 1997, when these two parties won control of the national legislative branch, PRD and PAN politicians governed half of Mexico's population.

During the many decades in which the PRI dominated Mexican politics, the Mexican federal bureaucracy became the favored source of political leadership. The reason for this is that in reality, the legislative and judicial branches remained weak, and local and state governments were staffed by individuals who owed their careers to state and national leaders, respectively. Even the party's own leadership came from career bureaucrats beholden to Mexico's president.

The newness of the PRD (1989) makes it impossible to identify long-term recruitment trends, especially since many of its national leaders were former PRIistas. For most of its history, the National Action Party produced a different type of leadership, and therefore, stressed different recruitment institutions. It shared more similarities with U.S. political institutions, since its leaders competed vigorously within and outside of party ranks to be nominated and, more significantly, to defeat the PRI's candidates for various positions. Its prominent leaders have had predominantly local party careers, and have come from elective office.[5] Many of its top officials and candidates in the 1990s had been former congressman and, since the mid-1990s, governors. Vicente Fox himself illustrates this pattern, having served as a congressman and governor of his home state.

Indeed, an analysis of governors since 1997 clearly demonstrates the impact of a democratic setting on the recruitment and selection process, foreshadowing and replicating many of the characteristics Vicente Fox represents. Since the leading presidential contenders in the 2006 race from the

PRD and the PRI are also former governors, it further confirms the importance of such patterns. As the data in Table 5-2 suggest, the majority of new governors from all parties began their careers locally, emphasizing the importance of local political origins. Moreover, two-thirds of governors remain in their home states or nearby states for their college education, thus preventing networking ties with influential national politicians from Mexico City. Second, nearly 80 percent of governors have held elective office compared to only 8 percent of most national executive branch officials in the 1990s. Third, larger numbers of governors come from more modest socioeconomic backgrounds. Fourth, if we separate PAN governors from all other parties, we discover that they are not professional politicians; they made their living in the private sector and have had extensive experience in business as owners and managers. Many have also provided leadership in business interest group organizations.[6]

As party competition has increased, the PRI itself has been forced to emulate the recruitment patterns typical of PAN. In fact, now that it has lost control of the federal executive branch, the bureaucracy is no longer a natural source of PRI leadership. Instead, because it continues to control the

Table 5-2 Background Characteristics of Recent Mexican Governors

Characteristic	Percentage	PAN Governors Only
Precollege studies locally	90	89
Held elective office	77	56
Graduated from provincial university	64	33
Elected federal office	63	33
Middle-class origins	63	50
Professional politician	55	0
Born in small towns	43	33
Developmental poststate bureaucracy	40	22
Born in state capitals	37	63
State party leaders	33	33
Mayors	33	44
Nontraditional college degrees	33	44
Law degree	32	11
Business career	29	56
Attended private university	21	30
Led business organization	20	44
Graduate degrees	20	22
No college degrees	20	33
Working-class origins	25	25
Graduate work abroad	17	22
No government experience	10	33

Note: Based on a survey of thirty-four governors who took office between 1997 and 2004. Only one governor is excluded from the sample, that of Tabasco (PRI), for insufficient information.

majority of state governorships, political recruitment patterns within the PRI will shift back to state elective and appointive careers, and to a lesser degree to local experience. This pattern was more common in the party's early history in the 1930s and 1940s. The important shift in recruitment patterns can be seen in the careers of the three major parties' presidential contenders in 2000. All three had been governors of their home state. In no presidential race since 1964 had more than one presidential candidate served as governor.

THE INFORMAL RULES: WHAT IS
NECESSARY TO RISE TO THE TOP

Regardless of which individuals do the actual recruiting of future figures in prominent national political offices, certain institutional settings facilitate that process, making the contacts between certain persons possible. Strangely, the most important institution in the initial recruitment of Mexico's national political leaders in the twentieth century is the university.

Mexico's postrevolutionary leadership, building on the concept of a National Preparatory School introduced by the liberals in the mid-nineteenth century, used public education as a means of preparing and identifying future politicians. In the nineteenth century, many of the prerevolutionary leaders were educated at the National Preparatory School, and it continued to function in this way after 1920. Some politicians who served in national posts in the 1920s and 1930s never obtained higher education; they were self-made, largely on revolutionary battlefields from 1910 to 1920. Many continued as career military officers in the new postrevolutionary army.

A rapid shift occurred in credentials between the revolutionary generation of political leaders (holding office from 1920 to 1946) and the postrevolutionary generation (holding office from 1946 through the 1960s). The importance of higher education in political recruitment and the rapid decline of battlefield experiences are clearly illustrated by the personal experiences of presidents Lázaro Cárdenas (1934–1940) and Miguel Alemán (1946–1952) and the persons they recruited to political office. More than half of all national officeholders from 1920 to 1934 had fought in the revolution. Cárdenas joined the revolution as a young man and rose through the ranks to become a division general, Mexico's highest-ranking officer. He had no formal education beyond primary school in his hometown. Although he pursued a political career in the 1920s, he remained in the army, eventually serving as secretary of national defense. On the other hand, Miguel Alemán, son of a prominent general, was too young to have fought in the revolution. Encour-

Table 5-3 Political Recruitment Sources for Presidents Cárdenas and Alemán

President	Revolution (%)	State (%)	Bureaucracy (%)	Party (%)	School (%)	Relatives (%)
	Sources of Initial Recruitment					
Cárdenas	34	18	26	0	18	3
Alemán	0	10	3	3	85	0

Source: Roderic Ai Camp, *Mexico's Leaders, Their Education and Recruitment* (Tucson: University of Arizona Press, 1980), 22.

aged by his father to obtain a good education, he was sent to Mexico City where he studied at the National Preparatory School and then the National School of Law, graduating in 1929.

The personal experiences of a president influences his sources of initial political recruitment (see Table 5-3). In the case of Cárdenas, the revolution was central. After all, men under battle conditions develop trust in one another and respect for survival skills. A third of Cárdenas's collaborators had come in contact with him through shared service in the revolution. Once Cárdenas began his political career, he met other men in the bureaucracy who accompanied him up the political ladder. Although relatively unschooled, when he was governor of his home state, he held weekly seminars for students and professors from the local university, forming close ties with people whom he brought into political life later on. Cárdenas served as president of the National Revolutionary Party (PNR), an antecedent of the PRI, but did not recruit from this source. The contrast between him and Alemán could not be more remarkable. Over four-fifths of Alemán's chosen political associates had been classmates or professors at the two schools he had attended in Mexico City.

Alemán established the overwhelming value of preparatory and university education as the institutional locus of Mexican political recruitment. Its importance increased as greater numbers of future politicians began to attend the National Preparatory School and, more significant, the National University. Having attended the former reached an all-time high during the 1958–1964 administration, in which 58 percent of the politicians were graduates. Graduates of the National University reached their highest level under President de la Madrid (1982–1988), when they accounted for 56 percent of his college-educated officeholders. Midway through the Salinas administration, National University graduates continued to account for half of all national politicians. Indeed, among Zedillo's cabinet, over 70 percent were alumni.

Table 5-4 University Graduates by Presidential Administration, 1920–1991

	Institution			
President	Universidad Nacional Autónomo de Mexico (%)	Military (%)	Private (%)	Other (%)
Obregón, 1920–1924	50	9	0	41
Calles, 1924–1928	37	0	5	58
Portes Gil, 1929–1930	33	0	0	67
Ortiz Rubio, 1930–1932	43	21	0	26
Rodríguez, 1932–1934	50	0	0	50
Cárdenas, 1934–1930	27	7	3	74
Avila Camacho 1940–1946	36	7	4	53
Alemán, 1946–1952	50	5	4	41
Ruiz Cortines, 1952–1958	36	8	1	55
López Mateos, 1958–1964	47	7	1	45
Díaz Ordaz, 1964–1970	51	7	1	41
Echeverría, 1970–1976	54	7	2	37
López Portillo, 1976–1982	52	7	2	39
De la Madrid, 1982–1988	56	5	6	33
Salinas, 1988–1991	51	9	13	27

Source: Roderic Ai Camp, *Mexican Political Biography Project,* 1995.

The university and preparatory school became important sources of political recruitment for two reasons (see Table 5-4). Many future politicians taught at these two institutions, generally a single course. Three-quarters of national political figures have taught at the college level. Salinas was an adjunct professor at his alma mater, the National University, and President Zedillo taught at two of Mexico's leading institutions. Politicians use academia in part as a means to teach students intellectual and political skills, helping them get started in a public career. Typically, they place a student in a government internship or part-time job, followed by a full-time position after graduation. Miguel de la Madrid (1982–1988) is an excellent illustration of this, having started his career in the Bank of Mexico (Mexico's "federal reserve bank") on the recommendation of an economics professor.[7]

Vicente Fox does not continue the tradition of college teaching typical of his predecessors; he only completed his degree while campaigning for president. Nevertheless, his educational experiences at the prestigious Ibero-American University produced several influential ties to future, prominent Mexicans. More importantly, many of his cabinet members have been part- or full-time academics, including his treasury and foreign relations secretaries. What is distinctive about Fox's administration educationally is the fact that many top appointees graduated from or taught at distinguished private institutions, especially the Monterrey Technological Institute for Higher Studies (ITESM) in Nuevo León, popularly known as

"Monterrey Tech," and the Autonomous Technological Institute of Mexico (ITAM), in the Federal District.

As suggested above, the second institution most influential in the initial recruitment of national politicians is the federal bureaucracy. Numerous prominent figures have begun their careers in lesser agency posts, sometimes as advisers or technical experts. If they decide to make politics their career, they develop contacts with other ambitious figures, typically a superior in their own agency or in a related organization. That individual, similar to the politician-teacher, initiates their rise within the national bureaucracy. In spite of the inroads made by local and state party and governmental bureaucracies, and by the PAN national party organization, the federal bureaucracy continues to rank second only to the university as a source of political recruitment. In contrast to the United States, the Democratic and Republican parties are often the source of nationally prominent politicians because they have traditionally been formative in the candidate-selection process and in the competition for offices that influence policymaking.

An examination of Mexico's most influential politicians from 1970 to 2000, reinforces this interpretation. Mexican politicians rely on informal, personal contacts to develop their ties to a politician-teacher or a superior, which sociologists call networking. Ambitious Mexicans form strong personal ties to an individual mentor and may have different mentors at various stages of their careers. These networking patterns, which are examined in some detail below, occur in three common settings (Table 5-5): educational

Table 5-5 How Mentor-Disciples Among the Mexican Elites Meet

	Sources of Mentor-Disciple Relationships		
	Education	Career	Family
Type of Power Elite	(percentages)		
Political	45	42	13
Intellectual	76	15	9
Capitalist	1	5	94
Military	31	69	0
Clergy	63	25	11

Note: (N = 398) Data based on known relationships between a mentor and disciple among Mexico's power elite. *Education* refers to a mentor-disciple contact that occurred in any educational setting, typically between a student and a professor, between any two students, or between professorial peers. *Career* refers to a mentor-disciple contact that took place in an occupational setting, typically between two individuals working in an organizational bureaucracy, often in a superior-subordinate relationship. *Family* refers to mentor-disciple relationships established within the immediate family, including mentors who were grandparents, in-laws, aunts and uncles, or parents.
Source: Roderic Ai Camp, *Mexico's Mandarins, Crafting a Power Elite for the Twenty-first Century* (Berkeley: University of California Press, 2002).

institutions, career positions (primarily the bureaucracy), and within the family.

In Mexico few *national* politicians have been recruited through party channels, especially at the local and state levels, with the exception of prominent PAN party figures and, to a lesser extent, younger leaders of the PRD. Many prominent figures at the state and local levels are recruited in such fashion. Because decision making was centralized in the executive branch rather than in the legislative bodies, a career in the national bureaucracy was the foremost means of ascent.

The salience of the federal bureaucracy in the recruitment process contributes to another informal characteristic of upward political mobility in Mexico: the significance of Mexico City. Politicians who come from Mexico City, in spite of its tremendous size, are overrepresented in the national political leadership. This was true before the revolution of 1910, but those violent events introduced a leadership whose birthplaces deemphasized the importance of the capital (see Table 5-6). That remained true until the 1940s, when the presence of Mexico City in the backgrounds of national politicians increased substantially. By the presidency of Luis Echeverría (1970–1976), when fewer than one in ten citizens was born in Mexico City, one in four national political figures named it as a place of birth. In the past twenty years, that figure increased dramatically: Mexico City was the birthplace of nearly half of President Salinas's appointees who held national office for the first time, nearly four times that of the general population of the same age. The government has not provided comparable data on national politicians since 1994, but an examination of the Zedillo and Fox cabinets suggests a gradual, but important decline in the importance of the Federal District in the backgrounds of Mexico's most influential political figures (Table 5-7). In Zedillo's cabinet, more than two-thirds of his collaborators were born in the Federal District, a figure that dropped to 60 percent under Fox. The reason for this decline is clear: Fox recruited his cabinet from institutional settings other than the federal bureaucracy, thus giving greater prominence to other cities and regions. As elective office becomes more common in the background of aspiring politicians, the prominence of the Federal District is likely to continue to decline.

In all political systems, whom one knows has much to do with political recruitment and with appointment to an important political office. U.S. politics is replete with examples of prominent figures who sought out old friends to fill responsible political offices. In fact, knowing someone is often a means for obtaining employment in the private sector as well. In Mexico, whom one knows in public life is even more telling, given the fact that incumbent office-holders often decide who obtains influential posts. Mexicans with political

Table 5-6 Region of Birth of First-Time National Officeholders by Presidential Administration, 1884–1991

Presidential Administration	Federal District	East Central	West	North	South	Gulf	West Central	Foreign
	Region of Birth (%)							
Díaz	15	13	15	15	12	18	11	1
1889–	7	10	19	16	19	19	10	0
1893–	12	24	6	15	15	9	18	0
1897–	13	11	11	16	4	31	13	0
1901–	22	5	5	24	8	22	11	3
1905	14	9	11	29	11	17	9	0
1910–	23	6	0	35	0	24	6	6
De la Barra	6	22	28	28	6	0	11	0
Madero	13	13	20	18	6	20	9	0
Huerta	16	10	16	24	8	12	16	0
Convention	5	11	19	32	5	5	22	0
Carranza	4	17	16	26	10	13	12	1
Obregón	6	14	19	19	13	21	8	0
Calles	3	15	18	20	13	12	18	0
Portes Gil	0	21	14	29	0	29	7	0
Ortiz Rubio	8	8	12	28	4	12	28	0
Rodríguez	0	15	0	46	17	0	8	0
Cárdenas	6	20	15	13	13	13	20	1
Avila Camacho	10	20	15	16	10	11	25	1
Alemán	11	15	12	20	9	16	15	1
Ruiz Cortines	3	18	20	16	12	17	17	1
López Mateos	9	19	16	17	10	11	15	0
Díaz Ordaz	8	11	23	15	7	15	12	0
Echeverría	24	15	14	13	9	12	13	1
López Portillo	26	12	13	13	8	13	12	3
De la Madrid	39	13	11	11	8	6	10	1
Salinas	45	6	11	15	2	13	4	4
Total	16	14	15	15	9	14	13	1
1910 Census[a]	5	22	16	11	14	12	21	
1950 Census[a]	12	18	14	15	13	12	17	

Source: Roderic A. Camp, *Mexican Political Biography Project,* 1995.
[a]Percentage of general population from each region.

ambitions can enhance personal contacts at school, in the university, or during their professional and public careers through family ties (Table 5-5).

Americans have produced a few notable political families, say, the Adamses and Kennedys, and George W. Bush is the son of a president and grandson of a U.S. senator, but such families are numerous in Mexico. One reason, as studies of British and U.S. politicians have shown, is that children of political activists are more likely to see politics as a potential career than are children reared in a nonpolitical environment.[8] It is natural that a youngster growing up in a political family would come in contact with many polit-

Table 5-7 General Characteristics of the Fox and Zedillo Cabinets

	Place of Origin		University Attended		Undergraduate Degree			Graduate Work			Career		Electoral Experience	
	Federal District	Province	Private	Public	Economics[a]	Law	Other	United States	England/ Europe	Mexico	Private Sector	Public Sector	Elective Office	None
Zedillo	68	32	18	82	36	32	32	50	32	18	0	100	23	77
Fox	60	40	44	56	32	29	39	48	19	33	68	32	32	68

[a]Economics includes CPAs and business administration degrees.
[b]Based on a comparison of both presidents' first cabinet-level appointees.

ical figures. More than one in eight Mexican national politicians from 1970 through 1988, including President Salinas, were the children of nationally prominent political figures. Salinas's father, who served in the cabinet in the 1960s, helped his son's early career. Cuauhtémoc Cárdenas, PRD's leading figure, is the son of President Lázaro Cárdenas. If extended family ties are considered, between one-fifth and one-third of all politicians were related to national political figures during the same period. Numerous PAN leaders are the children of its founders and early presidential candidates. The same is true on the state level and has been documented in detail by Javier Hurtado in his examination of Jalisco, an important western state.[9]

Politically active families are not the only factor that makes family background important. Social and economic status is another. Studies of politicians worldwide, in both socialist and nonsocialist societies, reveal the importance of middle- and upper-middle-class backgrounds.[10] In Third World countries without competitive political structures, family origins become even more significant to career success.

Higher socioeconomic backgrounds are helpful in political life because well-off parents provide opportunities for their children. Education is such a significant means of political recruitment that *access* to it enables making the right contacts and obtaining the necessary, informal credentials. Some Mexicans from working-class backgrounds manage to attend preparatory school and even a university, but few actually complete degree programs. Family socioeconomic status has increased in significance, as private schooling has increased its presence among all politicians, and particularly among Panistas. Scholarships to private institutions are the exception, not the norm. This explains why Mexico's youngest generation of national politicians, those born since 1940 (Presidents Salinas's, Zedillo's, and Fox's generation), are almost exclusively from middle- and upper-middle-class backgrounds. President Zedillo, however, is an exception, the first chief executive in decades to come from a working-class family of modest means. Fox, on the other hand, fits the recent pattern.

THE RISE OF WOMEN

Another informal credential universal to political leadership in all countries is gender. Politics has been, and remains, dominated by men. Nevertheless, women have made substantial inroads in national political office. On the whole, women have been far more successful politically in Mexico than in many other countries, including the United States. For example, several women served on the supreme court in Mexico, long before Sandra Day

O'Connor was appointed by President Reagan. Numerous women have held senate positions. In the 1990s, women accounted for 15 and 18 percent of Senate and congressional seats compared to only 9 and 13 percent, respectively, in the United States.[11] Cabinet posts have occasionally been filled by women, but men have a virtual lock on that domain, especially in the major agencies. President Zedillo increased the number of women in his cabinet to three, the highest ever, a figure equalled by president Fox. Most important, in 1998, Rosario Green became secretary of foreign relations, the first woman to hold a significant cabinet post.

Slightly different recruitment patterns have traditionally been followed by women interested in politics. This fact worked against their obtaining the higher positions because they did not come in contact with current and future political figures who could assist them up the bureaucratic ladder.[12] Typically, women politicians have been found far more frequently in party posts and in the legislative branch, and they have not had the same type or level of education (see Table 5-8). Younger women who are politically ambitious are now taking on many of the characteristics of their male peers. Among younger political figures (born after 1950) at the national level, women now

Table 5-8 Credentials of First-Time Officeholders by Gender, 1934–1991

Credential	Women (%)	Men (%)
Education		
Primary, secondary, preparatory only	22	19
Normal only	22	5
University	32	51
Graduate	26	25
Degree earned		
None	43	27
Law	38	51
Economics	19	12
Medicine	6	9
Engineering	5	14
Other	32	15
Political office		
Private secretary	3	9
Union leader	13	13
Kinship ties		
Relative in public office	15	28
Father in politics	8	9
Party office		
President of PRI	0	1
Secretary of PRI	6	8
Federal District director	0	1
State director	8	4
Other post	43	17
All PRI posts combined	50	22

Source: Roderic A. Camp, *Mexican Political Biography Project,* 1995.

Table 5-9 Women's Recruitment to National Political
Office by Administration, 1935–1991

President	Percentage of Women in Administration
Cárdenas, 1934–1940	0
Avila Camacho, 1940–1946	1
Alemán, 1946–1952	2
Ruiz Cortines, 1952–1958	4
López Mateos, 1958–1964	4
Díaz Ordaz, 1964–1970	6
Echeverría, 1970–1976	8
López Portillo, 1976–1982	19
De la Madrid, 1982–1988	17
Salinas, 1988–1991	11

Source: Roderic A. Camp, *Mexican Political Biography Project,* 1995.

account for one in four. The representation of women in national political offices (cabinet, subcabinet, and top judicial and legislative posts) increased substantially after 1976, during the administration of José López Portillo (see Table 5-9). The lower figure for Salinas does not necessarily represent a decline in the representation of women, as the data are for only the first half of his administration. For example, among all officials in the Salinas administration, 12 percent of the legislative branch, 12 percent of the judicial branch, and 6 percent of the executive branch were women.[13] In the legislative branch during the Zedillo administration (1994–2000), women accounted for 16 percent of the deputies and 9 percent of the senators. Under Fox, those figures rose again, to 20 and 20 percent, respectively. (See Table 5-10). Among the major political parties, in the National Executive Committee, women controlled 24, 13, and 11 percent, respectively, of the PRD, PRI, and PAN posts. The PRD, similar to some Scandinavian parties, began experimenting with a quota system. In 1993, they instituted a 30 percent rule, guaranteeing women that level of representation among the party's candidates for office. After the implementation of this rule, women deputies from the PRD increased from 8 to 23 percent.

In the 2003 congressional elections, after the implementation of the new federal quota legislation, the number of female deputies increased significantly (see Table 5-10). In spite of this notable improvement, the implementation of the spirit of the law varied from party to party. Party candidates chosen in direct elections for congressional and senate seats need not comply with the quota. Among the three major parties, 49 percent of their candidates were chosen through direct election. In spite of the fact that the gender quotas applied to only half of the candidates, women won 23 percent of the seats in the 2003–2006 legislature, moving Mexico's ranking of the per-

Table 5-10 Women's Recruitment to National Legislative
Office by Administration, 1952–2006

	Percentage of Women in Office	
Administration	Chamber of Deputies	Senate
1952–1958	2	0
1958–1964	5	0
1964–1970	6	3
1970–1976	7	3
1976–1982	9	6
1982–1988	11	9
1988–1994	10	11
1994–2000	16	9
2000–2006	20	20

Source: Adapted from Anna M. Fernández Poncela, "The Political Participation of Women in Mexico Today," in *Changing Structure of Mexico: Political, Social and Economic Prospects* (Armonk, N.Y.: Sharpe, 1996), 307–14;
Este País, September 2000, 23; *Quién es quién en el congreso* (Mexico:
IETD, 2002).

centage of women in the legislative branch worldwide from 55 to 23, equal
to Switzerland.[14]

Women in the 1980s and 1990s began to acquire men's credentials,
thus increasing their opportunities for closer contact with potential future
politicians. Women traditionally have not been as well educated as men, but
younger women have received much more university training, putting them
on par with men holding influential posts in the 1970s and 1980s. In 1995,
women were only two-tenths of a year behind men in their average number
of years of schooling.[15] The major difference in recruitment qualities among
female and male politicians today is that women are not receiving the same
level of graduate education and, more important, are attending graduate
schools that are no longer considered prestigious by men. But women continue to have much broader and deeper experiences in their parties and in
civic and nongovernmental organizations. These career differences, though
working against female political recruitment in the past, may very well give
women stronger skills in a changing, plural political context and thus an
advantage in an increasingly democratic Mexico.[16]

THE CAMARILLA: GROUP POLITICS IN MEXICO

Perhaps the most distinctive characteristic of Mexican politics, knowledge
of which is essential to understanding the recruitment process, is the politi-

cal clique, the *camarilla.* It has determined prior to 2000, more than any other variable discussed, who goes to the top of the political ladder, what paths are taken, and the specific posts they are assigned. Many of the features of Mexican political culture predispose the political system to rely on camarillas. A camarilla is a group of people who have political interests in common and rely on one another to improve their chances within the political leadership (see Table 5-11).

The fundamental question that the PAN presidential victory raises for this unique, informal process of Mexican political life is: Will the camarilla system continue to play a crucial role? The camarilla system will be altered substantially by the structural changes that the PRI defeat introduces, but it is unlikely to disappear altogether. The reasons why these informal, personal linkages are unlikely to disappear altogether include the following. First, the underlying cement of the camarilla system is the mentor-disciple relationship. As a recent study of Mexico's most influential leaders from all professions, including the armed forces, the clergy, cultural elites, capitalists, and politicians, illustrates, prominent Mexicans have relied heavily on mentors, who often were equally influential themselves, to promote their career success.[17] In fact, six out of seven influential Mexicans were known to have a

Table 5-11 Characteristics of Mexican Camarillas in the Twenty-first Century

1. The structural basis of the camarilla system is a mentor-disciple relationship, which has many similarities to the patron-client culture throughout Latin America.
2. The camarilla system is extremely fluid, and camarillas are not exclusive but overlapping, relying on networking techniques found in other societies.
3. Most successful politicians are the products of multiple mentors and camarillas, that is, rarely does a politician remain within a single camarilla from beginning to the end of his or her career.
4. The larger the camarilla, the more influential its leader and, likewise, his disciples.
5. Some camarillas are characterized by an ideological flavor, but other personal qualities determine disciple ties to a mentor.
6. Disciples often surpass the political careers of their mentors, thus reversing the benefits of the camarilla's relationship and the logical order of camarilla influence.
7. Camarillas increasingly will be formed in diverse institutional environments, including state bureaucracies, the corporate world, international agencies, civic organizations, as well as federal bureaucratic agencies.
8. Superior-subordinate institutional relationships will increasingly displace the importance of educational and familial contacts.
9. Most politicians continue to carry with them membership in an educational camarilla, represented by their preparatory, professional, and graduate school generation.
10. The rise of the nonprofessional politician increases the potential importance of networking across influential groups and professions.

Source: Roderic Ai Camp, *Mexico's Mandarins, Crafting a Power Elite for the Twenty-first Century* (Berkeley: University of California Press, 2002); and "Camarillas in Mexican Politics: The Case of the Salinas Cabinet," *Mexican Studies* 6 (Winter 1990), 106–7.

mentor. Among politicians, the figure is 100 percent. Second, even if camarillas were to disappear altogether within the federal bureaucracy, an unlikely situation, they would still function at the state level, where PRI continues to control the majority of governorships and, therefore, state patronage. Third, personal loyalties are a fact of Mexican life. Individuals are likely to rely on personal relationships to foster their career success, even if the rewards are altered by structural changes within the Mexican system.

A camarilla is often formed early, even while the members are still in college. The members place considerable trust in one another. Using a group of friends to accomplish professional objectives is a feature found in other sectors of Mexican society, including academia and the business community. A camarilla has a leader who acts as a political mentor to other members of

---

Camarilla: a group of persons who share political interests, and rely on one another to improve their chances in the political leadership.

---

the group. He typically is more successful than his peers and uses his own career as a means of furthering the careers of other group members. As the leader of a camarilla ascends in an institution, he places members of his group, when possible, in other influential positions either within his organization or outside it. The higher he rises, the more positions he can fill.[18]

All of the qualities described in Table 5-11 remain true for most national government officeholders. But the universality of these qualities will break down as PAN and PRD members acquire more posts, especially if those individuals are not career politicians, but have moved laterally into politics from other professions. Camarillas will not disappear, but other characteristics will increase in importance and other variables will moderate camarillas' influence.[19]

The role of the mentor and the political groups he creates take on added importance because the mentor establishes the criteria by which he chooses his disciples and because he plays a formative role in socializing his disciples. The implications for political recruitment are crucial. It has been shown that politicians, like most people, tend to recruit those with similar credentials or experience, who in many ways mirror themselves.[20] Over time, mentors can structure the recruitment process to favor certain credentials. In the past, the most successful camarillas reached the presidency. Presidents, because they exercise the most comprehensive influence over political appointments, have the greatest impact on the recruitment process, affecting the entire political system.

The demise of PRI's monopoly completely alters this pattern. The recruitment and promotion criteria will no longer be universal, but dispersed, depending on the political setting from which an individual emerges, for example, from state politics, the congress, the bureaucracy, or from a nonpolitical career in business and civic organizations. Furthermore, President Fox has not shown a strong tendency to appoint influential cabinet members who mirror his career and political experience. Instead, he has diversified the recruitment process by selecting a range of individuals to direct governmental agencies who differ in their career experiences. These individuals, in turn, have the greatest opportunity to fill subordinate posts with their own choices. It remains to be seen whether they too will follow the pattern of their predecessors in choosing like types for the most influential positions. In the foreseeable future, the majority of mid-to upper-level positions are still likely to be filled by individuals who have come from careers in the bureaucracy, since they have the expertise and experience necessary for many of these positions.

Significant changes in broad recruitment patterns historically, the result of preferences by leading mentors, are easily documented. For example, President Alemán surrounded himself with a new type of politician, giving his collaborators an opportunity to reinforce their same credentials. From the 1940s through the 1970s, as the camarillas introduced by Alemán and his generation rose to the top, certain credentials became increasingly important: a college education, preferably from the National University; an urban birthplace, preferably Mexico City; a career in national politics, preferably the federal bureaucracy; pursuit of a law degree and legal career; and entrance into public service at a young age, often while still in college.

In the 1980s, and in some instances earlier, a change began to occur in the informal credentials required of the most successful politicians. A policy setting forth these changing requirements was not established; rather, they emerged naturally as the politicians themselves changed their credentials. Those recent trends became sharper and more easily recognized under Salinas and Zedillo.

Politicians' educational and career characteristics have changed markedly in the past two decades. The most persistent change has been the constant increase in *level* of education. Not only are all national political leaders, with a few exceptions in the legislative branch, college educated, but graduate education has reached new highs. De la Madrid, Salinas, and Zedillo obtained graduate degrees. De la Madrid has an M.A. degree in public administration from Harvard; his disciple and successor, Salinas, has two M.A. degrees as well as a Ph.D. degree from Harvard; and Salinas' successor, Zedillo, received his M.A. and Ph.D. from Yale. President Fox does not continue the pattern established by his predecessors, having completed only an undergraduate business administration degree. Because he was not a professional politician, nor employed in the federal bureaucracy, the broad recruitment criteria established by influential political mentors and presidents did not influence his preparation. Fox's three predecessors reflect the importance given to advanced education in Mexican politics. Of the *new* national officeholders under de la Madrid, nearly half, like the president, had graduate degrees. Only six years later, beginning with the Salinas administration in 1988, 70 percent had received graduate training; many of them with Ph.D.s. Of Zedillo's cabinet members, 66 percent claimed such educational credentials. Graduate education has become such a preferred credential that top political figures have been known to lie about having it. For example, there was a scandal involving Zedillo's first education secretary, who never completed his B.A. or his Ph.D.[21]

De la Madrid and Salinas introduced another informal credential into the recruitment process. Their camarilla selections emphasized politicians who had been educated outside Mexico, particularly at the graduate level. Zedillo did likewise. It can be said that Salinas was following in the footsteps of his father, who also graduated from Harvard with an advanced degree. Zedillo followed in the footsteps of his mentor, economist Leopoldo Solís, a Yale graduate. Even Fox, although he did not earn a graduate degree, obtained a diploma in advanced management from Harvard. The point is that numerous political figures began to study abroad, generally at the most prestigious universities in the United States. In Salinas's administration Harvard and Yale graduates were the most common. These patterns have been carefully traced since the 1970s. In 1972, 58 percent of Mexico's national political figures with Ph.D.s received them from the National University, and only 13 percent from U.S. universities. By 1989, only 29 percent had graduated from an institution in their native country, compared with 48 percent from U.S. institutions.[22] In the 1990s, 55 percent of national politicians received their Ph.D.s in the United States.

A third change in the educational background of contemporary politicians, and perhaps the most significant, is the discipline studied. Law, as in the United States, has always been the field of study of most future politicians, with engineering and medicine coming in second. This means that law school is the most likely place to meet future politicians and political mentors. The most remarkable change is a shift from law to economics in politicians' educational backgrounds. Salinas was the first president with that specialty, and his political generation was the first to count as many economists as lawyers among its members. Zedillo duplicated this pattern personally and among his collaborators. Fox's degree in business administration is closely linked to the emphasis on economics, and one out of three members of his cabinet graduated in economically related disciplines, (Table 5-7).

The new emphasis on economics has led to another significant change in recruitment characteristics: the elevation of private over public education. This characteristic is less pervasive than the others but even more remarkable. Between the administration of de la Madrid and Salinas, a sixfold increase in the percentage of private-school graduates took place. Instead of the National University and public universities maintaining their level of dominance, private institutions have begun to make serious inroads. This trend is enhanced by the fact that many PAN politicians are private school graduates, and as more businesspeople choose political careers, private university graduates will increase. Vicente Fox is a case in point. His educational origins are reflected in his cabinet choices. Nearly half have graduated from private schools, with Ibero-American University, his alma mater, the Monterrey Technological Institute of Higher Studies, the Free Law School, the Autonomous Technological University of Mexico, and Anahuac University, the most important. Even more remarkable, three of his cabinet members obtained undergraduate degrees from private universities in the United States. This is significant for political recruitment because it will change not only informal credentials, but also the locations where recruitment takes place. In fact, it contributes to the diversity of the recruitment process, a process that traditionally has relied on fewer, concentrated, public educational sources.

THE RISE AND DECLINE OF THE TECHNOCRAT

As the recruitment process changed and the credentials of future politicians were modified, some scholars labeled the younger generation of politicians in Mexico as technocrats, *técnicos*. The rise of technocratic leadership took place throughout Latin America. A number of attributes have been associated with this class of leaders in Brazil and Chile, and many have been mistakenly applied to Mexico's leaders. This has generated some confusion about technocrats.[23]

Mexico's technocratic leadership is characterized by new developments in their informal credentials. In particular, they are seen as well educated in technologically sophisticated fields; as spending most of their careers in the national bureaucracy; as having come from large urban centers, notably Mexico City; as having middle- and upper-middle-class backgrounds; and as having studied abroad (see Table 5-12). By implication, in

Table 5-12 Characteristics of Mexico's Politician-Technocrats in
the 1990s

Characteristic	Percentage Having
Urban birthplace	94
Male	87
Middle-class parents	85
College educated	83
Graduate of the National University	58
Taught	57
Prior national political post	56
Born between 1920 and 1939	52
Graduate education	46
Lawyer	37
Taught at the National University	37
Graduate of the National Preparatory School	29
Ph.D. degree	20
Graduate work in the United States	19
Economist	16

Source: Roderic A. Camp, *Mexican Political Biography Project,* 1995.

contrast to the more traditional Mexican politician, they have few direct ties
to the masses and, in terms of career experience, lack elective office-holding
and grassroots party experience.

For some years the typical Mexican politician had been a hybrid,
exhibiting characteristics found among *técnicos* and traditional politicians.
The assertion by some scholars that technocrats lack political skills is incor-
rect and misleading. Technocrats as a group do not have an identifiable ideology. The political-technocrat, a more apt label, is primarily distinguished
from the politician of the 1960s or 1970s by lack of party experience, by the
fact that he or she has never held elective office, and by specialized education abroad. These characteristics, for example, are found in President
Zedillo's own career (see Table 5-13). The implication of these three characteristics is that the politician-technocrat, although highly skilled, does not
possess the same political bargaining skills as does the peer who has had a
different career track and that such a person *may* be more receptive to political and economic strategies used in other cultures as a consequence of foreign education.

It has been convincingly argued that Salinas's economic cabinet,
including Zedillo, whose members shared these technocratic characteristics,
welcomed the economic liberalization philosophy of western Europe and
the United States because of their economic background and education
abroad. As economists, they identified with an international profession
based in the United States, with tools and concepts that were believed to be

Table 5-13 Career Progression of Ernesto Zedillo Ponce de León, Technocrat President

1992–1993	Secretary of Public Education[a]
1988–1992	Secretary of Programming and Budgeting[b]
1987–1988	Subsecretary of Programming and Budgeting
1983–1987	Director, Exchange Risks Trust Fund, Bank of Mexico
1982–1983	Assistant Manager, Treasury Research, Bank of Mexico
1981–1983	Professor, economics, El Colegio de México
1978–1982	Economist, Bank of Mexico
1978–1980	Professor, economics, National Polytechnic Institute (IPN)
1974–1978	M.A. and Ph.D., economics, Yale University
1973–1974	Professor, economics, National Polytechnic Institute (IPN)
1973	Studies, University of Bradford, England
1971–1974	Researcher, Economic and Social Planning Division, Secretariat of the Presidency
1969–1971	Accounting assistant, Bank of the Army and Navy
1969–1972	Economics studies, National Polytechnic Institute
1967–1969	Vocational School No. 5, National Polytechnic Institute (IPN), Mexico City
1964–1967	Public School No. 18, Mexicali
1958–1964	Leona Vicario and Cuauhtémoc Schools, Mexicali, Baja California

[a]Zedillo became Luis Donaldo Colosio's campaign manager in 1993/1994, making him one of the few prominent figures eligible constitutionally in March 1994 to become the new PRI candidate.
[b]This secretariat was incorporated into the Treasury in 1992.

universally—and locally—transferable, and with the methodology and ideology dominant in leading Ivy League graduate programs.[24]

Much of the dissension in the Mexican establishment political leadership in the 1990s can be attributed to a division between the technocratic leadership and traditional political figures, popularly called *los dinos,* or dinosaurs. Essentially, the argument was that the *técnicos* replaced the traditional politicians; devalued their skills and experiences, primarily their electoral and party experiences; and opposed their unprogressive authoritarian practices with modernizing political and economic alternatives. The crux of the divisions was the alleged ideological differences between the two groups. In reality, as Miguel Centeno pointed out, the central issue introduced by this technocratic elite was not "an ideology of answers or issues but . . . an ideology of method. The ideological cohesion of the new elite was not necessarily based on philosophical agreements on policy but an agreement on how such a policy ought to be pursued."[25]

The fundamental issue dividing the technocrat from the traditional political leadership, as is so often the case, was access to power. The traditional politician did not want to give up his control over the political system and PRI leadership to a technocratic elite, regardless of different ideological preferences. The dominance of the technocrats in the 1990s introduced an additional characteristic, a belief that the institutions they led were the undisputed arbiters of economic and political decision making. Even so, they showed an inability to listen and an intolerance of their domestic opponents. This pattern increasingly isolated the technocratic leaders from other groups, both within and outside Mexico's leadership prior to 2000. Technocrats like Zedillo had smaller and smaller camarillas because their relative youth afforded them less political experience, and this experience covered a narrower range of institutions and agencies.

Technocratic leadership might have remained entrenched for many years if PRI had retained its dominance over national political leadership and a technocrat had been PRI's presidential candidate. Fox's presidential victory, however, ensured the rapid decline of technocratic control over national political institutions. Fox's own career, when contrasted with that of Zedillo, makes the differences between the two men patently clear (Table 5-14). Zedillo, who moved to Mexico City to continue his education, began a career in the federal bureaucracy even before he completed his undergraduate economics degree. Fox, on the other hand, remained in León, his home town, for most of his education, and only upon graduation from college did he begin a career in the private sector. Zedillo quickly ended up in the forefront of the programming and budgeting secretariat, a crucial agency in the development of Mexican technocrats.[26] Fox, instead, spent his formative years working up the ladder of a multi-national corporation, Coca Cola of Mexico. Zedillo left Mexico in the 1970s to earn two graduate degrees from Yale and, like so many of his peers, began teaching part-time. Fox obtained a diploma from a short advanced management course at Harvard, but continued as a full-time employee of Coca Cola, becoming its CEO. Zedillo continued his career in the Mexican federal government in a progression of

Table 5-14 Career Progression of Vicente Fox Quesada, Democratic President

1997–1999	Governor of Guanajuato
1991–	PAN candidate for Governor of Guanajuato
1988–1991	Federal Deputy from Guanajuato, District 3
1988–	Secretary of Agriculture in PAN shadow cabinet (Manuel Clouthier)
1988–	Joined PAN
1979–1988	Owner and CEO Grupo Fox, Frozen Vegetable Export Firm
1975–1979	CEO of Coca Cola of Mexico
1969–1975	Operations Manager, Coca Cola of Mexico
1969	Zone Manager, Coca Cola of Mexico
1965–1969	Joined Coca Cola as a route supervisor
1960–1964	Business Administration studies, Ibero-American University (Jesuit)
1953–1960	Instituto Lux (Jesuit), León, Guanajuato
1947–1952	Instituto Mayllén (La Sallists), León, Guanajuato

posts, while Fox left Coca Cola to go into business for himself. Zedillo joined Salinas' cabinet in 1988, and Fox won election as a congressman from his home state, before becoming governor in the 1990s.

In certain respects, Fox represents some of the same trends occurring within the PRI itself. The increased pluralization of the political system, and the intense electoral competition in the 1990s, contributed to the rise of politicians from all parties who had experience in electoral politics. These structural changes also promoted the careers of politicians with broad experience, rather than a narrow range of technocratic career experience. Fox himself, and some of the collaborators he appointed, broadened the scope of these experiences further to include representatives of the private sector and even individuals with careers in international organizations (Table 5-7). For example, more than two-thirds of his cabinet had previously pursued careers in the private sector.

Fox appointed several technocrats to his cabinet, notably his treasury secretary, and another technocrat continued his term as head of the Bank of Mexico. An international technocrat was in charge of his economic development agency. Technocratic types have retained considerable influence in economic decision making, but they have lost control over the national political system. This does not mean, however, that some of the characteristics that technocrats reinforced or introduced have also disappeared. Among the characteristics that are in decline are the predominance of the Federal District in the backgrounds of national leadership, the importance of graduate work abroad, and public bureaucratic careers. Among those qualities that continue to be preeminent are the increasing importance of private university education and the growth of economics or economically related disciplines in politicians' educational backgrounds. The most dramatic changes from Zedillo's to Fox's cabinet are that nearly half of Fox's collaborators are the product of private schools, and two-thirds are businessmen contrasted to none under Zedillo, a radical shift from six years earlier.

CONCLUSION

Prior to 2000, the formal structure of Mexico's political system shed little light on how interested Mexicans pursued successful political careers. The political recruitment process was strongly affected by the centralization of political authority and the characteristics fostered by incumbent selection. Informal credentials typically replaced formal requirements as helpful or essential to the recruitment process. The PAN presidential victory, the PAN and PRD control over the national legislative branch, and the breadth of their influence at the state and local levels introduced different leadership characteristics and legitimized new recruitment practices. Democracy does alter recruitment patterns.

Informal credentials have long been associated with generations of political leaders since the 1920s. As mentors changed their own credentials, they passed on those changes to succeeding generations of politicians. They were responsible for such trends as higher levels of education, graduate education abroad, private undergraduate education, the importance of economics, the role of university teaching, and the impact of economic agencies in the federal government. All of these qualities, with the exception of the influence of federal economic agencies, remain influential since 2000. The continuation of their influence, however, depends on the nature of leadership at all levels of the federal government. It is too soon to determine if the diversity represented in Fox's cabinet has filtered down to the department and division level in the national bureaucracy.

In the past, the political clique or camarilla was the essential ingredient in the recruitment process. As we have seen, it is an informal structure built on several characteristics of the general culture, a structure emphasizing the use of a group of friends to enhance career success. The political camarilla, as crafted prior to 2000, will decline in importance, as new leadership types take over national positions. Fox himself, and many of his collaborators, suggests the continued importance of informal processes, including networking. These new politicians elevate networking that goes beyond the formation of political groups to establishing linkages between politicians and leaders from other sectors of society, including influential businesspeople and clergy. Recent studies demonstrate unequivocally that many of Mexico's leaders in the twenty-first century have extensive ties, established through educational experiences, family, and career, with prominent figures from other leadership groups. For example, Fox went to school and became close friends with three members of Mexico's most influential capitalist families. Fox also became involved with a pro-democratic civic action organization, the San Angel Group, where he made contact with prominent intellectuals and civic leaders, including two of his future cabinet members.

Changes in the recruitment process, brought about by alterations in the political structure and type of leadership, have already introduced several important trends, particularly the importance of individuals from provincial and private sector backgrounds and the increase in private university training. These two features have several potential consequences. In the first place, the continued importance of private university education enhances the likelihood that Mexicans from business or professional backgrounds in the private sector will pursue political careers, since many of them come from those educational institutions. On the other hand, the exclusive nature of private institution student bodies, given the socioeconomic inequalities in Mexico and the lack of scholarship opportunities, will actually narrow rather than increase the range of recruitment pools especially if they increase their dominance over most levels of national political recruitment. If having a provincial background becomes increasingly important, and the next generation of mentors have this background, then subsequent leaders are also likely to come from the provinces rather than from the Federal District. This is part of a decentralization trend arising from democratization. It remains to be seen, however, if this pattern is not just sustained, but increased. If the electoral process remains highly competitive, then mayoral, gubernatorial, and national legislative careers, all emphasizing geographic origins outside of Mexico's capital, will flourish.

NOTES

1. Lester G. Seligman, *Recruiting Political Elites* (New York: General Learning Press, 1971).

2. Kenneth Prewitt, *The Recruitment of Political Leaders: A Study of Citizen-Politicians* (Indianapolis: Bobbs-Merrill, 1970), 13.

3. See Ralph Turner, "Sponsored and Contest Mobility and the School System," *American Sociological Review* 25 (December 1960): 855–56.

4. George W. Grayson, *A Guide to the November 7, 1999, PRI Presidential Primary* (Washington, D.C.: CSIS, 1999).

5. For more detailed information about the recruitment characteristics of PAN and PRD members, see Roderic A. Camp, "The PAN's Social Bases: Implications for Leadership," in *Opposition Government in Mexico,* eds. Victoria Rodríguez and Peter M. Ward (Albuquerque: University of New Mexico Press, 1995), 65–80, and "The Opposition: An Alternative Path to Leadership?" in my *Political Recruitment Across Two Centuries, Mexico, 1884–1993* (Austin: University of Texas Press, 1995), 194–215.

6. Roderic Ai Camp, "Political Recruitment, Governance, and Leadership, Has Democracy Made a Difference," in *Pathways to Power: Political Recruitment and Candidate Selection in Latin America,* ed. Peter Siavelis and Scott Morgenstern (forthcoming).

7. Interview with Miguel de la Madrid, Mexico City, 1991.

8. See, for example, Richard Rose's statement that "the number of politicians from political families is disproportionately high in every Cabinet." *Politics in England: Change and Persistence,* 5th ed. (Boston: Little, Brown, 1989), 177. For the United States, see Alfred Clubok et al., "Family Relationships, Congressional

6

Groups and the State: What Is the Relationship?

> The growth of electoral competition in Mexico has had uneven and ambiguous consequences on the role and shape of clientelistic interest-intermediation arrangements. As elsewhere in Latin America, democratization has clearly failed to destroy the political centrality of clientelistic structures. Rising electoral competition has not left, however, clientelism unchanged. The combination of more open political contestation, fiscal stringency and market reform has introduced major changes in the nature and scope of clientelistic arrangements.
>
> BLANCA HEREDIA, *"Clientelism in Flux"*

All political systems, regardless of whether the struggle for political power is highly competitive or strongly monopolized by a small leadership group or single party, must cope with political interests and groups. In the United States various interest groups, as they are labeled, express their demands to the executive and legislative branches and contribute significant sums of money to parties and candidates. In Mexico, because the political system's structure is different from that of the United States, both the type of groups and their means for influencing public policy are not the same.

THE RESIDUE OF CORPORATISM

The importance of corporatism to the Mexican political culture and pre-2000 model was noted earlier.[1] Corporatism describes the more formal relationship between selected groups or institutions and the government or state. Since the revolution—that is, for most of the twentieth century—Mexico used an interesting structure to channel the most influential groups' demands, enabling the government to monitor the demands and mediate among them. The government has sought to act as the ultimate arbiter and to see to it that no one group becomes predominant.

The corporatist structure was largely devised and put in place under President Lázaro Cárdenas (1934–1940). Cárdenas wanted to strengthen the state's hand in order to protect the interests of the ordinary worker and peasant, but he ironically created a structure that for the most part benefited the interests of the middle classes and the wealthy, not unlike that of many other political systems.[2] The reason for this outcome is that Cárdenas' commitment to the social welfare of the less well off has not been shared by most of his successors, who have responded to other concerns and groups.

What is important, however, is that although the ideological orientation has changed and various economic strategies have been experimented with since the 1930s, the arrangement remained largely intact until the 1990s.[3] Only under President Salinas was there some interest in restructuring the corporatist relationship,[4] in response to Salinas's promises of political modernization and democracy. Critics argued that the corporatist structures provided the greatest stumbling block to a functioning Mexican democracy.[5] Some changes in the corporatist structure were introduced by recent presidents. Others, however, were the result of larger economic and political changes. Not only did the government have fewer resources to offer various groups, but its electoral competitors achieved huge inroads on PRI's monopoly regionally.[6] Fox's presidential victory clinched the demise of the corporatist system, depriving a PRI-controlled federal government from subsidizing or rewarding various groups.

Historically, the corporatist features of the political system allowed two types of channels for making political demands, and consequently two types of institutional representatives emerged prior to the 1990s. The institutional relationship with the government under this type of system was traditionally a formal one: The state established an organization, requiring those persons meeting the criteria of a special interest to belong to it. For example, the state created several business organizations to which businesses employing a certain number of employees must belong.[7] The state, however, even when PRI enjoyed a political monopoly, was not able to control all institutions representing various groups. Those it controlled were considered to be quasi-governmental interest organizations, part of the traditional corporatist structure.

Some interest groups increased their influence over time, becoming more autonomous. They created their own organizations, as would typically be the case in the United States, which were independent of the government. For example, the business community established the Mexican Association of Employers (Coparmex), an influential private-sector voice, frequently voicing public opposition to government economic policies. Many of their members played a crucial role in supporting PAN electoral victories at the state and local level, especially in northern Mexico.[8]

The other kind of channel is the informal channel, which is characteristic of all government models. Certain groups in Mexico do not use formal institutions, independent or governmental, to exercise their considerable influence, but instead use informal channels. The informal channels may be incorporated in the governmental structure or remain independent of it. We cannot assert with complete certainty that the informal channels are more significant than the formal channels, but given the lack of relevant studies, most observers of Mexican politics believe that to be the case.

INSTITUTIONAL VOICES

The range of interest groups in the United States is formidable because of the political system's openness and the ability of multitudes of like-minded citizens and institutions to organize. Such collectivities in Mexico are fewer and weak, and do not figure as significantly in decision making.[9] Remember that decision making remains centered in the executive branch, thus blocking the ability of diverse interests to pressure the legislative branch despite its growing influence. Further, the prohibition against running consecutively for legislative seats limits the potential threat that interests can level against individual members of Congress. Nevertheless, interest groups have gradually increased in number and influence, addressing their concerns to congress as it initiates greater numbers of bills. As members of PAN and PRD have taken over as chairs of the committee structure in congress, they have shown an interest and autonomy in pursuing policy issues related to certain groups, including the armed forces and the Zapatista guerrillas. As a leading student of the congress concluded, "the long period during which congress neither mattered nor paid attention to government actions has come to an end."[10] This will have a significant impact on future group relations with the state.

The most important groups incorporated formally and informally in Mexico's interest group structure are the military, the Catholic Church, business, organized labor, intellectuals and the media, nongovernmental organizations, and guerrillas. Each has a somewhat different institutional relationship to the government.[11] Most have stood out historically in other Latin American countries, suggesting the significance of similar past experiences and the influence of the colonial heritage on contemporary politics in the region.

The Military

No group has played a more significant role in Latin American political life than the military. However, since the 1930s its pattern of influence in Mexico has been quite different from that found elsewhere in Latin America. Most important, the military has found it necessary to intervene politically in every Latin American country except Mexico since that decade, and in most countries the military seized power in the 1970s and 1980s.[12]

The military's relationship to the Mexican state or government is different from that of most other groups. The reason is that the military does not function as a separate political actor; rather, it is part of the government apparatus and operates under civilian leadership. This does not mean that the military does not have institutional interests; rather, it publically subsumes its differences from those of the state.

Since the 1930s Mexico's civil-military relationship has been increasingly characterized by subordination of the military and of its interests to those of society as defined by the civilian leadership.[13] Aside from Costa Rica, which has operated without an army since the late 1940s Mexico is an exception. How did its unusual relationship come about?

When Cárdenas became president—and he was part of the generation that had participated in Mexico's civil war—he incorporated the military into the recently established government party, the National Revolutionary Party (PNR). He wanted to balance the military against the agrarian and labor sectors within the party and thus lessen its overall political influence.[14]

Cárdenas's successor in the presidency, General Manuel Avila Camacho, altered this major characteristic of the early corporatist structure by removing the military as a separate party sector.[15] Basically, he did not want to recognize the military as having a public, political voice and did not want to give it equal standing with other notable interest groups. From the 1940s to the present, then, the military's relationship to the government has been determined by its formal structural ties to the executive branch and through informal channels.

The political leadership gradually reduced the military's political influence through a variety of techniques. In the first place, as James Wilkie showed, each successive government reduced the military's allocation as a percentage of the federal budget from 1921 to 1964.[16] The size of the military in relation to population, and the sum budgeted to the military per capita, was among the lowest worldwide, far below the figures for the United States,[17] but has risen significantly in the 1990s. Under Zedillo, military expenditures averaged 5 percent instead of 2 to 3 percent, placing it midway among countries' per capita expenditures. The armed forces were

Table 6-1 Changes in Mexico's Armed Forces by Administration

Administration	Size Last Year of Administration	Percentage Increase
2000–2003	241,143	1.7
1994–2000	237,025	9.7
1988–1994	214,681	16.4
1982–1988	179,305	35.2
1976–1982	116,050	29.3
1970–1976	82,500	18.3
1964–1970	67,100	37.3

Sources: George W. Grayson, *Mexico's Armed Forces, A Fact Book* (Washington, D.C.: CSIS, 1999), 39; and Ernesto Zedillo, *Sexto Informe, Anexo Estadístico*, Disco 11, 2000.

179,000 in 1988, and reached 215,000 in 1994. They now number approximately 241,000 (see Table 6-1).[18]

As the political leadership gradually reduced the size and potential influence of the military, it strengthened the legitimacy of political institutions, including the official party (PRI). Government politicians had the advantage of operating in a semiauthoritarian fashion within the electoral arena. Military intervention is generally facilitated by competing political groups in a society that are seeking allies in the military. In Mexico, however, the military had to be either for the establishment—that is, the civilian leadership—or against it, and it had no outside civilian allies after 1952. During the 1940s, 1950s, and 1960s, military officers who pursued political careers helped bridge the gap between civilian and military officials. In other words, these political military officers provided a significant, *informal* channel of communication, allowing the civilian leadership to solidify its control and to establish its legitimacy.

Civilian leadership also cemented its control over the military through the professional socialization process. Civilian politicians established several military schools, most notably the Heroic Military College, the Superior War College, and in 1981 the National Defense College, to train officers. One of the most important themes in the curriculum of the schools is respect for authority, for one's superior officer, and for the commander in chief, the president. All military schools tend to drill in their cadets the concept of subordination to authority, but Mexican military academies are famous for the level of discipline they instill. An American officer, a graduate of a U.S. military academy, wrote that the dominant value would be the individual's willingness to subordinate himself totally to those in authority over him and the expectation that submission would be rewarded and independence would be severely punished. An officer's primary motivation would be to secure the rewards that the system has to offer.[19]

Colonel Steven Wager, one of the most knowledgeable Mexican military analysts, argued:

> Most of the political influence the military has attained since World War II has derived from its crisis management role, which has been fairly limited. However, that role has more often served as a double-edged sword for the army, rather than the distinct advantage some experts have perceived. Since the unfortunate incidents during the student uprisings in 1968, military leaders have been reluctant to participate in crisis situations, preferring to leave police actions to local and state authorities. The irony is that only by defending the state in a major crisis can the army substantially augment its power and prestige within the Mexican system.[20]

For these reasons and many others, the military is clearly subordinate to the civilian political leadership in Mexico. This does not mean that it has little or no influence on the government. The military has served the government in many capacities other than those traditionally subscribed to by the military in the United States.[21] The Mexican military's primary responsibility has not been national defense; rather, it has operated in many realms as an internal police force devoted to national security.[22] Not only does it provide the government with political intelligence, but it also has been used to maintain electoral peace, to settle contentious strikes, and, in the 1980s and 1990s, to carry out antinarcotics raids and repress incipient guerrillas.

The activities that will most affect the military's relationship to the state and increase or decrease its potential influence over the decision-making process are its roles in the anti-drug-trafficking campaign and in maintaining public security, which emerged in the 1990s as national security issues of significant proportions.[23] This led to a public debate on the militarization of society.[24] The United States not only has generated demand for illegal drugs, but by restricting sea and land routes through the Caribbean, the Drug Enforcement Agency increased the number of locations in Mexico used in drug transshipments from Latin America. The alleged connection of drug trafficking and drug monies to the assassinations of the PRI's presidential candidate, the Tijuana police chief, and Cardinal Posadas in Guadalajara during the 1990s, indicates the depth to which drug-related corruption has penetrated the Mexican political establishment.[25] In response to growing levels of crime and drug-related violence, President Zedillo established a National Public Security Council in 1996, giving for the first time "Mexico's military a role in decision making and policy-setting in important domestic public security matters."[26] Fox, responding to the public's concern for personal security, created a new cabinet-level agency, National Public Security, in 2000 (see Table 6-2).

The decision of the Mexican government to use the Mexican armed forces in drug interdiction missions has exposed the military at all levels to drug-related corruption. Salinas fired his navy secretary midway through his administration when it became apparent that naval officials were using military installations and ports to transport drugs. Zedillo removed his first highly touted drug czar, General Jesús Gutiérrez Rebollo, just weeks after his appointment in 1997, when it became apparent that he too was in the pay of a drug cartel. Finally, officials under President Fox, only four months into his administration, arrested a commander of a mechanize brigade along the Texas border for providing protection from arrest to drug traffickers.[27] The degree to which various units of the military are compromised by drug corruption increases their autonomy from civilian authorities and their own superiors, provokes interagency rivalries, and hastens the decline of military institutional integrity. Given the amounts of money involved and the constant demand from the United States, this is a serious, deeply troubling issue that will not disappear in the foreseeable future. It contributes heavily to political instability and to problems in the military-civilian relationship and the societal-institutional relationship generally.[28] Fox promised to withdraw the armed forces from their drug missions during his presidential campaign, but on taking office found he could not replace them with other agencies.

The expanded military role in national security matters raises international and human rights issues too. In 1997 and 1998, according to the *Washington Post,* some 1,067 Mexican officers were trained at United States bases, and the Central Intelligence Agency instructed 90 officers in intelligence-gathering courses to enhance their participation in counter-narcotics activities. Critics charge that equipment supplied to the armed forces for anti-drug trafficking use can be applied indiscriminately against ordinary citizens or guerrilla sympathizers.[29]

Table 6-2 Deaths of Mexican Soldiers in the War on Drugs

Administration	Troops and Officers Who Died Combating Drug Traffickers
López Portillo	38
De la Madrid	103
Salinas	135
Zedillo	85
Fox	55[a]

[a]As of July 2003.
Source: www.sedena.gob.mx, transparency request, folio 0000700031503, July 14, 2003.

Drug corruption and its consequences will be the most intractable problem facing Mexico's leaders for the forseeable future, but the country's most immediate political issue refocusing attention on civil-military relations was the attack by the Zapatista Army of National Liberation (EZLN) on January 1, 1994, on army encampments in the highlands of Chiapas. The military had provided accurate intelligence on the Zapatistas' activities long before their surprise attack, but civilian intelligence authorities in the Secretariat of Government either chose to ignore that information or convinced themselves that they could delay resolving festering conflicts in the region, despite evidence to the contrary. The response of the Mexican army was swift and repressive and led to numerous allegations of human rights abuses and summary executions. However, because of the extraordinary Mexican and foreign media coverage, President Salinas quickly reined in the military.

The armed forces used extreme force against the Zapatista attacks, but it has not been anxious to suppress large groups of Mexicans in response to mishandled civilian policies since the debacle of the 1968 student massacre. This decision has led military leaders to demand a larger voice in formulating government security policy, rather than merely acting as a tool for resolving civilian mistakes.[30] According to one analyst, a high-ranking army officer publicly declared that the army would not attack the Zapatistas unless the EZLN attacked first and more important, it would do so only if Congress approved.[31] The military lost the public relations war to the Zapatistas in 1994, damaging in the process its institutional and self-image. Thus, because of the price it paid for civilian failures, it asked for and received a larger role in the policy process under the Zedillo administration.

The situation with the Zapatistas remains unsettled, but army troops have had to respond to a smaller and more widespread guerrilla organization, the People's Revolutionary Army (ERP), which emerged in the summer of 1996 and has operated in numerous states, as far north as the border state of Tamaulipas. According to General Clemente Vega Garcia, the Secretary of National Defense, it is the ERP, not the EZLN, which the armed forces considers a national security threat.[32] Accordingly, the military not only demanded a higher price from the government for its continued loyalty, but perhaps more important, because of the increasing political pluralization, supported the legitimacy of Vicente Fox's presidential election. The pluralist environment in Congress, and the strength of PAN and PRD, do offer the military the option for the first time in Mexico's recent history of forming alliances outside the government, thereby placing in jeopardy its traditional relationship with executive branch authorities.

The armed forces has been undergoing many subtle internal changes in response to problems that have surfaced in the last few years. It has had to cope with dissident officers complaining publicly about due process within the military justice system, it has raised the issue of concentrated decision-making in the hands of the secretariat of national defense, it has made an effort to increase its professionalization, including its capabilities in electronic warfare and public relations, it has sought to expand the number of civilian employees inside the military, and it has increased its formal contacts with civilian government employees in the recent graduating classes from the presitigious National Defense College.[33]

President Fox has signaled his decision to work closely with the armed forces and to give them a broader role in national security concerns, appointing for the first time in many decades a senior military officer to a nonmilitary cabinet post, that of attorney general. Civil-military relations have changed significantly under President Fox's administration. The secretary of the navy and, to a lesser extent, the secretary of national defense have instituted internal, structural changes affecting the promotion process, human rights training, and, in the case of the navy, drastic reductions in the top naval bureaucracy and a radical reduction in the number of admirals on active duty. The relationship between the attorney general and the armed forces has been stronger under Fox than any recent president and has led to extensive collaboration in the armed forces' anti-drug mission. The application of the new transparency law beginning in June 2003 has opened the military to greater public scrutiny by the media and scholars. The increasing interest of the legislative branch in military affairs resulted, for the first time in history, to testimony by a secretary of national defense in the legislative chambers, during which various deputies, with the media present, questioned the secretary extensively on a wide range of controversial issues. Finally, the military has continued to maintain and improve its public image. In a 2004 poll it shared top ranking (60 percent) with the Catholic Church (64 percent) and the Federal Electoral Institute (61 percent) in favorable opinions among ordinary citizens expressing a good or very good opinion of the institution. Moreover, among all the institutions listed, it had the lowest percentage of negative ratings.[34]

The Church

Mexico legally established and, in practice, enjoys freedom of religion, yet Mexicans, as we noted in Chapter 4, are overwhelmingly Catholic, products of a Catholic, Christian culture.[35] The Catholic Church exercised extraordinary political influence in Mexico and elsewhere in the region during the colonial period and continued to do so in much of the nineteenth century and part of the twentieth.[36]

The government broke this pattern of influence by implementing virulent anticlerical provisions in the 1917 Constitution in an attempt to limit the church's ideological influence over the socialization of citizen values. Articles 3 and 130 specified these restrictive clauses, which limited religious influence in education, spelled out numerous restrictions on clergy's political involvement, and clearly established state superiority over the church. Clergy's and Catholics's resistance to the implementation of these provisions under President Calles led to the Cristero War from 1926 to 1929, during which time many priests were persecuted, masses were suspended, and seminaries were closed.

The church, unlike the military, operated as an institution fully independent of the government yet severely hampered in theory and practice by the constitution. The state reached an informal understanding with the church after 1930 that in effect allowed it to carry out the spiritual and pastoral functions within the purview of all churches in return for its remaining publicly quiet about political and social issues. The understanding remained in effect until 1992 and in practice was fairly well followed by both parties until the early 1980s.

The church's role as an interest group was limited because of the antichurch rhetoric that was incorporated into the public education of each child in Mexico. The church and clergy were at a disadvantage compared with some other groups in the corporatist arrangement because of the legal limbo they occupied. For example, the church as an institution had no legal standing until 1992, the only institution among the organized groups under discussion. Before 1992, clergy of all faiths did not have a legal right to vote, although many actually did.[37]

As Chapter 4 pointed out, Mexicans nonetheless remain very religious: Many are practicing Catholics, and most have a high regard for clergy and the church as an institution. Half of all Mexicans attend church regularly, about the same percentage as in the United States.[38] Because respect for the church is high and political organizations did not provide adequate channels for people to express their political demands, some Mexicans turned to the church for guidance and, more important, as an institutional vehicle to convey their political frustrations. This trend is reinforced by the fact that Mexican priests support such a posture (Table 6-3). Catholic bishops have begun to speak regularly and critically, illustrating the view expressed by Cardinal Norberto Rivera Carrera of the Mexico City archdiocese that a "silent Church does not serve God nor humanity."[39]

The church, as is true of other groups, such as businessmen, does not speak with a single voice. Despite its image as a centralized, hierarchical institution, it is decentralized at the level of individual dioceses, of which there are seventy-three in Mexico. Dioceses and archdioceses are territorial subdivisions that serve as organizational units, and each is governed by a

Table 6-3 Attitudes of Parish Priests Toward Democracy and Political Participation

Questions Asked	Agree	Disagree	No Opinion	Don't Know
			(percentages)	
The Church should support democratization even though it might produce conflicts with the government	88	5	4	3
The new evangelization requires an open promise from the church for a more just and democratic society in spite of the fact that it might produce conflicts with the government	81	4	3	12

Source: Adapted from Oscar Aguilar Ascencio, "La iglesia católica y la democratización en México," in *La iglesia católica y la política en el México de hoy,* ed. José de Jesús Legoretta Zepeda (Mexico: Ibero-American University, 2000), 171.

bishop or archbishop. Collectively, these men are the extremely autonomous hierarchy of the church.

The leadership of the church in Mexico in terms of policy influence is the episcopate—the body of bishops, archbishops, and cardinals—which in conference recommends policies on issues ranging from the purely theological to foreign debt, the maldistribution of income, and drugs. The episcopal meetings result in the publication of pastoral letters and enunciations of recommended positions.

It is apparent from recent events in Mexico that the geography and the social and economic composition of a diocese often affect the attitude and orientation of its priests and bishops. The most extreme example of this recently was, of course, Bishop Samuel Ruiz in Chiapas, whose clergy represented rural, indigenous interests in San Cristóbal de las Casas. Ruiz's firm stance in defense of the Indians, both before and after the Zapatista uprising, engendered criticism as well as support within episcopal ranks.[40] The Vatican has ordered his diocese to stop ordaining secular Indian deacons in an effort to dismantle Ruiz's ideological influence.[41]

The most important issue in the 1990s that unified bishops nationally, however, was the issue of democratization. Not only did individual bishops issue numerous pastoral letters on this topic, as early as the late 1980s, but the episcopate itself adopted several of these letters as its official position. In particular, bishops addressed several specific issues, especially the obligation to vote, electoral fraud, and the so-called "fear vote." The episocpate declared in 2000, shortly before the election, that it was a sin for any party to use scare tactics as a means of encouraging partisan support.[42] The Mexican Episcopate, recognizing the importance of the 2000 presidential race, produced a pamphlet entitled *Democracy Isn't Possible Without You,* in which it urged all Mexicans to vote according to their conscience and to select candidates they believed most ideal to serve the nation.[43]

The tone of many bishops' commentaries have also changed in recent years. Numerous bishops now believe it is their responsibility to take stands on significant social, economic, and political issues, a belief that has produced implicit and explicit criticism of government actions. In fact, the episcopate warned the Fox government not to fail to help the citizenry, especially poorer Mexicans.[44] One bishop commented:

> One point that is important to make which is independent of the present condition in Mexico is that the Church, both the bishops and priests, consider it necessary to socialize the people about their civic obligations regardless of what the political situation might be. The people are very ignorant of their civic responsibilities. From a moral point of view, we need to create a sense of consciousness. All of this can be badly interpreted by the government, which may see us wanting to reestablish political privileges we have had historically. For us, however, it is obvious that we have no desire to make policy decisions that are handled presently by the government. We only believe we have a responsibility to defend the people. Who else is there?[45]

Bishops have continued this critical posture throughout the Fox administration, raising critical questions about such issues as the government's labor reforms and complete liberty of expression for all Mexicans, including clergy.

Some bishops have strengthened their positions by joining together to explain their views. The most memorable instance in recent years was that of the northern bishops, led by Archbishop Adalberto Almeida of Chihuahua; they condemned election fraud in Chihuahua in 1986 and called on the administration of Miguel de la Madrid to annul the results and hold new elections.[46] The bishops threatened to stop saying mass until the government responded to their demands. The pope intervened to prevent their carrying out the threat, but the bishops' public posture, in direct violation of the constitution, illustrated their potential influence.

President Salinas moved, as part of his modernization plans, to make the Catholic Church a more open actor in the political system. Many politicians resisted any changes in the constitutional restrictions on the church, but Salinas believed the relationship was outdated and needed refashioning. Demonstrating his new posture, he invited leading clergy to attend his inauguration in December 1988 and then appointed a former political figure as his personal representative to the Vatican. He also made Pope John Paul a welcome guest in Mexico in the summer of 1991, creating even closer relations between the government and the church. In 1992, Salinas revised several major constitutional provisions, one of which now permits recognition of all churches as legal entities. However, the reforms did leave several major constitutional issues unresolved, among them "religious education in public schools, access to electronic means of mass communication, [and] fiscal measures for religious associations."[47]

The church generally does not openly lobby for its political positions; rather, it requests and receives audiences with the state officials. Typically, party presidential candidates meet with bishops during their campaigns.[48] Fox even sent a ten-point proposal to the Catholic and evangelical hierarchy two months before the election.[49] Church personnel also meet with various members of the executive branch on matters of mutual concern. On the state level, bishops frequently exchange views with state governors and collaborate with the government on social welfare projects. Relations are good as a rule and have improved considerably since 1989, but at the local level in certain instances, such as in the southern state of Chiapas, they may be quite conflictual. Chiapas has witnessed the deportation of priests, armed attacks on the bishop, conflicts among various religious groups, and the intervention of various outside national and international actors, including the Vatican envoy. The San Cristóbal de las Casas diocese has become deeply embroiled in the Chiapan conflict, involving indigenous peasants, mestizo ranchers, the government, paramilitary groups, and the army. With bishop Samuel Ruiz's retirement in 2000, and Fox's efforts to reduce potential sources of friction, conflicts there have declined.

The open posture of church leaders in advocating civic participation, and stating their views on broad national policy, has extended to the position of individual politicians too. Leading bishops have called on politicians to profess openly their religious faith, thus setting a spiritual example for other Mexicans.[50] President Fox himself provides the most prominent example of this recent pattern. When the pope visited Mexico in 2002 in celebration of the canonization of a Mexican saint, critics charged that Fox, the first president to attend a public religious act presided over by the pope, should not have attended the mass nor demonstrated publicly his respect for the pope by kissing his hand. The Mexican public, however, overwhelming supported (more than 80 percent) the president attending the mass, publicly demonstrating his religious devotion, and exercising the same religious rights as any ordinary Mexican.[51]

Raising the visibility of religious beliefs among the population at large, and politicians specifically, might well affect public policy. A unique study of Mexican congresspersons demonstrates significant differences in their levels of religiosity, measured by Church attendance. (Table 6-4) PAN members of congress are more religious and more Catholic than the Mexican population. Ninety-seven percent are Catholic and 3 percent Protestant.

Table 6-4 Religious Attendance Among Members of Congress

Party Affiliation	Frequence of Attendance (percentages)				
	Once a Week	Monthly	Infrequently	Rarely	Never
PRI	13	9	28	34	16
PAN	58	27	8	7	0
PRD	5	0	13	22	60

Source: Based on interviews with members of the 1994–1997 Legislature. See Antonia Martínez, "Diputados, clivajes (cleavages) y polarizacíon en México," *Perfiles latinoamericanos*, 11 (December, 1997), 57.

PRD congresspersons, on the other hand, express low levels of religiosity, with two-thirds declaring no religious affiliation; the other third are Catholic. The PRIista deputies are most representative of the population generally, with 87 percent Catholics, 10 percent no religion, and 3 percent Protestants. The attendance patterns reflected in Table 6-4 demonstrate that PAN politicians practice their religious faith more intensely. These religious beliefs, as the author of this research argues, may affect politicians' views on important issues, including such controversial topics as divorce and abortion, on which the deputies from each party take substantially different positions.

The constitutional reforms of 1992 effectively legitimized the church's institutional role.[52] Some observers believe the constitutional reforms decrease the church's autonomy, but in practice the state actually legitimized it, decreasing the negative impact of the liberal heritage and allowing the church a greater part in nonspiritual matters. The church is unlikely to confront antagonistically the state on secular matters, but it has become a more influential actor and will make its voice heard on national issues as societal dissension heats up.[53] The church does not foment dissent; rather, it mirrors its constituency's existing frustrations. The church's openly critical posture on policy issues, when it deems it necessary, has continued under Fox, and has led to petitions to both the Vatican and the government to prevent bishops from interfering in internal political affairs.[54]

Business

The private business sector combines some of the features of a governmental institution, the military, with those of an autonomous institution, the Church. As pointed out earlier, an array of its organizations present its demands to the government. The most important quasi-governmental organizations, established by the government itself, are a group of federations that include the National Chamber of Industries (Canacintra, or CNIT), the National Chamber of Commerce (Concanaco), and the National Federation of Chamber of Industries (Concamin). These organizations have been considerably weakened since 1996, when the Supreme Court ruled against obligatory chamber membership, leaving them insufficient revenues from membership fees and dependent on secretary of commerce subsidies. The most important autonomous organizations, in addition to Coparmex, are the Mexican Insurance Association (AMIS), the Mexican Council of Businessmen (CMHN), and, the Mexican Bankers Association.

When Cárdenas established some of these quasi-governmental business groups, the private sector was rather weak. As it has grown, it has not only developed other organizations to represent its own interests, but has often taken positions on economic policies different from those advocated by the government.[55] The private sector, however, has labored under conditions similar to the constraints on the church, although not nearly as extreme. The government prior to 2000 allowed labor, professional organizations, and peasants to be formally represented in the PRI, but it purposely excluded the private sector. It did so because private-sector interests did not coincide with the rhetoric of the postrevolutionary leadership, even if in reality their interests have been shared.

The quasi-governmental organizations are not the most important means for expressing private-sector demands. Again, the significance of *informal* channels to express those demands becomes apparent. One prominent businessman described the actuality:

> Sometimes it is the business groups which approach the government concerning policy questions, and in other situations it is the government which takes the initiative with the private sector through the individual chambers. It is really what you might call a corporatist situation in which the government and the private sector are tied together as far as interest representation. The difference between our system and that in your country is that here we try to influence directly the minister of the appropriate secretariat rather than going through the legislative branch. Normally, even though we try to directly influence the minister in charge, we first go through the chamber before approaching the individual personally.[56]

Recognizing the advantage of collective representation, at least on certain issues, businessmen created a unitary body to represent the top organizations: the Businessmen's Coordinating Council (CCE). The CCE, however, is not representative of its own members, even though it speaks for them. The most influential business organization in Mexico is the semi-secret CMHN, which is made up of thirty-nine prominent capitalists. The members meet frequently with cabinet members, and occasionally with the president. Just three weeks after his election, president-elect Fox met with members of the council at the Bankers Club. The meeting was arranged by one of its members, a long-time friend and school companion of Fox from the Ibero-American University.[57] It is clear from the literature that the CMHN rarely makes direct demands on the government or the president; rather, membership in this elite organization is used to gain individual access to the president or the appropriate government official.[58] What is ignored by analysts, however, is the fact that the council serves as an influential vehicle through which capitalists network and advance their own business interests. In short, it functions as an informal interest group between politicians and leading capitalists and a crucial personal link between capitalists. Another informal group, known as the "21 Group," is even more discrete. Founded in 1992, and including some of the same members as the CMHN, it supported President Fox's preference for a new international airport in late 2001.[59] The CMHN shares certain similarities to the Japanese *Keidanren,* a super-business organization.[60]

A structural condition in Mexico that explains the added importance of capitalists, and facilitates informal processes, including business-government networking, is the fact that the majority of Mexico's top corporations remain in the hands of a small number of wealthy families. Whether they are listed on the stock exchange in Mexico or in New York, these families dominate Mexico's manufacturing, industrial, and technological economy. Consequently, individual capitalists influence corporate decision-making to a greater extent than found in most post-industrial societies, including the United States.

Until the 1970s, business and government maintained a relatively stable and symbiotic relationship, although tensions did exist.[61] By the end of Luis Echeverría's administration in 1976, these tensions were increasing as the government began to expand its economic role, buying up privately operated enterprises and initiating policies that ran counter to private-sector interests. This culminated in the 1982 decision by President José López Portillo (1976–1982) to nationalize privately owned banks. There followed a significant break between the private sector and the government and the former's great distrust of the latter.[62]

President Miguel de la Madrid worked assiduously in the 1980s to repair the damaged relationship and partially succeeded. Nevertheless, smaller independent business groups under Coparmex's vociferous leadership advocated a more energetic political activism for businessmen, including open support for opposition parties. These groups began to campaign for candidates of the National Action Party, and members even ran for state and local offices, especially in northern Mexico.[63] Their position was symbolized in the 1988 presidential race when a successful northern businessman, Manuel Clouthier, a former president of both Coparmex and the CCE, opposed Salinas on the PAN ticket. Clouthier's candidacy had even longer-term significance, since one of the businessmen he recruited was none other than Vicente Fox. Bussinessmen's commitment became more intense and had positive results in the 1992 Chihuahua gubernatorial campaign, in which many of their members supported the PAN's victorious candidate, Francisco Barrio. The direct involvement of businessmen in political campaigns has continued and increased, and several prominent businessmen served as advisers to Fox during his presidential race, becoming members of his administration after his election. These radically changing patterns are illustrated by the fact that among the thirty-four newly elected governors from 1997 to 2004, nearly half of the PAN governors were local or national leaders of Coparmex or other business organizations. Among all governors from this period, three out of ten came from business backgrounds (see Table 5-2).

PAN was not the only party which made inroads in the traditional government-business alliance. Dissident members of Canacintra, opposed to the entire formal, corporatist arrangement between business organizations and the state prior to 1996, found a strong ally in the PRD. As one observer argues, "PRD officials saw an opportunity to broaden the party's base of support to include one faction of business. Thus, the PRD integrated the private sector dissendents' anti-corporatist campaign with their own on-going criticisms of the state's liberal economic policies and authoritarian practices."[64]

Businessmen, more than any other group in Mexico with the exception of the political leaders themselves, have the capability of influencing government decisions, especially in the economic realm. They have not been able to do so consistently or to a meaningful degree. This can be seen most vividly in the private sector's open criticism of Zedillo's austerity policy, thereby jeopardizing its success. Government economic policy, which has favored business's interests more frequently than those of organized labor, has emerged as much from the self-interest or preferences of government leaders as from private-sector pressures. Given Fox's macro-economic preferences, and his business background, this is not likely to change in the forseeable future. On the other hand, numerous conflicts have occurred between the Fox administration and the private sector over major policy issues, indicative of divisions within the business community.[65]

The overt participation of entrepreneurs in the electoral arena has changed the traditional relationship between business and government.[66] Entrepreneurs' support was crucial to the PAN's successes and strengthened the opposition generally before 2000. As individual businesses or business groups become directly tied to the electoral process and to the fortunes of political candidates, they acquire powerful political capital that they can use to negotiate with the state. In turn, governments must pay closer attention to business's demands, especially given the increasing electoral competitiveness and business's greater ability to determine the outcome of elections. Organized business groups that collectively support candidacies and parties are likely to expand their influence too.[67] Because the former quasi-governmental organizations have formed alliances with the autonomous groups to criticize government economic policies, business organizations no longer can even be considered remotely corporatist.[68] This greater activity marks a significant change in entrepreneurial political behavior and, if adapted elsewhere in Mexico, will cause major alterations in state-group relations.

Organized Labor

Of all the groups with political influence in Mexico, organized labor best met the criteria of an ideal, traditional corporatist group. One of the contributing causes of the Mexican Revolution was the suppression of the working class under the Porfiriato. General Obregón recognized the political importance of labor and relied on labor's support in his struggles against President Venustiano Carranza. The labor movement started to grow in the 1920s, and in the next decade membership in labor organizations reached 15.4 percent of the economically active workforce. It has not grown in percentage terms since 1940 and by 1970 began to decline.[69]

Organized labor in Mexico is quite different from that in the United States. The first distinguishing characteristic is the preponderance of government employees, most of them federal, who account for more than a third of all organized workers. The second characteristic is that organized labor is made up of unions called confederations, similar to the chambers of the business organizations. Nearly half of organized laborers are members of these broad confederations. The third differentiating characteristic of labor is the lesser presence of purely industrial-based unions such as those of miners, electricians, and petroleum workers. These characteristics are undergoing significant change since PRI's defeat in 2000.

The most important labor organization, the Mexican Federation of Labor (CTM), was established under President Cárdenas. He and his successors maintained a close relationship with union leaders that amounted to government control.[70] The control was cemented by incorporating the CTM as the foundation of one of the three sectoral pillars of the National Revolutionary Party—a role that continues to this day. The CTM was led from the 1940s to 1997 by Fidel Velázquez, giving him considerable stature and influence in the labor movement.[71] More than any other characteristic, organized labor's status within the party placed it in the semi-corporatist fold. Unlike business, the church, or even the military, which is incorporated into the state itself, organized labor has had a prominent role in the PRI. Between 1979 and 1988, for example, 21 to 25 percent of the PRI's congressional candidates were labor leaders, most commonly from the CTM.[72] Since President Fox's election, the percentage of labor deputies as a proportion of PRI members of congress has declined dramatically, accounting for a mere 9 percent in 2003.[73] This does not mean that it influenced the decision-making process but, rather, that its relationship with the government, through the party, was formalized, legitimized, and visible.

A small but growing percentage of unions in Mexico are independent of PRI control. One of the most interesting consequences of the North American Free Trade Agreement's (NAFTA) labor provisions is the impact on labor-government relations generally, and specifically on legitimizing independent organizations. In 1997, for the first time in history, a PRI-affiliated union was decertified in favor of an independent union among the 2,700 assembly (maquiladora) plants. In some cases their leadership has been able to obtain better benefits for members than have government-controlled unions. On the other hand, previous studies of independent unions in Mexico reveal that democratically elected leaders typically do not better represent the demands of the rank and file than do the designated leaders in government-controlled unions. This pattern has changed under Fox. It is apparent that even international protests against conditions in multinational corporations in Mexico has led to newly independent union representation among some firms, and that their leadership, at least initially, is responsive to worker demands.[74] It became clear that independent unions would make significant inroads after 2001, when the Supreme Court, following a series of other court decisions, ruled against provisions in the Federal Labor Law giving preference to the established, corporatist unions.[75]

The government prior to 2000 used unions to prevent the mobilization of large-scale opposition. "The government treats labor as a firm parent would a teenager. When it needs support in family crises and labor quickly provides it, it rewards the action. But when labor strays away from the family fold, it is scolded in a variety of ways. The government, not organized labor, controls the relationship."[76]

In the past, the government often promoted new unions and leaders to keep established unions in line. The removal of PRI-affiliated politicians from the national government in 2000, however, has effectively eliminated the ability of the government to continue such policies. The corporatist system of integrating most of organized labor within the PRI required that it control the government bureaucracy, providing resources for patronage and the establishment of new unions. The government also subsidized favored unions, creating a dependent relationship, because most unions were unable to charge dues.[77] Since 1997, within months of Fidel Velasquez's death, other labor leaders formed the National Workers Union (UNT), an umbrella organization composed of 110 unions and two million workers, to oppose the CTM. The UNT has a different agenda from the traditional trade unions. In 2002, the long-time leader of the telephone workers' union and seccretary general of the UNT resigned from the PRI and established a new organization.

Even the more cohesive National Teachers Union (SNTE) has been faced with numerous dissident movements in response to President Fox negotiating a salary increase with the former union head without involving its national leadership. Perhaps the most influential sources of change within the labor movement are recent decisions by the Supreme Court. In April 2001, for example, the court ruled against the existing federal labor law, which allowed employees to be fired if they left the union that held a collective contract with the employer. This and other decisions are significantly changing Mexican labor culture. In response to these decisions, the Federal Workers Union (FSTSE) recently told members they could affiliate with any party of their choice.[78]

The National Teachers Union is the largest single organization among government workers' unions, and one of the most important groups in Mexico. A study of it provides interesting data on its techniques for conveying demands to the private sector and the government (see Table 6-5). Mexican unions must convince the government that their demands are legitimate; otherwise, they cannot legally strike. Determinations of legality are made by conciliation and arbitration boards, on which the government representative holds the deciding vote. The strike is only one means of conveying demands; marches and demonstrations have become increasingly common. But strike threats bring pressure to bear on both government and private-sector management.

Because teachers were federal employees when the data were compiled, it is revealing to examine how the government itself responded to labor demands (see Table 6-6). Rarely did it actually raise salaries; rather, it provided low-cost benefits—such as discounts for married teachers at government stores—or relied on dialogue or promises to resolve complaints. If it decided not to negotiate, the government then took a hard line, either refusing to discuss the issues or threatening to fire striking teachers.

The current relationship between labor and the state is the result of two important trends since the 1980s, economic crisis and political liberalization. The economic liberalization policies introduced by Miguel de la Madrid in

Table 6-5 Means Used by Organized Labor in Mexico to
Convey Demands: National Teachers Union

Union Means of Action	Percentage of Total
Partial strike	21
Meetings, marches, demonstrations	21
Strike	17
Indefinite strike	7
Parade in front of public buildings	6
Call for a demonstration	6
Rejection of salary increases	6
Denunciations in press conferences	5
Block streets and highways	4
Occupy educational institutions	4
Block access to offices	3
List of demands to authorities	2
Hunger strikes	1

Source: Este País, June 1991, 32–34; based on an analysis of 237 newspaper
articles, January–April 1991.

the mid-1980s, expanded by Salinas and Zedillo, have had "profound implications for the state-labor alliance which has been so central to the Mexican
regime" since the original formation of the corporatist strategy.[79] As Ruth
Berins Collier observed, the established relationship, based on the state's
protection of labor, has now lost its logic. From an economic perspective, it
is clear that over the last two decades labor never benefited in real terms from
rising wages, although the government did provide some subsidies for consumer goods and housing. In real terms, the minimum wage is less today than
it was in 1970. Politically, the government under PRI rewarded labor leadership with positions in the legislative branch and, to a lesser degree, in the

Table 6-6 Government Responses to Organized Labor Demands:
National Teachers Union

Government Response to Union Demands	Percentage of Total
Married teachers will receive discounts	42
Dialogue	15
Shut off dialogue	13
Promise to resolve issues	9
No funds available	9
Will fire teachers who miss three days	7
Offer a small salary increase	3
Reject violent actions	1
Reject actions	1

Source: Este País, June 1991, 32.

party itself. Given the fact that PRI is just one of three major parties, it cannot rely on government subsidies. Its economic philosophy more closely approximates that of PAN, therefore labor has more in common with the PRD. Some unions may remain closely affiliated with the PRI because it can still offer certain rewards at the state and local level, and others, with stronger ideological concerns, may ally with the PRD. The competitive political process, and the need for all parties to capture large groups of voters, now gives unions viable political alternatives and a noncorporatist path.

Intellectuals and the Media

The intellectual community has an amorphous relationship with the government. Some of its formal organizations are patronized by the state; others are independent. None speaks for the intellectual community, but they do provide some public prestige. The most salient quasi-governmental organization is the National College, a publicly supported institution founded in 1946, whose purpose is to disseminate its members' work. Members are prominent figures in all fields, including law, sciences, humanities, social sciences, and fine arts.

The relationship of the intellectual community to the state is much more a product of the relationship between the government and intellectual employment than between the government and intellectuals' organizations. Three sectors of the economy employ the vast majority of intellectuals: government, academia, and publishing. Unlike intellectuals in the United States, Latin American intellectuals—Mexican intellectuals among them—have a long history of employment in public life, either in a federal bureaucracy, especially the Secretariats of Foreign Affairs and Education, or in various political posts as governors, party leaders, and cabinet members.[80]

The lack of employment opportunities in Mexico has encouraged intellectuals to work for the government. This means that the government does not have to incorporate intellectuals formally into institutional relationships with the state because the majority have been state employees since the 1920s. Many intellectuals, desirous of maintaining greater autonomy, have sought employment in the most prestigious universities, especially those in Mexico City. They hold teaching and administrative positions at the National Autonomous University, the Autonomous Technological Institute of Mexico, the Ibero-American University, and at the Colegio de México. Intellectuals have advantageous ties to the government because many were classmates of future politicians and others have been their teachers. Politicians often identify prominent intellectuals as having been their most influential professors.

If intellectuals influence societal ideas, they do so through the written word. Intellectuals in Mexico, as in the United States and other countries, establish magazines to circulate their views. Magazines dedicated to particular schools of thought are typically the product of a group of people who share certain ideological principles. One Mexican described the phenomenon:

> There are some good papers and excellent magazines here, but each one tends to be controlled by some group or interest. All of these, such as *Excélsior,* or the publications of the Colegio de México and the Fondo de Cultura Económica, are publications of elite groups. It is very difficult for a person who writes to publish in them if [he or she does] not belong to the group in control of that publication. . . . These groups exist because most intellectuals are receptive to ideas paralleling their own preferences. . . . Actually there are very few independent intellectuals in Mexico, or intellectuals who have not formed groups.[81]

Some of the more prominent contemporary intellectual groups in Mexico include those of the late Octavio Paz, who contributed to his journal *Vuelta* and its successor, *Letras Libres,* headed by Enrique Krause; Héctor Aguilar Camín, who from 1983 to 1995 directed the popular monthly *Nexos;* Julio Scherer García, president of the board of *Proceso;* and Federico Reyes Heroles, who is an editorial board member of *Este País,* Mexico's first magazine devoted to survey research, but with a strong intellectual bent. Other groups are associated with newspapers, and many intellectuals earn a portion of their income contributing essays to editorial pages.

The intellectual community has increasingly sought new channels in the electronic media, mainly in television. Some prominent Mexican figures, including Enrique Krause, Octavio Paz, and Rolando Cordera, have used this medium to reach a larger audience and to discuss controversial political and social topics. The proliferation of public opinion polls, the association of some leading figures with these survey research efforts, and most important, their analysis of the findings in both the print and electronic media extend the intellectuals' influence to the electoral arena, as polling results become identified with the party and the candidate.[82] In a recent survey among Mexico City residents of the impact of opinion polls, over half reported hearing about or reading the results of such polls, two-fifths indicated they believed in the result somewhat or a lot, half thought it would influence how people voted, but only a tiny minority, 10 percent said the results would determine the party they would vote for or if they would vote.[83]

The government's relationship to the intellectual community is also reflected in its attitude toward the media.[84] Mexico has freedom of speech. Freedom of the press, however, does not have a strong tradition and is affected somewhat by the medium. Government controls over radio and television programing are quite strict. Since the 1990s, radio call-in shows have become quite popular, and the spontaneity of the process has made it possible to voice political and social criticism, thus circumventing traditional restrictions. Television is the most important medium politically, and selected intellectuals and commentators have developed national recognition. Television is significant because it is second only to family as a basic source of political attitudes.[85] The print media, which has operated under far fewer restrictions, has existed within a professional culture that has not advocated investigative journalism. On the other hand, the government rarely provided adequate information about its budget or policies, a pattern which has changed dramatically since 2003, when the Fox administration implemented the new Transparency Law, giving ordinary citizens and reporters access to a wide range of governmental information and statistics. These practices, combined with government payments, subsidies, and favors, led to a press that was largely pro-PRI during elections. Most of the censorship in Mexico today is self-censorship from publishers who are afraid to antagonize their sources, governmental and nongovernmental, or advertisers.[86]

The influence of censorship and self-censorship on politics can be better understood by exploring the media's coverage of various parties in the electoral process. A number of studies examined both television and print media coverage of the candidates in the 1994 elections. These studies found qualitative biases in the media's presentation of the various parties or candidates, and in addition, the quantitative biases in the coverage were extreme. For example, in a study of two leading television news programs, *24 Horas* and *Hechos,* from January to April 1994, the authors discovered that on *24 Horas* the amount of time given to the PRI candidate compared with that given to his major rivals was in a ratio of 46 to 1. The parties did better, but on both programs, the PRI received far more attention than did the PAN or the PRD.[87] The same was true of the print media, which gave the PRI candidate 44 percent of their coverage, compared with 24 percent and 20 percent for the PRD and the PAN, respectively.

Overall, despite these conditions, media professionalism is on the upswing. *Reforma,* a major Mexican daily owned by a Monterrey-based publisher, accepts no government advertising and has strict journalistic guidelines. Televisa, a private television monopoly with an openly declared government bias in the past, not only has faced intense competition from the Azteca chain, but its leadership changed significantly in 1997.[88] Journalists, according to a study by Sallie Hughes, have begun to emulate journalistic practices in the United States. Many of them were impelled to make these changes by specific political events in the 1990s, such as the Zapatista uprising and because of influences from the United States.[89]

The impact of this changing pattern in television coverage is starkly illustrated by Chappell Lawson's examination of 402 voters in Mexico City during the contentious 1997 race for head of the Federal District. Lawson interviewed the respondents when the candidates were announced, after a debate on television, and immediately following the elections. He discovered a marked change among Televisa viewers who initially favored PRI. More than half of those voters abandoned the PRI for another party's candidate (see Table 6-7). Televisa coverage, balanced quantitatively among the leading candidates, significantly altered the outcome of the election.[90]

Television appears to have played a significant role in the 2000 presidential election. During the campaign, 84 percent of the voters watched television news, and two-thirds of those viewed news programs at least four or more times weekly. Several NGOs, and the Federal Electoral Institute examined media bias. The parties and candidates can obtain television and other media coverage in two primary ways: advertising and news commentaries. Because of significant changes in the electoral laws, the major parties in 2000 were roughly equal in their ability to advertise, especially on the dominant television networks. Even when coverage is equitably distributed, it may well be biased. In a comprehensive examination of television news coverage in the 2000 election, Hughes and Lawson discovered that privately owned stations offered more balanced political news than state-run stations, that both were subject to bias, and that the inclinations and values of owners and journalists influenced electoral coverage.[91] Most Mexicans believed that Francisco Labastida received more coverage on television. However, when they were asked if they saw advertisements for the leading candidates, an equal number, half, saw announcements for both Fox and Labastida. By the end of the campaign, three-quarters of the voters could identity Fox's slogan "now is the time for change," a slightly higher percentage than those voters who recognized Labastida's motto.

The dependence of intellectuals and journalists and the institutions that employ them on the largesse of the state affected their relationship to the government. But the coming to power of a different political party elimi-

Table 6-7 The Impact of Media on Voter Preferences in Mexico, 1997

Viewer Preference	Percent Favoring PRI	Percent Voting for PRI
Televisa Viewers	28	13
Televisión Azteca Viewers	14	14
All Viewers	21	14

Source: Adapted from Chappell Lawson, "Building the Fourth Estate, Democratization and Media Opening in Mexico," Ph.D. dissertation, Stanford University, 1999, p 268.

nates the monopoly of a single party-state relationship over time. Furthermore, the increasing professionalization in television and the media increasingly restricts governmental influence from any one source. Finally, the rise of independent educational institutions, as alternative sources of employment for future intellectuals, also provides greater potential autonomy in intellectual employment. Nevertheless, some sectors of the intellectual community continue to rely heavily on the government to support their activities, thus continuing a pattern of dependence.

VOICES OF DISSENT

Even when Mexico's political model was a more or less orthodox example of a corporatist structure, the government never successfully incorporated all potentially influential groups into its fold, nor all members of the groups just discussed. Indeed, many of those who opposed the government politically were formerly its supporters. These included both intellectuals and political opposition leaders.

Mexico allowed dissent, but successfully controlled its level and tone prior to 2000. The government had a structural advantage in terms of continuity of leadership and the dominance of its party, the PRI, over the voting process. In an underdeveloped economy, the state's economic resources are overwhelming, and in Mexico those resources were used to disarm and co-opt dissidents, be they peasant leaders, lawyers, labor organizers, or intellectuals. Yet the state, including the presidency and the federal bureaucratic leadership—contrary to its impression as a monolithic and all powerful institution—demonstrated in practice that it was "a heterogeneous concoction of social classes and political factions holding little consensus over critical issues."[92] In the past, the government often coopted dissidents. Cooptation is the process by which the government incorporates an individual person or

---

Cooptation: the process by which the government successfully incorporates an individual person or group into its ranks.

---

group into its ranks. Groups find it difficult to counter government influence over their leaders. Few people can resist the attraction of political power or money, and the government often rewards cooperation with prestigious posts. Some persons accept posts for financial reasons; others because of the possibility of working within rather than outside the system.

On the whole, the government dealt well with contending groups until the 1990s, maneuvering them against one another when it believed that was necessary or creating intragroup competition to diminish the strength of a single recalcitrant leader or organization. The attitudes of each administration toward various groups and individual leaders varied. Since 1989, the state gave greater attention and consequently prestige to business, the military, and the church, and less attention to labor. It remains to be seen if Fox will continue that pattern. It is definitely the case, however, that he will pay more attention to the voices of dissent, since his own election in 2000 legitimized their existence.

Nongovernmental Organizations

Mexico has witnessed a flowering of popular movements since 1989. This is not a new phenomenon. Many groups with political, economic, and social interests grew out of the general malaise of the 1968 student movement and the subsequent government repression, and such organizations were given an additional boost in Mexico City after the 1985 earthquake. Also, after 1968, women were given more influential roles in these organizations, particularly in urban areas. In the 1988 presidential elections, many of these movements began linking themselves more closely to political parties.[93]

Critical voices have been a presence among most of these groups for decades. But a set of organizations over which the government has been unable to exercise much control has been nongovernmental organizations. Nongovernmental organizations range in scope from civic action groups, similar to the League of Women Voters in the United States, to religiously affiliated human rights advocacy organizations. By the mid-1990s, more than 5,000 such groups existed in Mexico, half of them in Mexico City, and an additional 25 percent in four cities: Guadalajara, Tijuana, Oaxaca, and Saltillo (Table 6-8). They are largely "urban phenomena, a result of the action of elite economic and cultural groups."[94]

As the 1994 presidential elections approached, many civic organizations were formed specifically to observe and evaluate the electoral process. Among the most notable of these organizations was an umbrella group, the *Alianza Cívica,* or Civic Alliance, which coordinated dozens of other organizations. Directed by Sergio Aguayo, a leading Mexican intellectual and human rights activist, Civic Alliance represented Mexicans seeking democratic change, in particular clean and fair elections. It recruited election observers from four hundred nongovernmental and civic groups to watch five thousand polling places. In 2000, it concentrated its electoral observation program on 200 districts in 27 states, using more than 7,000 volunteers.

Table 6-8 Nongovernmental Organizations in Mexico

Type of Organization	Number of Organizations
Welfare & assistance	1,883
Environmental	1,027
Human rights	952
Women	437
Indigenous services	270
Art, culture & science	248
Rural development	200
Total	5,017

Source: Adapted from Alberto Olvera, "Civil Society in Mexico at Century's End," in *Dilemmas of Political Change in Mexico,* ed. Kevin Middlebrook (La Jolla: U.S.-Mexico Studies Center, 2004), 428.

Even intellectuals became involved in the electoral outcome, when a loosely organized elite, calling itself the San Angel group, acted as a watchdog.

The San Angel group, small in numbers, but bringing together an extraordinary collection of intellectuals, politicians, and professionals favoring democracy, illustrates the potential influence of even the smallest organization. Vicente Fox was a member when he met Jorge Castañeda, Adolfo Aguilar Zinser, and Carlos Fuentes, all leading intellectuals, and Santiago Creel and Alejandro Gertz. Three of these individuals, Castañeda, Creel, and Gertz, became his secretaries of foreign relations, government, and public security, respectively, and Aguilar Zinser became ambassador to the United Nations. Fox himself admitted that meetings with the San Angel group help sustain his battle for democracy in Mexico.[95]

Another notable example, made up of individuals and groups who were part of the old corporatatist structure, is the El Barzón movement, composed of small businessmen, agriculturalists, and middle-class people opposed to government financial policies. Specifically, many people were caught in a credit crunch and became part of a broad, debtors' protest. Analysts claimed that they may have reached as many as two million members by the late 1990s. What is significant about this group is that it transformed itself into a typical interest organization, making demands on state and federal governments, and using a range of techniques to express its views. More importantly, it created a multiplier effect, because it weaved "together, more or less simultaneously, events ongoing in the farthest corners of Mexico."[96]

The political changes introduced since the 1988 presidential elections, as well as President Salinas's dismantling of certain features and structures of established state-group relations, contributed to the increasing growth and strength of nongovernmental organizations and to links with peer groups in other countries, ranging from environmental to human rights allies. Human rights organizations in Mexico, both independent and affiliated with the Catholic Church, were especially effective in obtaining media attention and support for their agendas, thereby becoming important actors in the political and social arenas.

Human rights groups, during the first two years of the Fox administration, have been among the most influential organizations in effecting changes in domestic policies. Among the most important of these changes has been increased access to government files, similar to the U.S. freedom of information legislation. This new access has led to numerous revelations about past abuses, including the massacre of student demonstrators in Mexico City in 1968, and the disappearance of leftist and alleged leftist activists in the 1970s and 1980s, during Mexico's own version of the region's "dirty wars." The President appointed a special prosecutor and promised to prosecute and punish officials responsible for the murders. Many human rights activists remain critical of the Fox administration for the slow pace of reforms, and the inadequacy of protection for activists and judges citing the murder of a leading human rights figure, Digna Ochoa, in October 2001 in the capital, and two federal judges in Mazatlan.

Nongovernmental groups, without a doubt, played a crucial role in the increasing competitiveness of Mexico's electoral process and in Vicente Fox's electoral victory. Their growth is one of the most significant political changes in Mexico since 1988, and they are likely to play a critical role in contributing to the give and take of democratic politics, especially in their relationship to the legislative branch. In recognition of this role, the Chamber of Deputies passed a law in 2004 "to Encourage Citizen Activities Performed by Civil Organizations, which sets forth certain benefits such organizations may obtain from the government, as well as establishing opportunities for collaboration between civil associations and the government. In short, such groups are now formally registered."[97] At present, however, most nongovernmental groups are characterized by their lack of partisan political attachments. They also have created a network of channels from which to work outside the party system altogether. Finally, they have contributed significantly to an expansion of international influences in Mexico.[98] For example, Global Exchange, a U.S. NGO that established a relationship with the Civic Alliance, made a long-term, sustained political investment in working with Mexican partners and became one of the pro-democratic movements' most consistent civil society allies.[99]

Guerrillas

The failure of Mexican administrations—local, state, and national—to resolve many long-standing problems, particularly in rural communities, came to a head on January 1, 1994, with far-reaching national and international consequences. A different kind of popular movement, willing to use force to obtain redress for decades of abuse and exploitation of indigenous peasants in the highlands of Chiapas, emerged in the form of the Zapatista Army of National Liberation (EZLN), which launched guerrilla attacks and seized villages near San Cristóbal de las Casas.[100]

The Zapatistas' beliefs are laid out very clearly in their official paper, *El Despertador Mexicano* and their website, and cover many issues, including women's rights. Their principal focus is on agrarian and economic reform, and some of their requests echo the voice of their inspiration, Emiliano Zapata, such as limits on land ownership and the redistribution of excessive land holdings.[101] The rebellion had at least three underlying causes: disappointment with the government for changing the provisions for agrarian reform in Article 27 and ignoring peasants as a client group, the peasants' declining economic status in the rural community, and their exclusion from the political process.[102]

The enigmatic spokesperson for the EZLN, Subcomandante Marcos, later identified as Rafael Sebastián Guillén, a former university professor and non-Indian, captured the national and international media's attention.[103] It immediately became clear that although most Mexicans opposed the guerrillas' use of force, they sympathized strongly with their goals. The EZLN uprising influenced the pace of electoral change for the remainder of 1994, leading to more electoral reforms favorable to the opposition parties, and it also set the tone for this period as one of increasing political instability and violence, especially after the PRI presidential candidate, Luis Donaldo Colosio, was assassinated. The Zapatistas showed other popular movements that even small, well-organized groups can have tremendous political influence. The guerrillas demonstrated the importance of electronic media, illustrating their ability to defeat the military and the government in the media war, affiliating themselves with national and international NGOs through e-mail. They continue to maintain an updated web site.[104]

The government and the Zapatistas signed an agreement in February 1996, the San Andrés accords, but President Zedillo never implemented these provisions. The division between executive branch and legislative branch control from 1997 to 2000 further complicated compromise on the accords. Among the provisions, the government agreed to permit the Indian communities to establish local governments, to educate themselves using indigenous languages, and to mandate indigeneous representation in legislative bodies. President Fox made settling the Zapatista impasse a primary campaign issue, stating publicly in a nonchalant fashion that he would settle this issue "in 15 minutes." In spite of many concessions, including withdrawing the military in 2001, the guerrillas remain intractable. Further debate of constitutional reforms linked to a National Indigenous Law (2001) suggest the consequences of democratic pluralism in addressing these and other long-neglected issues.

The continued lack of resolution of the Zapatista issue, and the activities of paramilitary groups, often in the employ of local economic interests and political officials, contributed to increased violence in Chiapas. Most notably, a paramilitary group in the employ of a local PRI leader attacked the village of Acteal in December 1997, murdering forty-five indigenous people, including children.[105]

The emergence of the Zapatistas produced an environment more favorable to other groups willing to use violence to achieve their goals. In the summer of 1996, an organization calling itself the People's Revolutionary Army (ERP) initated attacks on isolated police outposts and military patrols in the southern state of Oaxaca and elsewhere in central Mexico. They have been traced back to dissident leftist groups founded in the 1960s, and to an organization associated with Lucio Cabañas, a guerrilla leader killed in Guerrero in the 1970s. Unlike the Zapatistas, the ERP has been unwilling to negotiate with the government. Small affiliated groups have continued their attacks in seventeen different states. Other armed groups are also operating in many rural regions. None of these groups achieved the Zaptista's level of success politically, nor has any established international linkages.[106] Increased participation and democratic competition since 2000 have not necessarily provided adequate channels for the demands of all Mexicans.

CONCLUSION

From the leadership's viewpoint prior to the 1990s, Mexico developed a successful corporatist structure for engaging and controlling society's most important interest groups. The corporatist system was never comprehensive or complete, but channeled many political demands through quasi-governmental institutions. It was an essential ingredient in Mexico's one-party state.

Various groups in Mexico, including the military, the Church, business, labor, intellectuals, and the media, have maintained somewhat different relations with the government, depending on the legal and institutional role given to them by society. Interestingly, whether their relationship is established and visible or more autonomous and independent, the informal channels that their leaders use carry more weight in the decision-making process than do the formal channels. The political system used and abused interest-group institutions to mobilize the rank and file for their own purposes rather than, for the most part, to hear group demands. The removal of a single-party elite from controlling the state, and electoral competition, destroys this well-established pattern of interest-group relations.

The groups having the most institutionalized relationship with the government through their incorporation in the PRI party structure had the least influence, on the whole, on the decision-making process. Groups excluded from the party, such as business, the Church, and the military, have influenced the decision-making process more heavily. Of the major interest groups in most Western polities, business has had the most influence on Mexican government policies, primarily in the area of economic policy. Electoral competition, and the increasing strength of the legislative branch, will continue to enhance the importance of these three institutional actors, but especially the Catholic Church and business.

The state itself has often pursued its own policies, not in response to demands or pressures from any particular group, but because of self-interest or its interpretation of societal interests.[107] In this sense, the state too has been an actor in the decision-making process. It has had the greatest potential for influencing the outcome of policy making because it operated in a semiauthoritarian environment prior to 2000, and it mediated among the more traditional, competing interests.

Electoral democracy, multi-party control, and different executive branch leadership have dealt a death blow to the traditional, semi-corporatist structure in Mexican politics. The most influential structural change that alters this relationship is that the state and the party are no longer interchangeable. The ability of a small, circulating elite, affiliated with the same political organization, to retain control for decades over the federal bureaucracy, was the source of this pattern in state-groups relations. The PRI itself was a hollow skeleton, funded by the largesse of the state. Breaking that link destroyed the ability of government officials to keep groups loyal to their party or to the state. It is possible that on the state and local level, certain groups, especially labor, may retain ties to specific political parties, including the PRI, but the competition for interest group loyalties has intensified, making such linkages difficult.

The pattern that is least likely to be affected in state-interest group relations in the short run, at least until the legislative branch unequivocally demonstrates its decision-making influence on the national level, is the informal process through which elites use their networking ties to raise issues, seek out crucial information, and obtain access to critical policymakers. Certain institutions, however, are well placed to continue using the elite networking patterns to convey their demands, especially capitalists in the private sector, while at the same time participating in a partisan manner as individuals or groups in the electoral process. The Catholic Church also has demonstrated before and after Fox's election that it is an influential actor. More than any other interest group, it has a reservoir of support among average Mexicans, and it often articulates the interests of less influential Mexicans, rather than just its own institutional self-interest. Consequently it will remain the most critical voice of government economic policies that do not address the issue of poverty and redistribution of wealth. Finally, NGOs, if they decide to pursue partisan political issues as part of their mission, and develop the skills to do so, will increase their role in a more open, competitive setting at the state, national, and international levels.

NOTES

1. For the Mexican version, see Ruth J. Spalding, "State Power and its Limits: Corporatism in Mexico," *Comparative Political Studies* 14 (July 1981): 139–61.

2. Nora Hamilton, *The Limits of State Autonomy: Post Revolutionary Mexico* (Princeton, N.J.: Princeton University Press, 1982), describes this early pattern. Presidents Adolfo López Mateos (1958–1964) and Luis Echeverría (1970–1976) also responded more strongly to working-class interests.

3. For an interpretation that identifies cracks in the corporatist edifice in the mid-1980s, see Howard J. Wiarda, "Mexico: The Unravelling of a Corporatist Regime?" *Journal of Inter-American Studies and World Affairs* 30 (Winter 1988–1989): 1–28.

4. Luis Rubio, "Economic Reform and Political Liberalization," in *The Politics of Economic Liberalization in Mexico,* ed. Riordan Roett (Boulder, Colo.: Lynne Rienner, 1993), 35–50.

5. James Sánchez Susarrey, "Corporativismo o democracia?" *Vuelta* 12 (March 1988): 12–19.

6. Blanca Heredia, "Clientelism in Flux: Democratization and Interest Intermediation in Contemporary Mexico," paper presented at the National Latin American Studies Association, Guadalajara, 1997.

7. Robert J. Shafer, *Mexican Business Organizations* (Syracuse, N.Y.: Syracuse University Press, 1973), explains these requirements in some detail.

8. For detailed evidence of this influence, see Vikram K. Chand, *Mexico's Political Awakening* (Notre Dame: University of Notre Dame Press, 2001), 208 ff; and Yemille Mizrahi, "Entrepreneurs in Opposition: Modes of Political Participation in Chihuahua," in *Opposition Government in Mexico,* eds. Peter Ward and Victoria Rodríguez (Albuquerque: University of New Mexico Press, 1995), 81–96.

9. Judith A. Teichman, *Policymaking in Mexico: From Boom to Crisis* (Boston: Allen & Unwin, 1988).

10. Luis Carlos Ugalde, *The Mexican Congress: Old Player, New Player* (Washington, D.C.: CSIS, 2000), 160.

11. Miguel Basáñez, *La lucha por la hegemonía en México, 1968–1990,* 8th ed. (Mexico City: Siglo XXI, 1990), 35ff.

12. Abraham Lowenthal and J. Samuel Fitch, *Armies and Politics in Latin America,* rev. ed. (New York: Holmes & Meier, 1986), 4ff.

13. Franklin D. Margiotta, "Civilian Control and the Mexican Military: Changing Patterns of Political Influence," in *Civilian Control of the Military: Theories and Cases from Developing Countries,* ed. Claude E. Welch Jr. (Albany: State University of New York Press, 1976).

14. Gordon C. Schloming, "Civil-Military Relations in Mexico, 1910–1940: A Case Study" (Ph.D. diss., Columbia University, 1974), 297.

15. Jorge Lozoya, *El ejécito mexicano (1911–1965)* (Mexico City: El Colegio de México, 1970), 64.

16. James W. Wilkie, *The Mexican Revolution: Federal Expenditure and Social Change Since 1910,* 2d ed. (Berkeley and Los Angeles: University of California Press, 1970), 100–6.

17. Merilee Grindle, "Civil-Military Relations and Budget Politics in Latin America," *Armed Forces and Society* 13 (Winter 1987): 255–75.

18. Roderic Ai Camp, "Militarizing Mexico, Where is the Officer Corps Going?," (Washington, D.C.: CSIS, 1999).

19. Michael J. Dziedzic, "Mexico's Converging Challenges: Problems, Prospects, and Implications," unpublished manuscript, U.S. Air Force Academy, April 1989, 34.

20. Stephen J. Wager, "The Mexican Military Approaches the 21st Century: Coping with a New World Order," *Special Report* (Carlisle, Pa.: U.S. Army War College, 1994), 15.

21. See Roderic A. Camp, *Generals in the Palacio: The Military in Modern Mexico* (New York: Oxford University Press, 1992), for an analysis of these roles.

22. Phylis Greene Walker, "The Modern Mexican Military: Political Influence and Institutional Interests" (master's thesis, American University, 1987), 76.

23. For evidence of this, see José Luis Reyna, "Narcotics as a Destabilizing Force for Source Countries and Non-Source Countries," in *The Latin American Narcotics Trade and United States National Security,* ed. Donald A. Mabry (Westport, Conn.: Greenwood Press, 1989), 123–35.

24. Roderic Ai Camp, "Mexico's Armed Forces, March to a Democratic Tune?" in *Dilemmas of Political Change in Mexico,* ed. Kevin Middlebrook (London: Institute of Latin American Studies, University of London, 2004), 169.

25. The most pessimistic view, backed by considerable evidence of corruption in the Salinas and de la Madrid administrations, reaching the top levels, is offered in Christopher Whalen's "México: El narcosistema," *Dinero,* November 1994, 162–76.

26. Eric L. Olson, "The Evolving Role of Mexico's Military in Public Security and Antinarcotics Programs," Washington Office on Latin America, May 1996, 4; and Graham H. Turbiville, Jr., "Law Enforcement and the Mexican Armed Forces: New Internal Security Missions Challenge the Military," *Low Intensity Conflict & Law Enforcement,* 6 (Autumn 1997), 69–83.

27. Tim Weiner, "Mexico's Image Is Buffed and Tarnished With Military Drug Arrests," *The New York Times,* April 7, 2001, www.nytimes.com.

28. David Mares, "U.S. Drug Policy and Mexican Civil-Military Relations," *Crime, Law & Social Change* 40 (July 2003): 61–75; Raúl Benítez Manaut, *National Security and Armed Forces in Mexico: Challenges and Scenarios at the End of the Century,* Working Paper Series, Woodrow Wilson Center, Washington, D.C., 1998.

29. Douglas Farah and Dana Priest, "Mexican Drug Force Is U.S.-Bred," *Washington Post,* February 26, 1998, 1A.

30. I present these arguments in my "The Sword and the Cross, New Battlefields in Chiapas?" "Enfoque," *Reforma,* February 20, 1994, 16–20.

31. Stephen J. Wager, "The Mexican Military: The Dilemma of Functioning in a One-Party System," in *Beyond Praetorianism: The Latin American Military in Transition,* ed. Richard Millett and Michael Gold-Bliss (Miami: North-South Center Press, 1996), 125.

32. Roderic Ai Camp, *The Mexican Military on the Democratic Stage* (Washington, D.C.: Center for Strategic and International Studies and Praeger, 2005).

33. For discussions about these dissident officers, who allied themselves with several PRD politicians in an open march down Mexico City's main thoroughfare, see Sergio Aguayo, "La protesta militar," *Diaro de Yucatán,* December 31, 1998, www.sureste.com.; "Militares presos se quejan de juicios prolongaods," *Proceso,* January 17, 1999, www.proceso.com.mx.; and Ginger Thompson, "Mexico Army Protestor Goes Loudly into Hiding," *The New York Times,* December 29, 1998, www.nytimes.com. For the changes in professionalization, see the author's *Militarizing Mexico: Where is the Officer Corps Going?*

34. Bimsa, "Encuesta nacional en vivienda: imagen del ejército," August 13–17, 2004, 3.5+/– margin of error.

35. Soledad Loaeza, "La iglesia católica y el reformismo autoritario," *Foro Internacional* 25 (October-December 1984): 142.

36. The relationship is outlined in Karl Schmitt, "Church and State in Mexico: A Corporatist Relationship," *Americas* 40 (January 1984): 349–76.

37. For an excellent example, see Matt Moffet, "In Catholic Mexico, a Priest's Power Is Limited to Prayer," *Wall Street Journal,* December 6, 1989.

38. "La religiosidad en México," *Este País,* (March 2001), 72.

39. "Una Iglesia muda no sirve, dice Mons. Rivera," *Diario de Yucatán,* September 6, 1999, www.yucatan.com.mx.

40. The best analysis of church involvement in base communities and the internal and external consequences of Bishop Ruiz's role in Chiapas can be found in Michael Tangeman (longtime correspondent for the *Catholic National Review*), *Mexico at the Crossroads, Politics, the Church, and the Poor* (Maryknoll, N.Y.: Orbis Books, 1994). For the political involvement of CEBs, see Elsa Guzmán and Christopher Martin, "Back to Basics Mexican Style: Radical Catholicism and Survival on the Margins," *Bulletin of Latin American Research* 16, (1997): 351–66.

41. Ginger Thompson, "Vatican Seeks to Curb Mexico's Indian Deacons," *New York Times,* March 12, 2002.

42. "También es un pecado grave saber que ocurre esa y no denunciarla, censura de la Iglesia al vote del miedo," *Diario de Yucátan,* May 10, 2000, www.yucatan.com.mx.

43. Conferencia del Episcopado Mexicano, *La democracia no se puede dar sin ti, elecciones del 2000* (Mexico: CEM, 2000), 12.

44. For examples of the potential political conflict, see Claude Pomerlau, "The Changing Church in Mexico and Its Challenge to the State," *Review of Politics* 43 (October 1981): 540–59.

45. Interview with Abelardo Alvardo Alcantara, auxiliary bishop of Mexico City, June 2, 1987.

46. Dennis M. Hanratty, "The Church," in *Prospects for Democracy in Mexico,* ed. George Grayson (New Brunswick, N.J.: Transaction Books, 1990), 118.

47. Roberto Blancarte, "Religion and Constitutional Change in Mexico, 1988–1992," *Social Compass* 40 (1993): 567.

48. Interviews with former presidents José López Portillo and Miguel de la Madrid, Mexico City, summer 1990.

49. "Las 10 propuestas de Fox Quesada a las iglesias," *Diario de Yucatán,* May 8, 2000, www.yucatan.com.mx.

50. "Los políticos deben profesar públicamente su fe," *Diario de Yucatán,* November 6, 2000, www.yucatan.com.mx.

51. "La visita del Papa y el respeto a la ley," *Este País,* September 2002, 53–54.

52. For an excellent description of church-state relations under Salinas before the reforms, see Allan Metz, "Mexican Church-State Relations Under President Carlos Salinas de Gortari," *Journal of Church and State* 34 (Winter 1992): 111–30.

53. Evidence of this, based on numerous interviews with higher clergy, can be found in my *Crossing Swords: Politics and Religion in Mexico* (New York: Oxford University Press, 1997).

54. A PAN sympathizer successfully requested that the Vatican prevent bishop Onésimo Cepeda Silva, president of the episcopate's Social Communication Committee, and an open partisan of PRI's presidential candidate, from speaking in the name of the episcopate in September 2000. The PRD formally asked the secretary of government to call to Cardinal Rivera Carrera's attention his potential violation of the constitution by involving himself in internal party matters. See "Una misiva del Vaticano, prohiben a Mons. Cepeda Silva hablar en nombre del Episcopado," *Diario de Yucatán,* September 7, 2000, *www.yucatan.com.mx;* and "El PRD pide a Gobernación que 'meta en orden' al Cardenal Rivera Carrera," *Diario de Yucatán,* August 29, 2000, www.yucatan.com.mx. For examples of more recent complaints, including a priest who held an open forum for local candidates on church property, see Chris Kraul, "Priest's Election Activity Derided in Mexico," *Los Angeles Times,* July 1, 2003; and "Castigo a los obispos que tomen parte en la política," *Diario de Yucatán,* May 27, 2003.

55. The best analysis in English of these industrial groups is by Dale Story, *Industry, the State, and Public Policy in Mexico* (Austin: University of Texas Press, 1986). An updated analysis of their current roles are well-analyzed in Strom C.

Thacker, *Big Business, the State, and Free Trade, Constructing Coalitions in Mexico* (Cambridge: Cambridge University Press, 2000).

56. Roderic Ai Camp, *Entrepreneurs and Politics in Twentieth Century Mexico* (New York: Oxford University Press, 1989), 141–42.

57. *Reforma,* June 10, 1996, A1.

58. Alicia Ortiz Rivera, "Consejo Mexicano de Hombres de Negocios," MA Thesis, Instituto Mora, Mexico City, 1998; and Ben Ross Schneider, "Why Is Mexican Business So Organized?" *Latin American Research Review* 37, no. 1 (2002): 77–118.

59. Roderic Ai Camp, *Mexico's Mandarins: Crafting a Power Elite for the Twenty-First Century* (Berkeley: University of California Press, 2002), "El 'Grupo 21,'" *El Diario de Yucatán,* November 27, 2001, www.yucatan.com.mx.

60. Harold R. Kerbo and John A. McKinestry, *Who Rules Japan? The Inner Circles of Economic and Political Power* (Westport: Praeger, 1995), 122.

61. John Womack, "The Spoils of the Mexican Revolution," *Foreign Affairs* 48 (July 1970): 677–87.

62. Saúl Escobar Toledo, "Rifts in the Mexican Power Elite, 1976–1986," in *Government and the Private Sector in Contemporary Mexico,* ed. Sylvia Maxfield (La Jolla, Calif.: Center for U.S.–Mexican Studies, UCSD, 1987), 79.

63. Graciela Guadarrama S., "Entrepreneurs and Politics: Businessmen in Electoral Contests in Sonora and Nuevo León," in *Electoral Patterns and Perspectives in Mexico,* ed. Arturo Alvarado (La Jolla, Calif.: Center for U.S.–Mexican Studies, UCSD, 1987), 83ff.

64. Kenneth C. Shadlen, *Democratization Without Representation, the Politics of Small Industry in Mexico* (University Park: Pennsylvania State University Press, 2004). In 2000, the former president of the CCE, Eduardo Bours, used his position to seek funds for Francisco Labastida's candidacy, and later became his campaign finance secretary.

65. Matilde Luna, "Business and Politics in Mexico," in *Dilemmas of Political Change in Mexico*, ed. Kevin J. Middlebrook (London: Institute of Latin American Studies, University of London, 2004), 350.

66. See Yemile Mizrahi, *From Martyrdom to Power, the Partido Acción Nacional* (Notre Dame: University of Notre Dame Press, 2003), 68ff.

67. Strom C. Thacker, *Big Business, the State, and Free Trade: Constructing Coalitions in Mexico, 207.*

68. For an excellent appraisal of these recent alliances and partisan activities, see Kristin Johnson Ceva, "Business-Government Relations in Mexico Since 1990: NAFTA, Economic Crisis, and the Reorganization of Business Interests," in *Mexico's Private Sector: Recent History, Future Challenges,* ed. Riordan Roett (Boulder: Lynne Rienner, 1998), 125–157.

69. Howard Handleman, "The Politics of Labor Protest in Mexico: Two Case Studies," *Journal of Inter-American Studies and World Affairs* 18 (August 1976): 267–94.

70. George W. Grayson, *The Mexican Labor Machine: Power, Politics, and Patronage,* Significant Issues Series 19 (Washington, D.C.: CSIS, 1989), 12.

71. For background, see Kevin J. Middlebrook, "State-Labor Relations in Mexico: The Changing Economic and Political Context," in *Unions, Workers, and the State in Mexico,* ed. Kevin J. Middlebrook (La Jolla, Calif.: Center for U.S.–Mexican Studies, UCSD, 1991), 1–26.

72. Juan Reyes del Campillo, "El movimiento obrero en la Cámara de Diputados (1979–1988)," *Revista Mexicana de Sociología* 52 (July–September 1990): 139–60.

73. Graciela Bensusán, "A New Scenario for Mexican Trade Unions: Changes in the Structure of Political and Economic Opportunities," in *Dilemmas of Political Change in Mexico,* ed. Kevin J. Middlebrook (London: Institute of Latin American Studies, University of London, 2004), 254.

74. Sam Dillon, "Mexican Factory to Recognize Independent Union Severing Ties to Government," *New York Times,* December 14, 1997; Ginger Thompson, "Mexican Labor Protest Gets Results," *New York Times,* October 8, 2001, www.nytimes.com.

75. Katrina Burgess, "Mexican Labor at a Crossroads," in *Mexico's Politics and Society in Transition,* ed. Joseph S. Tulchin and Andrew D. Selee (Boulder, Colo: Lynne Rienner, 2003), 99.

76. Roderic A. Camp, "Organized Labor and the Mexican State: A Symbiotic Relationship?" *Mexican Forum* 4 (October 1984): 4.

77. Kevin J. Middlebrook, "The Political Economy of State-Labor Relations in Mexico," paper presented at the National Latin American Studies Association, Washington, D.C., March 1982, and "The Sounds of Silence: Organised Labour's Response to Economic Crisis in Mexico," *Journal of Latin American Studies* 21 (May 1989): 195–220.

78. See "Labor, Another Flank Demanding Reform," *Review of the Economic Situation of Mexico,* (May 2001), 207–208. If five consecutive appeals are made against that portion of the labor law, and the court provides the same ruling, it will become invalid. "Las negociaciones SPE-SNTE, 'una pantomina'," *El Diairo de Yucatán,* May 16, 2001, www.yucatan.com.mx.

79. Ruth Berins Collier, *The Contradictory Alliance: State-Labor Relations and Regime Change in Mexico* (Berkeley: International and Area Studies, University of California, 1992), 156.

80. Fred P. Ellison, "The Writer," in *Continuity and Change in Latin America,* ed. John J. Johnson (Stanford, Calif.: Stanford University Press, 1964), 84.

81. Roderic A. Camp, *Intellectuals and the State in Twentieth-Century Mexico* (Austin: University of Texas Press, 1985), 131. An excellent update on the relationship in the Fox era can be found in Yvon Grenier, "Octavio Paz and the Changing Role of Intellectuals in Mexico," *Discourse* 23 (Spring 2001): 124–143.

82. For discussions of its influence, see Juan Carlos Gamboa, "Media, Public Opinion Polls, and the 1994 Mexican Presidential Election," in *Polling for Democracy: Public Opinion and Political Liberalization in Mexico,* ed. Roderic Ai Camp (Wilmington: Scholarly Resources, 1996), 17–36.

83. Roy Campos, "Una Encuesta sobre las encuestas," *Este País,* March 2003, 55.

84. Albert L. Hester and Richard R. Cole, eds., *Mass Communications in Mexico* (Brookings, S.D.: Association for Education in Journalism, 1975).

85. Roderic Ai Camp, "Learning Democracy in Mexico and the United States," *Mexican Studies* 19, no. 1 (Winter 2003), 17.

86. The details of these machinations are fully explained by Jeffrey Staub (a former reporter for the paper), in "Self-Censorship and the Mexican Press," *Mexico Policy News,* no. 9, fall 1993, 30–34. Background information on these relationships can be found in Ilya Adler, "Press-Government Relations in Mexico: A Study of Freedom of the Mexican Press and Press Criticism of Government Institutions," *Studies in Latin American Popular Culture* 12 (1993): 1–29.

87. See Mexican Academy of Human Rights, "The Media and the 1994 Federal Elections in Mexico, a Content Analysis of Television News Coverage of the Political Parties and Presidential Candidates," May 19, 1994, 3.

88. For the impact of *Reforma,* see Murray Fromson, "Mexico's Struggle for a Free Press," in *Communications in Latin America: Journalism, Mass Media, and Society* (Wilmington: Scholarly Resources, 1996), 115–37.

89. Sallie Hughes, "From the Inside Out: How Institutional Entrepreneurs Transformed Mexican Journalism," *Harvard International Journal of Press/Politics* 8, no. 3 (2003): 87–117.

90. Chappell H. Lawson, "Building the Fourth Estate: Media Opening and Democratization in Mexico," in *Dilemmas of Political Change in Mexico*, ed. Kevin J. Middlebrook (London: Institute of Latin American Studies, University of London, 2004), 373–402.

91. Sallie Hughes and Chappell Lawson, "Propaganda and Crony Capitalism: Partisan Bias in Mexican Television News," *Latin American Research Review* 39, no. 3 (October 2004), 82.

92. Diane E. Davis provides the most thorough case study of policymaking in Mexico, focusing particularly on the Federal District Department and government strategies in Mexico City. See *Urban Leviathan: Mexico City in the Twentieth Century* (Philadelphia: Temple University Press, 1994), 320.

93. These and other arguments are developed by contributors to Joe Foweraker and Ann L. Craig, eds., *Popular Movements and Political Change in Mexico* (Boulder, Colo.: Lynne Rienner, 1990); and Maria Lorena Cook, Kevin J. Middlebrook, and Juan Molinar Horcasitas, eds., *The Politics of Economic Restructuring, State-Society Relations and Regime Change in Mexico* (La Jolla, Calif.: Center for U.S.–Mexican Studies, UCSD, 1994). For human rights, see Edward L. Cleary, "Human Rights Organizations in Mexico: Growth in Turbulence," *Journal of Church and State* 37 (Autumn 1995): 793–812.

94. Alberto Olvera, "Civil Society in Mexico at Century's End," in *Dilemmas of Political Change in Mexico,* ed. Kevin Middlebrook (London: Institute of Latin American Studies, University of London, 2004).

95. "Tensiones, diferencias y recelos entre Fox y el PAN," *Proceso,* July 16, 2000. www.proceso.com.mx.

96. Gabriel Torres, "The El Barzón Debtors' Movement: From the Local to the National in Protest Politics," in *Subnational Politics and Democratization in Mexico,*

Wayne A. Cornelius, Todd A. Eisenstadt, and Jane Hindley, eds. (La Jolla: Center for U.S.-Mexican Studies, UCSD, 1999), 146.

97. Cristina Puga, "Associations and Governance in Mexico," paper presented at the Latin American Studies Association, Las Vegas, Nevada, October 2004, 10–11. For additional background, see Alberto J. Olvera's excellent "Civil Society in Mexico at Century's End," in *Dilemmas of Political Change in Mexico*, ed. Kevin J. Middlebrook (London: Institute of Latin American Studies, University of London, 2004), 403–39.

98. For an excellent summary of the changes wrought by NGOs, see Douglas A. Chalmers and Kerianne Piester, "Nongovernmental Organizations and the Changing Structure of Mexican Politics," in *Changing Structure of Mexico: Political, Social and Economic Prospects,* ed. Laura Randall (New York: M.E. Sharpe, 1996) 253–61.

99. Jonathan Fox, "Assessing Binational Civil Society Coalitions," in *Dilemmas of Political Change in Mexico,* ed. Kevin Middlebrook (London: Institute of Latin American Studies, University of London, 2004), 466–522.

100. Some of the best background information on this movement can be found in Thomas Benjamin, *A Rich Land a Poor People: Politics and Society in Modern Chiapas* (Albuquerque: University of New Mexico Press, 1989); and Tom Barry's perceptive exploration of the agrarian issues in *Zapata's Revenge: Free Trade and the Farm Crisis in Mexico* (Boston: South End Press, 1995).

101. *El despertador mexicano,* no. 1, December 1993, 1–20.

102. See George A. Collier's "The New Politics of Exclusion: Antecedents to the Rebellion in Mexico," *Dialectical Anthropology* 19 (May 1994): 1–44. Other explanations, focused on its being a response to postmodernism, can be found in Carlos Arriola, *Chiapas 1994: The Enemies of Modernity* (Mexico City: M. A. Porrúa, 1994); and Roger Burback, "Roots of the Postmodern Rebellion in Chiapas," *New Left Review,* May–June 1994, 113–24.

103. Revealing portraits of Marcos can be found in Alma Guillermoprieto, "The Unmasking," as well as her earlier essay in the *New Yorker,* March 13, 1995, 40–47; and Ann Louise Bardach, "Mexico's Poet Rebel," *Vanity Fair,* June 1994, 69–74, 130–35.

104. See Ruth Urry, "Rebels, Technology, and Mass Communications: A Comparative Analysis of EZLN and FMLN Media Strategy," Tulane University, 1996.

105. For a brief discussion of such groups, see Mary Beth Sheridan, "Pro-PRI Gangs Breed Fear, Potential Chaos in Chiapas," *Los Angeles Times,* January 25, 1998, 1A.

106. Gustavo Hirales Morán, "Radical Groups in Mexico Today," Policy Papers on the Americas, Center for Strategic and International Studies, Washington, D.C., September 2003.

107. For support of this view, see Rose J. Spalding, "State Power and Its Limits: Corporatism in Mexico."

7

Who Governs? The Structure of Decision Making

> Previous studies of democratization in Mexico have focused mainly on top-down analyses of political change. From this perspective, democratization in the highly centralized Mexican political system was said to flow from the president and his cohort of reform-minded politicians. This view of Mexican politics is not necessarily wrong, but it distorts what is happening in Mexico in two ways. First, it ignores crucial social and political processes at the regional and local levels that have been gnawing at the foundations of Mexico's authoritarian system. These processes involve growing political consciousness among ordinary citizens; increasingly competitive elections; stronger opposition political parties; a more vigorous associational life; and growing activism by the Catholic Church after many decades of quiescence. Second, the top-down perspective fails to come to grips with the role of bottom-up pressures in compelling the president and his allies to promote political opening.
>
> VIKRAM K. CHAND, *Mexico's Political Awakening*

Every political system devises a set of structures and institutions to facilitate political decision making. Studies of decision making reveal that there are a number of interrelated steps in the process. The steps begin with a problem requiring a political solution and pass through a series of institutions in which the problem is ignored or resolved, often legislatively. Some institutions primarily channel demands from society through the political system. Other institutions contribute to the selection and election of political leadership. Still others carry out the solutions proposed by the political system.

Each political model performs the steps in decision making differently, although many models have certain similarities. For example, in the United States, the legislative branch plays a critical role in the formulation of laws and as a focus of interest-group activity. In the United Kingdom, although Parliament plays a critical role in approving legislation, most of its formulation and lobbying are done through the executive branch. The cabinet, however, is a product of the legislative branch; that is, its members are members of Parliament, and so election to Parliament determines who will make many government decisions.

Mexico, as has been suggested earlier, evolved a political system that formally resembles that of the United States but centralized much greater authority in the executive branch. The powers of the executive branch combined with the dominance of a leadership group represented by a single party—the PRI and its antecedents—led to a government dominated by the executive, largely in the person of the president.

THE EXECUTIVE BRANCH

The seat of the Mexican government is Mexico City, in the Federal District, a jurisdiction with certain similarities to the District of Columbia in the United States. Mexico City, however, unlike Washington, D.C., combines the qualities of New York City, Chicago, and Los Angeles, for Mexico's political capital is also its intellectual and economic capital.

The executive branch of the government houses two types of agencies: those that have counterparts in most First and Third World countries, such as departments of foreign relations and national defense, and others that are idiosyncratically Mexican, sometimes called decentralized or parastatal agencies, somewhat analogous to the Tennessee Valley Authority in the United States. Parastatal agencies are a product of Mexican nationalism, Mexicanization, and state expansion from the 1940s through the 1980s, culminating in the nationalization of private, domestically owned banks in 1982.[1]

The preeminent parastatal agency in Mexico, recognized internationally, is Petroleos Mexicanos (Pemex), the national petroleum company. Pemex was born when President Lázaro Cárdenas nationalized foreign-owned petroleum companies in 1938.[2] Since then the government has controlled the development of petroleum resources, including exploration and drilling, and the domestic retailing of petroleum products. Because of the vast Mexican oil reserves and their rapid exploitation in the 1970s and 1980s, Pemex became Mexico's number-one company. Its sales at their apex accounted for more than three-quarters of export revenues.

Among the fifty leading firms (excluding banks) in Mexico during the 1980s, a fourth were government owned. Other important government entities included the Federal Electric Commission, which develops and distributes electricity; the National Bank of Foreign Commerce, designed to promote trade; the National Finance Bank (Nacional Financiera), a developmental bank; and many other companies in utilities, communications, transportation, minerals, fertilizers, and so on. Their numbers have declined dramatically due to privatization programs since 1989, but the agencies mentioned here have semicabinet status, and the president announces his appointees to them simultaneously with those of formal cabinet members.[3]

The formal cabinet has nineteen agencies: Attorney General of the Republic; Secretariat of Public Functions; Secretariat of Agrarian Reform; Secretariat of Tourism; Secretariat of Agriculture, Livestock, Rural Development, Fishing and Nutrition; Secretariat of Communications and Transportation; Secretariat of Foreign Relations; Secretariat of Government; Secretariat of Energy; Secretariat of Health and Welfare; Secretariat of Labor and Social Welfare; Secretariat of National Defense; Secretariat of the Navy; Secretariat of Social Development; Secretariat of Public Education; Secretariat of the Economy; Secretariat of Public Security and Justice Services; Secretariat of the Environment and Natural Resources; and Secretariat of the Treasury and Public Credit.

An examination of the major agencies suggests some interesting aspects of Mexican policy issues and the importance of specific economic problems. For example, the historic impact of agrarian issues and agrarian reform after the revolution can be seen in the fact that *two* cabinet-level agencies are devoted to agriculture, one specifically to agrarian reform, and until recently, hydraulic resources were the purview of a separate agency. Nevertheless, it would be misleading to say that any president since Lázaro Cárdenas has given priority to agrarian issues. In fact, the desire of the Salinas administration to eliminate land-tenure problems generated by village-held land titles (*ejidos*), incorporated in constitutional reforms of Article 27, may mean the eventual disappearance of the Secretariat of Agrarian Reform. The newest cabinet agency, reflecting an unfortunate recent trend in Mexican social conditions, is the Secretariat of Public Security. Public security issues related to crime and drug trafficking are among the most significant policy problems in Mexico since 1994. In fact, among residents in the Federal District, public security is overwhelmingly the most important issue.[4] The public's concern with personal safety, the low esteem in which police are held by Mexicans, and the lack of coordination among federal, state, civil, and military agencies responsible for the lower incidence of crime, all led to President Fox's decision to add this new cabinet position.

The agencies of greatest standing in the executive branch are those with long histories. In the 1920s, 1930s, and 1940s, the Secretariat of National Defense carried far more weight than it does today, not because of its impact on day-to-day policies but because it often was the source of presidential leadership, given the control exercised by revolutionary generals. With the centralization of power in the hands of the president and, as we have seen, the importance of individual, federal bureaucratic agencies as sources of political recruitment prior to 2000, some relationship developed between decision-making influence and the degree to which individual agencies were the source of high-level personnel. In the 1950s and 1960s, the Secretariat of Government, an agency devoted to internal political affairs, replaced the Secretariat of National Defense as a source of presidential leadership and as a major voice in policy decisions.[5]

Despite the roles played by the Secretariat of National Defense and the Secretariat of Government, the Secretariat of the Treasury wielded considerable influence, and its head received much attention in each cabinet. President Cárdenas enhanced both Treasury's authority and its leader by permitting him to act as an arbiter in the allocation of funds to other agencies and to state governors in connection with the federal revenue-sharing program.[6] Thus, other than the president, the treasury secretary became the key figure in distributing economic resources, as well as in determining financial policies.

Economic agencies in the government increased their influence with the onset of hard times. By the 1980s, the Secretariat of Programming and Budgeting (combined with Treasury in 1992), the Secretariat of the Treasury, and the Bank of Mexico (the federal reserve bank) became the troika in setting economic policy.[7]

The most interesting of these three agencies, and the most politically influential during its short life (1977–1992), was the Secretariat of Programming and Budgeting, which produced three consecutive presidents: de la Madrid, Salinas, and Zedillo. More important, it produced a cadre of important political-technocrats who dominated the Salinas-Zedillo camarillas, their political generation, and economic decision making.[8] One of their members, Francisco Gil Díaz, became Fox's treasury secretary.[9] It is ironic, therefore, that this agency and the presidents it produced both expanded statist economic intervention in the form of hundreds of government-owned enterprises—whose budgets the new secretariat managed, and then presided over its eventual disappearance as a budgeting agency.[10] The president's desire to streamline economic policy-making and the ultimate decline of technocrats among the political leadership ensured the demise of this agency.[11]

To streamline cabinet coordination and facilitate policymaking, Miguel de la Madrid organized subcabinet groups along policy lines, including an economic cabinet. These groups were more active under Salinas and Zedillo, and Salinas added another category, national security, giving it heightened visibility. It includes the Secretariats of Government, Foreign Relations, National Defense, Navy, Public Security, and the Attorney General of the Republic. This subcabinet group provided the basis for Fox's new public security secretariat.

Groups in Mexican society who want some part in national policy decisions must make their concerns and interests known to the executive branch at the highest possible level. Yet as Daniel Levy and Gabriel Szekely observed, this is difficult to accomplish:

> As most important legislation is initiated and carried through to approval by the president, hardly any opportunity exists for effective interaction between citizens and their representatives during the lawmaking process. However, groups and individuals may occasionally influence the way in which laws and policies are actually implemented. A common element of day-to-day politics in Mexico is the presentation of demands to local and state governments, to departments of the federal bureaucracy, and even directly to the president.[12]

The cabinet secretary is the key figure in initiating policy proposals, and his staff thoroughly studies the issues and collects information relevant to the formulation of policy. He may be responding to a presidential request or pursuing matters associated with his agency's mandate under broad guidelines outlined to him by the president and the presidential advisers.[13] The persons who have access to the president himself are even more successful in influencing decisions than are those whose highest-level contacts are cabinet figures.

Because the decision-making structure has been so hierarchical and the president exercised so much influence (or presently is expected to exercise authority over the system), considerable pressure is put on channels of access to the presidency. The president's private secretary, who functions as a chief of staff and whose position is essentially a cabinet-level appointment, has the complete confidence of the president. Because he acts as a gatekeeper in denying or granting requests to see the president, he performs a crucial role in the decision-making process.

President Fox introduced few changes to the formal cabinet structure in Mexico, continuing the concept of interagency coordination first introduced by President de la Madrid, dividing his cabinet into three broad groups: economic, political and security, and social. However, he created an entirely new arrangement of formal advisers, called coordinators, who report to an overall Coordinator of Public Policies, who in turn reports directly to the president. Fox used these coordinators to draw attention to major policy issues, appointing a number of prominent figures to these posts. For example, Adolfo Aguilar Zinser, a leading intellectual and independent politician, served as his coordinator of national security, and Luis H. Alvarez, a distinguished PAN leader and former presidential candidate, coordinated his negotiations in Chiapas with the Zapatistas. Most observers have concluded that these coordinators, many of whom resigned during the first half of Fox's administration, never exerted significant influence on policy, and that the traditional cabinet agency leadership has continued to maintain its preeminence in the executive branch decision-making process.[14]

Prior to Fox's electoral victory in 2000, the presidency specifically, and the executive branch generally, were viewed as the primary voice in the decision-making process. Analysts described the Mexican presidency as having "meta" constitutional powers, or as "hyper" presidentialism. The president's and the executive branch's role in the decision-making process could be illustrated with two pre-2000 examples. The worst fears of critics of the Mexican semiauthoritarian decision-making process were borne out in 1982 when President José López Portillo announced without warning the nationalization of the banks. The circumstances surrounding the decision have been well documented, and according to the few people López Portillo consulted, he did not consider the views of any of the groups that would be affected.[15] The fact that a single political actor, in consultation with two or three others, could make a decision that would have major reverberations throughout the economy and bring relations between the private sector and the state to a breaking point demonstrates the dangers inherent in centralized power.[16] This can also occur in the political realm, as illustrated in the manner in which the incumbent president has been able to designate his own successor. This power was magnified in 1994, when the PRI's presidential candidate was assassinated, and the president had to decide quickly, and very much in the public eye, on a successor, Ernesto Zedillo, without the charade of the party itself making such a choice.

Typically, however, presidents have not operated in solitary splendor. Diane Davis, in the only case study of recent presidential decision-making even before Fox took office, discovered that the president often failed to get his way.[17] There is no question that until 2000, decision-making was centralized and that the president personally had greater influence over the outcome of policies than does a U.S. president. Even with the advent of multiple-party control in the Chamber of Deputies, the percentage of legislation passed initiated by the executive branch remained remarkably high, with the executive branch having a success rate of 99 percent from 1994–1997, and

Table 7-1 The Role of the Mexican Executive Branch in the Legislative Process

Measurements of Activity	1994–1997 Legislature	1997–2000 Legislature	2000–2003 Legislature
Bills presented	223 (N)	674 (N)	1128 (N)
Deputy success rate	16	21	13
Executive success rate	99	90	67

Source: Adapted from Jeffrey A. Weldon, "The Fall 2003 Term of the Mexican Congress," *Mexican Congressional Report Series* (Washington, D.C.: CSIS, 2004), 23.

90 percent from 1997–2000 (Table 7-1). Such a rate of passage would be the envy of any leader in a typical democratic, presidential model.

Under President Fox, however, the 2000–2003 legislature was even more divided than it was under Zedillo. Moreover, the president, unlike his predecessors, has little control over the members of his own party. In his first year in office, Fox faced considerable opposition from his own party's ranks to his major policy proposals, including his value-added tax bill and his indigenous rights legislation. This is not surprising given the fact that a study of the 1997–2000 legislature revealed that the entire PAN delegation stuck together on a legislative vote only 63 percent of the time compared with 91 percent for PRI.[18]

The data in Table 7-1, however, illustrate the significant changes that impact on the importance of the executive branch in the decision-making process and the increasing balance between it and the legislative branch. For example, the number of legislative proposals increased dramatically— nearly 150 percent—from the 1994–1997 to the 1997–2000 session. After Fox became president, the total number of bills presented before congress exploded, reaching a total of 1128 at the end of 58th congress (2000–2003), compared to only 233 and 674 in the two preceding periods (1994–1997, 1997–2000). The approval rate overall declined to 19 percent, although President Fox was able to receive approval for two-thirds of his bills, compared to only 13 percent for members of congress. Jeffrey Weldon, a leading student of congressional decision-making, believes that the 2003–2006 congress may be more productive, but the divisions between and within parties continue unabated, making legislative coalitions and compromises difficult to achieve.[19]

A comparison of the number of initiatives per member of congress reveals that the legislative branch had not achieved such a comparable level since the 1920s, before the PRI existed. These figures demonstrate that competitive elections, a multi-party system, and shared legislative control, will expand the number and range of sources for legislative proposals, thereby expanding access to the decision-making process among various groups, including political parties, interest groups, and legislators themselves. Caroline Beer, in a recent study of this phenomenon at the state level, demonstrated a pronounced increase in legislative staff, bills and discussion in those states where electoral competition was intense.[20]

Presidentialism, which has been the cornerstone of the Mexican political system and the decision-making process, has taken on many new features during the Fox administration.[21] It is readily apparent that the president and his individual cabinet members face many difficulties in persuading congress to approve their legislative proposals, and success will require considerable political skills and negotiation. The fact that many policy debates are now within the public's view and are extensively covered in the media affects the style of the decision-making process. Given the presidency's long history of dominance, however, the expectation still exists in many quarters that the president remains a strong figure and that the presidency, not the legislative branch, should continue to initiate the most influential bills. However, after Fox's disappointing performance, citizens have expressed strong criticisms of both branches of government.

THE LEGISLATIVE BRANCH

Mexico's national legislature is bicameral, with a Chamber of Deputies and the Senate. Deputies are elected on the basis of roughly equally populated districts, of which there are three hundred. In 1970 one hundred seats were added for deputies selected from party lists based on the proportion of the votes cast for the parties. The purpose of the increment was to increase the opposition's representation, owing to the overwhelming dominance of the PRI in the regular legislative seats. In the reforms in the 1980s, another hundred seats were added; now three hundred deputies represent districts and two hundred represent parties. These party or plurinominal deputies are elected at large, based on the proportion of votes received in five regions each containing forty seats. A case can be made for the benefits of plurinominal seats, but in Mexico, as one astute observer concludes: "In terms of democracy . . . , proportional representation exacts a heavy cost for minimal benefits. Formulas which ensure minority representation, while bringing opposition to the legislature, are at best distorting and at worst antidemocratic."[22] This system breaks the link between voters and their representatives. Even more surprising, all three parties are using these relatively "safe seats" to elect party leaders to the Chamber, a pattern continued in the 2000–2003 and 2003–2006 legislatures.[23]

The Senate, which has fewer powers than the Chamber of Deputies, has two senators from each state and the Federal District, a total of sixty-four, and in 1994 added sixty-four additional seats, thirty-two to be assigned to the party with the second highest vote count in each state in 1994, and the remaining thirty-two as national proportional representation seats in 1997, for a grand total of 128. Senators are elected for six-year terms, all of which came up for election in 2000. The Chamber of Deputies and the Senate each have numerous committees, some with names like those in the U.S. Congress.

Deputies and senators cannot be reelected to consecutive terms, seniority does not exist, at least regarding committees, for all members are new to a particular legislature. Some critics argue that one means of enhancing legislative powers in Mexico is to allow consecutive reelection, which would permit members to develop stronger ties with their constituencies. Interestingly, many Americans would like to see a limit set on congressional terms. Mexican legislators proposed eliminating the reelection prohibition in 1995. The view that legislators should be allowed to be reelected, even among PRI members, has again gained support in the 2000–2003 legislature. More than two-thirds of both chambers favored such a change, a figure sufficient to amend the constitution, but the reelection prohibition remains in place.

The legislative branch was long controlled by the PRI, whose members accounted for more than 90 percent of the district seats in the Chamber of Deputies and, until 1988, all Senate seats (see Table 7-2). Until 1997, when PRI lost majority control of the lower chamber, the president appointed a congressional leader (equivalent to the majority leader in the U.S. Congress), who headed all the state delegations. Each state's delegation in the Chamber was usually headed by someone who had served before or by a rising star who was given the post for the first time. Many deputies from the PRI complained that decisions were made in an authoritarian fashion by the leadership and that as individuals they played a minor role.[24] Since the PRD and PAN won control of the Chamber of Deputies in 1997, the deputies have elected their own leader. PAN and PRD members now chair and serve on the various committees. Committee chairs play a significant role in the legislative process.[25] The Senate also has a leader, and the senior senators from each state form the internal governing body. The Senate has taken on a more plural character since 1994, when the PAN and PRD obtained thirty-two party seats, 25 percent of the total, a figure they increased in the 2000 elections to sixty-eight seats, or 53 percent.

Table 7-2 Representation in the Legislative Branch, Mexico, 1994–2006

| | Deputies | | | | | | | | | | | | | | Senators | | | | | | | | | | | | | |
| | District Seats | | | | Party Seats | | | | Total | | | | State Seats[b] | | Party Seats | | | Total | | | |
Party[a]	1994	1997	2000	2003	1994	1997	2000	2003	1994	1997	2000	1994	2000	1994	1997[c]	2000	1994	1997	2000	2003
PRI	277	165	131	163	23	74	78	61	300	239	209	64	32	32	13	28	96	77	60	60
PAN	18	64	141	82	101	57	67	71	119	121	208	0	28	24	9	23	24	33	51	46
PRD	5	70	28	55	66	55	23	40	71	125	51	0	4	8	8	13	8	16	17	16
PT	0	1	0	—	10	6	9	—	10	7	9	0	0	0	1	0	0	1	0	0
PVEM		0	0	—		8	15	—		8	15		0		1	0		1	0	5
Others				—			8	28			8		0			0			0	1
Total	300	300	300	300	200	200	200	200	500	500	500	64	64	64	32	64	128	128	128	128

[a]PRI = Institutional Revolutionary Party, PAN = National Action Party, PRD = Democratic Revolutionary Party, PT = Labor Party, PVEM = Green Party.
[b]The state seats were all elected in 1994.
[c]Only 32 seats were allocated in 1997.

Earlier discussion indicated that the legislative branch traditionally had little to say in the decision-making process, unlike the U.S. Congress. The reason for this was that each legislator who was a member of the PRI was beholden to the political leadership, and indirectly the president, for his or her position. If such a legislator wanted to pursue a public career, he or she needed to follow presidential directives. The post-2000 legislators are not controlled by the president, regardless of their party affiliation. Even the members of PRI who were elected to the 2000–2003 legislature were not beholden to President Zedillo or to the losing PRI presidential candidate. None of the three parties obtained a simple majority of seats, thus legislative alliances became a fact of life in passing legislation in the Fox administration.

The role of the legislative branch in the Mexican decision-making process has changed dramatically since late 1997. In the past, congress primarily examined presidential legislative initiatives and made recommendations to the executive branch for alterations. Theoretically it could have rejected a presidential initiative, but most presidential legislation as we have seen was approved, typically overwhelmingly (see Table 7-1).

The dominance of parties in the legislative branch that do not control the executive branch have led to other important changes. The legislators have significantly altered bills proposed by the executive before their approval. Indeed, the legislative branch has either modified or rejected all of Fox's major bills, including his crucial tax reform package. They have created a much more contentious environment for debates, and they have increased attention to bills that originate from within the Chamber. Given their importance, members of the Fox cabinet have sought to court them, using many of the same techniques found in the relationship between the executive and legislative branches in the United States. "Lobbyists who used to focus all their efforts on the president now schmooze with members of Congress."[26] Nearly two-thirds of deputies reported some or a lot of lobbying in the Chamber (see Table 7-3).

The legislative branch also serves to legitimize, rather than just approve executive legislation. One of the potential consequences of the elections since 1988, when opposition parties began obtaining significant representation in the Chamber of Deputies, was that the government lost its ability to amend the constitution; the PRI did not have two-thirds of the seats in the lower chamber, the number necessary to do so. Mexican presidents and the executive branch have used constitutional amendments to give major, controversial legislation an extra measure of legitimacy. The government cannot any longer use this technique without first achieving a coalition.

A change introduced by the Zedillo administration considerably strengthens the opposition's voice in the Chamber of Deputies and signifi-

Table 7-3 Legislator's Attitudes in Mexico

Attitude	Deputies in 2000	Deputies in 2003
Most important task		
Representing constituency	64	72
Public finance	44	38
Most important consideration when voting		
Electorate	57	69
Ideological posture		
Left	11	13
Center-left	39	31
Center	34	28
Center-right	16	20
Right	1	2
Policy positions		
The wealthiest should pay the most taxes	—	81
Abortion should be illegal if a woman's life is not in danger	—	39
Men are better leaders than women	—	89

Source: Alejandro Moreno and Eduardo Fragoso, "La ideología en San Lázaro," *Enfoque* February 8, 2004. Interviews with 187 deputies, +/–6.5 percent margin of error.

cantly increased the importance of the judicial branch. According to the *Diario Oficial,* on December 31, 1994, Article 105 of the constitution was modified to grant the equivalent of 33 percent of the members of the Chamber of Deputies, the Senate, or local state legislators the right, within thirty days of passing a law, to question the constitutionality of such legislation before the supreme court.[27] Given the increased willingness of the Supreme Court to discuss legal issues with significant political implications, parties that are not in control of the executive branch now have an alternative legal recourse to test controversial legislation.

There are two important structural conditions which contribute to the legislative branch's weaker policy-making position compared to Mexico's executive. The first of these, mentioned above, is the continued prohibition on consecutive reelection, which limits the expertise among legislators.[28] In the 1997–2000 session only 16 percent of members of congress had any previous state or national legislative experience, and in the 2000–2003 session, that figure dropped to 15 percent.[29] Although the deputies themselves have raised the issue of eliminating the prohibition on immediate reelection, the Mexican public is definitely opposed to such a reform. In a comprehensive poll in 2005, more than two-thirds of Mexicans were against the immediate reelection of federal deputies and senators, and nearly equal numbers were against the reelection of mayors, governors, and the president. The only structural change in the chamber of deputies the public appears to favor is reducing its size (60 percent favor 100 or 200 deputies instead of 300), suggesting, in part, the low esteem in which the legislative branch is held.[30] The importance of legislative staff is becoming a hallmark of the new, democratic era, even at the state level. Staff sizes are likely to increase significantly among all parties in the congress, and a staff culture in legislative bodies will become the norm, as in the case of similar institutions in the United States. The second condition is the limited budget devoted to congressional staff. The Chamber has approximately sixty researchers for five hundred legislators, and like their employers, many leave at the end of three years. By contrast, the executive branch has several thousand full-time permanent staff. Since 1999, when congress passed a new law for the legislative branch, the research and analysis services have expanded substantially, and they have begun to provide committees with research reports.[31]

The legislative branch is also a training ground for future political leaders and an important source of political patronage. It has been used in the past to reward people prominent in quasi-governmental interest groups and among the labor, peasant, and popular, professional sectors.[32] Among some opposition parties, such as the PRD, and now the PRI, it remains the only national venue for their leaders. Professional people predominate among the legislators, but peasant and labor leaders, as well as women, who might not obtain higher political office in the executive branch, are well represented. In fact, more women now serve in Mexico's congress than in the U.S. Congress, 23 percent of members in the 2003–2006 legislature. It now ranks 23rd in the world, along with Switzerland.[33] In the Senate, women hold 18 percent of the seats. Even more important, the legislative branch provides upward mobility to a different type of politician: those who are more likely to have come from a working-class background, from the provinces (because of the district representation), from electoral careers, and with less formal education (see Table 7-4). In short, greater percentages of persons who are excluded from executive branch careers, even at the departmental level, can find places in the legislative branch. The fact that some channels are open to these kinds of Mexicans, who in many background characteristics correspond more closely to the population in general, is important to social mobility and leadership fluidity. This recruitment function is more significant since 2000 because holding a national, legislative post is increasingly significant in the policy process.

The legislative branch also is a school for political skills. Among national government institutions, some opposition leaders and parties are represented only in the legislative branch. Negotiating skills will be more and more valued in the decision-making process as legislative seats remain divided among various parties. Most officials in the executive branch have little or no experience in such skills; hence persons whose careers have

Table 7-4 Legislators and Executive-Branch Officials, 1994

Background Variable	Legislators (%)	Executive Branch Officials (%)
Gender		
Female	8	7
Education		
Preparatory or less	20	1
Career Experience		
Political parties	85	43
Unions	59	16
Elective posts	57	10
Parents' Occupation		
Peasant	5	1
Laborer	3	1
Birthplace		
Federal District	16	55

Source: Diccionario biográfico del gobierno mexicano (Mexico: Presidencia de la República, 1994); based on 1,100 officials and 549 legislators.

brought them through the legislative bodies are likely to be in greater demand in the future.

THE JUDICIAL BRANCH

A major principle in the U.S. government structure is the balance of power. The founding fathers were concerned that the executive branch might take on dictatorial aspects and hence sought to apportion power among the executive, legislative, and judicial branches in such fashion that none would dominate. Mexico's judicial branch, while sharing some structural similarities to its counterpart in the United States, plays a significantly different role in governance. The Constitution of 1917 assigns the Supreme Court power over the judicial structure, which consists of the Supreme Court, circuit courts, and district courts.

The Supreme Court, according to Article 94, consists of twenty-one justices. When it meets, its hearings are open to the public, except in special cases. Justices are appointed by the president of Mexico with the approval of the Senate. Circuit court judges and district court judges are appointed by the Supreme Court to a four-year term, after which they may be reappointed. Each justice is responsible for a certain number of circuit and district courts, and inspects them periodically, to assure they are performing their duties as prescribed by law.

A judicial branch influences the decision-making process when it is independent of legislative and executive authority and when it can legislate through judicial rulings. The U.S. Supreme Court can declare a law unconstitutional, after which Congress can devise other legislation to achieve its goal if it so wishes. U.S. courts hand down rulings that bear on future cases and also on legislation regarding the issues involved. Mexico's legal system is less adversarial than that of the United States, and was designed to supplement a system of administrative laws and procedures, thus channeling legal conflicts into this domain rather than the judicial system. The federal court system considers legal disputes that arise out of actions or laws by government authorities that violate individual guarantees spelled out in the Constitution; actions or laws by federal authorities that encroach on the sovereignty of states; and actions or laws by states that invade federal authority. Legislating through judicial precedent has not been a viable procedure in Mexico. For the Supreme Court to establish a binding precedent, it was required repeatedly to reach identical conclusions about precisely the same issue. In other words, the decision would only affect the appealing party, not any other citizen. The high bench typically has ruled on appeals of individual persons, not on matters of constitutionality, and they have not ventured into political issues.

The remaining serious limitation of the judicial system is that the lower levels are tainted by corruption and outside political manipulation. An absence of consistency and integrity makes it difficult, if not impossible, for the average citizen to resort to the system to protect his or her rights. The criminal justice subsystem has incorporated the use of torture in obtaining confessions. These circumstances combine to create a lack of respect for the law, a crucial element in a viable legal system and democracy.

In spite of these limitations, and the fact that prior to 1994, the executive branch controlled appointees to the supreme court given the fact that it also controlled the legislative branch and could amend the constitution to thwart a constitutional ruling, the Supreme Court often ruled against the government, especially in matters dealing with administrative procedures related to expropriations and taxes. In politically charged issues, on the other hand, the court rarely ruled against the government.

The court began to take on a more influential role in the governing process after 1994, when a series of judicial reforms were introduced. The first of these reforms, passed with the support of PAN, altered the control that the president exercised over Supreme Court appointees, requiring that he obtain a two-thirds majority in the Senate and that appointees could not hold influential political office in the year immediately prior to their nomination. Even more important, the law introduced a new form of judicial review, the "action of unconstitutionality," which allowed the court to declare laws or administrative acts unconstitutional. If a required number of justices support the decision, it becomes the law for all citizens. Only specified government officials and legislators may initiate this type of case.[34]

Symbolically, the court's independent and activist role began to receive attention from the public when it "stunned Mexicans by ruling against Zedillo in a dispute with Congress [similarly increasing the autonomy of the legislative branch]. The court ordered Zedillo's administration to release records from Banco Unión, which was part of a massive government bailout of failed banks in 1995."[35] Under Fox, the court blocked the president's attempt to make minor changes to the rules on private electricity generation.

The data presented in Table 7-5 support the conclusions of recent scholars that the Supreme Court indeed has become an effective political force in Mexico. This new role is indicated dramatically in the increase of constitutional cases, using the actions of unconstitutionality law, since Fox became president. Furthermore, the rulings themselves show a dramatic increase in favor of the plaintiff versus the government, from only 2 percent from 1995 to 1997 to 9 percent from 1997 to 2000 to 25 percent from 2000 to 2003.[36]

Presidents Zedillo and Fox, recognizing the lack of respect for the legal system, have attempted to make the culture of law a crucial element in their presidencies. President Fox made the institutionalization of the legal system a hallmark of his first months in office by refusing to settle a dispute in a state electoral body, instead referring it to the Supreme Court, which ruled in favor of the Federal Electoral Institute. Furthermore, he has openly praised the high court, assuring Mexicans that it has not received a political line from any source.[37] Fox also proposed additional reforms to the justice system in 2004, including making legal proceedings public, introducing plea bargaining, and making the attorney general's office a strictly investigative agency.[38] It is apparent that the court has taken a more activist role, and it has further strengthened the circuit courts, giving them complete

Table 7-5 Recent Decisions by Mexico's Supreme Court

Important Cases	1994–1997	1997–2000	2000–2003
Constitutional controversies	3	2	23
Actions of unconstitutionality	9	13	21
Totals	12	15	44

Source: Julio Ríos-Figueroa, "A Minimum Condition for the Judiciary to Become an Effective Power, the Mexican Supreme Court, 1994–2002," paper presented at the Midwest Political Science Association meeting, Chicago, Illinois, April 15–18, 2004.

autonomy to decide the constitutionality of local laws.[39] Despite these significant changes, the judicial system faces an uphill battle against a criminal justice system and police agencies riddled with corruption.[40]

FEDERALISM

Technically, Mexico's 1917 Constitution established a federal system, which allocated certain rights to states and municipalities. After all, municipal autonomy from federal control was an important issue raised by northern revolutionaries. The basic structure of municipal and state governments is established in Article 115 of the Constitution. Each municipality is governed by a municipal president and a council chosen by direct popular election. Municipalities are autonomous in the administration of their finances, but the taxes they collect are decided upon by the state legislatures, not the municipality itself. Similarly, governors and state legislatures are chosen by direct popular election. The same prohibition against reelection applies to governors (who are elected for a six-year term) and municipal presidents (who are elected for a three-year term) as applied to national elective offices. State legislators may be reelected, but not consecutively.

Historically, however, the federal executive branch, similar to its control over the other national branches of government, exercised highly centralized control over the states and municipalities. Prior to 1994, it accomplished this control in several ways. First, in terms of state political leadership, the president typically chose or influenced the choice of state governors. It is important to recall that no governor from an opposition party won office from 1929 to 1989, thus giving PRI a monopoly over state governments. The governor of each state exercised control over the legislative and judicial systems analogous to presidential control over the federal branches of government. Moreover, the relationship between municipal leadership and the state executive branch was equally analogous to the relationship between the federal executive and state leadership.

Fiscal policy was an equally important variable in determining the subordinate relationship among local, state, and federal authorities. According to students of intergovernmental fiscal relations, a decision reached at the 1947 national tax convention became the driving force behind the loss of local autonomy. That meeting "proposed that local governments be given exclusive authority to the federal government in exchange for a guaranteed share of federal tax revenues. In later years, the federal government further concentrated financial authority in its hands," culminating in the creation of a National Tax Coordination System, which guaranteed states a share of the federal value added tax provided they relinquished authority over additional state-level taxes.[41] Although the constitution did not force state politicians to accept this offer, given PRI's monopoly over successful state and national political careers, few were willing to risk such a loss in revenues. Essentially, given the extensive control the federal government had over the allocation of tax revenues, it basically could determine the funding for most government initiated projects at the state and local levels, accounting for 85 percent or more of the public revenues. Since the 1920s, the federal government has often allocated a disproportionate share of income to the wealthier states, thus reinforcing their economic position, while simultaneously depriving poorer states adequate funding. Beginning in the 1990s, this pattern changed, and poorer states began receiving larger shares of federal funds.

The fundamental issue in decentralizing decision-making from the federal to the state and local level since PRI's monopoly was broken is the distribution of fiscal resources. Shortly before the end of the Zedillo administration, the governors collectively, in collaboration with the legislative leaders from PAN, PRD, PT, and PVEM, asked the federal executive branch to set aside more monies for the states. Public sentiment also favors the federal government allocating more of its revenues to the states to decide how those monies should be spent. The federal executive's position is enhanced in the overall process because revenues are collected by the executive branch and then reallocated back to the states. Under multiple party control since 1997, congress has changed these figures twice, reducing the federal portion to 75 percent. By 2004, the federal government was transferring 31 percent of the national budget directly to the states. Municipalities depend on the federal government for two-thirds of their total funds.[42] In 2002, a group of twenty-two governors from PRI and PRD formed a National Conference of Governors (CONAGO) to lobby the executive branch and congress for more funds and to continue increasing the percentage of transfers. This organization now includes governors from all three parties and has become a significant voice in federal-state relations.

Increased control over a larger share of revenues provides an incentive for individuals, institutions, and groups to seek help from state and local governments and to influence the outcome of state legislation beneficial to their interests. Since Fox won the presidency, however, states and municipalities increasingly have exerted an influence on national policy, especially fiscal policy. By 2005, state governorships were roughly divided between those controlled by PAN and PRD and those controlled by PRI. The majority of governorships were controlled by parties other than PAN, setting the stage for policy conflicts between states and the federal government. The

Table 7-6 Attendance at Municipal Council Meetings

Country	Percentage Who Attend
Panama	6
Costa Rica	7
El Salvador	13
Mexico	**13**
Honduras	15
Nicaragua	16
Guatemala	17

Source: Jorge Buendía, Alejandro Moreno, and Mitchell A. Seligson, *La cultura política de la democracia en México, 2004* (Nashville: Vanderbilt University, Public Opinión Project of Latin America, 2004).

distribution of party control in state legislatures in 2005 were 42 percent PRI, 28 percent PAN, and 20 percent PRD, with other parties capturing 1 percent of the seats and plurinominal deputies the remaining 9 percent.

Citizen attitudes toward state and local governments suggest some interesting patterns. In the first place, ordinary Mexicans know even less about their local than their national political institutions. For example, in 2005 only half of all Mexicans were sure that state legislatures actually existed. Since an equal number were aware that it was the responsibility of the national congress to make laws, it is unlikely that few would know the role of the state legislatures. Indeed, the principles of the separation of powers and federalism are not well understood by the average citizen since one-third believed the state legislature was dependent on the national congress, and only a fourth knew definitively that it was independent of the national congress. Moreover, only 38 percent believed that congress was independent of the president, and 36 percent believed the state legislature was independent of the governor. Interestingly, Mexicans have slightly more confidence in their state legislatures than the national congress (30 to 24 percent), although their overall confidence in both is low, as is the case of most political institutions. What is most important, however, is that nearly twice as many Mexicans believed their state legislator is more concerned with problems in their state than their federal representative (27 versus 15 percent), suggesting the greater potential for taking their problems to their state rather than to their national representative.[43] At the local level, Mexicans, similar to other Latin Americans, do attend municipal council meetings. As the data in Table 7-6 show, Mexican attendance is average compared to Central American countries. But as the authors of the survey note, 13 percent of Mexicans over the age of eighteen account for eight to nine million active citizens.

The revival of Mexican federalism, accompanied by the process of political decentralization, while undoubtedly enhancing the decision-making influence of new institutions, faces some serious problems, captured in a critique by Alberto Díaz Cayeros:

> .... The centralization of revenue collection and the large dependence of subnational governments on federal transfers, is something that happened because local political actors were willing to abdicate on their tax authority, while in the last years they pressed the federal government for greater resources. The system of revenue sharing was constructed from the regions up, in the sense that state and municipal tax authority was gradually eroded, and federal transfers substituted their own revenue. The recent trend towards decentralization through federal transfers has been constructed more from the federation down, in the sense that it has been a very fast divesting of responsibilities in expenditure that have led to greater local responsibility. However, there is a very strong mismatch between the character of this system and the evolution of the political forces in the states and municipalities.[44]

As states strengthen their autonomy from the federal government, governors and mayors will play a more influential role in the political process. Recent case studies demonstrate that, in spite of the fiscal limitations, these actors are undergoing significant transformation, as various groups present their demands to a new tier of decision-makers.[45] It is also apparent that policies originating at the state or local level are beginning to be transferred to, and have an impact on, the national policy agenda.[46]

CONCLUSION

Decision-making in Mexico is still dominated by the executive branch, centralized in the person of the president. As economic problems have overshadowed all other issues, the influence of the economic cabinet has expanded. President Fox's electoral victory has contributed to a decentralizing pattern in decision-making begun by his predecessor. The actor with the most rapidly expanding role in policy making is the national legislature. Since 1997, its influence has been apparent, whether it initiates, alters, or approves legislation. The expanding role of the legislative branch contributes to a changing role in group-state relations. As the analysis of interest groups in the preceding chapter suggests, leaders have sought out individual decision-makers in the executive branch, but since 2000, they are increasingly likely to make their demands on legislative leaders and committee chairs.

Mexico is rebuilding its political institutions structurally and symbolically. Many of these institutions retain vestiges from the past. For example, now that the electoral process is competitive, the rationale for having 200 plurinominal deputies remains questionable. The parties, as one observer concluded, are using these positions as an internal "family affair" to place party loyalists in legislative posts.[47] Two-fifths of the lower chamber are not accountable to any specific constituency. By 1998, Mexicans had accepted the belief that congress should be stronger than the presidency, a concept totally foreign to their experience and in spite of the fact that nearly half of all Mexicans believe they were badly represented by their congressperson.[48] Initially, when the new legislature was sworn in during September 2000, 57 percent of Mexicans thought it would perform better than its predecessor. By 2004, approval ratings of congress were averaging 23 percent, compared to 49 percent for the President Fox.[49]

The dramatic rise of the role of the legislative branch, while fulfilling the expectations of democratic theory, has created numerous political difficulties for Mexico's consolidating democracy and for the policy process. In the first congressional session (2000–2003), a stalemate emerged between the president and the Chamber of Deputies over significant policy issues, complicated by the president's difficult relations with his own party. The PRI faction in congress issued a statement spelling out mechanisms for improving political negotiations and achieving policy consensus between the two branches of government. Among them they included new channels for direct exchanges between the legislative and executive branches, direct dialogue between state governors and the executive branch so that state officials could present their policy preferences to the federal government, and a requirement that executive branch priorities be fully transparent to the public.[50] Although the electorate assigned blame for the policy failures to both branches, they punished the incumbent PAN party in the 2003 congressional elections, reducing its representation in the Chamber of Deputies by fifty-one seats. Fox frankly admitted these failures in his State of the Union address, calling on all actors to "accept negotiation as an essential political practice and not as an act of weakness."[51] Unfortunately, instead of pursuing a strategy of cooperation, executive-legislative relations continued to be embroiled in controversy, repeating the pre-2003 pattern. Most notably, the Chamber of Deputies reallocated 7.8 billion of the government's proposed 158 billion budget, bringing their relationship with the president to "a new level of acrimony" and sending the message to the president that he is not in charge. Fox complained that the authoritarian presidency was in danger of being "replaced with an inflexible Congress."[52] The executive branch decided to appeal what they viewed as a legislative abuse of power to the

Supreme Court, essentially asking the court to establish the two branches respective roles in the budget-making process.[53]

Groups or individuals desirous of influencing the decision-making process have an increasing number of avenues to use to affect institutions that determine actual policy outcomes. They may continue using informal forms of access more than formal, open channels, regardless of their greater opportunities. An expanded legislative and judicial role in decision-making also increases the potential of groups, less influential in the past, such as NGOs, to enhance their impact on the policy-making process. However, it is not likely in the foreseeable future for individual voters to channel their demands through the legislative branch. Two out of five Mexicans cannot name any branch of government, only one in three knows the senate is part of the legislative branch, only 15 percent know their deputy, three-quarters could not name a single member of congress, and 92 percent could not name a senator. The most well known member of the chamber of deputies and the senate were named by 2 and 7 percent of respondents, respectively.[54] State governors have also increased their influence on national policy, adding to the expanding list of political actors. Indeed, by 2004, state governors were receiving higher approval ratings than the president, and six out of ten Mexicans gave them favorable ratings, reinforcing their ability to exercise a greater voice in Mexican democracy.[55]

NOTES

1. For an analysis of how this sector has functioned, see the case study by William P. Glade, "Entrepreneurship in the State Sector: Conasupo of Mexico," in *Entrepreneurship in Cultural Context,* ed. Sidney Greenfield et al. (Albuquerque: University of New Mexico Press, 1979), 191–222.

2. For background, see George Grayson, *The Politics of Mexican Oil* (Pittsburgh: University of Pittsburgh Press, 1980); Edward J. Williams, *The Rebirth of the Mexican Petroleum Industry* (Lexington, Mass.: Heath, 1979).

3. Judith A. Teichman, *Privatization and Political Change in Mexico* (Pittsburgh: University of Pittsburgh Press, 1995), 159.

4. According to a *Reforma* poll, 71 percent of residents in the spring of 2001 thought public security was the number one issue in the capital, a fifth had been a victim of crime in the last three months, and over half thought it was useless to file a complaint with the police. A survey of 855 residents, April 21–22, 2001, +/–3.5 percent margin of error. May 9, 2001.

5. Miguel Alemán, 1946–1952; Adolfo Ruiz Cortines, 1952–1958; Gustavo Díaz Ordaz, 1964–1970; and Luis Echeverría, 1970–1976, are presidents indicative

of this changing institutional influence and the rise of civilian leadership; they came from the Secretariat of Government.

6. See the introduction by Antonio Carrillo Flores in Eduardo Suárez, *Comentarios y recuerdos, 1926–1946* (Mexico City: Porrúa, 1977).

7. For background on the rise of the Secretariat of Programming and Budgeting, see John J. Bailey's excellent "Presidency, Bureaucracy, and Administrative Reform in Mexico: The Secretariat of Programming and Budgeting," *Inter-American Economic Affairs* 34 (Summer 1980): 27–59.

8. Miguel Angel Centeno and Sylvia Maxfield, "The Marriage of Finance and Order: Changes in the Mexican Political Elite," *Journal of Latin American Studies* 24 (February 1992): 84.

9. Francisco Gil Díaz was part of the original group of economists in the presidency in the early 1970s. He was the teacher of Pedro Aspe, the architect of economic neoliberalism under President Salinas, and was responsible for obtaining a position for Zedillo early in his career. *Proceso* (January 13, 1992), 13.

10. Julie A. Erfani, *The Paradox of the Mexican State: Rereading Sovereignty from Independence to NAFTA* (Boulder, Colo.: Lynne Rienner, 1995), 127ff.

11. Eduardo Torres Espinosa, *Bureaucracy and Politics in Mexico: The Case of the Secretariat of Programming and Budget* (Aldershot: Ashgate, 1999), 227.

12. Daniel Levy and Gabriel Székely, *Mexico: Paradoxes of Stability and Change,* 2d ed. (Boulder, Colo.: Westview Press, 1987), 49–50.

13. For case studies in education, hydraulic resources, and agricultural policy, see Guy Benveniste, *Bureaucracy and National Planning: A Sociological Case Study in Mexico* (New York: Praeger, 1970); Martin H. Greenberg, *Bureaucracy and Development: A Mexican Case Study* (Lexington, Mass.: Heath, 1970); Merilee S. Grindle, *Bureaucrats, Politicians, and Peasants in Mexico: A Case Study in Public Policy* (Berkeley and Los Angeles: University of California Press, 1977). A new examination of oil policy formulation concluded that "conflict, lobbying, and coalition building between patron-client pyramids, or bargaining" were typical. See María de la Luz Valverde, "A Heuristic Model of Mexican Public Policymaking," paper presented at the Latin American Studies Association, Los Angeles, 1992, 19.

14. For a complete description of these coordinators, and the administrative lines of communication, see *Review of the Economic Situation of Mexico,* (December 2000), 499.

15. Carlos Tello, *La nacionalización de la banca en México* (Mexico City: Siglo XXI, 1984).

16. Roderic Ai Camp, *Entrepreneurs and the State in Twentieth Century Mexico* (New York: Oxford University Press, 1989), 128–33.

17. Diane E. Davis, *Urban Leviathan, Mexico City in the Twentieth Century* (Philadelphia: Temple University Press, 1994), 316.

18. Alonso Lujambio, "Adiós a la excepcionalidad, régimen presidencial y gobierno dividido en México," *Este País* (February 2000), 9.

19. "The Legislative Balance: Agenda for the 59th," *Review of the Economic Situation of Mexico,* October 2003, 340–43; and Jeffrey A. Weldon, "The Fall 2003

Term of the Mexican Congress," Mexican Congressional Report Series (Washington, D.C.: CSIS, 2004), 23.

20. Caroline Beer, *Electoral Competition and Institutional Change in Mexico*, (Notre Dame: University of Notre Dame Press, 2003).

21. Jeffrey Weldon, "The Political Sources of *Presidencialismo* in Mexico," in *Presidentialism and Democracy in Latin America*, ed. Scott Mainwaring and Matthew Shugart (Cambridge: Cambridge University Press, 1997), 225–58.

22. For excellent background on the legislative structure, see Michael C. Taylor, "Constitutional Crisis: How Reforms to the Legislature Have Doomed Mexico," *Mexican Studies* 13 (Summer 1997): 319.

23. "Tres secretarios de Estado, aspiran a senadores 29 ex gobernadores del PRI," *Diario de Yucatán*, March 11, 2000, www.yucatan.com.mx.

24. The best analysis to date is Alonso Lujambio's excellent *Federalismo y congreso en el cambio político de México* (Mexico: UNAM, 1995); and Luis Carlos Ugalde, *The Mexican Congress: Old Player, New Power* (Washington, D.C.: CSIS, 2000).

25. See the excellent essay by Jeffrey A. Weldon, "Committee Power in the Mexican Chamber of Deputies," Paper presented at the National Latin American Studies Association, Chicago, September 1998.

26. Kevin Sullivan, "Gentrifying Mexico's 'Bronx,' With Power Shifting, Backbenchers Mind Their Manners," *Washington Post*, April 27, 2001, A18; "Encuesta a legisladores," *Reforma*, December 16, 2001. A survey of 130 deputies and 49 senators, October 21 to December 5, 2001.

27. *Diario Oficial*, December 31, 1994, 2–6.

28. For a discussion of this issue, see my "Mexico's Legislature: Missing the Democratic Lockstep," in *Legislatures and the New Democracies in Latin America*, ed. David Close (Boulder: Lynne Rienner, 1995), 17–36.

29. Rosa María Mirón Lince, "El PRI post-hegemónico: liderazgos y decisiones en el Congreso," paper presented at the Latin American Studies Association, Las Vegas, Nevada, October 7–9, 2004, 19.

30. "Encuesta Nacional: Reforma del Congreso," Bimsa, April 1–5, 2005, 1000 interviews, +/–3.5 percent margin of error.

31. Dulce María Liahut Baldomar, "The Role of the Research Services in the Modernization of the Mexican Congress," paper presented at the 66th IFLA Council and General Conference, Jerusalem, Israel, August 13–18, 2000.

32. See Peter H. Smith, *Labyrinths of Power: Political Recruitment in Twentieth-Century Mexico* (Princeton, N.J.: Princeton University Press, 1979), 217ff.

33. As Lisa Baldez has demonstrated, the application of quota laws, while imperfect, produced a dramatic change in the percentage of women holding seats in the Chamber of Deputies, up from only 16 percent in the previous legislature. Since future national figures in the executive branch and state governorships are more likely to come from elective positions, this change improves women's opportunities politically. See her excellent "Elected Bodies: The Gender Quota Law for Legislative Candidates in Mexico," *Legislative Studies Quarterly* 29, no. 2 (May 2004), 251.

Of the 228 female candidates, 48, or 21 percent, were elected. By party, the success rate was PRI, 33 percent; PAN, 21 percent; and PRD, 14 percent. At the state legislative level, in 2003, women held 14 percent of the 1064 seats nationally.

34. An excellent discussion of these changes can be found in Fabrice Lehoucq et al., "Political Institutions, Policymaking Processes, and Policy Outcomes in Mexico," (Mexico: CIDE, 2005), 44ff.

35. Kevin Sullivan and Mary Jordan, "Mexican Supreme Court Refuses to Take Back Seat," *Washington Post*, September 10, 2000, A31.

36. For detailed analyses of the court's growing independence, see Pilar Domingo, "Judicial Independence: The Politics of the Supreme Court of Mexico," *Journal of Latin American Studies* 32 (2000), 705–35; Jodi Finkel, "Supreme Court Decisions on Electoral Rules After Mexico's Judicial Reform: An Empowered Court," *Journal of Latin American Studies* 35 (2003), 777–99.

37. "El Tribunal, última instancia ante los excesos del poder público," *Diario de Yucatán*, April 19, 2001.

38. Chris Kraul, "Fox Tries to Balance Scales of Mexican Justice," *Los Angeles Times*, March 30, 2004, A3.

39. "Inconstitucionalidad de leyes," *Diario de Yucatán*, September 18, 2000.

40. George Grayson argues that the case of an angry mob in Mexico City beating, lynching, and burning to death two Mexican federal agents is an example of the disdain of poorer Mexicans toward law enforcement, a view confirmed in surveys year after year. Such perceptions affect overall reactions to the judicial process. "Running After a Fallen Fox," *Harvard International Review* (Spring 2005), 22.

41. Fabrice Lehoucq, "Political Institutes, Policymaking Processes, and Policy Outcomes in Mexico," 47.

42. Carlos Rosales, "Mexican Federalism and Municipal Finance: Bases for Interpretation," *Review of the Economic Situation of Mexico*, April 2003, 156–61.

43. "Percepión del Congreso de la Unión y los Congresos Estatales," www.Parametria.com.mx, 960 respondents, +/–3.2 percent, November 2004.

44. Alberto Díaz-Cayeros, "Decentralization, Democratization, and Federalism in Mexico," in *Dilemmas of Change in Mexican Politics*, ed. Kevin Middlebrook (London: Institute of Latin American Studies, University of London, 2004), 198–236.

45. For several excellent case studies, see Peter M. Ward and Victoria E. Rodríguez, "New Federalism, Intra-governmental Relations and Co-governance in Mexico," *Journal of Latin American Studies,* 31 (1999), 673–710; and Peter M. Ward and Elizabeth Durden, "Government and Democracy in Mexico's Federal District: Cárdenas, the PRD, and the Curate's Egg," *Bulletin of Latin American Research* 21, no. 1 (2002), 1–39.

46. Caroline Beer, *Electoral Competition and Institutional Change in Mexico*, 192, notes that Guanajuato became the first state in Mexico to publish public accounts on the Internet, a policy that Fox has transferred to the national financial system.

47. Luis Carlos Ugalde, "El Congreso mexicano, una mirada a la última década," *Este País,* (April 2001), 102.

48 "Democracy Through Latin American Lenses," Grant, Hewlett Foundation, principal investigator, Roderic Ai Camp, June 1998.

49. "Evaluación de autoridades: ejecutivo y legislativo," Carta Paramétria, July 2, 2004, www.parametria.com.mx.

50. "La oposición exige al President que ponga las bases para lograr acuerdos," *Diario de Yucatán*, March 9, 2002, www.yucatan.com.mx.

51. Richard Boudreaux, "Mexico Demands Better,' Fox Says in Midterm Speech," *Los Angeles Times*, September 2, 2003; Kevin Sullivan, "Fox Offers Frank View of Mexico's Problems," *Washington Post*, September 2, 2003, A16.

52. Richard Boudreaux, "Fox Loses Mexico Budget Battle," *Los Angeles Times*, November 21, 2004, A19; Nydia Iglesias, "The Political Scene," *Review of the Economic Situation of Mexico*, December 2004.

53. Nydia Iglesias, "The Political Environment," *Review of the Economic Situation of Mexico*, February 2005, 72–75.

54. "El poder legislativo en México," Consulta Mitofsky, April 2005. 1000 interviews from 100 legislative districts, April 23–27, 2005, +/–3.5 percent margin of error.

55. "Encuesta: aprobación presidencial y de los gobernadores," Ipsos Bimsa, November 9, 2004.

8

Expanding Participation: The Electoral Process

> The victory of the PAN at the Presidential level is a watershed in Mexico's political history. On one level, it marks the conclusion of a prolonged transition to democracy. The election of Vicente Fox is in effect the last brick in the centripetal path to democracy, one started at the local level and gradually moved toward the center. By accepting its defeat, the PRI acknowledged that fair elections are now the only legitimate means of gaining access to power. Although this seems obvious and simple, it is quite a substantial accomplishment if one considers that only a few years ago there was not a general and accepted consensus in the country on this matter. Today, electoral democracy and the institutions that support it are fully consolidated.
>
> YEMILLE MIZRAHI, "From Martyrdom to Power"

A little over a decade ago, most political analysis would have given little space to elections and electoral politics in Mexico. Elections have been a feature of the political landscape since the time of Porfirio Díaz, but with the exception of Francisco Madero's election in 1911, they never functioned as the crucial determinant of political leadership or furnished a policy mandate.

Beginning in the mid-1970s, elections took on a new dimension. At first, the uncharacteristic emphasis could be tied to the desire of some establishment figures to strengthen the PRI's image and that of the political system by promoting the opposition's fortunes. In other words, the government itself, through a series of electoral reforms, tried to stimulate the opposition. It provided opposition parties with an incentive to challenge the PRI's dominance by increasing their potential rewards but without extending the possibility of real victory. The single-party dominance of the system and election results was brought home when the National Action Party (PAN), frustrated by the futility of opposition, as well as differences among party leadership as to its

202

electoral role, refused to nominate a candidate to run against José López Portillo in the 1976 presidential race.

ELECTORAL REFORMS

Some government strategists believed it was smart politics to increase opposition representation in the Chamber of Deputies through implementation of a plurinominal deputy system (deputies selected on the basis of their party's total regional vote); others were committed to actual reforms. The latter, who hoped to democratize the elections, believed that genuine competition would strengthen the political model and increase participation, a change for which they believed Mexicans were ready. One of the architects of these earlier reforms, Secretary of Government Jesús Reyes Heroles, introduced enabling legislation in 1977 under President José López Portillo (1976–1982).[1]

The 1977 reforms, incorporated into the Federal Law of Political Organizations and Electoral Processes (LOPPE), altered several constitutional provisions. The law increased majority districts for federal deputies (similar to United States congressional districts) from approximately two hundred to exactly three hundred seats. It also specified that an additional one hundred seats be assigned to opposition parties in the Chamber of Deputies through a complex mathematical formula that allocated seats proportional to each party's national vote totals. Under the party-deputy arrangement in effect from the 1964 through the 1976 national elections, opposition parties were

---

Majority districts: legislative districts of roughly equal populations whose congressional representative wins the largest number of votes cast within the district.

---

allocated thirty to forty seats, also on the basis of each party's national vote totals. From the mid-1960s to the mid-1970s the opposition, combining party and majority deputies, averaged about 17 percent of the seats in the lower house but none in the Senate. The 1977 law, however, set aside *all* one hundred seats for this purpose, requiring them to be divided proportionately among the opposition parties. In effect, this meant that opposition parties, after the LOPPE went into effect, garnered approximately 26 percent of the seats in the lower house and were guaranteed a minimum of one-quarter of all the seats.

The 1977 reforms, while giving some encouragement to opposition parties, providing them with more seats in the Chamber of Deputies and allowing them greater access to the media during campaigns, lost their impetus after 1979, when Reyes Heroles left his post. Both the reforms in the early 1960s, which first introduced the party deputy system, and the 1977 electoral

---

Proportional representation: a system for allocating legislative seats to parties on the basis of the national or regional vote cast for all of the party's legislative candidates.

---

law, which created the plurinominal deputy system, stabilized opposition gains at a given level during the life of the legislation. In other words, opposition representation within the two periods (1964–1976 and 1979–1985) remained stable at approximately 17 and 26 percent respectively, suggesting—at least on the basis of official tabulations—that the opposition parties experienced little growth.

When President de la Madrid took office in 1982, he seemed to indicate a new posture toward the opposition. Specifically, his administration initially tolerated intense electoral competition at the local level. Wayne Cornelius argued:

> Even more significantly, de la Madrid established a new policy regarding municipal elections: henceforth, municipal-level victories by opposition party candidates would be recognized, wherever they occurred. During the first ten months of his administration, the PRI conceded defeat in municipal elections held in seven major cities, including five state capitals and Ciudad Juárez, a large city on the U.S.–Mexican border. Virtually no electoral fraud was reported in these key municipal contests of 1983. As one high-ranking PAN official recalled, "It was like Switzerland up there. There was no interference in the voting, and the ballot count was absolutely clean."[2]

In 1986 de la Madrid introduced his own electoral law, which had significant consequences in the 1988 presidential elections, the first to test it. The 1986 electoral code included the following provisions:

1. The winning or majority party is never to obtain more than 70 percent of the seats in the lower chamber.
2. Three hundred deputies are to be elected by a relative majority based on individual congressional districts (similar to the United States).
3. The seats allotted to deputies on the basis of a proportional percentage of their total national vote are to be increased from 100 to 200, increasing the total number of seats from 400 to 500 (300 by district and 200 by proportional representation).

4. Opposition parties may obtain 40 percent of the seats without winning a single majority district (200 of the 500 seats).

5. The party winning the greatest number of majority seats is to retain a simple majority in the entire chamber; that is, the party is to be allotted seats through the proportional representation system sufficient to obtain an absolute majority in the lower house.

6. Half the Senate is to be renewed triennially instead of the entire chamber every six years (the first change in senatorial elections since 1934).[3]

Compared with the two earlier laws, these reforms reduce the proportion of the majority party (then the PRI) in the Chamber of Deputies, which ranged from 83 percent to 74 percent, to 70 percent or less. The 1986 law also reduced the overall importance of majority districts, which were generally won by the PRI (usually 95 percent or more, see Table 8-1). Again, the law increased the opposition's presence in the Chamber of Deputies, but it was an increase *allocated by the government,* rather than an increase that the government permitted the opposition to earn.

It can be argued that economic and political conditions did more to boost opposition fortunes and to give elections greater political importance in Mexico than did internal reforms during this interim. As the economic crisis worsened in the early 1980s, the opposition on the state and local levels thrived. Opposition-party candidates were winning local-level executive positions and seats on municipal councils. The PAN in particular was placing its members in important city posts in state capitals.

The declining legitimacy of the presidency, in combination with the declining legitimacy of the government itself, began to take a toll by the 1985 and 1986 elections. Although some of the smaller leftist parties were beneficiaries of these trends, the party capturing the greatest number of local seats was the PAN. The PRI worked hard to recoup the losses, in some cases by using such techniques as missing ballot boxes, duplication of registered voters, counting votes of citizens who had not voted, last-minute disqualifications of opposition poll watchers, and last-minute changes in the location of polling booths.[4]

The imposition of PRI victories on the subnational level reached a high point with the gubernatorial and local elections in the state of Chihuahua, a next-door neighbor of Texas. Ciudad Juárez, one of Mexico's largest cities, lies on the border and is traditionally a PAN stronghold. The PRI claimed victories in the state capital and in Ciudad Juárez, as well as in the state gubernatorial race.[5] The scope of fraud was so great and citizen resistance so palpable that prominent intellectuals and Catholic bishops denounced the results in a full-page ad in Mexico's leading daily, *Excélsior,* and called for the election to be annulled. As mentioned earlier, northern bishops

Table 8-1 Seats in the Chamber of Deputies by Party, 1949–2006

Year	PRI	PAN	PPS	PARM	PDM	PSUM	PST[f]	PRT	PMT	PRD	PT	PVEM	Totals
1949 Districts	142	4	1	—	—	—	—	—	—	—	—	—	147
1952[b] Districts	152	5	2	—	—	—	—	—	—	—	—	—	159
1955 Districts	155	6	1	—	—	—	—	—	—	—	—	—	162
1958[b] Districts	153	6	1	1	—.	—	—	—	—	—	—	—	161
1961 Districts	172	5	1	—	—	—	—	—	—	—	—	—	178
1964 Districts	175	2	1	—	—	—	—	—	—	—	—	—	178
Party	—	18	9	5	—	—	—	—	—	—	—	—	36
1967 Districts	177	1	0	0	—	—	—	—	—	—	—	—	178
Party Districts	—	19	10	5	—	—	—	—	—	—	—	—	34
1970 Districts	178	0	0	0	—	—	—	—	—	—	—	—	178
Party	—	20	10	5	—	—	—	—	—	—	—	—	35
1973 Districts	189	4	—	1	—	—	—	—	—	—	—	—	194
Party	—	21	10	6	—	—	—	—	—	—	—	—	37
1976 Districts	195	—	—	2	—	—	—	—	—	—	—	—	197
Party	—	20	12	9	—	—	—	—	—	—	—	—	41
1979 Districts	296	4	—	—	—	—	—	—	—	—	—	—	300
Plurinominal	—	39	11	12	10	18	10	—	—	—	—	—	
1982 Districts	299	1	—	—	—	—	—	—	—	—	—	—	
Plurinominal	—	50	10	0	12	17	11	—	—	—	—	—	
1985 Districts	289	9	—	2	—	—	—	—	—	—	—	—	
Plurinominal	—	32	11	9	12	12	12	6	6	—	—	—	
1988[c] Districts	233	38	4	5	—	—	5	—	—	15	—	—	
Plurinominal	27	63	27	23	—	—	46	—	—	11	—	—	
1991 Districts	290	10	—	—	—	—	23	—	—	—	—	—	
Plurinominal	31	80	12	14	—	—	—	—	—	40	—	—	
1994 Districts	277	18	—	—	—	—	—	—	—	5	—	—	
Plurinominal	23	101	—	—	—	—	—	—	—	66	10	—	
1997 Districts	164	65	—	—	—	—	—	—	—	70	1	—	
Plurinominal	74	57	—	—	—	—	—	—	—	55	6	8	
2000 Districts	131	141	—	—	—	—	—	—	—	28	—	—	
Plurinominal[d]	78	67	—	—	—	—	—	—	—	23	9	15	
2003 Districts	160	80	—	—	—	—	—	55	—	—	3		
Plurinominal[e]	62	71								40	6	14	

Source: Adapted from Héctor Zamitiz and Carlos Hernández, "La composición política de la Cámara de Diputados, 1949–1989," *Revista de Ciencias Políticas y Sociales* 36 (January–March 1990): 97–108; "Electoral Analysis: How the Votes were Cast," *Review of the Economic Situation of Mexico,* July 2000, 257–263.

[a]PRI = Institutional Revolutionary Party; PAN = National Action Party; PPS = Popular Socialist Party; PARM = Authentic Party of the Mexican Revolution; PDM = Democratic Mexican Party; PSUM = Mexico's United Socialist Party; PST = Socialist Workers Party; PRT = Revolutionary Workers Party; PMT = Mexican Workers Party; PRD = Democratic Revolutionary Party; PVEM = Green Party.

[b]Three other seats were won by members of the Federación de Partidos Populares Mexicanos and the Partido Nacionalista Mexicano.

[c]Three deputies were classified as independents, and one deputy among the PRD majority transferred his loyalty to the PRD after being elected on the PRI ticket.

[d]The Convergence for Democracy (part of the PRD Alliance for Mexico), obtained 3 seats; the Nationalist Society Party (part of the PRD Alliance for Mexico), obtained 3 seats, and the Social Alliance Party (part of the PRD Alliance for Mexico), obtained 2 seats.

[e]The Convergence for Democracy obtained 5 seats.

[f]The PST changed its name to the PFCRN (Cardenista Front for National Reconstruction Party) in 1988.

announced they would cancel masses if the federal government did not respond. The Vatican delegate to Mexico, at the prompting of Mexico's secretary of government, persuaded the clergy to withdraw their threat.[6] The overall political environment laid the groundwork for the most significant change in the PRI and led to the events that characterized the 1988 presidential election, a benchmark in Mexican electoral politics. Certain persons in the establishment leadership, in disagreement with the economic direction of the de la Madrid government and the timidity of his reforms, attempted a reform of the party's structure. In 1986 they constituted themselves as the Democratic Current. Among the most prominent members were Cuauhtémoc Cárdenas, a former governor of Michoacán and son of President Lázaro Cárdenas, the major political figure in the 1930s, and Porfirio Muñoz Ledo, a former cabinet official and president of the National Executive Committee of the PRI. This group and other party figures and intellectuals kept up a running criticism of the government's failure to implement genuine democratic reforms. At first they were tolerated, but their dissenting voice became intolerable to the party and government leadership during the 1987 presidential succession, and their party memberships were revoked.

Cárdenas, Muñoz Ledo, and other PRI dissidents formed the National Democratic Front (FDN), selecting Cárdenas as its presidential candidate. Because the FDN joined the race too late to have its credentials legally recognized, several of the PRI's tiny splinter parties, the Authentic Party of the Mexican Revolution (PARM), the Popular Socialist Party (PPS), and the Socialist Workers Party (PST), which became the Cardenista Front for National Reconstruction Party (PFCRN), selected Cárdenas as its nominee, thus giving the FDN a place on the ballot. The FDN's formation occurred at a time when internal contention over the selection of the PRI's candidate broke into the open. Carlos Salinas de Gortari, the programming and budget secretary, was seen by most observers as a man who would continue de la Madrid's economic philosophy. This suggested that the PRI's populist wing, represented by such persons as Cuauhtémoc Cárdenas, would not have a presence in his administration.[7] The fact that Salinas had no prior electoral or grassroots political experience marked the ascendancy of the technocratic leadership within the PRI.[8]

THE 1988 AND 1994 PRESIDENTIAL ELECTIONS

The 1988 presidential election illustrated a longtime pattern in Mexican electoral politics: The strongest opposition movements were often led by dissidents from within the PRI. As will be seen in the brief histories of several major opposition parties, most were founded by persons who abandoned government leadership because of policy and personal disagreements. This was true of the PAN and the PRD. Opposition party building did, however, include grass-roots components, too.

The 1988 presidential election took place when the government and the PRI were at a low in terms of their legitimacy among the people. The selection of Salinas as the PRI candidate, the least popular choice among party leaders, further eroded the PRI's position. Given these conditions, the opposition began a vigorous campaign against Salinas. The PAN selected a charismatic businessman from the north, Manuel J. Clouthier, who provided energetic, if somewhat bombastic, leadership during the contest. Cárdenas was off to a rocky start, but with his name recognition, notably in rural Mexico, he began to build a following. Three leftist parties, which typically had attracted only small numbers of Mexican voters (see Table 8-1), eventually joined Cárdenas's battle against the PRI candidate: the Popular Socialist Party (PPS); the Cardenista Front for National Reconstruction Party (PFCRN); and the Mexican Socialist Party (PMS). Of the eight parties on the 1988 presidential ballot, four supported Cárdenas.

To most analysts' genuine surprise, the populist and leftist Cárdenas alliance generated a widespread response among Mexican voters. Cárdenas, according to official tallies, received 31 percent of the vote, the highest figure given to an opposition presidential candidate since the revolution; Salinas obtained 51 percent, barely a simple majority; and Clouthier captured 17 percent, the typical PAN percentage in a presidential election. Contrary to most observers's expectations, the Left, not the Right, altered the face of the election. In other words, the 1982 voters who defected from the PRI six years later cast their ballots for Cárdenas, not the PAN.

It is important to remember that the 1988 election took place under the 1986 law, which allowed, for the first time, the majority party (the PRI) to increase its representation in the Chamber of Deputies from some of the 200 plurinominal seats. The PRI needed to implement the provision because it obtained only 233 majority district seats, 18 short of a simple majority of 251. It allocated itself 27 plurinominal seats, which added to the 233 majority district seats gave it a slight majority (260 out of 500). Table 8-2 illustrates the extraordinary shift in the parties' representation in the legislative branch. Up to 1988 the highest percentage of seats obtained by the opposition, combining majority districts and plurinominal seats, was 28 percent. In 1988, however, the opposition achieved 48 percent of the total, a 71 percent increase in three years.

Most observers of the 1988 election believe that the PRI engaged in fraudulent practices. Some—PRD figures among them—believe that Cár-

Table 8-2 Percentage of Total Vote Won by Candidates for Congress, by Major Party, 1961–2003

Election Year	Party[a]												
	PRI	PAN	PPS	PARM	PDM	PSUM	PST	PRT	PMT	PRD	PFCRN	PT	PVEM
1961	90.2	7.6	1.0	0.5	—	—	—	—	—	—	—	—	—
1964	86.3	11.5	1.4	0.7	—	—	—	—	—	—	—	—	—
1967	83.3	12.4	2.8	1.3	—	—	—	—	—	—	—	—	—
1970	80.1	13.9	1.4	0.8	—	—	—	—	—	—	—	—	—
1973	69.7	14.7	3.6	1.9	—	—	—	—	—	—	—	—	—
1976	80.1	8.5	3.0	2.5	—	—	—	—	—	—	—	—	—
1979	69.7	10.8	2.6	1.8	2.1	4.9	2.7	—	—	—	—	—	—
1982	69.3	17.5	1.9	1.4	2.2	4.4	1.8	1.3	—	—	—	—	—
1985	65.0	15.5	2.0	1.7	2.7	3.2	2.5	1.3	1.5	—	—	—	—
1988	50.4	17.1	10.5	6.2	0.4	3.6[b]	—	0.4	—	—	10.5	—	—
1991	61.4	17.7	1.8	2.1	1.1	—	—	0.6	—	8.3	4.4	—	—
1994[c]	50.3	25.8	0.7	0.9	0.4	—	—	—	—	16.1	1.1	2.9	—
1997	39.1	26.6	0.3	0.7	—	—	—	—	—	25.7	—	2.5	3.8
2000[d]	36.9	38.2	—	0.7	—	—	—	—	—	18.7	—	—	—
2003[e]	36.5	30.6	—	—	—	—	—	—	—	17.7	—	2.4	3.9

Sources: Delal Baer, "The 1991 Mexican Midterm Elections," CSIS Latin American Election Study Series (October 1, 1991), 31; federal election data, Mexican Embassy, Washington, D.C.; Instituto Federal Electoral, *Elecciones federales 1994* (August 28, 1994); "The Composition of the New Federal Congress," *Review of the Economic Situation of Mexico,* July 2000, 269; "Balances and Consequences of July 6," *Review of the Economic Situation of Mexico* (July 2003), 288–92; and George Grayson, "Beyond the Midterm Elections," *Western Hemisphere Election Studies* (Washington, D.C.: SIS, 2003).

[a]PRI = Institutional Revolutionary Party; PAN = National Action Party; PPS = Popular Socialist Party; PARM = Authentic Party of the Mexican Revolution; PDM = Democratic Mexican Party; PSUM = Mexico's United Socialist Party; PST = Socialist Workers Party; PRT = Revolutionary Workers Party; PMT = Mexican Workers Party; PRD = Democratic Revolutionary Party; PFCRN = Cardenista Front for National Reconstruction Party; PT = Labor Party; PVEM = Green Party.

[b]Votes for the PSUM in 1988 were for the Mexican Socialist Party (PMS).

[c]Several minor parties, obtaining fewer than 2 percent of the vote, are not reported in these figures.

[d]The Federal Electoral Institute calculated the percentages on the basis of the electoral alliances, therefore, the PVEM percentage is incorporated with PAN, as the Alliance for Change; and the percentage for the PT, the CD (Convergence for Democracy), the PSN (National Socialist Party), and the PAS (Social Alliance Party) are reported under the PRD, as the Alliance for Mexico.

[e]All other parties earned 8.9 percent.

denas actually won. The majority, however, although agreeing with charges of fraud, believe that Salinas actually did win—but that his percentage of the total vote was lower.

The 1988 elections appeared to suggest the end of Mexico's one party-dominant system, the increased importance of pluralism in the political culture, and, as suggested in Chapter 7, the greater importance of the legislative branch, where the PRI would have to negotiate with the opposition to obtain alliances sufficient to gain passage of major legislation. The 1988 elections were a departure from a pattern, but the 1991 congressional elections temporarily dampened expectations of a permanent augmentation of opposition strength.

The PRI claimed 61.4 percent of the vote in the 1991 elections, a step back from 1988's brink but still within the pattern of decline since 1961 (see Table 8-2). These elections wrought changes. First, whereas the PRI was on the verge of becoming merely a plurality party, controlling the electorate through the largest number of votes rather than exceeding a majority, it recovered its majority status. Second, the PAN basically remained at the same level as in 1982 and 1988, retaining its position as the second-ranking party, the key opposition party for three decades. Third, the PRD, the major beneficiary of PRI defectors in 1988, was the primary source of PRI returnees in 1991. The PRD did not win a majority of votes in a single state in 1991, including those it had dominated in 1988 (Michoacán, México, Morelos, and the Federal District). Overall, its vote declined from nearly a third in 1988 to only 8 percent. Finally, instead of increasing the legislative branch's importance, the PRI's renewed dominance reinforced its weakness.

The 1994 elections established a new benchmark in the Mexican electoral process. First, the political context was more challenging and less stable than in 1988. Beginning with the surprise uprising of the Zapatista Army of National Liberation on January 1, 1994, followed two months later by the assassination of PRI's presidential candidate in Tijuana, Baja California, on March 23, in midcampaign (the first presidential candidate to be assassinated since 1929), the fear of political instability became widespread among all social classes. Among urban Mexicans polled in February 1994, 42 percent believed that the situation in Chiapas would lead to important changes. Two months later, shortly after Colosio's murder, 30 percent of urban Mexicans perceived the country's situation as very grave, and 39 percent as grave.[9] Second, before these events, the congress introduced several significant reforms in the COFIPE, including eliminating the right of the plurality party to guarantee itself a simple majority, preventing any party from winning more than 315 of the 500 seats in the Chamber of Deputies, doubling the number of seats in the Senate from 64 to 128, establishing the Federal Electoral Institute (IFE) as the arbiter of all federal elections, introducing campaign-spending limits, and improving access to media. Third, these events led to the formation of the Pact for Peace, Justice, and Democracy by eight political parties to promote electoral reforms, later approved by the congress. In addition to these changes, the congress altered the composition of the IFE, giving to six "citizen" councillors, who had no party affiliation, the balance of power in the eleven-member body.[10]

The election results themselves were widely anticipated not only in Mexico but abroad as well. Public opinion polls taken immediately before election day predicted a PRI victory, but what was not expected was the extraordinary turnout, 78 percent, of registered voters, the highest ever recorded in Mexico and well above national averages elsewhere; the active participation of independent voters; and the proportion of independent voters casting ballots in favor of the PRI. Most analysts had expected the PRI to win with only 45 percent of the vote, but Zedillo captured approximately the same percentage of voters as did his predecessor (50 percent). Moreover, most Mexicans believed that the PRI actually won these elections, an important change in the credibility of the electoral process.[11]

The presence of international and trained national observers from numerous civic and nongovernmental organizations helped validate the outcome, despite the evidence of some fraud, the lack of secrecy in casting actual ballots, and many technical violations. In retrospect, most critics agreed that although the voting on election day itself was among the cleanest in recent Mexican history, the larger electoral context, including financing and access to media, created an unfair playing field favoring the PRI's fortunes.[12]

The 1994 presidential elections also demonstrated an ideological trend toward the center-right, even though half the voters cast their ballots for someone other than the PRI candidate. Diego Fernández de Cevallos, the PAN presidential contender, obtained 26 percent of the vote, firmly establishing the PAN as Mexico's second party. These elections also confirmed the declining fortunes of the PRD, whose candidate, Cuauhtémoc Cárdenas, was unable to capitalize on his earlier popularity in 1988, earning a distinct third place with 17 percent of the vote. The PAN also continued to do very well in the north, as it did in 1988, although it lost those states in which it won its first gubernatorial elections.

These losses also demonstrated that the opposition by no means had a lock on repeated electoral victories and that the PRI, because of the differing local circumstances, could recover. Finally, the pollster for *Reforma,* Mexico City's leading independent newspaper, found that uneducated voters, fearful of violence, voted in significantly larger numbers for the PRI. This finding also was evident in an August 12 poll taken shortly before the election, in which 54 percent of the citizens questioned agreed that they would "prefer that PRI win to continue the advances that have been achieved," compared with only 36 percent who favored change directed by an opposition party.[13]

In the 1988 and especially the 1991 and 1994 elections, Mexico's proximity to the United States played a special role. In 1988 the government became increasingly sensitive to charges of pervasive election fraud from abroad, especially from the United States media.[14] By 1991 Mexico's conduct in the electoral arena came under severe scrutiny in the U.S. Congress and in the media as discussions of the North American Free-Trade Agreement (NAFTA) continued. American critics of the agreement charged that the United States should not be a party to it in light of Mexico's antidemocratic practices. Even with NAFTA going into effect on January 1, 1994, the United States' interest, governmental and public, remained high.

The 1997 congressional and state gubernatorial elections reinforced more strongly the declining fortunes of the PRI and reversed PRI's recovery in the 1994 presidential elections. In 1996, the PRI-controlled congress passed further electoral reforms.[15] Among these, the IFE was further modified, becoming completely independent of government control. The General Council increased from six to nine independent citizens, party representatives were removed as voting members, and an independent was appointed head of IFE. As Armand Peschard suggests, perhaps most important among these reforms was the decision to allocate larger amounts of public monies for campaign expenditures, approximately 264 million dollars, 30 percent distributed equally among eight contending parties, and 70 percent according to their share of votes in the 1994 election.[16] The IFE provided free television and radio advertising, also allocated on the same 30/70 percent formula. Finally, for the first time in many years, majority congressional districts were reallocated to correspond more closely to shifting demographic patterns. The most important changes were in the Federal District, which lost 25 percent of its seats (from forty to thirty); Chiapas, which increased its seats by the same percentage (from nine to twelve); México, which gained two seats, replacing the Federal District as the most populous entity in Mexico; and Guanajuato, which also gained two additional seats.

Despite the fact that the 1997 elections involved congressional and gubernatorial races only, 58 percent of the electorate voted, an unusually high figure for midterm elections. More important, in response to the economic crisis, the government austerity program, conflicts within the PRI, and severe social problems, particularly urban crime and violence, the opposition won the largest number of congressional seats ever, 136 of the 300 majority districts.[17] Combined with their plurinominal seats, the four opposition parties, PAN, PRD, PT (the Labor Party), and PVEM (the Green Party), controlled 262 of the 500 seats and, for the first time, the Chamber of Deputies. The PRD also made a significant comeback, as did the party's standard-bearer, Cuauhtémoc Cárdenas, who, with 48 percent of the vote, handily defeated both PRI and PAN as the first elected head of government of the Federal District since the 1920s. The PRD replaced PAN in congress as the number-two party. The PAN, which barely lost its position as the number-two party nationally, increased its strength in congress and won two important gubernatorial races, one in the important industrial border state of Nuevo León and the other in the central state of Querétaro, a traditional PRI stronghold.

The 1997 elections confirmed the importance Mexican citizens attribute to the electoral process, which increasingly became more competitive and clean. Nevertheless, Mexicans continued to remain skeptical, despite growing opposition victories. More than half of all Mexicans (56 percent) considered those elections to have been fradulent.[18] Prior to the 2000 presidential elections, two-fifths of Mexicans continued to believe elections would be unfair. Attitudes toward elections are crucial to Mexican conceptions of democracy. When asked what was most important to achieve a better democracy, nearly two-thirds of all Mexicans said clean elections.[19]

THE 2000 PRESIDENTIAL ELECTION, A POLITICAL LANDMARK

Throughout the preceding chapters, frequent reference has been made to the presidential victory of Vicente Fox and the PAN in the July 2000 elections. This election is a landmark in Mexico's political evolution for many reasons. The victory of a party other than PRI essentially stood the Mexican political model on its head, destroying permanently the incestuous, monopolistic relationship between state and party. Such a relationship no longer exists. The future of the Mexican electoral process from 2000 forward relies heavily on the behavior and organizational strength of the three leading political parties, the PAN, PRI, and PRD, and on citizen perceptions of their candidates. It also relies on citizen views of the performance of the parties' candidates in office, particularly in executive posts. Obviously, the party controlling the national executive branch, the PAN, has the most to lose or gain by its performance. Nevertheless, the performance of PRD and PRI politicians in gubernatorial and mayoralty positions is also important to their fortunes, especially in such populous states as México and the Federal District. A PRD politician currently is in charge of the Federal District, which is the residence of one out of six Mexicans.

Initial analyses of the PAN electoral victory in 2000 suggest a number of explanations for Vicente Fox's defeat of the PRI's candidate, the first time this party lost a presidential race since 1929. The most obvious explanations for the Fox victory are fascinating, but many of them are part of much longer-term trends in Mexican politics, trends that explain the rise of the opposition generally and of PAN specifically. These trends extend back to the 1940s. Three variables contributed to the evolution that led to the 2000 PAN victory. They are regionalism, urbanization, and level of economic and social development.[20]

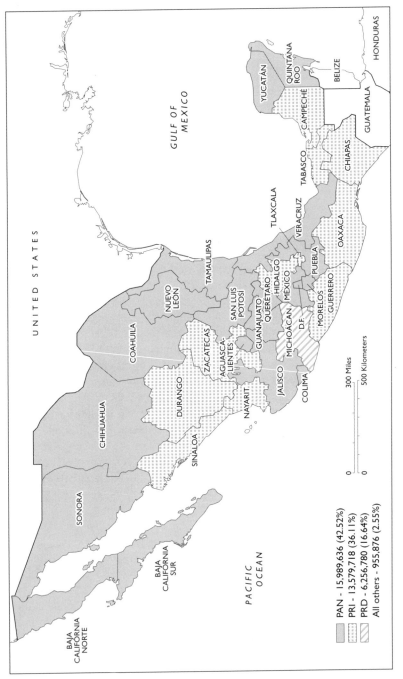

Party Winning the Most Votes by State in the 2000 Election

PAN - 15,989,636 (42.52%)
PRI - 13,579,718 (36.11%)
PRD - 6,256,780 (16.64%)
All others - 955,876 (2.55%)

Opposition has often coalesced around individual candidates and temporary party organizations, such as those of José Vasconcelos in 1929 and General Miguel Henríquez Guzmán in 1952, but opposition tendencies have remained strong in certain states and regions for many decades, indicating a permanence extending beyond any single issue or personality. An examination of the four presidential elections prior to 1994, in 1946, 1952, 1982, and 1988, when the opposition was strongest, reveals that the opposition collectively obtained at least 30 percent or more of the votes in seven states: Baja California, the Federal District, Guanajuato, Jalisco, México, Michoacán, and Morelos. In 1994, the opposition dominated in México, Jalisco, Morelos, the Federal District, and Michoacán, where it won more than half of the votes cast. It also won more than 45 percent of the vote in Guanajuato, but lost Baja California, Zedillo's home state. It 1997, it won the majority of congressional seats in each of those original seven states, and in 2000, of the 123 congressional seats distributed among those states, it captured 86 percent, and won all the seats in Baja California and the Federal District.

There are many reasons for the long opposition to the PRI in these states. For some—Baja California, the Federal District, Nuevo León, and México—growth, income, urbanization, and development are important, as they are among the seven states with the highest per capita income (see Table 8-3). Economic growth is likely to have the most influence on opposition strength over the long term. It has been argued that economic growth and development are statistically related to election results.[21] In the United States we know, for example, that when the economy does poorly, support for the president and his party generally declines; this was so for President

Table 8-3 PRI Vote by State Per Capita Income Level, 1976–2000

Jurisdiction[a]	Election Year							
	1976 (%)	1979 (%)	1982 (%)	1985 (%)	1988 (%)	1991 (%)	1994 (%)	2000 (%)
Nation	87	74	68	68	50	61	50	38
Low-income states	92	81	82	81	75	71	50	45
Medium-income states	93	78	73	68	56	66	49	36
High-income states	78	55	55	52	37	53	47	33

Sources: Adapted from Paulina Fernández Christlieb and Octavio Rodríguez Araujo, *Elecciones y partidos en México* (Mexico: El Caballito, 1986), 218, 223–24; Joseph Klesner, "Changing Patterns of Electoral Participation," in *Mexican Politics in Transition,* ed. Judith Gentleman (Boulder, Colo.: Westview Press, 1987), 1930, 139–141; *El Día,* July 16, 1988, 8; Instituto Federal Electoral, 1991 election data, district computations, courtesy of Luis Medina, Mexican Embassy, Washington, D.C.; 1994 data, Instituto Federal Electoral, August 28, 1994; *Review of the Economic Situation of Mexico,* July 2000, 273.
[a]High-income states typically = Baja California, Baja California Sur, Chihuahua, Federal District, Nuevo León, and Coahuila; low-income states = Chiapas, Hidalgo, Oaxaca, Puebla, Tlaxcala, Guerrero, Michoacán, Tabasco, Veracruz, and Zacatecas; medium-income states = the remaining states.

Bush in the fall of 1991 and into 1992. In Mexico, however, although strong economic performance in the short term increases voter satisfaction with the government, when economic performance translates into higher standards of living, those who live in regions benefiting most have voted for the opposition, contrary to expectations.

The region of the country that has best demonstrated this surprising voting behavior over time is the Federal District, which has always been among the high-per-capita-income states and has always recorded sizable votes for the opposition. The PAN has done extremely well in the capital for many years, as did the PRD during the 1988 presidential and 1997 congressional elections. In 2000, PAN captured 25 of 30 districts, and the PRD won the remainder.

To illustrate the relationship between economic development and support for the opposition, we can group Mexico's states according to per capita income and the percentage of votes for and against the PRI (see Table 8-3). In each election year since 1976, whether we are dealing with presidential or legislative candidates, the total percentage of votes for the PRI in high-income states typically was much lower than the national average. On the other hand, the PRI obtained a disproportionate amount of its support from low-income states.[22] This pattern held true in 2000, as well. PRI received 38 percent of the vote for the presidency, but only 33 percent came from the high-income states, a level comparable to what it had received in the 1988 race. It obtained a 25 percent higher proportion from the low-income states.

Over the last twenty-five years, the only time the PRI obtained balanced support from all states regardless of income, and especially strong support from high-income states relative to its national figures, was in 1994 (see Table 8-3). This is probably explained by the fact that on election day, an exit poll of 5,635 voters revealed that 53 percent considered Mexico's economic situation to have improved from 1988–1994. Of those voters, more than two-thirds voted for the PRI, suggesting the continued importance of a positive perception of economic conditions and partisanship.[23]

Why has the opposition been stronger in states benefiting economically under PRI's long leadership? A number of reasons stand out. First the PRI is much better organized in rural areas, and low-income states typically are the most agrarian. The PRI accentuated this relationship in the 1990s through resources allocated by Pronasol (Solidarity) and by Procampo, a peasant-subsidy program.[24] Second, educated Mexicans, who are more sophisticated about participation and more likely to vote for an opposition candidate, live in greater numbers in high-income states. Third, supervision of voting in urban centers, often located in the high-income states, is characterized by fewer reports of fraud and hence fairer.

Table 8-4 Patterns in Partisan Support, 1998–2000

	1998			2000		
Variable	PRI (%)	PAN (%)	PRD (%)	PRI (%)	PAN (%)	PRD (%)
Gender						
Men	33	28	21	28	31	11
Women	41	22	16	30	31	9
Place of Residence						
Metropolitan	24	31	21	19	31	17
Large city	35	28	19	31	30	7
Medium city	44	21	18	24	39	11
Small city	44	22	17	30	34	8
Rural	43	23	15	40	20	6
Level of Education						
Primary	43	19	16	39	25	9
Secondary	34	25	25	24	33	8
Preparatory+	29	41	13	18	40	12
Level of Income						
Low	42	20	18	32	28	9
Medium	33	23	18	21	40	10
High	29	34	15	19	35	15
Total	37	26	18	29	31	10

Note: Metropolitan = 1 million, Large = 100,000 to 1 million, Medium = 50,000 to 100,000, Small = 10,000 to 50,000, Rural = <10,000. Preparatory+ = preparatory or higher.
Source: "Democracy Through U.S. and Mexican Lenses," Grant, Hewlett Foundation, September 2000; "Democracy Through Latin American Lenses," Grant, Hewlett Foundation, June 1998.

It is also the case that frequent, severe economic crises, beginning in 1982 and continuing through 1995, contributed to PRI's declining legitimacy. Furthermore, the PRI-affiliated labor unions could no longer guarantee large blocks of loyal voters. Other variables complement or are integral to the regional income patterns. The data in Table 8-4 on location, level of education, and income suggest similar trends. On the basis of citizen party preferences, the PRD and PAN combined obtain their supporters in cities and have typically done poorly in rural areas, which are among the less developed economically. They also have done well, as we noted in Chapter 4, among the most educated voters, who naturally can be found in larger numbers in high-income states. Finally, the data also illustrate opposition support, even for the left of center PRD, among higher-income groups.

A state's geographic location also has been significant in contributing to opposition trends. For Baja California, and Nuevo León, proximity to the United States has played an important role. It is difficult to link empirically that proximity with Mexican voters' support for the opposition. However, it is a fact that Mexicans living along the border were most likely to support the PAN. There is little doubt, however, as we suggested earlier, that where Mexicans live affects their views of the United States and its political system, and their political values.[25] In fact, surveys show that the closer Mexicans live to the United States and the more they travel to it, the greater their admiration is.[26] In 2000, Mexicans who lived along the border were the least likely to view their country as democratic. Many of the prominent figures in the PAN are products of the border culture, including its 1988 presidential candidate, who attended high school in San Diego. In fact, Mexicans living in the United States repeatedly have requested the right to vote by absentee ballot, a request consistently denied until 2005. Observers argue that the government refusal was based on the high probability that the overwhelming majority would support opposition parties.[27] Polling data from the 2000 presidential election demonstrated that if they had been allowed to vote, they would have voted overwhelmingly for Fox. This group could have played a significant role in the 2006 presidential election, but approximately only 50,000 voters cast their ballots.

A geographic trend that is becoming a stronger and, in the view of some scholars, disturbing pattern in the democratic transition is the division of votes among the PRI, PAN and PRD. Joseph Klesner contends that "instead of a three-party system, two separate party systems seem to be developing in Mexico. In the north and west, the PAN and the PRI compete. In the areas south and east of the capital, excepting Yucatán, the PRD is the PRI's main adversary."[28] This regional separation remains, borne out by the 1997 congressional races. PAN did not win a single district in fourteen out of thirty-two states. PRD did not win a single district in twenty-two out of thirty-two states.[29] In 2000, PAN was able to improve its regional distribution, reducing the number of states where it won no districts to nine, but the PRD remained unrepresented in twenty-two states. Such a pattern accentuates regionalism and geographic partisanship, making national unity more difficult.

Historical experience also had much to do with the level of opposition support in various states, generally in connection with poor relationships. For example, Morelos, a state just south of Mexico City, gave birth to the most important agrarian movement during the 1910 Revolution, led by Emiliano Zapata. Zapata and his followers never pursued goals compatible with those of the Mexican government, even after the revolution's initial success in 1911 or its more institutional phase after 1916. Hence, tensions have always existed between the peasants in Morelos and national political leadership.

Strong opposition in Guanajuato, Jalisco, and Michoacán stem historically from the importance of Catholicism and church-state relations in those states during the 1920s. When the federal government strictly applied constitutional provisions relative to religion, it provoked resistance from staunch Catholics and some clergy in the region, including these three states. This movement in defense of religious rights became known as the Cristero rebellion. Memories of the events are still fresh in the minds of the people who were children in the 1920s. The region contributes heavily to the priesthood and hierarchy, and a disproportionate number of bishops are graduates of the Morelia seminary in the heart of Michoacán.

The long-term variables that contributed to the strength of the political opposition enhanced other, specific variables that made possible the PAN victory in 2000. Polls indicated that the PRI and PAN candidates were running neck-in-neck up to the day their campaigns officially ended. Who voted for Vicente Fox in 2000, and what were the special characteristics of the Fox voter? Among the traditional, historical variables determining opposition support, three stand out.

Educated voters were extremely influential in determining the outcome of the 2000 presidential race: 58 percent of Mexicans who voted in that election completed a secondary or higher education. These voters cast their ballots overwhelmingly for Fox. Fox, who received 42.5 percent of the vote nationally, obtained 49, 53, and 60 percent of the secondary, preparatory, and university educated voters, respectively. In contrast, Francisco Labastida, the PRI candidate, who won 36.1 percent of the national vote, obtained only 34, 28, and 22 percent, respectively, among the same three educational categories. Labastida did quite well among voters with a sixth grade or lower education, but they accounted for only two-fifths of the voters.

In terms of broad regions, Fox did well throughout Mexico, but especially in the north and center-west, the location of many of the same states that traditionally have supported opposition parties. The most important geographic factor, however, was not found among the voters in broad, multistate regions, but among those voters who live in areas the Mexican census classifies as urban, mixed (combined rural/urban populations), and rural, accounting for 70, 10, and 20 percent of the voters, respectively. Obviously, the party that does best among urban voters has the greatest potential for winning the largest number of votes. Fox did best among these voters, and interestingly, his pattern of support and that of his leading opponent, Francisco Labastida, were exactly the opposite of each other. Labastida did well in rural areas and poorly in urban centers. Fox did as well as Labastida in rural areas, but much better among urban voters, among whom he received nearly half of the votes.[30]

A different variable, or at least a variable that was measured for the first time, was the impact of those Mexicans who were most desirious of democracy. The growth of the opposition generally, and the change in the electoral playing field, encouraged many Mexicans' expectations about a democratic model. Those voters who believed that Mexico was not a democracy at the time of the election largely voted for PAN.

Just as a candidate's personality was important in the 1929, 1952, and 1988 elections, Vicente Fox's personality as a candidate played a critical role in the electoral outcome. PAN relied heavily on his charisma and personal, organizational skills to win the election. The fact that voters did not view the two leading candidates' professional abilities in a distinctive light allowed Fox to be considered as capable as the PRI's candidate. In the 1994 election, in every category voters ranked Zedillo more positively than the PAN candidate. It is possible to argue that Fox was more important to the PAN victory than was the party itself.

The most significant, unique influence on the outcome of the 2000 election was the voter who favored change, an individual most willing to risk change. The *Dallas Morning News* conducted a national survey one week prior to the election. They discovered two significant changes in voter attitudes that prompted them to predict Fox's victory. They found that 72 percent of the voters supported radical change, up from only half of all voters in December 1999. They also found that 43 percent of probable voters said they would never vote for PRI, up from only 30 percent seven months earlier.[31] Voters who were not risk-averse could be found in large numbers among both PAN and PRD sympathizers. These voters viewed Vicente Fox as the candidate of change, and this group voted overwhelmingly for Fox, many choosing him at the last minute. Many of these voters had identified themselves as independents, without giving pollsters a preference for a presidential candidate. Over half of the independent voters cast their ballots for PAN, more than twice that for PRI.[32]

Another group who influenced the 2000 electoral outcome was younger, first-time voters. In fact, voters who were 18 to 24 made up the largest, single age cohort among Mexican voters, a "baby boomer" group. This age group accounted for 18 percent of all voters. They have high expectations for Vicente Fox; and half of these young people, many of them students, voted for PAN. Fox did better than either of his competitors in every age group except the 55 or older Mexicans, who gave their vote disproportionately to the PRI candidate.

Significant changes in the electoral "playing field," notably public financing of the elections, media coverage of the candidates, and the independence of the Federal Electoral Institute, affected voter perceptions and participation in 2000. The most significant of these changes was public financing, which distributed the bulk of actual campaign monies more evenly among the three leading parties, based on absolute amounts for each party and on their performance in the 1997 elections. Only 10 percent of campaign funds may come from private sources. Because both the PAN and PRD formed electoral alliances, they increased their overall portion of public monies, which disproportionately favored the smaller parties. Therefore, although the PRI received the largest amount of funding, some $52,000,000, having obtained 40 percent of the vote in 1997, PAN's Alliance for Change received almost the same amount, but only had obtained 27 percent of the vote. PRD received only $4 million less than the other two parties.[33]

Fox also changed the image of PAN, broadening its appeal politically and socially, and strengthening its grassroots appeal through a personal organization, the Friends of Fox. Much of the grassroots support for PAN, and Fox's ability to increase PAN's appeal geographically in Mexico, stems from the impact of his personal organization. Much of PAN's partisan strength is recent and possibly tenuous, depending heavily on how citizens view him personally and their attachment to his Friends of Fox organization, not the PAN. Furthermore, this organization became a critical source of private campaign donations, adding to the PAN's significant level of public monies.

Perhaps the most influential long-term element in the PAN victory is the electorate's gradual move to center-right. PAN has become a major beneficiary of that shift because it, rather than the PRI, is now viewed as the party of the center, and the PRI of the far right. This shift in the ideological rankings of the parties had already taken place by 1997. A survey showed that on a 10-point scale, with the far right being a 10 and the far left a 1, PRI voters identified themselves ideologically as a 7.5 compared with only 6.0 for Panistas and 4.0 for PRD partisans. It is not entirely clear what Mexican citizens mean by "left and "right." Most analysts would probably suggest that "right" combined a preference for free markets with a preference for the regime status quo, while "left" combined economic statism with democracy.[34] Alejandro Moreno, the pollster for *Reforma*, discovered that Mexicans who went to the polls in July 2000, were not ideologically representative of the population as a whole. One explanation for this is that the presidential contest came down to a neck-and-neck race between the two candidates who represented the center-right and right parties; thus left-of-center voters had little incentive to participate.

The data in Table 8-5 illustrate some fascinating patterns that are not only revealing about the 2000 presidential election, but suggest important future trends as well. In the first place, Mexicans who perceive themselves as on the center and center-right of the political spectrum turned out in numbers different from their representation within the population at large immediately prior to the election. They accounted for 69 percent of potential vot-

Table 8-5 Ideological Identification and Partisan Preferences Before and After the July 2000 Elections

Voted for	Self-identification Ideologically				
	Left	Center-Left	Center	Center-Right	Right
PAN	50	54	51	59	30
PRI	17	19	32	34	57
PRD	32	24	15	6	12
Intended Voters	21	10	23	10	36
Actual Voters	11	6	25	19	39

Source: Personal communication from Alejandro Moreno, from pre-election and exit polls, *Reforma,* June and July 2000.

ers, but 83 percent of the voters who actually turned up at the polls were in these ideological categories. Second, PAN, among the three parties, obtained the most balanced support on the basis of voter ideological self-identification. In fact, in 2000, PAN appealed to half or more of the voters in four of the five ideological categories, including the left. Only among the far right did it not receive strong support. PRI, on the other hand, did extremely well among the far right, only modestly well among centrist voters, and poorly among the left. The PRD, which is perceived as being the left of center party, naturally appealed most strongly to the voters on the left. It did poorly among the center and center-right voters. Whatever shifts occured among voters during the 2000 election, it is critical to keep in mind that a third of all voters remain independent, and they will shift their party allegiance in future elections.

THE 2003 ELECTION AND THE PRESIDENTIAL RACE OF 2006

Given the performance of the Fox administration described in an earlier chapter, as well as his government's inability to pass major legislation and improve the economic performance significantly, it is not surprising that the PAN lost significant ground to the PRI and the PRD in the 2003 mid-term elections and the post-2000 governor races. The results of these congressional elections go well beyond an incumbent party and president's poor performance because of the historic role both played in bringing an end to a seven-decade incumbent. The 2003 elections not only have influential implications for the persistence and revival of a renewed PRI, but for voter confidence in the democratic model.

All three parties went into the election focused on addressing economic growth and poverty in Mexico. The voters themselves were overwhelmingly focused on these two issues, with 43 percent and 27 percent, respectively, indicating that they wanted the new congress to address these two issues. An additional 17 percent included fighting crime, and the remaining 13 percent included all other answers or no response.[35] Voters apparently were not choosing the parties on the basis of their agenda, but rather in the hope that a stronger PRI might be able to implement new legislation. PRI and PRD both improved their positions in relation to the PAN and dealt a telling political blow to Fox's prestige. PRI, however, similar to the PAN in the 2000 elections, was not able to translate their newfound support into a majority of the votes, obtaining a smaller percentage than did PAN itself in 2000 (see Table 8-6). At the district level, on the other hand, most winners received close to a majority of the votes, indicating a stronger level of victory by party. In only 10 percent of the districts did the winning deputy receive fewer than 39 percent of the votes.[36]

Mexican citizens' expectations of governmental performance had declined significantly since 2000. More than two-thirds of Mexicans believed the country was on the correct path in 2000, nearly the same as in 1994, but three years later, that figure declined to only 40 percent. Furthermore, the number of citizens who believed their personal situation had become worse increased almost twofold from 2000 to 2003 (18 to 36 percent), while the same percentage in both years (52 percent) continued to believe that the country's economic situation would improve.[37]

The composition of voters who cast their ballots for the PAN and the PRI suggests some interesting patterns about the Mexican electorate, from which some extrapolations can be drawn about the 2006 presidential race. Remarkably, in spite of the high expectations of policy reforms and the low performance of the executive and legislative branches, the absentee rate (58.2 percent) was the highest since 1946, which in the past has always favored PRI. Those individuals who did not vote expressed dissatisfaction with democracy, with the parties, and with congress itself. Two thirds of Mexicans who didn't vote said they were disillusioned with politics.[38] As many commentators have noted, most Mexicans do not believe they are well represented by their deputies and senators; indeed, few citizens know who their representatives are. Those Mexicans who discussed politics every day, however, were much more likely to vote for PAN than PRI (45 to 33 percent), while those Mexicans who never talked about political matters were equally likely to vote for PRI instead of PAN (44 to 27 percent). Older Mexicans over the age of 60 were much more likely to favor PRI over PAN (45 to 31 percent), as were Protestants (who typically are rural residents, a PRI stronghold).[39] PRI improved its postitions substantially over 2000 among those who had voted previously for Fox, among urban voters, among private sector and public sector professionals, and among independents (see Table 8-6). What is apparent from examining the national election data from 2003 and the local and municipal data from 1991 to 2003 is the decline of PRI and the rise of PAN, but also the fact that both parties are coming closer together in their overall support. By 2004, PAN controlled 18 percent of municipalities compared to 59 percent for PRI, which governed 30 and 48 percent of the population, respectively. Among local deputies elected from 2001 to 2004, PAN accounted for 23 percent, with essentially no increase since 2001, but PRI declined from 54 percent of the seats in 2001 to 50 percent in 2004. PRD decreased its percentage of seats slightly, to 19 percent. Nevertheless, PRI not only gained new ground in congress but continues to maintain a stronger presence at the local level than PAN, a presence that served as a base for its national ambitions. PRI has done equally well at the gubernatorial level, where it controls over half of all state leadership. It has demonstrated that it can defeat Fox's party in traditional PAN strongholds, such as the northern state of Chihuahua, the origin of the democratization movement in the 1980s. PRI has learned that strong candidates, with local roots, are more important than party labels.[40] Furthermore, ideologically speaking, the electorate has shifted slightly more to the right, and those who support PAN account for that shift. PRI, however, remains the party of the

Table 8-6 Comparison of Voter Support for Congress for PRI and PAN in 2000 and 2003

Group and % of Sample	PAN		PRI	
	2000	2003	2000	2003
			Percentages	
All voters	39	32	37	37
Men (52%)	42	32	32	38
Women (48%)	39	32	40	36
Age 39–49 (48%)	40	31	35	39
Urban residents	46	32	30	36
Middle-class urban	55	48	24	25
Working-class urban	40	30	33	37
Attended university (16%)	50	38	24	24
Professionals (5.9%)	49	30	27	36
Public professionals (1.5%)	45	23	32	44
Interested campaign	45	31	33	38
Independents (28%)	46	28	21	30
Voted for Fox (42%)	84	58	5	14
Catholics	42	34	36	37

Source: Adapted from Alejandro Moreno, "El viraje de las urnas," *Reforma*, July 13, 2003, www.reforma.mx.

right. PRD supporters have remained stable. As Alejandro Moreno notes, "the ideological center is, indeed, the most electorally profitable place in Mexican elections."[41] Finally, the geographic distribution of the vote continues to indicate that only PRI has a national base.

As Mexico prepared for the 2006 presidential race, the first presidential election since its citizenry had an opportunity to experience more deeply a democratic process with a divided executive and legislative branch, a number of important patterns became apparent, many of which may have medium to longer term implications for politics generally. In the first place, as commentators have noted in analyzing the results of the 2003 elections, Mexicans share extremely unfavorable views of all political parties. Two-fifths of Mexicans view them negatively, in contrast to only one-fifth who view parties positively. The most negative views of political parties are shared by those who live in the South; poorer, rural and indigenous people; independents; well-educated Mexicans; those who live in the center of the country (including the Federal District); and those who favor a PRD-controlled executive branch. In spite of their strongly negative views of political parties, only three out of ten Mexicans consider themselves non-partisan. As of 2005, PRI claims 28 percent of party loyalists, followed by 21 percent for PAN and 16 percent for PRD. However, among citizens who intended to vote in 2006, PRI received 31 percent to PAN's 27 percent. PRD, on the other hand, obtained 21 percent of the support. Furthermore, in what Mexicans call the *voto duro*, those individuals who always vote for the same party, PRI has an even stronger base, with 47 percent and 29 percent, respectively, voting for PRI and PAN. PRD earns 17 percent of these voters. Thus PRI had an advantage over PAN and PRD, measured by its core support, going into the presidential election. All parties need to attract significant support from independent voters, but PRI needs fewer of those than does PAN and especially PRD. Furthermore, local and state election data make clear that loyalty to incumbent parties has declined dramatically and that voters are concerned with a candidate's performance, not his or her party label. From 1988 through 2002, incumbent parties holding mayoralty posts were at an advantage over their opponents, but that advantage declined from their winning 90 percent of the time in 1988 to only 48 percent in 2003.[42]

When voters were asked to identify specific attributes with individual parties, surprisingly they made no distinctions among the three on good government or improving the future, nor significantly on the issue of being concerned with that particular ability. Major differences are associated with perceptions of corruption. Half of the respondents identified PRI with corruption, the highest single response associated with any party. Only 14 and 12 percent, respectively, identified this variable with PAN and PRD. On the issue of economic growth, PAN received stronger support, but PRD and PRI ranked similarly on that issue. Finally, nearly a third of the respondents identified PRI and the PRD as conflictual, compared to only 16 percent who gave PAN that label. As noted, independents, as they did in 2000, will likely determine the outcome of the 2006 election. When they were asked that same questions, they provided a decidedly different response on several crucial attributes, attributes that will affect their vote if these views continue through July 2006. They ranked PRI significantly lower in providing good government than PAN or PRD, and they ranked it equally low on producing a better future, while giving higher marks to PRD. Especially important is the fact that independents, by a huge margin, believed that PRD is interested in people like them (32 percent compared to only 16 percent for PAN and 12 percent for PRI). Independents, similar to all voters, view PAN as the party most strongly associated with economic growth and least identified with conflict.[43] As of 2006, voters were more likely to support PRI candidates for congress than PRD and PAN nominees, by a small margin.

The three leading presidential candidates were Manuel López Obrador of the PRD, Felipe Calderón of the PAN, and Roberto Madrazo of the PRI. Of the three, López Obrador was by far the most popular among the partisan voters of any party, and led in the presidential horserace in national polls for nearly two years. By the end of 2005, López Obrador and Calderón were neck and neck among voters. For the first three months of 2006, however, López Obrador built a solid lead over his competitors, reaching 8–10 percentage points ahead of Calderón by mid-March. But at the end of that month, once again, the two leading candidates were in a technical tie, with Madrazo closely behind. In one respect, the 2006 election parallels that of 2000. For any candidate to win the presidency, he would have to attract votes personally and carry his party to victory, similar to Fox. The PRD's candidate, however, has to increase his party's base most dramatically, given that PRD is a distant third among the three major parties in partisan supporters, whereas PAN provided Fox with a larger partisan base. As José Antonio Crespo has noted, López Obrador began organizing support committees in 2005, similar to the Friends of Fox, the crucial organization in Fox's campaign success in 2000.[44] Furthermore, even in the 2004 elections, after PRD improved its congressional representation a year earlier, it remained the most concentrated of regional parties, and in half of the states where elections took place, it received 10 percent or fewer of the votes. In 2005, probable voters gave more support to the PAN and the PRI than to their candidates.

In professional aptitudes, voters in 2006 ranked Calderón and López Obrador more positively than they did PRI's candidate, Roberto Madrazo. In 2000, it will be recalled, the candidates' professional abilities were not important variables in determining the outcome. The electorate has opened the door for another outside candidate, similar to Fox, indicating they would prefer a qualified citizen to a professional politician as their president (52 to 38 percent). They also desire a strong president who will pursue the appropriate policy even when it is unpopular. Interestingly, when asked to classify the three candidates as historical personages, half the voters identified Madrazo as a villain, and nearly a third identified López Obrador as a reformer and hero.[45]

López Obrador, the PRD candidate, took a strong lead among the presidential candidates by early 2004. One of the reasons his strength persisted is because a large percentage (42) of swing voters from the other parties and independents who voted for Fox in 2000 supported him. Equally important, López Obrador initially received strong support from the middle class. Although his support began to waver, Fox, with the help of PRI in congress, decided in 2005 to bring legal charges against López Obrador for abusing his power as governor of the Federal District by ignoring repeatedly a court order over a right of way. Although the legal violation was clear, and the legal matter itself, by Mexican standards, minor, the populace, and indeed many politicians, perceived the strategy against López Obrador to be entirely politically motivated, so as to remove him as a potential presidential candidate (candidates may not be under formal legal proceedings). The strategy backfired completely. López Obrador revived his candidacy and became a stronger frontrunner until April 2006.

The 2006 presidential race proved to be as exciting to observers as was the case six years earlier. Despite the fact that López Obrador took an early lead—in part because he demonstrated much stronger name recognition long before Calderón became a candidate—his PAN opponent was able late in the campaign to catch up and briefly took a small lead over López Obrador in April–May, 2006. For the last six months of the campaign, the PRI nominee, Roberto Madrazo, essentially remained a static candidate with a solid but unchanging percentage of support among slightly more than one fourth of intended voters, primarily PRI partisans. His candidacy, nevertheless, raises several implications for the electoral process. First, given the fact that Madrazo represents the traditional wing of his party, his poor showing in the race will force PRI's leadership to struggle over the kind of candidates they hope to nominate in the future. Unlike the other two political parties, support for PRI nationally has been essentially stronger than its candidate, and its congressional candidates have performed better than its presidential nominee (28 to 22 percent).

If we compare voter suppport for the leading candidates in 2006 with voter support for the PRI and PAN candidates in 2000, we can identify some significant strengths and weaknesses of the candidates. Fox received 43 percent of the vote in 2000, but he performed most successfully among the following groups: well-educated voters achieving high school, preparatory, and college educations (49 to 60 percent of voters); citizens residing in the North and the Center-West (49 percent); younger voters, ages eighteen to thirty-nine (47 to 50 percent); and urban residents (48 percent). Among actual voters on July 2, 2006, Calderón—who obtained almost 36 percent of the vote—received strong support from younger voters (who account for 79 percent of all voters) under age forty-nine (38 percent), those residing in the North and Center-West (43 and 47 percent), university-educated Mexicans (42 percent), higher-income voters (43 and 50 percent), urban residents (40 percent), beneficiaries of social programs (41 and 44 percent), and most decisively, those who thought their personal economic situation would improve (60 percent). López Obrador, in contrast, appealed to older voters (37 percent), lower income groups (34 and 39 percent), voters on the left (62 percent), independents (43 percent), residents of the Center and South (44 and 40 percent), and those Mexicans who expected their economic situation to worsen (52 percent).

The campaign itself became a crucial factor in determining the changing fortunes of the two leading candidates during the final weeks of the race. The months of April and May witnessed a change in the PRD candidate's growing lead. Data from survey research reveal shifting voter preferences during this brief period. The most notable changes among voter perceptions of the candidates in those weeks include the following. First, Madrazo's strongest base of support, other than voters who supported PRI's candidate in 2000, was among residents of the 7 northern states led by PRI governors. But his support there declined dramatically after March, shifting strongly in favor of Calderón. Between the last polls in mid-June and the vote on July 2, some 20 percent of his intended voters abandoned the PRI candidate, many of them in the North. On the other hand, Calderón, whose stronghold could be found in the 9 PAN-controlled states for most of the campaign, lost significant support there two months before the election, support which initially split in favor of the PRI and PRD candidates, but revived in favor of Calderón at the close of the presidential race. López Obrador witnessed declines in the PRD-controlled states and the PRI-dominated South-Center states, where he polled strongest. In general terms, from March to June, López Obrador converted more support from southern Mexico and Calderón acquired increased voter preferences from the North.

Unlike the presidential debates in the 2000 race, most pollsters believe the televised debates in 2006 did not produce a major shift in voter preferences. In the first debate, López Obrador, by declining to participate, reinforced a growing negative image among voters of a candidate who was arrogant, symbolized for all viewers to see by his empty podium. Calderón was perceived to have won the debate by a sizeable margin, but the small party candidates benefited most. López Obrador's decision to exclude himself, combined with his rude criticisms of President Fox, helped to reinforce an aggressive, negative PAN advertising campaign painting him as a "danger to the republic." Each of these factors contributed to López Obrador's decline in the polls. The second debate, in June, essentially reinforced existing voter perceptions, which already favored, once again, López Obrador, despite Calderón being perceived as the winner.

Learning a lesson from Calderón, López Obrador began his own negative advertising campaign against the PAN candidate, quadrupling his ads in May and June. This led to a major decline in how voters viewed Calderon's integrity, which prior to the ads was rated the most positive of the three leading candidates. Just three weeks before the election, López Obrador (compared to Calderón) was able to reestablish himself as being most capable or characterized by the following qualities: help people most (38 to 26 percent), most able to solve problems (28 to 19 percent), most able to improve your economic situation (32 to 29 percent), and most able to combat poverty (37 to 26 percent). The fact that 71 percent of López Obrador's supporters favored him since October 2005, compared to only 56 percent preferring Calderón, explains the weakness and fluidity of Calderón supporters.

Despite López Obrador's stronger showing in the final polls carried out in early to mid-June, at press time official results show that Calderón was able to eke out a narrow victory of one half of a percentage point over his opponent (35.88 percent over 35.31 percent, or approximately 240,000 votes). López Obrador has requested an official recount of the entire vote by the Federal Electoral Tribunal, a special election court, which has until September 6th to declare an official winner. However, given the strict legal procedures and specific requirements for the court to reopen and count any ballot boxes, it is unlikely that a total recount will occur—and, if so, that the result of the election will be altered.

What is most important about the 2006 elections is that regardless of which candidate is declared the official winner, no candidate won a simple majority of the votes and no party controls congress. If Mr. Calderón's narrow victory over López Obrador by one half percent of the vote is confirmed by the electoral court, it gives him the weakest mandate of any president in recent history, matched by a small plurality in the legislative branch (42 percent of the seats). Thus Mexico is likely to repeat the political impasse between the executive and legislative branches characterizing Fox's government after it took office on December 1, 2000. Such a small plurality reinforced by a three-party system does not augur well for governance or for Mexican democracy.

PARTIES: THEIR ORIGINS AND FUTURE

National Action Party

Mexican electoral politics is dominated by three parties: PAN, PRI, and the PRD. Given the persistence of electoral democracy, the parties' ability to survive, adjust, and eliminate their weaknesses will determine their success in the first decade of the twenty-first century. All three parties have something in common: their leadership is divided and they boast various factions favoring different party platforms. The most important of the three parties, given its control over the national executive branch, is the National Action Party, which, until its victory in 2000, was Mexico's longest-lived opposition party. The PAN was founded in 1939 by Manuel Gómez Morin, a former national figure in government economic policymaking, and Efraín González Luna, a lawyer and Catholic activist. As is true of so many of the opposition parties, leadership often came, at least initially, from disgruntled establishment elites. In some cases it is persons who have had their own political ambitions cut short; in other cases it is a question of policy differences. The PAN's formation is an example of the latter's bringing together diverse individuals who were against the statist, populist economic policies of President Lázaro Cárdenas (1934–1940).

The PAN first put up candidates against the PRI on the local level. Although it had supported several opposition presidential candidates, it did not run its own candidate until 1958. It put up a candidate in every election since then except 1976, when it protested the PRI's monopoly and electoral fraud by withdrawing from the presidential contest. Ten years after its founding, it captured less than 3 percent of the legislative seats (Table 8-2). After the first electoral reforms went into effect in 1964, it began obtaining roughly 10 percent of the seats, assisted by its share of party deputies. Its representation stabilized around that figure until 1988, when it doubled its share to 20 percent. In the 1991–1993 legislature it fell to 18 percent but rebounded to 24 and 26 percent in 1994 and 1997, respectively.

The PAN ideological banner has shifted over time. Initially, party leaders, many of whom were well connected financially or had ties to Catholic Action youth or other Catholic movements, were described as conservative, in some cases reactionary, pro-business, and pro-church. By the 1960s the party evolved gradually into a Mexican variant of a Christian Democratic organization.[46] However, like the PRI and especially the left-of-center parties, the PAN suffered from internal dissent. At various points its leadership wavered between those desirous of playing more or less by the rules of the political game, as set down by the government, and those who advocated a more aggressive stance vis-á-vis the PRI.

The new PAN activists since the 1980s, sometimes referred to as neo-Panistas, have taken a more conservative stance ideologically and have often allied themselves with combative businessmen willing to run under the PAN banner. As Soledad Loaeza suggested in her analysis of the 1988 presidential election, the neo-Panistas broke new ground "by challenging the unwritten rules of Mexican politics—in particular, the idea that industrialists should not participate in politics."[47] When President Salinas took some of the thunder out of traditional PAN issues, like statism, labor corruption, and outmoded church-state relations, the PAN centered its major criticism on political modernization, notably genuine electoral reform, a popular issue with the electorate.

The PAN's growth nationally was never dramatic. It remained the major opposition party, except during the 1988 presidential race, but its strength from 1982 to 1993 stabilized at approximately 17 percent. In 1994, it established a stronger presence, accounting for half of all opposition votes cast, a fourth of the electorate. National figures and figures from each of the three hundred majority districts suggest the regional quality of PAN support. Its organizational strength and the narrowness of its platform made it viable primarily in urban centers. Vicente Fox significantly increased PAN's support, especially strengthening the party in rural areas, although most new voters were supporting Fox, not the party. Indeed, it would be accurate to call the PAN a regional, urban party. In 1988, the first time that the PAN won more than 10 percent of the legislative majority districts, the thirty-eight seats it obtained were in the major cities, including Ciudad Juárez; Mexico City; León; Guadalajara, the capital of Jalisco; several districts in the industrialized section of the state of México; San Luis Potosí and Mérida, both state capitals; and Culiacán. In fact, four-fifths of its legislative seats were in just five Mexican cities. The PAN repeated the same pattern in 1994, but more than half its eighteen seats were from Jalisco and five from the north. Two-thirds of the districts it captured were from León, Guadalajara, and Mérida. In 1997, when it won sixty-five seats, more than half were from Jalisco, Guanajuato, México, Baja California, and Nuevo León. By 2000, it more than doubled the number of seats, to 141, and although Fox helped expand its representation to other districts, more than half the seats were from the Federal District, Guanajuato, Jalisco, and México. After 2003, however, PAN declined in the Federal District, while maintaining strong representation in México, Guanajuato, Veracruz, Jalisco, and Baja California.

PAN's potential in the future is strongest at the local and state levels. One might have expected it to grow most dramatically in the North, where many of its original supporters in the business community gave it national prominence.[48] Instead, PAN's strength has expanded to states in other regions as well. By 1997, it had elected mayors in 308 cities. In 2004, it controlled 276 municipalities (18 percent), where 18 million people reside. By 2005, PAN politicians had governed twelve different states, eight of them in regions other than the north.

PAN's national future, in spite of its presidential victory, is less sure. There are several reasons for this. First, Vicente Fox is an outsider, a populist version of a Panista, who used his personal charisma and his own organization to complement PAN's appeal, building on the small but solid base of partisan supporters. Three out of ten Mexicans were partisan supporters of PAN in 2000, but PAN will have to work hard to retain these Mexicans as core supporters. A third of its partisans converted to PAN in 2000. The 2003 elections demonstrated that PAN had not expanded beyond its core supporters.[49]

Second, PAN has preserved control of the party bureaucracy by promoting figures whose political experience was in the national, legislative branch. Most of these individuals boasted kinship or personal ties with the party's founders or leadership from earlier periods. PAN always has selected its presidential candidate democratically, but the selection process was internal, limited to a group of active party delegates. Some politicians inside the party want to renovate what they have described as an aristocracy among the leadership and to promote a more open process in policy debates and a direct, secret, universal vote of party members for both candidates and leaders. PAN has moved away from the more restrictive selection process to one that incorporates party activists generally, not just delegates. It has approved a process for the selection of its presidential candidate, in which all registered members of PAN may participate in the selection process. There will be a runoff if no candidate obtains an absolute majority.

The third reason why PAN faces an uphill battle to maintain and increase its national strength is the reason why most voters, other than traditional PAN partisans, voted for the party and its presidential candidate in 2000. The vast majority of new PAN partisans voted for the party because it represented a change from PRI. At least since 1990, many voters have viewed PAN as the primary alternative to PRI, rather than as a party whose ideology corresponds to their individual views. PAN's growth, therefore, depends heavily on its performance in office, whether it is at the national, state, or local levels. In the state where PAN has governed the longest (twelve years), Baja California, voters were asked in the summer of 2001 if they considered Panista governments to have been better, equal, or worse than Priista governments in their state. Only 36 percent replied that PAN produced better administrations, while 41 percent said they were equal, and 14 percent, worse. PAN, therefore, has not necessarily established an edge in future contests where it is the incumbent.[50] This argument is confirmed by the data presented earlier, which demonstrates that incumbency does not favor PAN or any party at the local level.

Democratic Revolutionary Party

The second national party is the Democratic Revolutionary Party. The PRD has a short history; it constructed itself on a foundation of smaller leftist parties that had flowered during the 1970s. Elements of the Mexican Communist Party (PCM), founded in 1919, and the Mexican Socialist Party (PMS), founded in 1987, provided the formal organizational basis. The PRD came into being after the 1988 presidential election. Many of its founders, as in the case of the PAN, were PRI dissidents.[51] Some of its members in the Chamber of Deputies and in the Senate previously held political posts as Priistas or as leftist-party members. In fact, so many figures resigned from the PRI to become contenders for PRD candidacies in gubernatorial races in 1998, that it provoked a negative reaction among many PRD leaders.

The results of the 1988 election were deceptive in terms of PRD strength. The immense popularity of candidate Cárdenas's father among many sectors of the population made it difficult to distinguish support for Cuauhtémoc Cárdenas as a symbol of his father from support for the principles of his coalition. Those who voted for the PRD, as in the case of the PAN, were primarily interested in change. But the PRD, even more than the PAN, owing to its origins in a loosely connected alliance of small parties, has found it difficult to maintain its cohesion.

By 1991 PRD electoral strength had declined precipitously to only 8 percent of the vote, a distant third to the PRI and the PAN (Table 8-1). The PRD faced electoral conditions involving fraud, and many of its active supporters were physically threatened, injured, or killed. In fact, PRD members constituted the single largest group of victims in national and international Human Rights Commission reports in the early 1990s. The PRI also was successful in 1994 in convincing many voters to associate electoral violence with the PRD. That fact, combined with Cárdenas's poor performance in the first televised presidential debate, ensured PRD's third-place position.

The 1997 midterm elections offered both Cárdenas and the PRD an opportunity to revive its electoral fortunes. Cárdenas became the party's standard-bearer in the most significant race, that of the newly elected head of the Federal District, Mexico's most influential urban center. Changing his campaign style and benefiting from deteriorating social and economic conditions, as well as a poor campaign by his PAN opponent, Cárdenas easily defeated PRI's candidate. Using the Federal District's thirty congressional seats as a base, the party swept to victory in twenty-nine districts and recaptured its original strength in México, Michoacán, and Morelos, states where it did well in 1988. It won nearly the same percentage of votes as PAN nationally, 26 percent, but it did slightly better in the plurinominal regions, thus receiving more seats and giving it second place after PRI in the Chamber of Deputies. In 2000, however, PRD's national strength remained stagnant at 17 percent of the vote for president (one-tenth of a percent less than in 1994), as PAN's increased and PRI's declined dramatically. PRD won only 28 districts in congress, one less than in 1997. It could claim significant representation congressionally only in Michoacán, Cárdenas' home state, Tabasco, and Zacatecas.

Cárdenas used his position as head of the Federal District to make a third run for the presidency in 2000. By imposing himself as the party's candidate, Cárdenas further accentuated divisions within its leadership. Those divisions spilled into the public arena. In addition to the serious problems inside the party, the PRD appeared hypocritical to many Mexicans, advocating democracy in the political arena, but not entertaining it within the party itself. PRD's candidate selection process contrasted with PRI's decision to hold an open primary, allowing any registered voter to cast a vote for its presidential candidate. In 2005, the PRD approved new internal regulations, including a decision to hold an open primary to select its presidential candidate. Unlike PRI's initial experience in 1999, the PRD also allows any individual who is not a PRD member, who meets the constitutional requirements, to compete against party members for the nomination.

After the party's poor performance in the 2000 presidential race, the leadership divisions multiplied in intensity and number. In 2001, three major groups existed within the party leadership: the Refoundation wing headed by Cuauhtémoc Cárdenas and Rosario Robles, the New Left group led by Jesús Ortega and Jesús Zambrano, and the Amalistas, directed by Amalia García, a former party president, and Raymundo Cárdenas. None of the three groups dominates the party, and therefore its governability relies on compromises among these three factions.[52] The party continued to be characterized by internal splits and dissension, but after the decision by PAN and PRI members of congress to deprive Manuel López Obrador of his immunity, party leadership put aside its differences and decided to maintain a united front through the 2006 presidential elections.

The PRD's ideology is difficult to characterize because the party's ranks are an amalgam of political groups professing views ranging from Marxist to populist. Some issues prominent in the PRD platform and that have distinguished it from the PRI include electoral reforms, fiscal reforms, broad social programs, women's rights, and free education. In short, the PRD advocated the diversification of economic relations, increased political pluralism in the electoral arena, programs to mitigate the negative effects of NAFTA, and thoroughgoing electoral reforms. With electoral democracy in place, PRD's most distinctive position is that it favors economic policies that cater less to business interests and advocates the traditional importance of the state in economic affairs.[53] At its sixth National Congress in 2001, the PRD leadership committed itself to "deepening the democratization of the state," to make "the struggle against social inequality a priority," and to confirm that it is "the genuine representative of Mexico's left."[54]

In an unusual interview with 484 PRD delegates at the VIII Congress in Mexico City in 2004, the delegates characterized the party in the following terms. (1) Three-fifths of those delegates identified at least eleven different political currents within the party, the largest being the New Left. (2) The delegates were most disgusted with the conflicts among the various leadership groups. (3) They considered their most important task to attract new voters. (4) The party should focus its resources on expanding its geographic base. (5) Two-thirds of the delegates believed PRD should maintain its political programs. (6) Four-fifths supported differentiating itself ideologically from the other parties. (7) 90 percent supported the candidacy of López Obrador as president. (8) Party members favored democracy followed by economic development as the priorities for the country but, at the same time, overwhelmingly favored social justice over economic development and democracy. (9) Party members agreed that the state had the responsibility for achieving social justice, even if it meant public instability.[55]

PRD's future is conditioned by three significant elements. First, it will depend on the ability of its leadership to resolve major issues in party governance after 2006. Second, it will have to reorganize from its grassroots base and rely on its local party activists and leaders for recruits to national political positions, just as its delegates suggested, reinforcing an earlier decision to use its base committees as the foundation for a bottom to top reorganization.[56] Third, voter support on the left represents a minority of Mexicans and shows no signs of expanding. Even though it increased the number of congressional districts it won in 2003 at the expense of PAN, PRD actually received 17.7 percent of the vote, 1 percent less than it did in 2000. As Mexico approached the 2006 presidential race, even though its candidate, López Obrador, initially led the field by a large margin, with 39 percent of the independent voters and 20 percent of Priistas indicating they would vote for him, at the same time, only 19 percent of the voters said they would vote for the PRD. López Obrador, as of mid-2006, demonstrated the same abilities as Fox in attracting support from partisans and independents alike. On the other hand, it is not clear that he could get his party's candidates elected to other offices. PRD does offer a platform distinct from the other two major national parties, but that platform, to date, appeals only to a limited number of voters. If the PRD leadership can maintain party unity, which it was able to do in 2005, it has the potential to continue exercising a decisive role in the national legislature between PAN and PRI. The party did make a crucial decision, however, not to share power in the executive branch, even when offered the opportunity, as was the case when Fox was forming his first cabinet.

Institutional Revolutionary Party

Much of the history of PRI, Mexico's third party, already has been discussed as a component of the evolution of Mexico's authoritarian governmental leadership. In the post-2000 electoral era, PRI shares similar problems with the other two parties. PRI went into the election as a transitional party whose leadership depended nearly completely on the incumbent president and whose candidates were selected internally by party leaders, the president, and PRI governors. PRI has been forced to cut its umbilical ties financially and structurally with the state. Since July 2000, it has begun operating as an independent political organization.

The party's leadership is broadly divided into two factions, a younger group who wants to transform the party into a competitive political organization by democratizing its leadership and making it responsive to its grassroots members. The second faction, dominated by a group of traditionalist governors, often referred to as dinosaurs, wants to keep the party's leadership under tighter control and continue some of the practices from the party's nondemocratic past. Ideologically, they are opposed to some of the features of economic neoliberalism. The democratic reformist wing, led by President Zedillo himself, partially transformed the image of the party by implementing, for the first time in the party's history, a democratic selection process for its presidential candidate. Critics charged that Zedillo's candidate was Francisco Labastida, who was thus favored by party insiders. Nevertheless, the party chose to use an open primary, the first time any party in Mexico had opened up its presidential candidacy to all registered voters. It could not hold a closed primary because it did not have a complete list of members. Labastida was opposed by the then PRI governor of Tabasco, Roberto Madrazo, a leading politician from the traditionalist wing, and the campaign was fierce.[57] Since then, under the leadership of Madrazo, PRI's presidential candidate in 2006, the party has withdrawn from its wide-open primary system, and instead implemented in 2005 a selection process long used previously by PAN, a secret vote of party delegates.[58]

The PRI's National Political Council met in 2001, and authorized its National Executive Committee to organize a national assembly at the end of the year. The assembly represented an innovative decision on the part of the party leadership because at least 30 percent of the participants were elected through a direct and secret vote at municipal and district assemblies. Furthermore, the party leadership, in recognition of Fox's appeal to younger voters, required that a third of the party activists attending the assembly be under 30 years of age. The party leadership also decided, after protests from PRI activists to expand the selection of the party's second in command, the secretary general, to an open, elective process inside the party.[59] After the party held its national assembly in November 2001, it passed several significant resolutions, among them that 40 percent of the party's candidates would be women and 30 percent would be individuals under 30 years of age.

A survey of delegates attending the PRI national assembly suggests another significant characteristic which has implications for partisan support. The delegates revealed that 37 percent describe themselves as center-left or left ideologically speaking. Similar to the data reported in Table 8-5, however, 50 percent of the party's sympathizers considered themselves on the center-right or right. These data indicate a major difference between the party's grass-roots leaders compared to its most likely supporters.

The question that interests most analysts of Mexico is what will happen to PRI now that it no longer controls the national executive branch and, therefore, is deprived of a huge source of patronage and financial influence. The party has demonstrated, in spite of its current leadership divisions, a continued ability to evolve into an independent political organization. If it truly relies on its grass-roots political activists, it will not only survive as Mexico's strongest national party, but has the potential to evolve and grow, solidifying its local and regional base.

Despite its dramatic defeat by PAN, PRI continues to maintain the strongest presence at the state level. It clearly demonstrated its political power to recover and to defeat the PAN in the 2003 congressional elections, winning 53 percent of the 300 districts, twice that of PAN. On the regional level, PRI continues to control 59 percent of Mexico's cities and over half of the state governships. In short, it remains a majority party at its base, but is unable to translate that strength into an equally strong presidential candidacy. To maintain this grass-roots strength, and to expand its base in the future, it needs to do what PAN accomplished in the previous decade—demonstrate to the electorate at the state and local level that it can govern effectively and be accountable to the people. Since 2002, it has demonstrated its ability to do that.

CONCLUSION

Mexico's electoral landscape has changed completely since July 2000. No party has a lock on Mexico's political future. In fact, one characteristic they all share is the fact that Mexicans have little confidence in political parties. This has been the case for years, and Fox's victory has not changed that view. Fewer than one out of four Mexicans has any confidence whatsoever in the three parties.[60] It is well to remember that even with the extraordinary advances of PAN, and to a much lesser extent the PRD at all levels—local, state, and national—no incumbent party is secure in any of its posts. Recent historical experience clearly demonstrates that despite their initial popularity, newly incumbent parties fail to convince voters to return them to office in the next election.[61] The reasons for voter disenchantment are often the same as those given for citizen dissatisfaction with PRI when it was the incumbent party: incompetence, unfulfilled campaign pledges, and corruption. Thus, PRI's ability to stage a comeback depends not only on its performance but on that of its opponents, once they have garnered elective office. PAN's loss to PRI in the 1998 Chihuahua gubernatorial race, returning the state to PRI control, illustrates the competitive nature of electoral competition. In fact, as one study concluded, "over 90 percent of the Mexican federal electoral districts are now competitive among two or more parties."[62]

PAN has three important advantages over PRI and PRD in the immediate future. First, as suggested above, the ideological preferences of the voters coincide with their view of PAN's ideology. That is not fixed forever. If PRI loses its image as a party opposed to democratic practices, in elections and elsewhere, it may shed its far-right label. That would expand its appeal among voters.

PAN also has an advantage over its two leading opponents because, as of the July 2000 elections, it established a firm base among younger voters, individuals who form a significant component of the electorate. If it can retain those voters, it has the potential for establishing lifelong partisans through the first half of the twenty-first century. However, its ability to accomplish that task, as Joseph Klesner suggests in his electoral analysis, will depend on the party's ability to retain voters who were recruited by the Amigos de Fox, which claimed as many as 4.5 million members shortly before the election.[63] PRI was able to erode its appeal to this group in 2003, demonstrating its fluidity.

Finally, PAN partisans are fewer than PRI's and more numerous than PRD's, but PRI is viewed most negatively in the context of controlling the national, executive branch. Furthermore, PRD and PRI both are viewed as obstructionist parties given their role in Fox's policy failures. Nevertheless, the unwillingness and inability of all the parties to negotiate policy solutions has worked to the detriment of political parties and democracy, reflected in the figures that 83 percent of Mexicans were dissatisfied with democracy and an equal number viewed the country as pursing the wrong path in 2005.[64]

The future of electoral politics in Mexico, regardless of each of the parties' individual strengths, is likely to remain divided among at least three major parties, and remain a contentious, multiple-party system. Many of Mexico's future national leaders will reflect much stronger party ties and experience and will achieve recognition as potential national figures because of demonstrated skills as legislative negotiators and gubernatorial executives.

NOTES

1. For background, see John Bailey, "Can the PRI be Reformed," in *Mexican Politics in Transition,* ed. Judith Gentleman (Boulder, Colo.: Westview Press, 1987), especially, 74–94.

2. Wayne Cornelius, "Political Liberalization in an Authoritarian Regime: Mexico, 1976–1985," in *Mexican Politics in Transition,* ed. Judith Gentleman (Boulder, Colo.: Westview Press, 1987), 22.

3. María Emilia Farias Mackey, *The Reform of Electoral Policy* (Mexico: Congreso de la Unión, 1987), 8–9. A detailed analysis of the motivations behind these changes are available in Silvia Gómez Tagle's "Electoral Reform and the Party System, 1977–90," in *Mexico: Dilemmas of Transition,* ed. Neil Harvey (London: Institute of Latin American Studies, 1993), 64–90.

4. Daniel Levy and Gabriel Székely, *Mexico: Paradoxes of Stability and Change,* 2d ed. (Boulder, Colo.: Westview Press, 1987), 68.

5. For detailed background, see Delal Baer, "The 1986 Mexican Elections, The Case of Chihuahua," CSIS Latin American Election Study Series (Washington, D.C.: Georgetown University, September 1986); and Vikram Khub Chand, "Politicization, Institutions, and Democratization in Mexico: The Politics of the State of Chihuahua in National Perspective" (Ph.D. diss., Harvard University, 1991).

6. For a detailed analysis of this conflict and its national consequences, see Vikram K. Chand, *Mexico's Political Awakening* (Notre Dame: University of Notre Dame Press, 2001).

7. For background, see Peter H. Smith, "The 1988 Presidential Succession in Historical Perspective," in *Mexico's Alternative Political Futures,* eds. Wayne Cornelius, Judith Gentleman, and Peter H. Smith (La Jolla, Calif.: U.S.–Mexico Studies Center, UCSD, 1989), 399ff.

8. Roderic Ai Camp, "Mexico," in *Latin America and Caribbean Contemporary Record*, eds. James M. Malloy and Eduardo A. Gamarra (New York: Holmes & Meier, 1990), B300.

9. MORI de México weekly poll for *Este País*, February 23 and April 20, 1994.

10. These and other changes are outlined in detail in George Grayson's excellent summary, *A Guide to the 1994 Mexican Presidential Election*, CSIS Election Studies Report (Washington, D.C.: CSIS, 1994), 8–10; and in John Bailey, *The 1994 Mexican Presidential Election*, CSIS Election Studies Series (Washington, D.C.: CSIS, 1994).

11. An excellent summary of opinions and discussion concerning the significance of the 1994 elections can be found in "Mexico's Electoral Aftermath and Political Future," summary of a conference at the Mexican Center, University of Texas, Austin, September 2–3, 1994; and in Enrique Calderón Alzati and Daniel Cazés, eds., *Las elecciones presidenciales de 1994* (Mexico: UNAM, 1996).

12. Numerous criticisms of the shortcomings of the 1994 election, before and during election day, can be found in Human Rights Watch/Americas, "Mexico at the Crossroads" 6 (August 1994): 1–24; Civic Alliance, "The Quality of the Election Day Process, August 21, 1994," September 19, 1994; "The Prospects for a Free, Fair and Honest Election in Mexico," A Report to the Business Coordinating Council, August 15, 1994; the Washington Office on Latin America, "The 1994 Mexican Election: A Question of Credibility," Washington, D.C., August 15, 1994; and the Instituto Federal Electoral, "Main Criticisms to the Electoral Roll and the Nominal Lists" (Mexico City: IFE, 1994).

13. Belden and Russonello, "Mexico 1994: A National Poll of the Mexican Electorate," Washington, D.C., August 10, 1994.

14. Leonardo French Iduarte, "The Mexican Presidential Election in the Mass Media of the United States," in *Sucesión Presidencial: The 1988 Mexican Presidential Election*, eds. Edgar W. Butler and Jorge A. Bustamante (Boulder, Colo.: Westview Press, 1991), 218.

15. For an excellent analysis, see Joseph Klesner, "Electoral Reform in Mexico's Hegemonic Party System: Perpetuation of Privilege or Democratic Advance? Paper presented at the American Political Science Association meeting, Washington, D.C., 1997.

16. Armand Peschard-Sverdrup, *The 1997 Mexican Midterm Elections: Post-Election Report*, Western Hemisphere Election Study Series (Washington, D.C.: CSIS, 1997), 6.

17. Partisans of all three parties ranked personal security, economic crisis, and unemployment as the principal issues in the election. *Este País*, July 1997, 37.

18. Ulises Beltrán et al., *Los mexicanos de los noventa* (Mexico: UNAM, 1996), 37.

19. *Este País*, May 1998, 16.

20. See my "Mexico's 1988 Elections: A Turning Point for Its Political Development and Foreign Relations," in *Sucesión Presidencial: The 1988 Mexican Presidential Elections*, eds. Edgar W. Butler and Jorge A. Bustamante (Boulder, Colo.: Westview Press, 1991), 98ff.

21. Barry Ames, "Bases of Support for Mexico's Dominant Party," *American Political Science Review* 64 (March 1970): 153–67.

22. For the most comprehensive analysis of these and other variables, see Joseph Klesner, "Electoral Reform in an Authoritarian Regime: The Case of Mexico" (Ph.D. diss., MIT, February 1988); for 1988, Antonia Martínez Rodríguez, "Que hable México: último gobierno priista?" *Revista de Estudios Políticos* 63 (January–March 1989): 251–58; and for 1991, see Joseph Klesner, "Realignment or Dealignment? Consequences of Economic Crisis and Restructuring for the Mexican Party System," in *The Politics of Economic Restructuring: State-Society Relations and Regime Change*, eds. Maria Lorena Cook, Kevin J. Middlebrook, and Juan Molinar (La Jolla, Calif.: Center for U.S.–Mexican Studies, UCSD, 1994), 159–94.

23. *New York Times*, August 23, 1994, 1, 8.

24. The most careful analysis of the relationship between government spending and PRI support between 1988 and 1991 found only a marginally significant connection. Kathleen Bruhn, "Social Spending and Political Support," *Comparative Politics* (January 1996): 151–77.

25. Alberto Hernández Hernández, "Political Attitudes Among Border Youth," in *Electoral Patterns and Perspectives in Mexico*, ed. Arturo Alvarado (La Jolla, Calif.: Center for U.S.–Mexican Studies, UCSD, 1987), 216.

26. William J. Millard, *Media Use by the Better-Educated in Major Mexican Cities* (Washington, D.C.: U.S. International Communications Agency, 1981); Alberto Hernández Medina and Luis Narro Rodríguez, eds. *Cómo somos los mexicanos* (Mexico City: CREA, 1987).

27. Comments, Symposium on Mexican Electoral Reform, Institute of Latin American Studies, University of Texas, March 1991, Austin.

28. Joseph Klesner, "The 1994 Mexican Elections: Manifestations of a Divided Society," *Mexican Studies* 11 (Winter 1995): 137–50.

29. *Review of the Economic Situation of Mexico*, September 1997, 363.

30. See "The Voter Profile," *Review of the Economic Situation of Mexico*, July 2000, 267.

31. "Los Antipriístas se inclinan por Fox," *Diario de Yucatán*, June 23, 2000. www.diariodeyucatan.com.mx.

32. "La perinola sigue girando," *Reforma*, July 29, 2000, www.reforma.com .mx. Alejandro Moreno, *El votante mexicano, democracia, actitudes políticas y conducta electoral* (Mexico: Fondo de Cultura Económica, 2003), 71, 108ff.

33. José Antonio Crespo, *Raising the Bar: The Next Generation of Electoral Reforms in Mexico* (Washington, D.C.: CSIS, 2000). For comparative figures from 1994 and 1997, see Mony de Swaan, "En busca de la equidad, financiamiento público a partidos políticos," *Este País*, (March 2000), 12–16.

34. Seymour Martin Lipset, Robert M. Worcester, and Frederick C. Turner, "Opening the Mexican Political System: Public Opinion and the Elections of 1994 and 1997," *Studies in Comparative International Development*, 33 (Fall 1998), 83.

35. Isabel Vázquez, "Political Parties and the Election Platforms," *Review of the Economic Situation of Mexico* (June 2003), 259.

36. Alejandro Poiré, "A Non-Majority Mandate in Mexico's 2003 Election?" unpublished paper, September 2003.

37. Andrés Albo, "The pre-Election Pulse," *Review of the Economic Situation of Mexico* (June 2003), 263–66.

38. Andrés Albo, "The Balance and Consequences of July 6," *Review of the Economic Situation of Mexico* (July 2003), 288–92.

39. "Elecciones 2003, encuesta sobre preferencias," *Reforma*, April 28, 2003.

40. Chris Kraul, "Fox's Party Suffers Defeat in Stronghold," *Los Angeles Times*, July 5, 2004, A3.

41. Alejandro Moreno, *El votante mexicano: democracia, actitudes políticas y conducta electoral* (Mexico: Fondo de Cultura Económica, 2003).

42. Carlo Varela, "The Electoral Processes Have Begun," *Review of the Economic Situation of Mexico* (June 2004), 220–24.

43. Bimsa, "Imagen de los partidos políticos," nactional poll, 1000 respondents, February 9–14, 2005, +/–3.1 margin of error.

44. José Antonio Crespo, "The Party System and Democratic Governance in Mexico," Policy Paper on the Americas (Washington, D.C.: CSIS, 2004), 35.

45. "Dividen votos por región," *Reforma*, February 28, 2005, 8A; and "Alcanza Calderón a AMLO," *Reforma*, November 21, 2005.

46. Donald Mabry, *Mexico's Acción Nacional: A Catholic Alternative to Revolution* (Syracuse, N.Y.: Syracuse University Press, 1973). For an update on the reasons for its growth, see Leticia Barraza and Ilán Bizberg, "El Partido Acción Nacional y el régimen político mexicano," *Foro Internacional* 31 (January–March 1991): 418–45.

47. Soledad Loaeza, "The Emergence and Legitimization of the Modern Right, 1970–1988," in *Mexico's Alternative Political Futures,* ed. Wayne Cornelius, Judith Gentleman, and Peter H. Smith (La Jolla, Calif.: Center for U.S.–Mexican Studies, 1989), 361.

48. See Yemile Mizrahi, *From Martyrdom to Power, The Partido Accióu Nacional in Mexico* (Notre Dame: University of Notre Dame Press, 2003), 68ff.

49. "Encuesta simpatizantes rumbo al 2006," *Reforma*, May 16, 2005, 6A.

50. Gallup Organization, exit poll, August 18, 1991. This was the first exit poll permitted by the Mexican government; and *Reforma,* June 29, 2001, poll of 1,004 adult residents of Baja California, June 22–24, 2001, +/–3 percent margin of error.

51. The evolution of the Democratic Current and the formation of the original electoral front, as described in detail by Cuauhtémoc Cárdenas in a lengthy interview with Carlos B. Gil, *Hope and Frustration: Interviews with Leaders of Mexico's Political Opposition* (Wilmington, Del.: Scholarly Resources, 1992), 155ff. This is the first work of its kind on Mexico and provides a broad sense of opposition views.

52. "PRD 6th National Congress," *Review of the Economic Situation of Mexico,* (May 2001), 198–200.

53. Javier Farrera Araujo and Diego Prieto Hernández, "Partido de la Revolución Democrática: Documentos básicos," *Revista Mexicana de Ciencias Políticas y Sociales* 36 (January-March 1990): 67–95. For a comparison with the PAN and other parties, see Federico Reyes Heroles, ed., *Los partidos politicos mexicanos en 1991*

(Mexico City: Fondo de Cultura Económica, 1991). For current positions, see the party's official website, www.prd.mx.gov.

54. "PRD 6th National Congress," 198–200.

55. "Estudio de opinión sobre el Partido de la Revolución Democrática," April 16, 2004, www.olivaresplata.com.

56. "PRD 6th National Congress," 199.

57. For interesting insights into the primary, see "PRI Primaries," *Review of the Economic Situation of Mexico,* (December 1999), 478–483; and "Votación abierta para elegir al candidato del PRI," *El Diario de Yucatán,* May 18, 1999, www.yucatan.com.mx.

58. Party statutes appoved by the 19th National Assembly of PRI and approved by IFE, April 2005. See www.pri.mx.gov.

59. "PRI," *Review of the Economic Situation of Mexico,* (May 2001), 201–202.

60. "Rumbo a la elección del 2000," *Este País,* (November 1999), 17.

61. For a discussion of the pragmatic consequences of holding versus obtaining office, see Yemile Mizrahi, "Dilemmas of the Opposition in Government: Chihuahua and Baja California," *Mexican Studies* 14 (Winter 1998): 151–89. For an excellent discussion of the problems PAN governors have faced, see David Shirk, *Mexico's New Politics, The PAN and Democratic Change* (Boulder, Colo.: Lynne Rienner, 2004).

62. Joseph Klesner, "Electoral Competition and the New Party System in Mexico," *Latin American Politics and Society* 47, no. 2 (Summer 2005): 103–42.

63. Joseph Klesner, *The 2000 Mexican Presidential and Congressional Elections: Pre-Election Report* (Washington, D.C.: CSIS, 2000), 7.

64. Emilio Salim Cabrera, "Autoritarismo irreflexivo o Gobernabilidad democrática," *Este País* (January 2005), 41–42.

9

External Politics: Relations with the United States

In the 1990s, the salience of U.S.-Mexican relations rose for both countries. Business firms profited, as did organized crime. Ordinary citizens crisscrossed the border legally and illegally. Nongovernmental organizations established transnational links to shape policies in both countries. This increasingly important and complex relationship multiplied the number of actors that sought participation and gain. This process led to a decentralization of decision-making from the public to the private arenas, from the capital cities to the states and local governments, from the executives to the legislatures and courts, and even within the executive branches of the respective national governments away from the foreign ministries. Political parties fractured over their views concerning this bilateral relationship; the mass media became suspicious and at times hostile toward the government and institutions of the other country. And yet, Mexico and the United States became closer and prospered more in the 1990s than at previous times in their shared history. One key to this successful outcome was the role of the presidents of the two countries in creating new means for policy coordination. Another key was the surprising statesmanship of U.S. and Mexican citizens who, better than those who claim to represent their interests, understood that these two peoples had much to gain from each other.

JORGE DOMINGUEZ & RAFAEL FERNANDEZ DE CASTRO,
The United States and Mexico

Throughout this book, beginning with Chapter 2, I have emphasized the impact of the United States on Mexico and the historical relations of the two countries. My focus has been on domestic politics, but the pervasive influence—if only psychological—of the United States, in addition to politics of place, culture, and economics, has helped mold indirectly and implicitly,

Mexican political behavior. This does not mean that Mexico is not concerned with foreign relations elsewhere in the region, particularly with Europe or Central America and the Pacific Rim. Rather, the dominance of the United States in foreign policy issues important to Mexico usually outweighs the latter's interests in other external actors. As the next chapter makes clear, Europe's rejection of Mexico's request for investment and aid in the late 1980s, in favor of concerns next door in eastern Europe, led the Mexican leadership to pursue a strategy of closer ties to the United States, thus ensuring even greater interdependency. Although Vicente Fox's administration has only accentuated a relationship begun by his predecessors, Fox attempted to diversify trade relations generally, and specifically with Europe, signing a European Union Free Trade Agreement in 2000. Nevertheless, the enormous growth in trade with the United States, as a result of NAFTA, reinforces Mexico's relationship with its neighbor.[1]

The proximity of the United States to Mexico has affected their relationship in the past, often to Mexico's disadvantage, and continues to determine their current relationship. Mexico always has struggled to retain a strong sense of self-identity in the shadow of its more powerful neighbor. Indeed, Mexico's nationalism is in part a response to its experiences with the United States, and Mexico's postrevolutionary foreign policy also, in part, is based on its relationship with the United States. For example, in both international and regional forums, such as the United Nations or the Organization of American States—the preeminent Western Hemisphere organization dominated by the United States—Mexico has tried to become an independent actor in foreign policy matters vis-à-vis the United States. In the 1980s, Mexico offered an important, autonomous voice in Central American politics, especially in regard to the United States' policies toward the civil war in El Salvador and the revolutionary Sandinista government in Nicaragua. Under Fox, Mexico won a temporary seat on the United Nations Security Council in 2001, reinforcing the president's desire to pursue a more active role in international politics. Mexico used its new position to oppose the U.S. position on Iraq, while at the same time it helped to forge a more moderate consensus among other Security Council members. On the other hand, Fox eventually fired his ambassador to the United Nations in 2003, after U.S. State Department protests when the ambassador publicly accused the United States government of desiring a "relationship of convenience, and subordination" and considering Mexico to be its backyard."[2]

Analysts of Mexican foreign policy have long argued that for many decades the Mexican government's nationalistic foreign policy stance permitted its leadership to grant concessions to the Mexican Left at little political cost. In other words, although the Mexican Left had few opportunities to pursue their agenda in strictly domestic politics, they could claim greater success in the foreign policy arena. Such concessions created friction with the United States, especially during the Reagan years, but it allowed the Mexican leadership to retain strong nationalistic symbols and to reinforce their legitimacy as a protector of Mexican sovereignty. Interestingly, Fox's appointment of Jorge Castañeda as his foreign minister in 2000 symbolically reflects this traditional pattern, since Castañeda, a prominent intellectual with long ties to the left, including the Mexican Communist party, has been an outspoken critic of the United States for decades. His appointment was roundly criticized by the policy community in Washington, D.C.[3]

Nationalism remains a significant issue in Mexico, especially in the context of the bilateral relationship with the United States. But as several scholars have noted recently, nationalism is much more complex in the twenty-first century than it was just a decade ago. The reason for this is the physical movement of vast numbers of Mexicans across the northern border. This has led to a number of fascinating consequences, complemented by increasing economic integration and even cultural influences fomented by technological change, the most influential of which is the Internet.

The Mexican government has recognized some components of this altered setting and has responded in several ways. One of the ways in which it responded formally, in view of the scope of the Mexican population in the United States, was to establish in 1990 a Program for Mexican Communities Abroad. This program officially took note of this "transborder embrace" in "an attempt to recruit migrants in the United States as members of the national diaspora."[4] Fox highlighted this commitment to Mexicans living in the United States, promising that he would implement a policy to allow such nationals to vote in Mexican presidential elections, a promise he fulfilled late in his term.

But perhaps the most significant transformation has occurred among Mexicans themselves, creating what David Gutiérrez masterfully describes as a Third Space. He argues that free-market global capitalism, the transnationalization of production processes and financial markets, the increasing utilization of multinational sources of labor, and the ongoing expansion of international communication networks, "have the inevitable effect of transnationalizing the identities of people who habitually travel through the social spaces transformed by these trends." As a result, the people who have grown up on both sides of the border often feel as "at home" in one place as another.[5]

In this contemporary, transnational context, traditional as well as new issues confront the bilateral agenda between the two countries. The most controversial issues facing Mexico and the United States in the first decade of the twenty-first century, however, are drug-trafficking and immigration. These two issues can be subsumed under three general categories, although at times specific issues cross these natural boundaries. Those broad categories describe national security concerns involving drug trafficking, terrorism, political corruption, and political development; basic economic issues, especially trade, investment, immigration, and debt; and difficult-to-measure cultural influences, especially values, language, and the arts.

NATIONAL SECURITY ISSUES

The national security issue of greatest significance and long duration in bilateral affairs is that of illegal drugs. The two countries have been collaborating for several decades in the battle against drug production and trafficking.[6] In the 1990s, Mexico shifted from a minor producer of drugs consumed in the United States, to an increasingly important source. By 1995, estimates suggested that between 20 and 30 percent of the cocaine consumed in the United States was produced in Mexico.[7] Even more importantly, because of the country's geographic location, it has become the major site for the transshipment of drugs from elsewhere in Latin America to the United States. More than two-thirds of the cocaine entering the United States is estimated to pass through Mexico.[8] It is very important to remember—and to stress from an objective as well as a Mexican point of view—that the drug problem originated in the United States, which is the largest illegal drug market in the world, where approximately one of six Americans uses illegal drugs. This fact explains why many analysts have argued that, "the U.S. government should focus its attention and resources on programs that fight domestic consumption, rather than pressuring Mexico and other nations to pursue policies likely to compromise their armed forces.[9]

Americans' demand for drugs has created many national security problems for Mexico and for Mexican-U.S. relations. Mexico has made considerable efforts to stop the shipment and production of illegal narcotics, but it has made little headway in stemming the flow of drugs across the border. The implementation of NAFTA has only made this easier.

For Mexico, drug trafficking has produced two consequences: First, because of the amounts of money changing hands and the profits to be made, corruption of government officials is inevitable, as is also true in the United States. Because Mexicans' income and standard of living are much lower than in the United States, this corruption has been both broader and deeper there. There is, therefore, widespread concern in Mexico that drug traffickers are establishing stronger ties to government officials. Indeed, in 1995, 42 percent of Mexicans polled believed such a link was strong, and 31 percent, somewhat strong.[10] Recent evidence from new investigations of the political assassinations in 1994—including one that seems to have been engineered by the brother of President Salinas—points to the involvement of drug money. These complex drug-related activities, involving United States actors, are no better illustrated than in the Tijuana border culture south of San Diego, California.[11] Thus, the very security of Mexico's national political life is at stake, and some analysts fear that the country is moving in the direction of Colombia, where drug producers dominate the fabric of political life. President Fox has promised to clean up government corruption, including drug-related corruption, through the attorney general's office. He appointed a tough, high-ranking officer to clean up those federal civilian agencies most responsible for the arrest and prosecution of drug traffickers. His administration achieved greater success in arresting major drug leaders and in improving cooperation between the attorney general, the armed forces, and the United States Drug Enforcement Agency in pursuit of drug traffickers. However, these successes have had little impact on the drug trade.

Mexicans also are concerned about issues of sovereignty in relation to combating drug trafficking in Mexico. The United States maintains a drug certification program which cites those countries that are doing their utmost to support the United States' effort to combat drugs. Mexicans see the irony of the United States making judgments about Mexican efforts—whatever their effectiveness—in confronting a problem created by and originating in the United States. This violation of Mexican sovereignty so rankles most Mexicans that it became a campaign issue in the 2000 presidential race. President Fox promised to make the removal of certification a primary issue in his bilateral agenda with the United States. He raised it directly in personal meetings with President Bush in the first six months of his administration. Members of the Senate Foreign Relations Committee were in favor of withdrawing the certification process. According to Senator Phil Gramm, an influential Republican from Texas, "It was a bad idea to begin with, President Fox wants to get rid of it. We want to get rid of it."[12] Nevertheless, despite repeated attempts to remove Mexico from the certification list, congress had not acted on this request as of 2006.

The second issue that drug trafficking raises in the bilateral relationship is one of collaboration between governmental agencies from both countries. Mexico's willingness to allow U.S. drug enforcement agents to operate on its soil has led to numerous controversies, all of which relate to sovereignty questions. The specific pattern between Mexico and the United States is part

of a transnational trend worldwide, as an influential country international-
izes its police and judicial arms in the battle against drugs in other countries.[13] As one Mexican analyst pointed out, "from the U.S. viewpoint it
would be inconceivable to have Mexican agents traveling freely in their
national territory searching for drug users."[14] Not surprisingly, extensive
drug use in American society is the behavior that Mexicans find most unat-
tractive about the United States. On the other hand, drug use in Mexico,
which traditionally has been low, is rising rapidly in poor urban neighbor-
hoods, leading to many social problems.

The third issue drug trafficking has raised in the bilateral relationship is
tied to the extradition policy between the two countries. A bilateral treaty has
existed between the two countries since 1980, but government officials
passed a domestic law prohibiting the extradition of a citizen in all cases to
any foreign country, including the United States. Under the Zedillo administration, the Mexican government began to make exceptions under "excep-
tional circumstances." But in January 2001, the Supreme Court ruled that the
extradition of a citizen does not violate the constitution, opening the door to
increased "binational cooperation in the future."[15] President Fox's administration has demonstrated that it is committed to a new policy of handing over
accused criminals, and it extradited a high-ranking member of the Tijuana
cartel just four months after the Supreme Court ruling. Typically, however, it
refuses to extradite persons who would be subject to a death or life sentence.
Fox believes that improved bilateral cooperation is the key in the fight against
drug trafficking and organized crime.[16]

In its long-term relationship with Latin America, including Mexico,
and the Third World generally, the United States has been primarily interested in political stability, not political liberalization. According to one
prominent historian,

> The nondemocratic nature of the Mexican political system has not been a sig-
> nificant factor in Mexican-U.S. relations, with the sole exception of the period
> in which the Mexican Revolution as an antiauthoritarian revolt coincided with
> the American reformism headed by President Wilson, and then only for a very
> short period.[17]

But this pattern began to change in the late 1980s, when Americans in general and some political figures in Congress took a greater interest in what
was happening in Mexico's internal politics.

The 1988 presidential elections in Mexico, which captured considerable media attention in the United States, served as a catalyst in making
domestic politics an important foreign policy issue. Encouraging United
States involvement in Mexican domestic politics became a significant for-

eign policy issue in the 1990s. From the point of view of the opposition parties, the United States' interest in the elections—given its open support for democratic elections elsewhere in the region—could be used to strengthen their ability to win in a "clean" electoral environment. This may be considered a foreign policy issue because many Mexican electoral groups, especially from opposition parties, sought the approval of foreign electoral observers to guarantee integrity at the ballot box. Mexico's government took the opposite point of view, claiming that such observers were tantamount to foreign interference in Mexican domestic affairs. Despite overwhelming sentiment among Mexican citizens in favor of increasing democratization and free elections, they, too, remained divided on the issue of international observers, with equal numbers for and against their presence in the 1994 presidential elections.

Beginning with the Bush senior administration, the American government publicly committed itself to free and fair elections in Mexico, even though its enthusiasm might have waned had Cuauhtémoc Cárdenas won the 1988 elections or regained his strength in 1994. Consequently, in the 1994 presidential elections—but at the very last minute and under intense international pressure—the Mexican government permitted both domestic and international observers. According to an independent observer, "Through its public statements, private diplomacy, and financial support for election-related activities, the Clinton administration went farther than any of its predecessors in setting forth a policy designed ostensibly to support the democratization process. On several fronts, however, this policy fell short of the mark."[18] The author went on to criticize American policy for glossing over major problems in the elections in its public statements; for supporting international observers primarily as a means of legitimizing the elections, rather than making them fairer; and for basing its political development strategy on getting NAFTA approved. In 2000, the government once again allowed international observers, some of whom were members of the U.S. Congress.

The electoral victory of Vicente Fox in July 2000, signalled an end to an era of explicit American interest in the nature of Mexico's political model, specifically the competitiveness of its elections. This event has moved the political development issue to a much less prominent position on the agenda of bilateral relations, but by no means has Mexican domestic politics been removed from the agenda altogether, either officially or unofficially. Two elements of Mexico's political development will continue to affect the relationship. First, many Americans and Mexicans have viewed political corruption as a leading domestic issue and have associated its presence, in part, with the authoritarian model. Thus, critics on both sides of the border will be looking closely at the demise of the semi-authoritarian state as a catalyst for declining levels of corruption. Such corruption, in a foreign policy context, have affected such diverse issues as collaborative anti-drug efforts or the effective implementation of the North American Free Trade Agreement (NAFTA) provisions, a topic discussed later in this chapter.

The most visible continuation of the political development agenda, however, is not likely to occur on a government to government level, but among nongovernmental organizations. On an unofficial level, Mexicans have involved a plethora of American and international agencies in domestic political affairs since 1988, creating a complex web of external domestic actors in Mexican politics. U.S. human rights and civic organizations' interest and published commentary regarding internal developments in Mexico have further complicated the official bilateral relationship between Mexico and the United States, since their executive branches and foreign relations agencies must consider all these other actors. These unofficial organizations are particularly adept at attracting media coverage. Of all the potential NGOs, the most important under the Fox administration will be the human rights groups. These groups will continue to be visible domestic and foreign policy actors because longstanding abuses within the legal justice system, especially at the state and local levels, will not be eliminated overnight. Furthermore, autonomous paramilitary actors in many parts of rural Mexico remain outside the control of federal government officials. Such groups have been a frequent source of human rights abuses, as in the case of Chiapas.

An excellent example of a domestic, national security issue that became an element in the bilateral relationship was the uprising led by the Zapatista Army for National Liberation (EZLN) in Chiapas in early 1994. It is a complex domestic issue that involved such international actors as the foreign media and NGOs. Indeed, as one analyst noted, its visibility and survival as a significant political actor was due, in part, to its sophisticated linkages with human rights and other groups.[19] It made skillful use of the Internet to establish and expand these international connections. Such transborder linkages are on the increase and will become more frequent in describing the actors in future bilateral issues, especially those related to national security, between the two countries.[20]

The presence of an active guerrilla group in Mexico not only created significant national security concerns internally but, because of Mexico's proximity to the United States, also raised grave concerns across the border. The United States thus implicitly became involved in the process by which Mexico chose to confront the rebels. Indeed, the reverberations of such a group extend well beyond traditional national security concerns in both countries, to the economic well-being of both Mexico and the United States.

For example, foreign investors' perceptions of the EZLN's continued presence in late 1994 and early 1995 had a significant effect on their confidence in the Mexican economy, continued investment, and the Mexican government's economic policy, leading to the worst crisis in recent Mexican history. The appearance of the Popular Revolutionary Army (ERP) in 1996, although far less visible, reinforces the image of social violence just below the surface of what appears to be a stable polity.

The conditions that produce guerrilla groups like the EZLN or the ERP, or that create extensive drug-related corruption, raise other issues on the bilateral agenda and involve other official and unofficial actors. Those problems that primarily have a strong security overtone are important to the intelligence and defense agencies. The degree to which American and Mexican intelligence organizations should collaborate is a thorny issue. It again raises sensitive sovereignty issues, though less so when it clearly focuses on alleged drug criminals. It becomes much more complex when it involves important groups of Mexicans who oppose governmental social and economic policies. Mexicans do not want the FBI or CIA involved directly in solving their national security problems any more than Americans want Mexican intelligence agencies intervening in U.S. domestic affairs. Unfortunately, transnational patterns include issues such as drug production and transportation that cross national borders and become the security problem of the country next door, or for that matter, thousands of miles away. As experts on United States-Mexican security issues warn, militarization of the border or the involvement of the U.S. military in the anti-drug struggle are just two possible future points of bilateral tensions.[21]

An entirely new issue in the bilateral national security agenda is international terrorism. It is an issue that is deeply enmeshed in other longstanding issues, including drug trafficking (as a means of financing such activities) and immigration (the ease with which individuals can cross into the United States from Mexico). The September 2001 terrorist attacks on the United States set off a series of reactions in Mexico that reflect the complexity and history of the two countries' relationship. Fox's first secretary of foreign relations, Jorge Castañeda, expressed strong support for the United States and for its right to defend itself, a position that was not widely supported by Mexicans. In response to public opinion, President Fox provided only tepid support for the United States.[22] Furthermore, Mexico announced its intentions in 2002 to withdraw from the Rio Treaty, a hemispheric defense pact negotiated in 1947, at such a difficult juncture. The relationship between the two countries continued to deteriorate as the Bush administration pursued an aggressive policy and initiated the war with Iraq, a war condemned by an overwhelming number of Mexicans. Indeed, three-quarters of

Mexicans disagreed with the U.S. decision to go to war with Iraq, and half supported a position of neutrality toward such a policy. Only 12 percent of Mexicans favored supporting the United States.[23]

Recent surveys provide some fascinating insights concerning Mexican and American views of foreign policy generally and the terrorism issue specifically. These surveys reinforce many of the perceptions described earlier. Contrary to what some public commentators might believe, Mexicans share similar concerns with Americans about national security issues. Ordinary citizens overwhelmingly believe drug trafficking, the world economic crisis, chemical and biological weapons, and international terrorism are major threats to Mexican security (see Table 9-1). Furthermore, they are much more likely to favor policies than their leaders, including collaboration with American officials. For example, they favor increased requirements for entering and exiting Mexico; increased control over goods through Mexico's borders, ports, and airports; and allowing American agents to work with Mexican counterparts to protect borders, airports, and ports.

Terrorism, and border security policies linked to that issue, have produced new institutional structures in the binational relationship. The establishment of a Homeland Security Agency, which coordinates numerous existing U.S. agencies, alters previously established institutional patterns. The potential terrorism threat implies increased collaboration among the armed forces, among health-related agencies that would cope with bioterrorism, and among intelligence agencies, just to name a few. Mexico's Cantarel oil field in the Gulf of Mexico, which supplies half of Mexico's oil production, is a much more likely target of terrorists since 2001.[24] Both countries are further linked together in solving these new bilateral issues

Table 9-1 Mexican and American Views of Critical Threats to Vital Interests

Threat (Percentage of respondents)	Mexicans	Americans
Drug trafficking	89	63
World economic crisis	86	—[a]
Chemical and biological weapons	86	66
International terrorism	81	75
World environmental problems	79	—[a]
Unfriendly countries becoming nuclear powers	—[a]	64

Source: Global Views 2004, Comparing Mexican and American Public Opinion and Foreign Policy (Chicago: Chicago Council on Foreign Relations, 2004), adapted from Figure 1-4, 16. When asked what should be very important goals of their foreign policy, 83 percent of Mexicans indicated stopping the flow of illegal drugs to the United States compared to 63 percent of Americans. Additionally, 77 percent and 73 percent of Mexicans and Americans, respectively, considered preventing the spread of nuclear weapons to be a significant goal.

Note: [a]Threat not asked in both countries.

because both countries citizens and infrastructure will have to bear the likely consequences of such attacks along the border.

CULTURAL INTERFACE

One salient contextual explanation of Mexico's willingness to consider an economic and even a political union with Canada and the United States is that some of the three countries' basic economic and political values are converging. For example, in eleven of fifteen values measured by the *World Values Survey* between 1981 and 1990, Ronald Inglehart and his collaborators discovered that the three countries were simultaneously moving in the same direction.[25] The three most important goals of Mexicans and Americans are the same: raise children, have a successful career, and be happily married. Even though Mexicans admire many qualities of their neighbor to the north, not least its political system, they have many reservations as well (see Tables 9-2 and 9-3).

Mexico's distrust of the United States because of the latter's involvement in Mexican affairs is complemented by cultural and economic relationships between the two countries. There is a lively commerce in ideas, music, art, fashion, and so on. The influence of U.S. culture can be found

Table 9-2 Mexicans' Positive Perceptions of the United States

What Mexicans Like Most	Percentage of Persons Interviewed	
	1989	1996
Economic opportunities	34	23
Cultural level	15	6
Democracy	14	6
Equality for all	8	4
Government protects the people	4	7
Its wealth	4	13
Good public services	3	10
Its liberty	2	2
Other reasons	1	11
Not sure	11	12
No answer	4	21

Source: Los Angeles Times poll, August 1989, courtesy of Miguel Basáñez. This poll is based on face-to-face interviews with 1,835 Mexican adults conducted from August 13th through 15th, 1989, in 42 randomly selected towns and cities throughout Mexico. It has a margin of error of 3 percent in either direction. *Los Angeles Times* poll, August 1996, 1,572 U.S. adults, August 3–6, 1996, +/–3 percent margin of error, and 1,500 Mexican adults, August 1–7, +/–3 percent margin of error.

Table 9-3 Mexicans' Negative Perceptions of the United States

What Mexicans Disliked Most	Percentage of Persons Interviewed
Racial discrimination	49
Government tries to dominate other countries	10
They think they are better than us	8
Drug/crime problem	8
People unfriendly	5
They think only about money	2
Families aren't strong	2
Military imperialists	2
Polluters	1
Resent influence of American TV and music	0
Too efficient	0
Other	0
Nothing/No answer	14
Don't know	12

Source: Los Angeles Times poll, August 1996.

worldwide, but it is more intense in Mexico by virtue of closeness. Heavy tourist traffic runs in both directions. More Americans report visiting Mexico than any other developing country or region. Of the 62 percent of Americans who traveled outside the United States, 48 percent visited Mexico, or about a third of the U.S. population. Mexico is only second to Canada of all countries visited.[26]

The reverse pattern is equally striking. One-fourth of all foreign visitors to the United States come from Mexico. By 1998, 278 million people a year entered the United States from Mexico. English is studied and spoken by many Mexicans. Spanish is the foreign language studied most often in U.S. high schools, and Spanish classes from even the smallest rural communities often take field trips to Mexico. American music permeates the airwaves. American performers from rock stars to magicians are headliners in major Mexican cities. Television is saturated with shows and movies from north of the border, and the well-to-do who subscribe to satellite reception have access to a complete range of news and entertainment programs. These circumstances and others have contributed to a condition whereby

the United States constitutes an almost unavoidable presence in the daily lives of most Mexicans. The music that is heard in the main urban centers of the country, the companies that dominate the billboards and television advertising, the entertainment and new broadcasts of the major media—all of these refer almost by necessity to the United States, creating a sense, however partial and distorted, of familiarity with U.S. society and culture.[27]

Throughout the twentieth century, especially since the 1930s, Mexicans have had to contend culturally and psychologically with American influence, which has had a serious impact on the structure of the intellectual community and on the content of university programs.[28] The proximity of place also has contributed to the fact that more Americans reside in Mexico than in any other Third World country, and more Mexicans reside in the United States than in any other country. Los Angeles has a higher concentration of people of Mexican descent than any city except Mexico City. It can be said that a greater percentage of Mexicans visited a First World country than did the citizens of any other Third World country. By 1989 one in three Mexicans had traveled to the United States, and nearly half said they had relatives living there.[29] Of those Mexicans who have relatives in the United States, nearly a third live in California. Mexicans establish personal links to the United States at a level unmatched by any other country with the possible exception of Israel.

We do not have comparable information on how Americans view Mexican values and societal qualities, but some data are available on the importance that U.S. citizens accord to Mexico and the issues most important to the two countries' bilateral relations. In general, many Americans have had some firsthand experience with Mexico or Mexicans. This does not necessarily mean that they understand Mexicans better or that it has made them more aware of the importance Mexico plays or might play in their economic and political future. Nevertheless, well before a free-trade agreement was contemplated, Americans understood the potential importance of Mexico's economic development to their own financial fortunes (see Table 9-4). To most Americans in 1990, immigration and political stability were the main issues confronting the United States' relations with Mexico. Today, most Americans, according to a *Wall Street Journal* poll, view Latin America, including Mexico, as a region with a severe drug-trafficking problem. They

Table 9-4 Americans' Perceptions of Mexico

Statement Asked	Percentage of Those Agreeing
Mexico's economic problems affect the U.S. economy	77
The U.S. should exert pressure to hold fair elections	54
The U.S. should limit Mexican immigration	43
Mexico is very important to the U.S.	40
Immigration is the most important issue	35
Political stability is the most important issue	32

Source: Data from Christine Contee, "U.S. Perceptions of United States-Mexican Relations," in *Images of Mexico in the United States,* ed. John H. Coatsworth and Carlos Rico (La Jolla, Calif.: Center for U.S.-Mexican Studies, 1989), 17–48.

not only blame the region for the United States' problem, but consider a reduction in drug trafficking their country's primary foreign policy objective.[30] In 2000, Californians considered immigration, drugs, and trade the most important issues in their state's relation with Mexico.[31]

Culturally, the relationship is unequal. Nevertheless, because Spanish is the second most frequently spoken language in the United States, and Mexicans—along with Central Americans, Cubans, and other Latin Americans—have spread throughout the United States, their culture is influencing the United States' culture.[32] It can be found in music (for example, in the popular song "La Bamba," of which a hundred versions exist in Mexico), food, art, and even language (*politico* comes to mind).[33] Some Americans have reacted with a heightened nationalism. The English First movement is an effort to reassert the supremacy of English and of traditional nonminority values in the face of what is deemed to be an onslaught of Hispanic values and language. Oscar Martínez writes,

> Groups such as U.S. English and English First have campaigned hard to convince a large portion of the American public that the use of languages other than English fosters fragmentation in the country and threatens future political stability. Led by California, by the mid-1980s about twelve states had declared English as their official language, sending a message to Hispanics and other language minority groups that they should rid themselves of their native tongues as quickly as possible. Thus far, similar measures in the legislatures of Texas, New Mexico, and Arizona have failed to pass, but the debate on the issue in these states is bound to increase in the future.[34]

The anti-immigration sentiment reached its apex with the establishment of a "voluntary militia" to patrol the border in 2004.

The cheek-by-jowl closeness of Mexico and the United States has given rise to what many observers believe to be a distinct hybrid border culture. The contiguous regions, which share a range of serious problems from unemployment to pollution, have begun to develop local solutions together that reflect the hybrid culture. The borderland has been given the name "MexAmerica" by Lester Langley, who thinks that few in the United States are ready to admit that Mexico might be a determinant of the kind of society we are becoming and the character of our politics.[35]

Politically and culturally it is the United States that has exercised the greatest long-term influence. Its position in the world gives it great prestige. This gives its political processes and to some extent its political values a certain degree of legitimacy in the eyes of many Mexicans, including politicians, hence the implicit influence of the United States model—especially as the international trend toward political liberalization, that is, democratization—continues.[36] This influence also generates resentment. Jorge Castañeda argued convincingly that some Mexicans have felt uncomfortable supporting democratization because they sense it is a goal of the United States.[37] In fact, the majority of Mexicans do not favor the United States policy of promoting democracy elsewhere in the world. Many Mexicans believe the United States exercises a significant influence on Mexican politics, especially those residing along the northern border. (see Table 9-5)

In the first two decades of the twenty-first century, however, it may be Mexicans who begin to exert a profound influence on the United States, especially in California and Texas. The growth in the Hispanic population generally, and Mexicans specifically, as reported in the demographic statistics from the 2000 census, have been nothing short of extraordinary. Some states, such as Iowa and Nebraska, experiencing declining populations, are actively recruiting immigrants, including Mexicans, to bolster their economically active populations. One might expect the Mexican influence to be substantial, based on its presence in certain regions. But in the first available comparative research on Mexicans, Mexican-Americans, and non-Mexican Americans, the findings demonstrate that on issues related to politics, generally Mexicans begin to take on the beliefs of other Americans, rather than altering American beliefs. This evolutionary pattern can clearly be seen among the three groups' views on the meaning of democracy (Table 9-6).

The data in Table 9-6 illustrate the transformation in political beliefs among Mexicans residing in the United States. They illustrate, for example, that once Mexicans move to the United States, they quickly begin to conceive of democracy as liberty, as do their American peers. Unlike their Mexican counterparts, they no longer give equal weight to equality and liberty and, instead, equality drops dramatically as an important concept. Finally, while voting and elections are important to Mexicans' definition of democracy, they drop significantly in importance among Mexican-Americans, who select them as their definition about as frequently as other Americans (Table 9-6).

Table 9-5 Mexican Views of Foreign Influence

Mexicans Who Believe Foreigners Have a Significant Influence on Domestic Politics:	Percentage Agreeing
Federal District	35
North	63
Center	35
South	36

Source: Este País, June, 1998, 37. National sample of 1,190 of Mexicans older than 18. Margin of error, +/–2.9 percent.

Table 9-6 Meaning of Democracy Among Mexicans, Mexican-Americans, and Americans

Meaning of Democracy	Group (percentages)		
	Mexicans	Mexican Americans	Other Americans
Liberty	25	42	64
Equality	26	15	8
Voting/elections	11	5	4
Type of government	9	7	2
Respect/lawfulness	8	3	4
Well-being/progress	7	8	1
Other	14	19	12
Don't know/No response	0	0	5

Note: The question asked: In one word, could you tell me what democracy means for you?
Source: "Democracy Through U.S. and Mexican Lenses," Grant, Hewlett Foundation, September 2000.

ECONOMIC LINKAGES

One of the most sensitive issues in the U.S.–Mexican relationship, because of its prominence as a cause of the Mexican Revolution, is economic imperialism. Even as late as the early twentieth century, some U.S. diplomatic representatives had personal economic interests in Mexico that influenced their recommendations. By the beginning of the revolution, U.S. investment in Mexico had reached staggering figures. Roger D. Hansen remarks that under Díaz, foreign capital (38 percent from the United States)

> flowed into the country in quantities proportionately much greater—in relation to national capital and the natural and human resources of Mexico—than the volume of European capital that entered the United States during its period of most intensive development. Only 100 million pesos as late as 1884, foreign investment rose to 3.4 billion by 1911.[38]

The ideology of Mexicanization, which grew out of the revolutionary struggle, traces its strongest roots to U.S. economic influence and the presence of American businessmen, managers, professionals, and landowners, especially in the north.[39] In formulating its economic development policies, while protecting the sovereignty of its decision making, Mexico has had to consider its economic relationship with the United States. President Salinas set in motion a revolutionary economic relationship between Mexico and the United States, encompassed in NAFTA. To accomplish this goal as part of his foreign and domestic policy agendas, he and his cabinet worked assiduously to persuade Mexicans that a formal economic linkage with the United States was beneficial financially and did not violate Mexican sovereignty. By the end of the 1990s, the majority of Mexicans had become convinced of NAFTA's benefits, viewing it positively from a variety of perspectives.[40] A decade after it went into effect, Mexicans express less positive views about NAFTA. Both Americans and Mexicans view its results as being more positive for their neighbor than for themselves (see Table 9-7).

Trade, foreign investment, and external debt affect the bilateral relationship directly and indirectly. The economic linkage between Mexico and the United States is so substantial that its impact on the formal linkages between the two countries—on the everyday lives of many citizens, especially Mexicans, and on sovereignty issues—is unavoidable. For many decades, the United States provided 60 to 70 percent of the merchandise imported by Mexico. In fact, by 1993, before its economic crises, Mexico was buying $42 billion of goods from its northern neighbor, or one-fourth of all goods sold by the United States in the Western Hemisphere. By the end of 1996, after NAFTA's implementation, the United States sold $67.5 billion in exports to Mexico, 9 percent of all its exports worldwide. Forty-four of fifty states experienced growth in export sales to Mexico from 1995 to 1996. It is figures like these that justify establishing a free-trade agreement between the two countries and Canada. Sidney Weintraub pointed out that

> world trade, in both goods and services, is growing more rapidly within major world regions than between them. For the United States, this reality emerges most clearly in trade with its two land neighbors, Canada and Mexico. The United States, therefore, has a major stake in the economic health of its neighbors; and not just Canada and Mexico, but also the rest of the Western Hemisphere, where the United States is the leading supplier of the region's exports, as it is not for the other major regions, either Asia or Europe.[41]

The anticipation and negotiations surrounding a free-trade agreement between Mexico and the United States dominated their bilateral agenda throughout the Bush and Salinas administrations, becoming a salient political issue in the 1992 United States presidential election. The main impact of NAFTA on bilateral relations before its passage in Congress and its implementation in January 1994 was the greater ability of the bilateral agenda in both countries, but especially in the United States, to frame many other issues in terms of their effect on the trade agreement and to increase speculation on how the completion of such an agreement might affect internal issues in both countries in the future, including those already on the bilateral agenda. President Salinas himself formulated much of his domestic program around the concept of NAFTA and its ultimate approval. Mexico's decision to interna-

Table 9-7 Mexican and American Views of NAFTA

Percentage of Mexicans and Americans Who View NAFTA as Good or Bad for
Each of the Following Issues

	Good		Bad	
	Mexicans	Americans	Mexicans	Americans
The U.S. economy	78	42	10	43
The Mexican economy	44	69	39	16
Mexican business (Mexico)/ American businesses (U.S.)	50	50	35	36
Creating jobs in U.S.	na	31	na	56
Creating jobs in Mexico	49	69	36	17
Your standard of living	41	51	35	33
The environment	39	34	39	48

Source: Global Views 2004, Comparing Mexican and American Public Opinion and Foreign Policy (Chicago: Chicago Council on Foreign Relations, 2004).

tionalize its economic development strategy and to form closer economic ties with its neighbors was seen by many in the United States international community as bringing Mexico closer in line with their own economic philosophy, thereby decreasing the potential for conflict on economic matters, at least from an ideological perspective. The actual linkages themselves highlighted other issues extending well beyond those purely "economic."[42]

The North American Free Trade Agreement is a complex document with implications for member countries' social policies. Management-labor relations provide a useful example of how a foreign economic policy agreement can have broader political implications domestically. In Mexico, many of the export-oriented companies employ unionized workers. The structural and legal pattern of labor-business relations enables a government official to provide the decisive vote in arbitrated disputes. One of the most controversial side agreements in NAFTA requires Mexico to conform to its own laws in protecting labor rights. The U.S. labor movement, though it opposed NAFTA, succeeded in obtaining certain agreements, which, if enforced, would strengthen workers' rights in Mexico. In April 1995, U.S. labor unions and human rights groups persuaded Robert Reich, the secretary of labor, to discuss with his Mexican counterpart the specific issue of workers in a Sony factory in Nuevo Laredo who had been prevented from establishing an independent union, thereby violating Mexico's own labor code.[43] The reverse is also true. In May 1998, four Mexican unions, with the support of the American teamsters union, filed a complaint against the Washington State apple industry for violating migrant worker rights, including safety and pay issues. The significance of this and other NAFTA side agreements is that they provide an important legal vehicle for American groups to become involved in numerous Mexican domestic issues, among them labor and environmental concerns, and for Mexicans to do the same in the United States. On the Mexican side, however, these legal changes have produced few successes in favor of labor rights.

The broader issue that economic and commercial agreements emphasize for both countries, but especially Mexico, is nationalism. Some analysts have gone as far as to argue that not only has NAFTA shrunk Mexican national sovereignty, but a decline in state sovereignty, engineered through international agreements, limits the country's ability to protect ordinary citizens' interests.[44] This interpretation can be disputed, but NAFTA and the increasing economic dependency of the two countries have determined other major policy decisions. The most striking example of such a consequence is the Clinton administration's financial rescue package offered in early 1995 after the devaluation of the peso led to extensive capital flight. Indeed, the size of the United States and international agency aid, some $49 billion, was in part based on Mexico's membership in NAFTA.[45] The package itself, because it required Mexico to guarantee repayment of its loans to the United States ($20 billion of the total), generated further concern in Mexico, because numerous Mexicans viewed the aid as further evidence of the United States' infringement on their sovereignty. The Mexicans repaid the loan early.[46] Another way of understanding its impact on Mexican sovereignty is legally. As one scholar argues, Mexico has undergone a transformation from "national sovereignty" to "constitutional sovereignty" in the sense that it has begun to alter its "standards of legitimacy and to increase the importance of international standards."[47]

The implementation of NAFTA entailed intense controversy on both sides of the border and became a significant presidential campaign issue for Bush and Zedillo in 1994. Analysts have noted that six years after its implementation, Mexican exports have more than doubled, while imports increased at a slightly lower rate. In fact, in 2001, Mexico replaced Japan as the number two destination of U.S. exports. Mexican goods now account for 10 percent of all U.S. imports. Mexico in 2006 ranked third as the United States' most important trade partner. In Mexico, exports account for one-third of its economy and half of the jobs created since NAFTA was implemented.[48] Yet the impact on Mexican living standards has been minimal. The minimum wage under Fox remains the same in real value as it was in 1980.[49] The agreement was sold to citizens of both countries as a policy to improve their standard of living. In Mexico, such improvements were linked to reducing immigration, which of course has not slowed. By 2002, one of the few successes Fox could claim from his bilateral agenda with the U.S.

was in reaching an agreement to open up U.S. highways to Mexican truckers, an unimplemented provision in the original NAFTA agreement.

The economically related issue generating the most controversy on the bilateral agenda, especially in the eyes of ordinary Americans and Mexicans, is immigration. It is revealing because its consequences invoke cultural, economic, and political issues, which become prominent on domestic agendas. Immigration has a long history, and only in recent years has the United States attempted comprehensively and formally to prevent the flow of Mexican immigrants. Mexicans crossed the border to work for decades after the mid-nineteenth century without controls.

Labor tends to follow capital, especially when unemployment and underemployment reach significant levels. Thus Mexicans went northward during difficult times in search of work. In the past some eventually became U.S. citizens, but most returned to their homeland after short stays. At other times when the United States faced labor shortages, especially of unskilled workers, it promoted controlled flows of such workers, which happened during World War II. What are the economic consequences of this relationship? For Mexico, it has meant increased economic opportunities for its people, in some cases the potential for learning new skills. Also, their wages in large part have been remitted to their places of origin, thereby creating local sources of capital. It has been estimated that in 2005 emigrants sent as much as $17 billion dollars back to Mexico. Mexico ranks second in the world in terms of income earned in foreign currencies. The potential impact of these remittances on the Mexican economy can be seen through comparisons with other sources generating dollar revenues. The subsecretary of migratory services in Mexico noted that in 2000, worker remittances from the United States were equal to 79 percent of petroleum exports, 93 percent of the income from tourism, and even 55 percent of foreign investment. By 2003, remittances were second only to petroleum exports. One out of twenty homes in Mexico received monies from the United States.[50] For the United States, the economic benefits have been substantial. Historically, most of the migrants have worked in agriculture, providing cheaper foodstuffs than would have been otherwise available. In recent years, Mexicans have contributed many workers to the service sector.

The political consequences of the relationship are numerous. Those consequences, on both sides of the border, will multiply as the population doubles in the next forty years, from 19 to 48 million people (see Table 9-8). For example, during periods of economic crisis in the 1980s in Mexico, millions of Mexicans sought employment in the United States, revealing the inability of the political model to manage the economy. Indirectly, then, the United States aided Mexican domestic stability by channeling discontent

Table 9-8 Growth of the Mexican-Origin Population in
the United States, 1995–2040

Year	Mexican Population	Hispanic Population
1995	16,135,000	26,936,000
2000	18,788,000	31,366,000
2010	24,642,000	41,139,000
2020	31,539,000	52,652,000
2030	39,276,000	65,570,000
2040	48,018,000	80,164,000

Source: Adapted from Jorge I. Domínguez and Rafael Fernández de Castro, *The United States and Mexico Between Partnership and Conflict*
(New York: Routledge, 2001), 153.

northward. Yet Mexican nationalism—given the historical relationship discussed previously—forces Mexico to express concern over the migration.
Some Mexicans have been maltreated in the United States or in crossing the
border. The crossing has become so dangerous that, on average, one person
a day dies in the attempt. Their exploitation pressures Mexico to place the
issue on the agenda of Mexican–United States relations.

The terrorist attacks in September 2001 added a new political perspective to the immigration issue, discussed earlier, of border security. Fox and
his first secretary of foreign relations made immigration reform the leading
issue on the bilateral agenda. Although it was never removed from the
agenda, the Bush administration essentially ignored that issue after 2001,
eventually leading to the resignation of Mexico's foreign relations secretary.
After continued pressure from the Mexican side, President Bush finally put
forward his own concept of a temporary workers' program in the United
States in his 2004 State of the Union address.[51]

Another political consequence affecting both sides of the border relates
to the political activity of this population. In 1998, the Mexican congress
granted dual nationality to Mexicans living abroad. Since 99 percent of all
Mexicans living abroad reside in the United States, the implications of this
legislation essentially are confined to the bilateral relationship. Politically,
dual nationality opens up the door to Mexicans abroad being able to vote in
Mexican elections. The Mexican government estimated that in 2000, 7.1
million adult Mexicans living abroad, and 2.8 million Americans of Mexican parentage, would take advantage of Mexican nationality.[52] In 2005, the
Chamber of Deputies overwhelmingly passed a bill giving the right to vote
in presidential elections to Mexicans abroad, in time for the 2006 presidential contest. Those eligible will be restricted to Mexicans who have or obtain
a voting credential before mid-February 2006 and apply for a mail-in ballot.

This group, although much smaller than their numbers suggest, could become decisive in Mexican elections, if their preferences differ significantly from their peers in Mexico. Mexican presidential candidates, already recognizing the importance of this group, have campaigned in the United States since Cuauhtémoc Cárdenas ran in 1988. In the 2000 race, both Fox and Cárdenas campaigned heavily in the United States and received contributions from Mexicans residing there. Under the new legislation, candidates could not advertise abroad, receive donations from abroad, or campaign in the United States in 2006. In future elections, domestic Mexican political campaigns in the United States, if permitted, especially if a foreign policy issue became part of their campaign issues, could have significant consequences for domestic American politics.

Immigrants already are politically active in both countries. In the United States, they have organized hundreds of groups, and their leaders have met with advisers to President Bush to push for immigration reform. On the Mexican side, they have formed political action committees and have sent delegations of campaign workers to help favored candidates. Some of these residents in the United States have returned to Mexico to compete for political office and have won a mayoralty race as well as a seat in the 2003–2006 congress. Manuel de la Cruz, the member of congress, is a legal resident of the United States from Norwalk, California.[53]

For the United States, the economic implications are obvious. Although the demand for unskilled workers now extends into a variety of occupational categories, critics charge that American workers go unemployed. Some groups in the United States resent what they see as their displacement by immigrant labor from Mexico. Moreover, employers are accused of hiring Mexican workers in order to avoid paying certain benefits and taxes. Finally, middle-class taxpayers have begun to view immigrants as a tremendous drain on welfare resources and public education, leading to the passage of California's Proposition 187 in 1994. In reality, Mexican immigrants are net tax contributors to the federal government, but at the state level, depending on services, their contributions vary. In New Jersey, they are net contributors; in California, they are net beneficiaries.

Proposition 187 is essentially anti-immigrant legislation designed to exclude Latinos from California's social services, specifically to remove children from public school classrooms and to prevent their parents seeking health care and unemployment benefits from the state. More than half of all Mexicans view this legislation as racist, and nine out of ten Mexicans strongly oppose similar legislation elsewhere in the United States.[54]

Culturally, immigration spills over into many of the issues affecting U.S.–Mexican relations. The English First movement came about largely through the rapid expansion of the U.S. Latino population, and the visible immigration of Mexicans and Central Americans into the Southwest. Immigration is a perceived cultural threat, which translates into local and state policy debates, often placed before voters. In Mexico, on the other hand, whole villages are literally ghost towns, as younger men and women leave for the United States. Children are often left in the hands of the mother alone or grandparents, breaking down the traditional family structure. Discouraged by the violence of U.S. cities, many migrant Mexicans who have children in the United States send them back to their home communities. But these children bring American values with them, threatening the integrity of the local culture.[55]

Immigration, trade, and investment have many more ramifications, both subtle and obvious. The point is that their proximity makes both countries prisoners, to some extent, of each other's problems. For example, Fox's ambitious policy agenda was adversely affected in 2001–2002 by the sharp downturn in Mexico's economy, heavily tied to the U.S. recession. And although Mexico labors under a much greater dependency and subordination, it affects the United States. The United States experienced an unexpected and immediate increase in its trade deficit in the months immediately following the devaluation of the Mexican peso in 1994 as United States exports became excessively expensive and Mexican imports relatively cheap. Mexico's political system must consider carefully the domestic issues and associated policies that bear on this relationship. The United States has no direct veto power over Mexican politics, but its presence casts a permanent shadow that the Mexican political leadership cannot ignore.

CONCLUSION

As this chapter makes clear, it is obvious that the United States exercises a significant role in Mexico, not only in its dominance over the focus of Mexican foreign policy, but in numerous other facets, social, cultural, and economic. The North American Free Trade Agreement only has reinforced a level of influence long apparent, implicitly and explicitly, in the relationship between Mexico and the United States. While it is true that Mexico's strong sense of nationalism was a natural response to its historical experience with the United States, Mexico has found it necessary, for important economic and social reasons, to modify its traditional posture in return for identifying its future development more closely with the fortunes of the United States.

Numerous issues affect the bilateral relationship between these two neighbors. This chapter touches only on those that are most prominent, particularly in the 2000s. The national security agenda between the two countries increasingly has taken precedence over other traditional issues, but the scope of national security concerns, because of increased linkages practically and formally, has broadened and deepened. Issues such as combating drug trafficking have gone well beyond social agendas typically associated with such problems to become inextricably intertwined with the very legitimacy of Mexican political institutions and the stability of its political system.

The intensity and breadth of the bilateral agenda, often involving issues affecting the domestic policy perspectives and postures of the two countries' voters and politicians, complicate their foreign relations.[56] Some of these issues, such as corruption and illegal immigration, evoke heated, emotional responses on both sides of the border. A strong temptation exists, particularly in the United States, for national legislators to impose moral and philosophical judgments on Mexico's political model, and specifically on the extent of corruption and on human rights issues. The increased involvement in Mexican domestic affairs by the U.S. media, and civic organizations such as human rights groups, ensures the U.S. government's continued and heightened involvement in Mexican matters.[57] At the same time, the expanding pluralization of Mexico's political process and the contentiousness of its differing political actors, nationally and regionally, further complicate relations between both countries. As individual states are linked more directly to Mexico, and as Mexicans have come to reside throughout the United States, state legislatures and governors have become significant actors. California, for example, has its own agency and legislative committee devoted to Mexican foreign relations.[58]

Foreign policy experts have raised a number of concerns about future issues on the bilateral agenda and about the inadequacies of the process through which they are dealt with by both countries. Many of these criticisms focus on security issues involving policing the border, drug enforcement corruption, and the lack of concern among U.S. officials toward the social and economic failures that have produced such movements as the EZLN in Chiapas.[59] These critics also point out, for example, the connection between the failures of U.S. domestic legislation in dealing with drug consumption, leading to many internal consequences for Mexico, and relations between the two countries. The U.S.'s failure to address this issue has generated serious national security problems for both countries.[60]

A hint of optimism is justified as far as the process is concerned. The strong personal connection between President Bush and President Fox, the leading political actors responsible for the bilateral agenda on both sides of the border, has increased their cooperation. Senator Jessie Helms, long a critic of Mexico, led a group of American legislators to Mexico in spring 2001. He told reporters that the legislators' meeting with their Mexican counterparts was "to the best of our knowledge, the first time in history that a committee of the U.S. Congress has held a joint meeting on foreign soil with a committee of another nation's congress or parliament."[61] Members of the Senate committee expressed a refreshing receptiveness to changing U.S. policies on several leading problems on the bilateral agenda, including President Fox's proposal that the two countries work out a joint guest worker program to eliminate the numerous consequences of illegal immigration. The September 11 terrorist attack set back the discussion of this and other issues on their bilateral agenda.

In spite of the closer relationship that has emerged between the two countries under presidents Fox and Bush, the terrorist attacks illustrate the substantial residue of traditional nationalism in Mexico. As noted earlier, Mexico's secretary of foreign relations immediately spoke strongly in support of the U.S., but President Fox did not publicly reinforce that position. Only later, after much criticism in the U.S. media, did he clarify his position. Fox's dilemma is a reflection of Mexican attitudes generally. Nearly three-quarters of the public believed Mexico should remain neutral. Thus, support for and suspicion of the U.S. continues to be an essential ingredient in the two countries' relationship.

NOTES

1. Javier Santismo, "Mexico's Economic Ties with Europe: Business as Usual?" in *Mexico's Democracy at Work, Political and Economic Dynamics*, ed. Russell Crandall, Guadalupe Paz, and Riordan Roett (Boulder, Colo: Lynne Rienner, 2005), 185.

2. Tim Weiner, "Mexico's Influence in Security Council Decision May Help Its Ties with U.S.," *New York Times*, November 9, 2002; and Kirk Semple, "Mexico's Ambassador to the United Nations Resigns," *New York Times*, November 21, 2003.

3. Castañeda was a member of the party from 1978–1980. His father, Jorge, Sr., was José López Portillo's foreign secretary from 1979–1982, when relations with the United States were strained over Central America. In spite of his assertive, nationalistic posture, Jorge, Jr. was adept at persuading the Bush administration to reconsider long standing policies that reinforce Mexican sovereignty prior to September 2001.

4. David Thelen, "Rethinking History and the Nation-State: Mexico and the United States," *The Journal of American History*, 86, no. 2 (September 1999), 439–455.

5. David G. Gutiérrez, "Migration, Emergent Ethnicity, and the 'Third Space': The Shifting Politics of Nationalism in Greater Mexico," *The Journal of American History*, 86, no. 2 (September 1999), 512–513.

6. See "The Fight Against Drugs," Mexico, Office of the President, September, 1997; *US/Mexico Bi-National Drug Strategy,* High Level Contact Group for Drug Control, U.S.-Mexico, February, 1998; and Executive Office of the President, Office of National Drug Control Policy, *Report to Congress* (Washington, D.C.: September, 1997).

7. K. Larry Storrs, "Mexico's Counter-Narcotics Efforts Under Zedillo, December 1994 to March 1999," *CRS Report for Congress,* (March 18, 1999) 2.

8. Silvana Paternostro, "Mexico as a Narco-democracy," *World Policy Journal* 12 (Spring 1995), 44.

9. "Mexico's Future Is Up for Grabs," *Orbis* 41 (Winter 1997), 100.

10. "Encuesta Metropolitana," *Este País,* April 5, 1995.

11. Sebastian Rotella, *Twilight on the Line: Underworlds and Politics on the Mexican Border* (New York: Norton, 1998).

12. "U.S Mexico Relations Strengthening," *The New York Times,* January 10, 2001, www.nytimes.com.

13. María Celia Toro, "The Internationalization of Police: The DEA in Mexico," *The Journal of American History,* 86 (September 1999), 640.

14. José Luis Reyna, "Narcotics as a Destabilizing Force for Source Countries and Non-source Countries," in *The Latin American Narcotics Trade and United States National Security,* ed. Donald Mabry (Westport, Conn.: Greenwood Press, 1989), 126.

15. John Bailey and Jorge Chabat, *Public Security and Democratic Governance: Challenges to Mexico and the United States* (Washington, D.C.: Georgetown University School of Foreign Service, 2001), 40.

16. Mary Jordan, "Mexico Sends Cartel Member to U.S. for Trial," *Washington Post,* May 6, 2001, A17.

17. Lorenzo Meyer, "Mexico: The Exception and the Rule," in *Exporting Democracy: the United States and Latin America,* ed. Abraham Lowenthal (Baltimore: Johns Hopkins University Press, 1991), 228.

18. Jared Kotler, *The Clinton Administration and the Mexican Elections* (Albuquerque: Resource Center Press, 1994), 28.

19. Markus S. Schulz, "Collective Action Across Borders: Opportunity Structures, Network Capacities, and Communicative Praxis in the Age of Advanced Globalization," *Sociological Perspectives* 41, no. 3 (1998), 605.

20. David Ronfeldt, et al., *The Zapatista Social Netwar in Mexico* (Santa Monica: RAND, 1998), provides a sophisticated theoretical and strategic analysis of the importance of this linkage for Mexican and U.S. national security.

21. John Bailey and Sergio Aguayo Quezada, eds., *Strategy and Security in U.S.-Mexican Relations Beyond the Cold War* (La Jolla: Center for U.S.–Mexican Studies, 1996), 3.

22. Pamela Starr, "U.S.-Mexico Relations," *Hemispheric Focus* 12, no. 2 (January 2004), 6.

23. "Conflicto entre EU e Iraq," *Reforma,* October 31, 2002.

24. *U.S.-Mexico Border Security and the Evolving Security Relationship, Recommendations for Policymakers* (Washington, D.C.: CSIS, 2004). This report pro-

vides an excellent overview of these issues and specific policy recommendations for both countries.

25. Ronald Inglehart, Miguel Basáñez, and Neil Nevitte, *Convergencia en Norte América, comercio, política y cultura* (Mexico City: Siglo XXI, 1994), 190–91.

26. Christine E. Contee, "U.S. Perceptions of United States–Mexican Relations," in *Images of Mexico in the United States,* ed. John H. Coatsworth and Carlos Rico (La Jolla, Calif.: Center for U.S.–Mexican Studies, 1989), 30.

27. Coatsworth and Rico, *Images of Mexico in the United States,* 10.

28. See Roderic Ai Camp, *Intellectuals and the State in Twentieth Century Mexico* (Austin: University of Texas Press, 1985), 79.

29. *New York Times* poll, October 28–November 4, 1986; *Los Angeles Times* poll, August 1989.

30. *Wall Street Journal,* April 16, 1998; and the original data, courtesy of Miguel Basáñez.

31. "Californians and Their Government," Poll conducted by the Public Policy Institute of California, 2,003 adults, July 28 to August 4, 2000, +/–2 percent margin of error. Californians, however, are fully aware of Mexico's impact on their future, since 88 percent believed that political and economic developments in Mexico were important to what went on in the state.

32. For excellent background on these issues, see Jaime Rodríguez and Kathryn Vincent, eds., *Common Border, Uncommon Paths* (Wilmington: Scholarly Resources, 1997).

33. For numerous examples of these special influences, see Tom Miller, *On the Border: Portraits of America's Southwestern Frontier* (Tucson: University of Arizona Press, 1985).

34. Oscar Martínez, *Troublesome Border* (Tucson: University of Arizona Press, 1988), 97.

35. Lester D. Langley, *MexAmerica: Two Countries, One Future* (New York: Crown Books, 1988), 7.

36. For an excellent discussion of the dilemmas facing the United States government in the promotion of the liberal model in Mexico, see Sergio Aguayo, "Mexico in Transition and the United States: Old Perceptions, New Problems," in *Mexico and the United States: Managing the Relationship,* ed. Riordan Roett (Boulder, Colo.: Westview Press, 1988), 157.

37. Jorge G. Castañeda, "The Choices Facing Mexico," in *Mexico in Transition: Implications for U.S. Policy,* ed. Susan K. Purcell (New York: Council on Foreign Relations, 1988), 26.

38. Roger D. Hansen, *The Politics of Mexican Development* (Baltimore: Johns Hopkins University Press, 1971), 15–17.

39. For its evolution, see Robert Freeman Smith, "The United States and the Mexican Revolution, 1921–1950," in *Myths, Misdeeds, and Misunderstandings,* eds. Jaime Rodríguez and Kathryn Vincent (Wilmington: Scholarly Resources, 1997), 181–98.

40. *Wall Street Journal,* April 16, 1998, poll of 13,000 adults in Latin America and the United States. +/–1 percent margin of error in Latin America.

41. Sidney Weintraub, *NAFTA: What Comes Next?* (Westport, Conn.: Praeger, 1994), 108; "NAFTA, the Standard for Free Trade," Mexico, Office of the President, September 1997.

42. For two excellent interpretations of the domestic political implications of NAFTA in Mexico, see Guy Poitras and Raymond Robsinson, "The Politics of NAFTA in Mexico," *Journal of Inter-American Studies and World Affairs* 36 (Spring 1994):1–35; and Jorge Castañeda, "Can NAFTA Change Mexico?" *Foreign Affairs,* 74 (September–October 1993): 66–80. A discussion of the implications and perceptions on both sides can be found in Ricardo Grinspun and Maxwell Cameron, eds., *The Political Economy of North American Free Trade* (New York: St. Martin's Press, 1993). Background on the negotiating and the side agreements is provided in George Grayson's excellent *The North American Free Trade Agreement: Regional Community and the New World Order* (Lanham, Md.: University Press of America, 1995).

43. Robert Bryce, "Gripe on Mexican Labor to Get NAFTA Hearing," *Christian Science Monitor,* April 26, 1995, 6.

44. Julie A. Erfani, *The Paradox of the Mexican State: Rereading Sovereignty from Independence to NAFTA* (Boulder, Colo.: Lynne Rienner, 1995), 178–79.

45. Sidney Weintraub, "Prospects for Hemispheric Trade and Economic Integration," CSIS Policy Paper on the Americas, 1995, 5. Also see Weintraub's "Mexico's Devaluation: Why and What Next?," CSIS, January 4, 1994, for an insightful explanation of how the devaluation came about. Mexico actually borrowed $13.5 billion, and repaid the amount in full, with interest, by January 1997.

46. Precise details of the agreement are provided in "Statement of Treasury Secretary Robert E. Rubin, Mexico Agreement Signing Ceremony," *Treasury News,* February 21, 1995. Nearly two-thirds of Mexicans polled at the time the peso rescue package was announced thought that it greatly compromised their sovereignty. MORI de México poll for *Este País,* February 1, 1995.

47. James Robinson, "NAFTA and Sovereignty," in *NAFTA's Impact on North America, the First* Decade, ed. Sidney Weintraub (Washington, D.C.: CSIS, 2004), 362.

48. "Mexicans Reap NAFTA Benefits," *Washington Post,* September 17, 2000, A22; and "NAFTA Has Doubled Trade," *El Financiero International,* January 3, 1999, 1.

49. Gary Gereffi and Martha A. Martínez, "Mexico's Economic Transformation under NAFTA," in *Mexico's Democracy at Work, Political and Economic Dynamics*, ed. Russell Crandall, Guadalupe Paz, and Riordan Roett (Boulder, Colo.: Lynne Rienner, 2005), 142–44.

50. "México, el país iberoamericano que más dinero recibe sus trabajdores en EE.UU.," *Diario de Yucatán,* January 29, 2000, www.yucatan.com.mx; "State of the Economy," *Review of Economic Stituation of Mexico* May 2004, 150–152.

51. U.S.-Mexico Binational Council, "Managing Mexican Migration to the United States, Recommendations for Policymakers," (Washington, D.C.: CSIS, 2004), 11.

52. "The Issue of Voting by Residents Abroad," *Review of the Economic Situation of Mexico,* (November 1998), 429–432.

53. Ginger Thompson, "Mexico's Migrants Profit from Dollars Sent Home," *New York Times*, February 23, 2005; and Jennifer Mena, "U.S. Citizen in Mexico's Congress," *Los Angeles Times*, February 2, 2004, B1.

54. MORI de México weekly poll for *Este País*, November 9 and November 23, 1994.

55. A vast literature exists on this topic. Some of the best work is discussed and analyzed objectively in David Fitzgerald, *Negotiating Extra-Territorial Citizenship, Mexican Migration and the Transnational Policies of Community* (La Jolla: Center for Comparative Immigration Studies, University of California, San Diego, 2000). For the darker side of immigration, including sexual slavery and sex tourism, see David Shirk and Alexandra Webber, "Human Trafficking in the U.S.-Mexican Context," paper presented at the Latin American Studies Association, Las Vegas, Nevada, October 2004.

56. An insightful inside analysis of some of these problems, including recommendations for solving some difficulties, is provided by Arturo Valenzuela, former Deputy Assistant Secretary of State for Inter-American Affairs, in *The Challenge of Mexico to U.S. Foreign Policy*, Occasional Paper Series, Overseas Development Council, Washington, D.C., June 1997.

57. Judith Adler Hellman, "Continuity and Change in the Mexican Political System: New Ways of Knowing a New Reality," *European Review of Latin American and Caribbean Studies* 63 (December 1997), 96.

58. Margaret Larragoite, "U.S. and Mexico State Legislatures Collaborate," *NAMINEWS*, no. 22 (Winter 1998), 2, 4.

59. Eric L. Olson, "Reconfiguring Mexico Policy," *Foreign Policy in Focus*, 4, no. 7 (February 1998), 1–7; Jacqueline Mazza, *Don't Disturb the Neighbors: The United States and Democracy in Mexico, 1980–1995* (New York: Routledge, 2001); and Peter Andreas' excellent analysis in *Border Games: Policing the U.S.–Mexico Divide* (Ithaca: Cornell University Press, 2000).

60. John Bailey and Roy Godson, eds., *Organized Crime and Democratic Governability: Mexico and the U.S.–Mexican Borderlands* (Pittsburgh: University of Pittsburgh Press, 2000); and Eva Bertram and Kenneth Sharpe, "Drug War Money Brings Ever More Corruption," *Los Angeles Times*, December 2, 1999, M2.

61. "Helms Leads Delegation to Mexico," *The New York Times*, April 16, 2001, www.nytimes.com.

10

Political and Economic Modernization: A Revolution?

The political question foremost in the minds of most observers and Mexican citizens alike is, What will be the influence of democracy and economic liberalism on Mexico's governmental model and its economic future? Many of the political and economic changes that have taken place in Eastern Europe since 1989 have far exceeded the expectations of most experts. Boundaries have been redrawn; political processes have been turned upside down; regional stability has been rendered problematic; and economic structures have collapsed or are tottering. Mexico has not been immune to the winds of change. Some analysts argue that international influences and world public opinion have strongly affected Mexico. Mexican architects of recent reforms and economic analysts consider Mexico to be part of "this vast process of world institutional evolution."[1]

BASES FOR ECONOMIC MODERNIZATION

For the average Mexican, the most important economic issues are employment and level of income. In 2001, Mexicans considered more sources of employment and better wages to be the most significant pending economic problems.[2] Mexico, like many other Third World nations, faces numerous challenges in stimulating economic growth, regardless of the strategy it chooses to pursue. Mexico's economy has changed significantly since the 1940s, in both size and the composition of its workforce. In the 1990s, Mexico had four times as many people in the economically active population as it did after World War II. From 1970, when Echeverría became president, to the late 1990s, Mexico tripled its workforce, from 12.9 million to 39.1 million.

Table 10-1 Mexico's Economically Active Population, by Economic Sector

Sector	1950	1970	1999	1950/1999 % Change
Agriculture	4,823,901	5,103,519	8,208,700	70.2
Petroleum and extractive	97,143	180,175	195,300	101.1
Manufacturing	972,542	2,169,074	7,282,800	650.5
Construction	224,512	571,006	2,158,000	861.2
Electric energy	24,966	53,285	193,100	672.0
Commerce	684,092	1,196,878	6,582,400	862.3
Transportation	210,592	368,813	1,544,400	631.8
Services	879,379	2,158,175	9,008,900	924.9
Government	—	406,607	1,728,300	—
Other	354,966	747,525	165,500	753.2
Total	8,272,093	12,955,057	39,069,100	372.3

Source: David E. Lorey, *The Rise of the Professions in Twentieth-Century Mexico, University Graduates and Occupational Change Since 1929,* 2d ed. (Los Angeles: UCLA Latin American Center, 1994), 137; and Mexico, Presidencia de la República, *Sexto informe de gobierno, anexo,* September 1, 2000, 40.
[a]Although no figures are available for 1950, the growth in government employees from 1940 through 1996 was 546.3 percent.

As the data in Table 10-1 demonstrate, Mexico has moved away from an agriculturally dominant society to an economy represented by manufacturing, commerce, and services. Mexico witnessed an increasing growth in ranching and agricultural workers from 1900 through 1960. As of 1960, such workers accounted for 54 percent of the economically active workforce, and until the mid-1980s, they were the single largest sector of the economy. But by the late 1990s, agricultural employees represented only 21 percent of the workforce, half the total workforce in 1960. Although they have grown only slowly in number since 1960, proportionately their reduction has been dramatic. In the past three decades, most of the new jobs in Mexico were in the manufacturing, commerce, construction, and transportation sectors. In volume, the service industry provided the most new jobs, 8.1 million, equal to the total population employed in agriculture. Today, services account for the largest single sector of the economy.

One social issue with important political ramifications is the ability of a country's economy and its economic model to produce upward social mobility and to increase the size of the middle class. A great danger in the austerity program (imposing strict controls over salary increases) introduced by President Zedillo is that measured by their income, many Mexicans joined the ranks of the poor. Mexico's National Institute of Statistics reported that Mexicans without sufficient food increased from 20 to 26 million from 1994 to 1999.[3] The data in Table 10-2 illustrate several features of

Table 10-2 Mexico's Class Structure from 1895 to 1990

Year	Class (%)					
	Upper	Change	Middle	Change	Lower	Change
1895	1.5	—	7.8	—	90.7	—
1940	2.9	93.3	12.6	61.5	84.5	−6.8
1950	1.7	−41.4	18.0	42.9	80.3	−5.0
1960	3.8	123.5	21.0	16.7	75.2	−6.4
1970	5.7	50.0	27.9	32.9	66.4	−11.7
1980	5.3	−7.0	33.0	18.3	61.8	−6.9
1990	6.8	28.3	38.2	15.8	55.0	−11.0

Source: Howard F. Cline, *Mexico: Revolution to Evolution, 1940–1960* (New York: Oxford University Press, 1963), 124; Stephanie Granato and Aida Mostkoff Linares, "The Class Structure of Mexico, 1895–1980," *Society and Economy in Mexico,* ed. James W. Wilkie (Los Angeles: UCLA Latin American Center, 1990); David Lorey and Aida Mostkoff Linares, "Mexico's Lost Decade," *Statistical Abstract of Latin America,* vol. 30, pt. 2 (Los Angeles: UCLA Latin American Center, 1994), 1339–60.

the Mexican class structure. Most important, the middle class has witnessed stable growth and, from the 1950s to the 1990s, doubled. The percentage of working-class Mexicans continues to fall, but the decline has been slow, particularly in the 1970s and early 1980s. The most dramatic change has been among Mexico's upper classes, which have tripled in size since 1950.

What these figures do not reveal are two significant patterns. First, the rapid growth of the Mexican population, especially since the 1950s, has created a working class and a marginal population, which in absolute numbers are far larger today than they were in the early part of the century. For example, of Mexico's current population, 98 million, 55 percent, or 53.9 million, are in the lower class, a figure larger than Mexico's entire population in 1960. What these figures also fail to show is the increasing concentration of wealth, as is true in the United States as well, among upper-income Mexicans. Thus even though the size of the lower class has continued to shrink, the quality of their life has worsened, not improved. In 2000, 46 percent of the population was considered to be living in high levels of marginalization.[4]

An important economic change that de la Madrid introduced and his successors have aggressively pursued is an increase in foreign investment. A major basis for the economic liberalization program is the generation of capital for the Mexican economy, especially foreign investment. The data in Table 10-3 show the growing importance of this variable in Mexico's economic development strategy. From 1988 to 1994, foreign investment increased fourfold. In 1993 alone, in anticipation of the North American Free-Trade Agreement, foreigners invested $15.6 billion, with U.S. investors accounting for 59 percent of investments since 1991. The Euro-

Table 10-3 Foreign Investment in Mexico

Administration	Totals (U.S. $ millions)	% Change
1970–1976	1,601.4	
1976–1982	5,470.6	241.7
1982–1988	13,455.4	146.0
1988–1994	60,565.5[a]	350.1
1994–2000	74,100.9	22.3
2000–2005[b]	85,418.0	15.2

Source: Crónica del gobierno de Carlos Salinas de Gortari, síntesis e indíce temático (Mexico City: Presidencia de la República, 1994), 441; and Mexico, Presidencia de la República, *Sexto informe de gobierno, anexo,* September 1, 2000, 132; www.inegi.gob.mx, June 2005; "Economic Indicators," *Review of the Economic Situation of Mexico* (June 2005), 195.
[a]Beginning in 1989, investment figures included those in the Mexican Stock Exchange; the data for 2000 are as of June 30.
[b]Data are through 1st quarter 2005.

pean Union is a distant second, with close to 20 percent, and Canada has become more important since NAFTA.[5]

ECONOMIC LIBERALIZATION

Whether the source of economic change in Mexico is international or domestic or both, there is no question that the administration of Carlos Salinas de Gortari instituted major economic reforms indicative of an altered government economic philosophy. As we argued earlier, the relationship between the state and the private sector had long been symbiotic and contentious. Its features emerged from a hybrid economic philosophy extending back to nineteenth-century laissez-faire liberalism and to social responsibility themes incorporated into the 1917 constitution.

For most of the twentieth century, the government offered a mixed private-public economic model, in which the state played a decisive, sometimes overpowering role. In the 1970s, under President Luis Echeverría (1970–1976), the legitimacy of the political model increasingly came into question. Echeverría's difficulties stemmed in part from the events of 1968, during which the army violently suppressed a student demonstration in the capital. He pursued various social and economic strategies to enhance presidential legitimacy and the political model's prestige.[6] Public employment was used to foster economic growth and stability, increasing opportunities for many Mexicans. One social scientist remarked, "Even though the public sector had had a relatively dynamic growth throughout the previous decade, during the first half of the 1970s it broke all precedents."[7]

During Echeverría's tenure, large reserves of petroleum were discovered. The government began exploiting those reserves and, on the basis of oils sales abroad, secured international loans to finance development projects.[8] During the early 1970s the government bought or gained control of hundreds of businesses and industries, placing more economic and human resources in the hands of government managers than at any time before. At the end of his administration Echeverría further alienated the private sector by attempting to expropriate valuable lands in the northwest.

Echeverría's successor, José López Portillo, a politician-technocrat experienced in the government financial sector, attempted to mend relations between the private and public sectors. Initially successful, he continued the pattern of borrowing large sums of money to invest in Mexico's economic infrastructure and development. When the oil boom abruptly ended and prices at the barrelhead plunged, the country found itself in serious trouble. It was hugely indebted to domestic and foreign bankers and was paying extraordinarily high interest.[9]

Instead of putting the brakes on the state's economic expansion, López Portillo actually stepped on the accelerator. In his last year in office, without warning or consultation, he announced the nationalization of the domestic banking system.[10] With a single decree, the president increased state control over the economy, of which bank-held mortgages increased it to somewhere between 75 and 85 percent. The move exacerbated the business community's lack of trust in the government and strongly encouraged the flight of capital from Mexico, primarily to the United States.[11] When López Portillo left office a few months later, the presidency was at its lowest ebb in decades; the business–government relationship was in great disrepair; and Mexico was in economic crisis.

López Portillo's successor, Miguel de la Madrid (1982–1988), like his mentor, was a product of the public financial sector, having worked in Mexico's equivalent of the U.S. Federal Reserve Bank, in the Secretariat of the Treasury, and as secretary of planning and budgeting. His economic philosophy, however, represented a different ideological wing of the government leadership. Essentially, he believed that the best strategy for rescuing Mexico from economic woe was to follow the strict, orthodox economic guidelines recommended by the International Monetary Fund (IMF): reduce government expenditures and impose controls on salaries, prices, and inflation.[12]

De la Madrid also introduced the most important element in Mexican economic liberalization: privatization. He actually wanted to undo the nationalization of the banks—which in itself would have had an immediate impact on government ownership—but believed that the mid-1980s were not a politically propitious time for the move.[13] Instead, he took several moderate steps that enabled joint private-public ownership of certain financial institutions. At the end of his administration, it became clear that some government-owned firms would be sold back to the private sector.

De la Madrid ensured the importance of privatization specifically and economic liberalism generally in selecting Salinas to follow him. The 1988 presidential succession took on great significance in the political leadership. In one sense, competition among contenders within the PRI represented a conflict between a more traditional economic philosophy, which favored state control and deficit-spending budget strategies, and the more orthodox private-sector emphasis that de la Madrid had reintroduced.[14] Although de la Madrid had improved the relationship between the private sector and the state, Salinas, by his second year in office, had established a clear-cut policy incorporating many ingredients of international economic liberalism.

It is very important to take note of U.S. influence on the Salinas policy. The United States did not play a direct role in the formulation of Mexico's economic policy. Nevertheless, both Reagan and Bush, Sr. pushed a more orthodox economic policy domestically and similar policies elsewhere, including that toward Mexico. Throughout the 1980s the United States expressed serious concern about Mexico's stability and its economic and political future. The American financial community, which held large portions of the Mexican government's debt portfolio, echoed this concern. Default might well have initiated a Latin American domino effect, with drastic consequences for the already shaky U.S. financial structure and the U.S. economy.[15] Salinas saw capital as essential to Mexico's economic recovery in the short term and international competition in the long term. When he realized that European governments and lenders were preoccupied with Eastern Europe, he turned to a free-trade agreement with the United States and Canada. Bush, who had close ties to Salinas, committed himself and the United States to approve such an agreement and encouraged Salinas to move ahead on it. In anticipation, Salinas and his economic team, most of whose members had studied in the United States, began to put many government-owned firms up for sale and to cut tariffs dramatically—many dropped from as high as 200 percent to an average of only 9 percent in 1992. The initiatives led to the return of some domestic capital and to new foreign investment—more than $60 billion by 1994 (see Table 10-3).

In late 1991 and early 1992 the government began to sell off the banks it had nationalized a decade earlier. It also put on the market several major corporations owned by the government, including Teléfonos de México

(Telmex), which had a monopoly on telephone communications in Mexico, and Mexicana Airlines, one of the two major domestic lines. In fact, of the 1,155 firms that the government owned as late as 1987, it retained control of only 286 in 1992, a drop of 80 percent. Critics also charged that the primary beneficiaries of the privatization program were friends of the president, including prominent businessmen who served on his campaign finance committee.[16]

The U.S. financial community responded favorably to these dramatic changes from a state-led to a free-market economy. Editorials in business-oriented publications like the *Wall Street Journal* praised Salinas and his collaborators. Other periodicals, such as *Business Week,* predicted a boom period for Mexico, making it attractive to investors. The Mexican government repeatedly cited its positive press as evidence supportive of its policies.

Yet critics charged that the state-controlled sector remained bloated. They argued that twelve of the twenty largest firms in terms of employees were still under state control. Indeed, state-owned firms employed 79 percent of all workers, and the size of all government workers was not much reduced from what it had been in 1987—from 4.4 to 4.1 million, largely the result of the sale of banks and government-owned companies.[17]

Parallel to his commitment to privatize and open up the economy to international competition, Salinas in 1992 startlingly proposed to overhaul the *ejido* land structure, a system of small-property holding controlled by each village. After the revolution, successive governments gave lands to individually operated *ejidos,* whose owners received use-right titles but not actual ownership from their local villages. Critics of agrarian reform charge that insufficient credit stems from an *ejidatarios*'s lack of collateral. Salinas's new legislation granted actual ownership and contract rights to these farmers. To keep farmers on the land and to assist in the transition to a more competitive market with U.S. imports, the government introduced Procampo, a program designed to eliminate its price supports for food by giving stipends (which would begin to drop after ten years and end in fifteen) directly to producers.[18]

Salinas introduced one other major social-economic policy soon after taking office, one closely linked to political liberalization. Known as the National Solidarity Program (Pronasol), or popularly as "Solidarity," it provided government seed money for local projects. Ostensibly, the philosophy behind the program was to encourage grassroots organization and local leadership. Thousands of farmers received loans; communities established rural medical clinics and renovated schools; and scholarships were awarded to promising students. By 1993 the government had spent 33 billion pesos on the program. Its supporters assert that it promoted grass-roots organization and leadership because local residents chose and prioritized the programs. Critics in opposition parties and some independent observers view Pronasol as a sophisticated, centrally controlled funding agency that built considerable electoral support for the PRI from 1989 to 2000. Procampo was accused of the same partisan linkage in the 1994 election. Still others believe that it was a means of enhancing the president's personal power and political influence.[19]

Regardless of the weaknesses and strengths of Salinas's economic policies, he pursued a consistent economic strategy, composed primarily of privatization, internationalization, and foreign investment. As part of his overall strategy to modernize Mexico, he was personally much more committed to economic than political liberalization. In fact, as he made clear, he intended to pursue modernization and, implicitly, the interrelationship of the two components.[20]

Salinas carefully planned his economic strategy and, more important, gave particular attention to the constituencies to whom it was addressed. His prudence paid off in considerable domestic and foreign support. He also used his economic successes—higher capital investment, lower inflation rates (reduced from 52 to 8 percent between 1988 and 1993), and increased dollar reserves—to mollify some of his domestic and many of his international critics, especially the United States.[21]

When Zedillo became the PRI candidate, he promised a ten-point program as his strategy for building on and continuing his predecessor's program. While praising the achievements of the preceding administration, Zedillo identified a number of problems that economic liberalization had not eliminated: insufficient jobs (with a 3 percent annual growth rate in the workforce, an average of 1 million new jobs are needed), a flat rate of productivity (only one-third of the population is economically active), and regional and sectoral inequities. Zedillo proposed boosting investment—public, private, and foreign—to increase money for education, altering the fiscal system to promote investment, encouraging saving, hastening deregulation, expanding new technological applications, broadening foreign competition, strengthening Procampo, and protecting the environment. Zedillo wanted an economic growth rate in 1995 twice that of the population growth rate, that is, 3.8 percent.[22]

But instead of having an opportunity to build on the economic structure left by his predecessor, Zedillo was confronted with a major economic crisis in the first month of his administration, the magnitude of which Mexico had not experienced even in the difficult days of the 1980s. Zedillo's economic team decided to devalue the Mexican peso against the dollar—a serious problem ignored by his predecessor—allowing it to float free (private market demand for pesos internationally).[23] Rather than the peso's stabilizing at a new exchange rate, which Mexican economists expected to be only 15 to 20 percent lower than the old rate, there was a run on the peso. According to some analysts, the New York financial community shares the responsibility for Mexico's crisis, having pressured the Mexicans—with the threat of withdrawing their investments—into issuing billions of dollars worth of dollar-denominated, short-term bonds, *tesebonos,* as a substitute for the peso-denominated investments, *cetes.* Investors liked the higher returns on the *cetes* before 1994, but the political situation in Mexico during 1994 and the declining dollar reserves made fund managers in New York worry about the security of Mexican peso bonds. Indeed, the Mexican government issued so many of the devaluation-proof *tesebonos* that ten billion became due between the end of December 1994 and March 1995.[24] It was able to meet its short-term obligations with the help of public, international financing.[25]

The result of the crises caused by the devaluation of the peso is that Mexico faced negative economic growth in 1995, a loss of somewhere between 250,000 and 1 million jobs before the end of the year, a reversal of foreign investment and capital flight, a dramatic rise in inflation exceeding 50 percent yearly, an extraordinary rise in private-bank interest for mortgages and loans far above the inflation rate, and numerous business closures and bankruptcies, including the threat of important state governments declaring financial insolvency.

After pursuing a severe austerity program for two years, and achieving a GDP of 7.5 percent and an inflation rate of 15.7 percent in 1997, Zedillo introduced PRONAFIDE, a medium-term economic program pursuing strategies designed to promote public and private savings and investment. The president introduced his own social programs, Progresa and Salud 2000, committed to increased spending in social development and health care. The federal budget's largest outlay in 1997, 56 percent, was for social programs.[26] In spite of Zedillo's increased outlays on social expenditures, according to a study of the Inter-American Development Bank, the end effect of the crisis was "a great loss of human capital." Many younger Mexicans were forced to abandon their studies and go to work. At the same time, many experienced workers in the 55 or older category lost their jobs. Half of those were unable to find new work.[27]

To what extent has economic liberalism, as pursued by each administration since 1982, improved the standard of living for most Mexicans? Each administration since 1946 has increased expenditures on social programs, such as health and education. Expenditures doubled in percentage terms in this category from 1946 to 1964, and increased dramatically from 1982 to the end of the century (Table 10-4). Despite economic statistics showing

Table 10-4 The Evolution of Federal Social Expenditures

		Expenditure Category (percent of total)		
Presidential Administration		Economic	Social	Administrative
Zedillo	1995–1996	31	53	16
Salinas	1989–1994	33	50	17
De la Madrid	1982–1988	39	41	20
López Portillo	1976–1982	41	33	26
Echeverría	1970–1976	62	29	9
Díaz Ordaz	1964–1970	55	32	13
López Mateos	1959–1964	39	19	42
Ruiz Cortines	1952–1958	53	14	33
Alemán	1946–1952	52	13	35

Source: Este País, (December 1999), 16.

improved productivity and growth, the record is not very encouraging. The distribution of income continues to favor wealthy Mexicans (see Table 10-5). Two-thirds of all income is distributed to 30 percent of the population. (In the United States, the top 20 percent of the population receive 55 percent of the national income.) The lowest 30 percent of the population, as measured by income, receives only 8 percent.[28] What is equally discouraging is that this pattern has remained unchanged since 1989. Furthermore, real salaries have continued to fall in Mexico since 1975, whether one looks at the minimum wage, which in 1993 was less than half of what it was in 1975, or contractual and assembly plant salaries. Per capita income in 2003 was $3,888. The United Nations estimated that the number of Mexicans living in conditions

Table 10-5 Distribution of Income in Mexico, 1984–2000 (in percent)

Family Income by Deciles, Lowest to Highest	1984	1989	1992	1998	2000
1	1.72	1.58	1.56	1.50	1.52
2	3.11	2.81	2.75	2.70	2.64
3	4.21	3.74	3.70	3.60	3.60
4	5.32	4.73	4.70	4.70	4.59
5	6.40	5.90	5.70	5.80	5.70
6	7.86	7.29	7.11	7.20	7.08
7	9.72	8.98	8.92	8.90	8.84
8	12.16	11.42	11.57	11.50	11.24
9	16.73	15.62	16.02	16.00	16.09
10	32.77	37.93	38.16	38.10	38.70

Source: Fernando Pérez Correa, "Modernización y mercado del trabajo," Este País, February 1995, 27; "Mexico: Income Distribution," Review of the Economic Situation of Mexico, October 2000, 416–418, August 2001, 358.

Income Levels Per Capita by State

Low-income states
Medium-income states
High-income states

300 Miles

500 Kilometers

of poverty, moderate poverty, and extreme poverty in 1999 totaled 57 percent, 15 percent and 28 percent of its population, respectively. The figures for those living in moderate and extreme poverty have taken a dramatic turn compared to 1997, when only 16 percent lived in extreme poverty and 30 percent in moderate poverty. Fifteen percent of Mexico's population earns less than a dollar a day.[29]

The pattern in Mexico's standard of living can also be examined from a more sophisticated perspective, more revealing than that of per capita income alone. The National Bank of Mexico, one of the country's most prominent financial institutions, has generated a Well-Being Index, composed of many variables related to an individual person's standard of living. Using their index, and statistics from the national census, they have constructed comparable data from the 1920s through the 1990s (see Table 10-6). Their data convincingly demonstrates strong growth from 1950 to 1980, and especially in the 1960s, with a 3.7 percent increase, but an extremely low level of well-being has been achieved since 1980.

Internationally, economists use a measurement, the Gini coefficient, to describe a country's overall inequality. What is unusual about the Mexican case is the dramatically increased concentration of wealth in the hands of the rich between 1984 and 2000. An insightful comparative analysis of Taiwan and Mexico, which shared comparable economic statistics in their early stages of development, is suggestive of what happened in Mexico. Taiwan overcame adverse conditions, while Mexico's economic development lagged behind. Taiwan's success compared with that of Mexico was achieved

Table 10-6 Mexico's Well-Being Index, 1925–1995 (in percent)

Year	Index[a]	Annual Growth Rate
1925	60.6	0.6
1930	62.3	1.6
1940	73.2	0.7
1950	78.5	2.4
1960	100.0	3.7
1970	144.1	2.3
1980	181.5	0.5
1990	190.5	1.0
1995	198.0	—

Source: Review of the Economic Situation of Mexico, March 1995, 83.
[a]The well-being index refers to basic necessities; it is an aggregate measure of prosperity using nineteen factors related to income, food consumption, health, education, clothing, and urbanization.

through several strategies, including land reform, labor-intensive exports, domestic saving, small- and medium-sized enterprises, and basic education. The authors of this comparative study believe that the role of human capital, and specifically education, was crucial in explaining Taiwan's success. Mexico's educational efforts did not produce similar results as those found in Taiwan because of higher population growth rates, a slower gross domestic product, and a higher proportion of families in the extreme poverty category. In their final analysis of all the variables that contributed to Taiwan's growth, the authors concluded that market-oriented growth does not automatically reduce inequality or poverty, but policies that redistribute land, improve skills, facilitate small enterprises, and increase savings, were instrumental in Taiwan's success.[30]

Human capital is affected by the interrelationship between income and education. Mexico has a low rate of matriculation in higher education. For example, only 1,600 young adults out of 100,000 register at universities and colleges, compared with 3,000 in Costa Rica and 5,300 in the United States.[31] Not surprisingly, the higher an individual's family income, the more likely he or she is to complete higher education. At the end of the twentieth century, the poorest 30 percent of the population in Mexico averaged only three years of education, while the wealthiest 10 percent achieved slightly more than twelve years.[32] What is potentially more devastating about the distribution of educational achievement in Mexico is the decline in upward social mobility through public institutions. If attendance at the National Preparatory School and the National Autonomous University of Mexico, the country's largest schools, are an indication, students whose parents had achieved only marginal levels of education declined dramatically from 1990 to 1999. For example, students enrolling at UNAM in 1990 reported that 37 and 50 percent of their fathers and mothers, respectively, had completed only a primary education. In a decade, those figures dropped to 22 and 31 percent, respectively, indicating that fewer students from moderate-income families were reaching the university in the twenty-first century.[33] National figures for the mid-1990s suggest that intergenerational mobility from the lowest to the highest schools remains limited, with only one-third of children born to parents with six or fewer years of education completing high school.[34]

Under the Fox administration Mexico's economy has grown, becoming the 9th largest in the world. With the impact of NAFTA, exports increased dramatically, but employment has not kept pace. Furthermore, the effects of NAFTA have devastated rural Mexico, the predominant source of the poorest families. At the same time Mexico has become less attractive to foreign investors, and many manufacturing companies are relocating their assembly plants to cheaper competitors, notably China. Many of the structural problems, as they relate to income distribution, poverty, and marginalization, remain relatively static. Mexico now ranks fifty-fourth in the United Nations human development ranking. To his credit, Fox, like his predecessor, has sought to increase the federal government's emphasis on social expenditures, and especially those expenditures that would help to alleviate poverty. For example, social spending was 19 percent higher in 2001 than in 1994, and Fox significantly expanded health expenditures for the poorest Mexicans. But as many economic analysts note, although a modest shift between those in the extreme poverty category in favor of the poverty category occurred, overall the total percentages of people in those categories remain roughly the same. Furthermore, the only income category that has shown any significant change since 1984 are households in the top 10 percent income bracket, having grown 6 percent, from 34 to 40 percent of national income. Those groups that have lost the greatest ground in family income in that shift are middle-income families.[35]

DEMOCRATIZATION

In Mexico, as elsewhere in the world, political liberalization has meant democratization. Thus, the international winds of change indicated a combined political-economic model, incorporating political democracy on the one hand and economic capitalism on the other. Mexicans had long expressed an interest in democratization, which flared up after independence, in the 1860s and 1870s, at the time of the revolution, and then again in the 1960s and 1970s.

As was true with the movement toward economic liberalization, President de la Madrid paved the way toward recent political events. Soon after taking office, as part of a moral renovation, he promised cleaner elections and decentralization of the candidate selection process within the government party. Initially, the promises translated into actual improvements, and opposition parties, especially the National Action Party, won many local elections in the mid-1980s. Surprised, government officials reversed the apparent opening by resorting to the "doctoring" of vote counts. The practice roused the Catholic hierarchy and the country's leading intellectuals to proclaim disbelief in government vote counts in the 1986 elections in Chihuahua.

Within the government leadership, a debate ensued as to future political and economic strategies. The debate centered on two primary, interrelated issues. First, should the government expand its commitment to the economic programs introduced gradually under de la Madrid, programs that reduced the standard of living of a fourth of Mexico's economically active population, or should it resort to spending programs to moderate the drastic effects of austerity and resist paying the international debt? Second, should the leadership open up the political system to widespread competition and report electoral results honestly or continue along the same road?

The political figures who wanted to return to deficit spending, economic nationalism, and strong state leadership, combined with electoral honesty, lost out in the internal battles for the presidency. In 1987 when they tried, particularly on the issue of democratizing the PRI, to pressure the leadership from within, they were summarily dismissed from PRI party ranks. Their decision to form an opposition movement under Cuauhtémoc Cárdenas provided a catalyst for the most important election in recent Mexican political history.

The presidential election of 1988 was a test of the legitimacy of the establishment leadership. Preelection polls indicated the strength of Cuauhtémoc Cárdenas, but most analysts underestimated his appeal to the electorate. It was clear that Salinas, the PRI's candidate, was the least popular choice among his own party rank and file, and he personally generated little additional support during the campaign. The official results show that Salinas won 51 percent of the vote; Cárdenas's alliance, 31 percent; and Manuel Clouthier, the National Action Party's candidate, 17 percent.

The official results were widely disputed in the media. As noted in the previous chapter, many independent observers and critics believe the figures were fraudulent, and many suggested that Cárdenas may actually have defeated Salinas. Most Mexicanists contend, and they are borne out by survey research, that Salinas won but with a much smaller margin than actually reported.[36] Even accepting the official results, the PRI and the establishment leadership gave up more seats in the Chamber of Deputies and, for the first time, in the Senate, than at any other point up to then.

The election of 1988 had numerous consequences. Among them, it provided a catalyst for the development of a new opposition party, the Democratic Revolutionary Party (PRD), which slipped from second to third place in 1991, and remains an important alternative to the PAN and PRI. The PRD was formed in 1988 after the demise of a temporary electoral alliance under Cárdenas. Second, the election gave greater prominence to the Chamber of Deputies, in which nearly half of the seats, proportional and district alike, went to the opposition. Third, it brought the populace's democratic demands to the fore and gave much greater visibility to desires that had been expressed electorally on the district and regional levels since the 1940s, but never so dramatically in a national election.[37] Fourth, it contributed to new political alliances, notably between the PAN and the PRD in the electoral arena, but only on the state level, and between the PAN and the PRI in the policy arena. Fifth, it paved the way for a series of gubernatorial elections, directly or indirectly leading to opposition victories in 1989, 1991, and 1992. Finally, it forced the government leadership to reformulate its political constituencies and, in doing so, introduced political changes as dramatic as those in the economic sphere.

Salinas took office in December 1988 with only a minimal level of political legitimacy. Having won or imposed the disputed election results, he faced—as no president in recent memory had faced—inauguration with very little public support. But Salinas confounded his detractors and supporters alike, moving quickly to establish a reputation as decisive. Instead of depending on the presidency to increase his political influence, Salinas enhanced the prestige of the presidency with his own power and strength. He did this in a series of deft decisions, including using the army to arrest a corrupt union leader and to seize a major drug trafficker, as well as arresting and prosecuting a well-known businessman for financial fraud.

Throughout his tenure Salinas used the presidency as the leading institution to implement his policies and to centralize control of decision making. One of the more interesting ironies of his administration was the concentration of decision-making authority in the presidency.[38] He streamlined the workings of the cabinet, removing the agency that both he and his mentor, de la Madrid—and his disciple, Zedillo—had used to rise to the top of the political ladder. Salinas eliminated programming and budgeting by joining it with the Secretariat of the Treasury. He further coordinated cabinet policymaking by expanding interagency planning through subcabinet groups.

There was a certain irony in Salinas's liberalization philosophy. Economically, he tried to demonstrate that Mexico was decentralizing, allocating decision-making authority to numerous independent enterprises. Politically, although he said he wanted liberalization for his own party leadership and in national politics, the results demonstrated otherwise: As the government decentralized economic decision making, it actually centralized political decision making even more.

Other characteristics of Salinas's political strategy illustrate the complexity of his policies and the contradictions in his goals. The most radical political policy of his administration involved long-standing church–state relations. Early on Salinas announced his desire to "modernize" church–state relations. In December 1991 Salinas proposed changes in the constitution in regard to church–state relations. Among the changes later approved by the Chamber of Deputies were recognizing all churches as legal entities;

allowing priests and ministers to vote and to run for political office if they had resigned from their clerical offices five years earlier; permitting churches and religious officials to offer primary and secondary education as long as they respected government-approved plans of study; allowing public celebrations of religious ceremonies; granting churches the right to own property; and explicitly separating churches from the state.

Clergy traditionally violated some constitutional provisions in practice, but the president confronted a highly emotional issue with deep roots in Mexican political liberalism. The proposals, however, not only modernized the relationship between religion and the state but they also conformed to explicit principles of democracy, particularly concerning the right to vote.

The presidential elections of 1994 returned Mexico to the electoral context of 1988 in regard to the level of support for the opposition. But as has been argued earlier, the outcome of the 1994 elections changed all previous patterns, including those recorded in 1988, in two potentially significant ways. First, the turnout was extraordinary and introduced a large minority of Mexicans directly into the political process. Their participation in the political process, even if only electorally, provided a base for future opposition growth. Second, although the proportion of voters casting their ballots for the PRI remained unchanged from 1988, the composition of the voters was quite different, especially in state income levels, rural and urban patterns, and region. Mexico witnessed an important change among the types of voters who supported opposition-party candidates. For example, the opposition demonstrated a substantial increase in support among rural voters and voters in the south, two traditionally "safe" groups for PRI.

When Zedillo took office, he reinforced the economic liberalization strategies of his predecessor, although as we suggested, he gave greater emphasis to redistribution policies, illustrated by his increased social expenditures. But he differed most strongly from Salinas in his political philosophy. Unlike his predecessor, he made it clear from the initial months of his administration that he would move away from a centralized, authoritarian executive with mega-constitutional powers. There is no question that he paved the way for Fox's electoral victory by changing the Mexican presidency's substance and tone.[39] He set in motion four fundamental patterns that altered the Mexican political context, all of which contributed to advances in democratization. First, he decentralized presidential decision-making, rarely intervening in political disputes. He symbolized this philosophy most notably and publicly in his decision to implement a PRI primary, thus ignoring the traditional presidential prerogative of designating his own successor. Second, he granted governors increased autonomy, thereby strengthening their political resources and encouraging federalism. The growth of federalism at the state and local level may well be the most influential characteristic of Mexican democratization in 2000. Third, he separated the party from the state, and by encouraging public campaign financing, eliminated the government party's financial advantages. Fourth, and finally, he strengthened other governmental institutions. Most importantly, he laid the groundwork for an independent judiciary and a stronger legislative branch. Electorally, he encouraged voter participation by guaranteeing the autonomy of the Federal Electoral Institute to oversee the election process.

The 2000 presidential election, as previously suggested, built on the patterns and trends introduced by the two preceding elections and the changes wrought by President Zedillo. The 2000 contest took Mexico's political development, in terms of democratization, to a higher plane, opening the door to structural, as distinct from just electoral, democracy. Structural democracy implies that Mexicans now have the opportunity to alter governmental institutions and to make their processes participatory and accountable. PAN's electoral victory legitimized the electoral process, demonstrating to the average voter that the will of the electorate can be achieved at the ballot box. The 2000 elections also reinforced trends in the distribution of support among various types of voters for the three leading parties. Again, for example, PAN further increased its strength among rural voters, as well as voters from the south, Mexico's poorest region, although PRI recovered some of these voters in 2003.

The most remarkable change resulting from the elections between 1988 and 2000 is the experience that Mexicans obtained at the local and state levels. Not only did the PAN and, to a lesser extent, the PRD defeat the PRI in numerous mayoral and gubernatorial races, but Mexicans were being exposed to alternative styles of executive-branch decision making on the local level. A major consequence of these experiences can be linked to a deconcentration of authority and a decentralization of political power. For example, after 1996, two-thirds of the social development budget, Mexico's largest line item, was devolved to municipal coffers.[40] PAN or PRD victories do not mean necessarily better government or more successful government.

A prominent emerging pattern is a revival of autonomy and independence at the local level.[41] This is demonstrated in the fact that local leaders, typically from opposition parties, are demanding more control over financial resources, the crucial variable in determining political influence. The mayor of Ciudad Juárez, Mexico's fourth largest city, demanded that the federal government turn over $4.9 million in revenues from tolls taken at the international bridge to its sister city, El Paso, Texas. The mayor, a PANista, set up municipal toll booths to take the money away from federally operated toll collectors.[42] Popular postures taken by local opposition-party leaders are being emulated by members of the government party in similar posts. The National Association of Governors called for an increase in the percentage of tax revenues going to states directly (from 20 to 23 percent), and increased control over social spending to prevent government programs being used to support partisan ends.[43]

By 2003, President Fox told the National Association of Governors that 35 percent of federal funds were allocated to state and local governments.

MEXICO'S FUTURE

With the election of Vicente Fox, Mexico now faces the final stage of democratization. Democracy, according to most analysts, goes well beyond the electoral process and includes the following features: policy debates and political competition, citizen participation, accountability for upholding the rule of law and representative mechanisms, civilian control over the military, and respect for the views and rights of others.[44] The behavior of the Fox administration reveals a positive attitude toward these fundamental components of democracy. The president has implemented legal changes to respond to several of these issues, and he has underscored their desirability through his personal declarations and behavior.

The presidency remains the most important institutional force in Mexican society and, as such, serves as the primary model for other forms of political and social behavior. If the president behaves in a paternalistic, interventionist, and controlling manner, even within the law, he sets the tone for the rest of the political system and society. As Mexico moves into the twenty-first century, a contradiction may appear between local and national trends. Different parties and leaders govern in numerous cities and states. Some of those leaders may pursue agendas that are less democratic and accountable than that of the president or PAN. These contradictions raise a fundamental and controversial issue that is a part of American political heritage, states' rights versus the federal government. In Mexico's transitional period since 1988, many state and local governments have increased democratization. In the next decade, other states and local governments might well do the opposite, dragging their feet on accountability and greater public participation.[45] The trend, however, appears to be in the democratic direction.

One of the most serious deficiencies in Mexico's democratic transformation since 1988 is its record on human rights. Amnesty International's representative has stated that "Mexico is a country with staggering levels of political violence." The abuses have been particularly commonplace in poor rural regions, including the states of Chiapas, Guerrero, and Oaxaca. Violations of rights in the criminal justice system have been identified as endemic in numerous international and domestic reports.[46] Most of the human rights abusers have been government respresentatives (see Table 10-7). Four years into the Fox administration, most Mexicans believe little respect for human rights still exists in their country, with nearly half believing no or little respects exists for such rights. The poor and indigenous receive the least respect, and when asked who least respects human rights, 36 percent specified the government or authorities, 10 percent said politicians, 14 percent said everyone or society, and 9 percent said the police.[47]

International pressure forced Salinas to establish the National Commission for Human Rights, initially presided over by Jorge Carpizo, a highly respected jurist and Supreme Court justice. The president's primary motivation was to temper worldwide disapproval of Mexico's human rights record in anticipation of public discussion and congressional hearings in the United States on the proposed free-trade agreement. The commission has investigated some complaints and protected the rights of some citizens, but overall, protections remain unsatisfactory, especially at the local level. Nevertheless, confidence in the Comisión itself has grown, with citizens ranking it below the Catholic Church and the Federal Electoral Institute, two of the most prestigious institutes, but well above the attorney general and the Supreme Court, two legal authorities that would be involved in protecting citizen rights.

The second important issue that remains unaddressed by the success of electoral democracy is the public's cynicism about governmental and party institutions because of pervasive corruption in public life. The most com-

Table 10-7 Sources of Human Rights Abuses in Mexico, 1997

Responsible Party	Percent
Army	27
State judicial police	14
Local police	14
Local authorities	11
Public security forces	9
Undetermined	9
Paramilitary groups	7
Secretariat of government	5
Attorney general	4

Source: Comisión Mexicana de Defensa y Promoción de los Derechos Humanos, *Guión* (January 1998), 31, based on 485 reported violations, January–December 1997.

Table 10-8 Mexican Views of Law and Corruption

Statement	Percentage in agreement
Violating the law isn't so terrible, what's bad is being caught by the authorities	65
When authorities cannot protect citizens, they should be able to take the law into their own hands	66
More democracy will guarantee better laws	25
Generally, those who violate the law are not caught or punished	29
We should obey only reasonable and just laws	37
Mexicans are basically honest, but it is the system that causes corruption	38
We should be guided by written and unwritten laws	52

Source: Este País, November 1997; October 1998.

prehensive examination of this issue concludes that organized crime's involvement in the political system at various levels significantly threatens public security and democratic government in Mexico.[48] Furthermore, a recent study concluded that levels of corruption at the state level are not affected by voting patterns, level of competitiveness, the party in power, or the power of incumbency.[49] It is not just obvious forms of corruption that detract from the integrity of the institutions and the leadership, but also corruption's detrimental effects on the sense of community interest and trust (Table 10-8). Thus, the pervasive corruption complements the belief that public life provides opportunities to benefit family and friends rather than to serve the interests of all Mexicans. This is not to say that all public officials in Mexico are dishonest, but to suggest that an ambience favorable to self-interest, dishonesty, and favoritism prevails in many areas and at numerous levels of the public sector. For example, in the Federal District, judicial agents are responsible for 80 percent of all kidnappings. The Mexican public believes that corruption is widespread. In fact, in 2002, 55 percent of Mexicans believed the majority of their fellow citizens were corrupt.[50] President Fox recognizes this issue and has made accountability and transparency a hallmark of his administration.[51] Whether he can substantially reduce its presence as part of the institutional culture, however, remains to be seen.

In recent years, under Fox and his predecessor, personal security has become a major issue. Two hundred and fifty thousand residents of the capital joined in a huge march to protest the increase in crime and lack of public safety in 2004. Thus the Fox administration has made little headway in reality or in public perception. Surveys demonstrate the following statistics about insecurity and crime in Mexico:

- The principle cause of crime in Mexico City is corrupt authorities and the police (52 percent)
- One in 7 homes reported at least one member of their household was a victim of crime in 2005
- 3.7 million people were victims of crime in 2003
- 44 percent feel somewhat or very unsafe in their state in 2003
- Only 17 of every 100 victims reported the crime to authorities
- 22 percent have modified their habits due to crime
- The fastest growing crimes are perceived to be drug trafficking and assault in public places[52]

Drug-related corruption has become Mexico's greatest threat. Popular musical groups such as the Tucanes, have used ballads to idolize the drug culture.[53] Drug consumption is also on the rise. Twenty-five percent of students over the age of twelve in Mexico City have tried drugs. Fox himself has alluded to this trend as a threat to Mexico's social fabric. It not only affects the social fabric of society, but increasingly impacts on domestic political stability. Many analysts believe that the high-profile assassinations of PRI's presidential candidate in 1994, the Cardinal of Guadalajara in 1993, and the secretary general of the PRI in 1994, were drug related. Some analysts fear that the levels of corruption in Mexico have reached deeply and broadly into the highest levels of government and the military and that Mexico is threatened with the possibility of the "Colombianization" of political life. There is no better example of this than Tijuana, the important border city near San Diego, California.[54] Mexico's banking and financial sectors have lacked "adequate controls on money laundering and [Tijuana] has become one of the most important money laundering centers in the western hemisphere."[55]

Fox has augmented the prestige of the rule of law, but it still has a long way to go. Analysts argue that the influx of foreign businesses and greater international competitiveness will encourage heavier reliance on the legal system to resolve disputes, given that these new phenomena traditionally used similar channels in their own cultures. This may well be the case, but for the average Mexican, the law provides few guarantees of equal treatment. As the human rights literature make clear, the criminal justice system is often the abuser of human rights, not their protector. The level of corruption also influences the legal system and the law's applicability to all citizens.[56]

For much of Latin America and many other Third World countries, civilian control over the military has rarely existed. The Mexican civilian sector, however, has had an exceedingly successful relationship with the military, especially since the 1930s, and has unquestionably maintained its supremacy. Even so, the relationship is quite complex and contains many variables. To achieve civilian supremacy, civilian leadership gave up a part of its autonomy regarding military matters, including promotions and the internal allocation of funding. Multiple-party control of the Chamber of Deputies, however, has enhanced legislative interest in military budget matters and even in what largely has been a pro-forma approval of promotions to general rank. Legislators have already broken with traditional deference to the defense secretary, requiring him and his naval counterpart to appear before the appropriate committees and answer queries openly and frankly.

Finally, as our earlier analysis of citizen political values and attitudes showed, most Mexicans share beliefs supportive of democratic behavior. However, portions of the populace and of the leadership, have not yet accepted the obligations of a democratic culture, one of which is tolerance of opposing political and social views. Leadership's positive actions toward its own members and toward members of the opposition can encourage this value. The degree to which the electoral process remains open and highly competitive also encourages this value.

Mexico's political development has taken some interesting turns in the 1990s. Its politicians and political process labor under a special burden with which few countries have had to cope: proximity to the United States. As noted in the discussion of the historical evolution of Mexico's political characteristics, just the geographic nearness of the United States and its historic involvement in internal Mexican affairs were part of Mexico's earlier history.

The United States continues to exercise considerable influence on Mexico's leadership, albeit usually implicit and indirect. In fact, if the United States were to attempt to influence Mexican political affairs directly, the effort would surely backfire. Nevertheless, the influence is obvious and many actors are involved. For example, U.S. media often criticize Mexico for its political failures, focusing in recent years on electoral fraud, corruption, and human rights abuses.[57]

The United States has exercised an indirect influence since the 1980s on many aspects of government policy through its drug interdiction program. Drug enforcement agents have worked closely with their Mexican counterparts to stanch the northward flow of drugs. The involvement of U.S. representatives in matters pertaining to Mexican national security often raises important political issues. And U.S. pressure pushed the Mexican government to expand its military's role in anti-narcotics missions.

Mexico's national leadership is truly committed to democratic reforms, and many forces within and outside Mexico are pushing it in that direction. Democracy's success will largely depend on its effectiveness as a governing process. Mexicans, having voted in a new leadership and a different political model, now expect concrete results. Their strongest expectations focus on economic growth, a decline in corruption, and personal security. Fox's five years in office clearly demonstrate that a multi-party system creates many obstacles in the policy process and that the executive branch faces an uphill battle in obtaining approval of its most significant legislative agenda.[58] The consequences of any failures on the part of the Fox government to implement its programs are not limited to the future electoral fortunes of his party but, given the initial experimentation with a democratic system, would deeply damage its appeal as a political model. When compared to other world regions, support for democracy in Mexico and Latin America is weak.[59] Strong support for democracy does lie with the next generation. Children between the ages of nine and sixteen, many of whom will vote for president and reaffirm the present model in 2006, overwhelmingly support democracy and believe their vote counts.[60] If Mexico can address both income inequality and political corruption in the next decade, democracy's future seems assured. If it fails to address these issues, its survival is questionable.

NOTES

1. Pedro Aspe, "Thoughts on the Structural Transformation in Mexico: The Case of Privatization of Public Sector Enterprises," speech to the World Affairs Council, Los Angeles, June 21, 1991, 6.

2. "Public Opinion: Balance and Expectations," *Review of the Economic Situation of Mexico* October 2001, 436.

3. "Zedillo Will Leave Behind More Poverty," *El Financiero International,* September 13, 1999, 11.

4. Isabel Vázquez, "Socio-Political Indicators: Poverty in Mexico," *Review of the Economic Situation of Mexico* (May 2002), 205.

5. CEPAL, *Foreign Investment in Latin America and the Caribbean, 1998 Report* (Santiago: CEPAL, 1998).

6. Samuel Schmidt, *The Deterioration of the Mexican Presidency: The Years of Luis Echeverría* (Tucson: University of Arizona Press, 1991).

7. Luis Rubio and Roberto Newell, *Mexico's Dilemma: The Political Origins of Economic Crisis* (Boulder, Colo.: Westview Press, 1984), 134.

8. George Grayson, *The Politics of Mexican Oil* (Pittsburgh: University of Pittsburgh Press, 1980), 119.

9. Sidney Weintraub, *A Marriage of Convenience: Relations Between Mexico and the United States* (New York: Oxford University Press, 1990), 134ff.

10. Sylvia Maxfield, "Introduction," in *Government and Private Sector in Contemporary Mexico,* eds. Sylvia Maxfield and Ricardo Anzaldúa Montoya (La Jolla, Calif.: Center for U.S.–Mexican Studies, UCSD, 1987), 18.

11. Daniel Levy and Gabriel Székely, *Mexico: Paradoxes of Stability and Change* (Boulder, Colo.: Westview Press, 1987), 157.

12. Wayne A. Cornelius, "The Political Economy of Mexico Under de la Madrid: Austerity, Routinized Crisis, and Nascent Recovery," *Mexican Studies/ Estudios Mexicanos* 1 (Winter 1985): 83–124.

13. Personal interview, Mexico City, July 20, 1984.

14. Peter H. Smith, "The 1988 Presidential Succession in Historical Perspective," in *Mexico's Alternative Political Futures,* eds. Wayne A. Cornelius, Judith Gentleman, and Peter H. Smith (La Jolla, Calif.: Center for U.S.–Mexican Studies, 1989), 402.

15. Tom Barry, ed., *Mexico: A Country Guide* (Albuquerque: Inter-Hemispheric Education Resource Guide, 1992), 86.

16. *Mexico Report,* February 10, 1992, 6; and Judith Teichman "Dismantling the Mexican State and the Role of The Private Sector," in *The Political Economy of North American Free Trade,* eds. Ricardo Grinspun and Maxwell Cameron (New York: St. Martin's Press, 1993), 177–92.

17. *Mexico Report,* February 10, 1992.

18. Sideny Weintraub, *NAFTA: What Comes Next?* (Washington, D.C.: CSIS, 1994), 53–54.

19. Raymundo Riva Palacio, "Mexico Is Not an Island," *El Financiero International,* February 24, 1992, 17; Sergio Sarmiento, "Solidarity Offers Hope for Votes," *El Financiero International,* September 30, 1991, 12.

20 "A New Hope for the Hemisphere," *New Perspective Quarterly,* 8 (Winter 1991): 128.

21. For some unusual insights into his strategy, see Robert A. Pastor, "Post-Revolutionary Mexico: The Salinas Opening," *Journal of Inter-American Studies and World Affairs* 32 (Fall 1990): 1–22.

22. Ernesto Zedillo, "A Strategy for Mexico's Economic Growth," June 6, 1994.

23. The clearest explanations of the devaluation decision and the mistakes made by both Salinas and Zedillo are explored briefly in Sidney Weintraub's "Mexico's Devaluation: Why and What Next?" (Washington, D.C.: CSIS, January 4, 1994), 1–7; Francisco Gil Díaz and Agustín Carstens, "Some Hypotheses Related to the Mexican 1994–1995 Crisis" (Mexico City: Bank of Mexico, 1996); and Nora Lustig, "Mexico in Crisis, The U.S. to the Rescue" (Washington, D.C.: Brookings Institution, 1996).

24. Douglas W. Payne, "Wall Street Blues," *The New Republic,* March 13, 1995, 20, 22.

25. Claire Poole, "Beast of Burden," *Mexico Business,* December 1996, 30, cites Carlos Marichal, an economic historian who argues that "Mexico's foreign debt load is the biggest ever in the history of Latin America, or for that matter, of any developing country."

26. Ernesto Zedillo, "Social Policy, a Commitment to Mexicans," September 1997.

27. Eduardo Lora and Gustavo Marquez, "The Scars of Volatility: Mexico 1994–1996," *Latin American Economic Policies 8* (Third Quarter 1999), 7–8.

28. For a discussion, see John Sheahan's excellent "Effects of Liberalization Programs on Poverty and Inequality: Chile, Mexico, and Peru," *Latin American Research Review* 37, 3 (1997): 7–37.

29. "Anti-poverty Program," *Review of the Economic Situation of Mexico,* September 1997, 369–72; *Este País,* September, 1999, 21.

30. H. Li, "Political Economy of Income Distribution: A Comparative Study of Taiwan and Mexico," Unpublished paper, Merrimack College, 1999.

31. Diego Valadés, "Pobreza, desarrollo y educación superior," *Este País,* (November 1999), 4.

32. "Indicators of Income Distribution," *Latin American Economic Policies,* no. 5 (Fourth Quarter 1998), 8.

33. Fernando Pérez Correa, "Crisis de la Universidad o crisis del sistema," *Este País,* (March 2000), 52.

34. Melissa Binder and Christopher Woodruff, "Intergenerational Mobility in Educational Attainment in Mexico," Unpublished paper, University of New Mexico, 1999, 18.

35. For comprehensive interpretations on these issues since 2000 and helpful economic data, see Russell Crandall, "Mexico's Domestic Economy: Policy Options and Choices," in *Mexico's Democracy at Work,* ed. Russell Crandall, Guadalupe Paz, and Riordan Roett (Boulder, Colo: Lynne Rienner, 2004), 61–88; Manuel Pastor and Carol Wise, "The Fox Administration and the Politics of Economic Transition," In *Mexico's Democracy at Work,* 89–118; Gary Gereffi and Martha A. Martínez, "Mexico's Economic Transformation Under NAFTA," in *Mexico's Democracy at Work,* 119–52; Manuel Pastor and Carol Wise, "A Long View of Mexico's Political Economy: What's Changed? What Are the Challenges?" in *Mexico's Politics and Society in Transition,* ed. Joseph Tulchin and Andrew D. Selee (Boulder, Colo.: Lynne Rienner, 2002), 179–214; Edna Jaime, "Fox's Economic Agenda: An Incomplete Transition," in *Mexico Under Fox,* ed. Luis Rubio and Susan Kaufman Purcell (Boulder, Colo.: Lynne Rienner, 2004), 35–64; Lourdes Rocha, "Competition Between Mexico and China in the U.S. Import Market for Manufacturers," *Review of the Economic Situation of Mexico* (April 2003), 162–70; and Sergio Sarmiento, "Mexico Alert, NAFTA and Mexico's Agriculture," *Hemisphere Focus* 9 (March 4, 2003).

36. For various analyses of the results, see Edgar W. Butler and Jorge A. Bustamante, eds., *Sucesión Presidencial: The 1988 Mexican Presidential Election* (Boulder, Colo.: Westview Press, 1991).

37. Roderic Ai Camp, "Mexico's 1988 Elections: A Turning Point for Its Political Development and Foreign Relations," in *Sucesión Presidencial: The 1988 Mexican Presidential Elections,* eds. Edgar W. Butler and Jorge A. Bustamante (Boulder, Colo.: Westview Press, 1990), 104–8.

38. For interesting insights into the issue of leadership, from the point of view of a Mexican intellectual, see Federico Reyes Heroles, "De la debilidad al liderazgo," *Este País,* September 1991, 3–10.

39. Pamela K. Starr, "Monetary Mismanagement and Inadvertent Democratization in Technocratic Mexico," *Studies in Comparative International Development* (Winter 1999), 35–65, provides the most insightful analysis of the interrelationship between economic and political liberalization from Salinas through Zedillo.

40. Víctor A. Espinoza Valle, "The New Federalism and Institutional Change in Mexico," *Enfoque*, (Fall 1996), 13.

41. The best case study is that of Chihuahua. See Victoria E. Rodríguez and Peter M. Ward, *Policymaking, Politics, and Urban Governance in Chihuahua: The Experience of Recent PANista Governments* (Austin: LBJ School of Public Affairs, University of Texas, 1992); and their more comprehensive work, especially Part 3, *Opposition Government in Mexico* (Albuquerque: University of New Mexico Press, 1994).

42. Carlos Vigueras, "Juárez Charges Own Border Tolls," *El Financiero International*, (April 16, 1995), 1.

43. "Un grupo de gobernadores pide que le transfieran recursos contra la pobreza," *La Jornada*, November 10, 2000. The system as of 2000 was the following: 20 percent of annual federal tax revenues are distributed to the states; 45 percent of it based on the state's proportion of the total population, 45 percent according to the proportion of taxes the individual state actually generates, and 10 percent allocated for balancing out inequities. Many state officials would like to take charge of collecting the taxes directly, rather than permitting the federal government to be in charge of the revenue collecting and distribution process. See "Local Taxation Dwarfed by Federation," *El Financiero International*, (November 1, 1999), 6.

44. Terry Lynn Karl, "Dilemmas of Democratization in Latin America," *Comparative Politics*, 23 (October 1990), 2–3; David Llehmann, *Democracy and Development in Latin America: Economics, Politics and Religion in the Postwar Period* (Philadelphia: Temple University Press, 1990), 206.

45. Richard Snyder makes this same point, concluding that "rather than leading to efficient allocation of resources by market forces, decentralizing reforms in places with powerful oligarchies may instead yield reregulated markets that generate monopoly rents for local elites. This finding challenges facile equations of decentralization with participatory governance that are common in the development literature." See his "After Neoliberalism, the Politics of Reregulation in Mexico," *World Politics* 51 (January 1999), 204.

46. House Committee on Foreign Affairs, *Hearing Before the Subcommittee on Human Rights and International Organizations, and on Western Hemisphere Affairs, September 12, 1990* (Washington, D.C.: GPO, 31).

47. Bimsa, "Derechos Humanos, Encuesta nacional trimestral de opinión pública," November 2004, 1000 interviews, November 5–10, 2004, +/–3.5 percent margin of error.

48. John Bailey and Roy Godson, *Organized Crime & Democratic Governability: Mexico and the U.S.–Mexican Borderlands* (Pittsburgh: University of Pittsburgh Press, 2000), 222.

49. Stephen D. Morris, "Political Corruption in Mexico: A Comparative State-

Level Analysis," paper presented as the Latin American Studies Association Meeting, Dallas, Texas, March 2003, 13–14.

50. Stephen D. Morris, *Corruption and Politics in Contemporary Mexico* (Tuscaloosa: University of Alabama Press, 1991), 103. Morris provides the most detailed analysis of corruption and politics in print. John Bailey and Roy Godson bring much of his substantive analysis up to date in *Organized Crime and Democratic Governability.* The best case study is Hans K. Hansen, "Government Mismanagement and Symbolic Violence: Discourses on Corruption in the Yucatán of the 1990's," *Bulletin of Latin American Research,* 17, no. 3 (September 1998), 367–386, who concludes that impunity is probably the most influential variable in perpetuating corruption. See also "La cultura del soborno y el conflicto en Pemex," *Este País* (November 2002), 48–49.

51. Andrés Albo, "Law on Transparency and Access to Information," *Review of the Economic Situation of Mexico* (May 2002), 195–96.

52. "Socio-Political Indicators: Insecurity," *Review of the Economic Situation of Mexico* (February 2003) 82–85 and (June 2002), 248–50; Consulta Mitofsky, "Uno de cada siete hogares ha sido víctima de algún delito," January 2005, www.consultamitofsky.com.mx.; Bimsa, "Encuesta telefónica: marcha contra la delincuencia," June 2004; and Maricarmen Hernández, "Democracy in Times of Insecurity," paper presented at the Latin American Studies Association, Las Vegas Nevada, October 2004.

53. Sam Dillon, "Mexico's Troubadors Turn From Amor to Drugs," *The New York Times,* February 19, 1999, www.nytimes.com.

54. Sebastian Rotella, *Twilight on the Line: Underworlds and Politics at the Mexican Border* (New York: Norton, 1997).

55. Douglas Payne, "Drugs into Money into Power: A Global Challenge," *Freedom Review* 27 (August 1996), 84.

56. One of the most informative and pragmatic discussions of the linkage between economic reform and political practices is presented in Luis Rubio, *The Mexican Democratic Quandary* (New York: Salomon Brothers, 1994), 40–43. The best comparative study is that by Judith Gentleman and Voytek Zubek, "International Integration and Democratic Development: The Cases of Poland and Mexico," *Journal of Inter-American Studies and World Affairs* 34 (Spring 1992): 59–109; and the excellent Juan D. Lindau and Timothy Cheek, eds., *Market Economics & Political Change: Comparing China and Mexico* (Lanham: Rowman & Littlefield, 1998).

57. Delal Baer, "Misreading Mexico," *Foreign Policy* (Fall 1997), 138–50.

58. For analyses of Fox's failures at the mid-point of his administration, see Chappell Lawson, "Fox's Mexico at Midterm," *Journal of Democracy* 15, no 1 (January 2004): 139–53; Carol Wise, "Mexico's Democratic Transition: The Search for New Reform Coalitions," in *Post-Stabilization Politics in Latin America,* ed. Carol Wise and Riordan Roett (Washington, D.C.: Brookings Institution Press, 2003); and Denise Dresser, "Mexico from PRI Predominance to Divided Democracy," in *Constructing Democratic Governance in Latin America,* ed. Jorge Domínguez and Michael Shifter (Baltimore: Johns Hopkins University Press, 2003), 321–437.

59. See Héctor Tobar, "Latin America Losing Faith in Democracy," *Los Angeles Times*, April 22, 2004, A3; and Alejandro Moreno and Patricia Méndez, "Attitudes Toward Democracy: Mexico in Comparative Perspective," *International Journal of Comparative Sociology* 43, no. 3–5 (2004): 350–67.

60. Eighty-one percent of the children in this age group said their vote counted, 75 percent thought democracy a good thing, 60 percent believe democracy is the best form of government, and 60 percent thought Mexico actually was a democracy. See the encuestas website, *Reforma,* reforma.com.mx. Poll was taken April 7 to 17, 2000, of 506 children nationally, +/– 4.5 percent margin of error.

Bibliographic Essay

For the student initially exploring Mexican politics, a voluminous literature exists in both Spanish and English. The purpose of this essay, however, is only to list sources that can lead to more detailed analyses for the general reader. Most of these sources are those readily available, generally in English, and published in the last decade.

For Latin American politics and Mexican politics specifically, an excellent place to start is David W. Dent, *Handbook of Political Science Research on Latin America, Trends from the 1960s to the 1990s* (Westport, Conn.: Greenwood Press, 1990), which includes chapters on various countries, several thematic topics, and two chapters on Mexico covering domestic and international affairs. For a more complete survey of recent material on Mexico, in all languages, with brief annotations, see my "Government and Politics, Mexico," in vol. 59 of *Handbook of Latin American Studies: Social Sciences*, ed. Lawrence Boudon (Austin: University of Texas Press, 2003), 429–54, as well as previous volumes. The *Handbook* is now accessible through CD-ROM at many research libraries, or on the internet at the Library of Congress, at www.lcweb2.loc.gov/hlas.

There also are some excellent broad surveys of various facets of Mexican politics, decision making, and political economy. Unfortunately, most of these monographs predate Fox's victory, and consequently, must be read with this limitation in mind. A good first source is Vikram K. Chand, *Mexico's Political Awakening* (Notre Dame: University of Notre Dame Press, 2001), which provides an overview up to but not including Fox's election. A helpful exploration of institutional decision-making is John Bailey, *Governing Mexico, the Statecraft of Crisis Management* (New York: St. Martin's Press, 1988), which examines the administrative and structural capabilities of the party and the state in the context of recent reforms. For a broad political, social, and economic overview, the best general survey is Daniel Levy and Kathleen Bruhn, *Mexico, The Struggle for Democratic Development*

(Berkeley: University of California Press, 2001), which also focuses on Mexico's relationship with the United States, providing a joint Mexican and North American interpretation. George Grayson offers a less in-depth appraisal, with a corporatist flavor, in *Mexico, From Corporatism to Pluralism?* (New York: Harcourt Brace, 1998). A view from a political-economic perspective can be found in Julie A. Erfani, *The Paradox of the Mexican State, Rereading Sovereignty from Independence to NAFTA* (Boulder, Colo.: Lynne Rienner, 1995), which concentrates on the evolution of the state.

Several edited collections provide recent, up-to-date interpretations of developments since the 1988 presidential election. These include Wayne A. Cornelius, Judith Gentleman, and Peter H. Smith, eds., *Mexico's Alternative Political Futures* (La Jolla, Calif.: Center for U.S.–Mexican Studies, UCSD, 1989); Maria Lorena Cook, Kevin J. Middlebrook, and Juan Molinar, eds., *The Politics of Economic Restructuring, State–Society Relations and Regime Change in Mexico* (La Jolla, Calif.: Center for U.S.–Mexican Studies, UCSD, 1994); Wayne A. Cornelius, Ann L. Craig, and Jonathan Fox, eds., *Transforming State–Society Relations in Mexico, the National Solidarity Strategy* (La Jolla, Calif.: Center for U.S.–Mexican Studies, UCSD, 1994); Wayne A. Cornelius, Todd A. Eisenstadt, and Jane Hindley, eds., *Subnational Politics and Democratization in Mexico* (La Jolla, Calif.: Center for U.S.–Mexican Studies, UCSD, 1999); Kevin Middlebrook, ed., *Dilemmas of Political Change in Mexico* (La Jolla, Calif.: Center for U.S.–Mexican Studies UCSD, 2004); Joseph Tulchin and Andrew D. Selee, eds., *Mexico's Politics and Society in Transition* (Boulder, Colo.: Lynne Rienner, 2002); Russell Crandall, Guadalupe Paz, and Riordan Roett, eds., *Mexico's Democracy at Work* (Boulder, Colo.: Lynne Rienner, 2004); Luis Rubio and Susan Kaufman Purcell, eds., *Mexico Under Fox* (Boulder, Colo.: Lynne Rienner, 2004); and Armand B. Peschard-Sverdrup and Sara R. Rioff, eds., *Mexican Governance, From Single-Party Rule to Divided Government* (Washington, D.C.: CSIS, 2005). These works contain some of the best interpretative essays on recent Mexico by North American and Mexican scholars.

The most extensive recent comparative analysis of Mexico and another country is that of China and Mexico, found in Juan D. Lindau and Timothy Cheek, eds., *Market Economics & Political Change: Comparing China and Mexico* (Lanham: Rowman & Littlefield, 1999). For more focused comparisons see an excellent work on labor by Karen E. Joyner, "Labor and Development in Poland and Mexico" (Master's thesis, Tulane University, 1993); and Edward L. Gibson, *The Populist Road to Market Reform: Policy and Electoral Coalitions in Argentina and Mexico* (Buenos Aires: Universidad Torcuato Di Tella, 1996). Of course, various edited collections include Mexico as part of a larger regional approach. Among the best are Daniel Levy and Kathleen Bruhn, "Mexico: Sustained Civilian Rule and the Question of

Democracy," in *Democracy in Developing Countries: Latin America,* 2nd edition, ed. Larry Diamond, Seymour Martin Lipset, Juan Linz, and Jonathan Hartlyn (Boulder, Colo.: Lynne Rienner, 1998); Alan Knight, "The Modern Mexican State," in *The Other Mirror,* ed. Miguel Centeño and Fernando López-Alves (Princeton: Princeton University Press, 2000); Carol Wise, "Mexico's Democratic Transition: The Search for New Reform Coalitions," in *Post-Stabilization Politics in Latin America,* ed. Carol Wise and Riordan Roett (Washington, D.C.: Brookings Institution Press, 2003); and Denise Dresser, "Mexico from PRI Predominance to Divided Democracy," in *Constructing Democratic Governance in Latin America,* ed. Jorge Domínguez and Michael Shifter (Baltimore: Johns Hopkins University Press, 2003), 321–437.

The historical literature on Mexico is extensive and detailed, although there are gaps for many topics and periods. The best comprehensive survey of Mexican history is that by Michael Meyer, William L. Sherman, and Susan M. Deeds, *The Course of Mexican History,* 7th ed. (New York: Oxford University Press, 2003), which lists readings for various periods and subjects, many of them classics. The most recent collection is Michael C. Meyer and William H. Beezley, eds., *The Oxford History of Mexico* (New York: Oxford University Press, 2000). A Mexican perspective is available in Héctor Aguilar Camín and Lorenzo Meyer, *In the Shadow of the Mexican Revolution, Contemporary Mexican History, 1910–1989* (Austin: University of Texas Press, 1993), and Enrique Krauze, *Mexico, Biography of Power: A History of Modern Mexico, 1810–1996* (New York: Harper Collins, 1997). For a historical survey focusing on popular culture and the perspective of the masses, see Colin MacLachlan and William H. Beezley, *El Gran Pueblo, A History of Greater Mexico* (Englewood Cliffs, N.J.: Prentice-Hall, 1994). Colin M. MacLachlan provides a broad overview of political characteristics stemming from the colonial system, in *Spain's Empire in the New World* (Berkeley: University of California Press, 1991). For the late-nineteenth-century political heritage, Charles A. Hale, *The Transformation of Liberalism in Late Nineteenth Century Mexico* (Princeton, N.J.: Princeton University Press, 1989), offers helpful interpretations. From a Mexican point of view, especially for understanding the political development and the importance of culture for politics, it is helpful to read Justo Sierra, *The Political Evolution of the Mexican People* (Austin: University of Texas Press, 1969); Samuel Ramos, *Profile of Man and Culture in Mexico* (Austin: University of Texas Press, 1962); and Octavio Paz, *The Labyrinth of Solitude, Life and Thought in Mexico* (New York: Grove Press, 1961), all of which are Mexican classics.

The subject of contemporary Mexican political culture has received more attention from Mexican than from U.S. analysts. The most recent comparative study is Roderic Ai Camp, ed., *Citizen Views of Democracy in Latin*

America (Pittsburgh: University of Pittsburgh Press, 2001), comparing democratic values in Chile, Costa Rica, and Mexico. A work focusing on international linkages is that by Ronald Inglehart, Neil Nevitte, and Miguel Basáñez, *The North American Trajectory, Cultural, Economic and Political Ties Among the United States, Canada, and Mexico.* (New York: Gruyter, 1996). Several excellent works have appeared in Mexico that provide data on changing Mexican social and political values. The three most comprehensive surveys are by Alberto Hernández Medina and Luis Narro Rodríguez, eds., *Como somos los mexicanos* (Mexico City: CREA, 1987); Enrique Alduncín, *Los valores de los mexicanos* (Mexico City: Fomento Cultural Banamex, 1986); Alejandro Moreno, *Nuestros valores* (Mexico City: Banamex, 2005). A much less comprehensive update can be found in Ulises Beltrán, *Los mexicanos de los noventa* (Mexico: UNAM, 1996).

On the relationship between cultural values and democracy, a good place to begin is Ronald Inglehart, "The Renaissance of Political Culture," *American Political Science Review* 82 (November 1988): 1203–30. For some useful comparisons with Mexico, see Mitchell Seligson, "Political Culture and Democratization in Latin America," in *Latin American and Caribbean Contemporary Record,* eds. James Malloy and Eduardo A. Gamarra (New York: Holmes & Meier, 1990), A49–65; the multi-Latin American survey by Miguel Basáñez, Marta Lagos, and Tatiana Beltrán, *Reporte 1995: encuesta latino barómetro* (1996); Roderic Ai Camp, ed., *Citizen Views of Democracy in Latin America;* and Alejandro Moreno and Patricia Méndez, "Attitudes Toward Democracy: Mexico in Comparative Perspective," *International Journal of Comparative Sociology* 43, no. 3–5 (2004), 350–67. Other recent views, based on survey research and public opinion polls, can be found in Roderic Ai Camp, ed., *Polling for Democracy: Public Opinion and Political Liberalization in Mexico* (Wilmington, Del.: Scholarly Resources, 1996).

In regard to the more specific issue of how values affect partisanship, alienation, and tolerance, there is very little literature on Mexico. One major study is that by Rafael Segovia, *La politización del niño mexicano* (Mexico City: El Colegio de México, 1975), which analyzes data on Mexico City schoolchildren, offering many useful comparisons with similar studies of the United States. The most important analyses are Timothy J. Power and Mary A. Clark, "Does Trust Matter?" in *Citizen Views of Democracy in Latin America*; Joseph L. Klesner, "Legacies of Authoritarianism," in *Citizen Views of Democracy in Latin America* and Alejandro Moreno, *Democracia, actitudes políticas y conducta electoral* (Mexico: Fondo de Cultura Económica, 2003). The best general analysis of this subject is still that by Ann Craig and Wayne Cornelius, "Political Culture in Mexico, Continuities and Revisionists Interpretations," in *The Civic Culture Revisited,* ed. Gabriel Almond and Sidney Verba (Boston: Little, Brown, 1980), 325–93.

For specific groups or issues tied to political behavior, few studies are available in English or in Spanish. Excellent new interpretations of specific elections are available in Jorge I. Domínguez and James A. McCann, "Shaping Mexico's Electoral Arena: The Construction of Partisan Cleavages in the 1988 and 1991 National Elections," *American Political Science Review* 89 (March 1995): 34–48 and their *Democratizing Mexico: Public Opinion and Electoral Choices* (Baltimore: Johns Hopkins University Press, 1996), Joseph Klesner, "The 1994 Elections, Manifestation of a Divided Society?" *Mexican Studies* 11 (Winter 1995): 137–49, and his "Democratic Transition? The 1997 Mexican Elections," *PS* 30 (December 1997): 703–11. For some variables which played a role in 2000, see various essays in Jorge Domínguez and Chappell Lawson, eds., *Mexico's Pivotal 2000 Election* (Stanford: Stanford University Press, 2004). For the impact of religion, see my "The Cross in the Polling Booth: Religion, Politics, and the Laity in Mexico," *Latin American Research Review* 29 (1994): 37–68; and Charles L. Davis, "Religion and Partisan Loyalty, the Case of Catholic Workers in Mexico," *Western Political Quarterly* 45 (March 1992): 275–97. On the subject of gender, the only recent analysis specifically on this topic is that by Victoria Rodríguez, ed., *Women's Participation in Mexican Political Life* (Boulder: Westview Press, 1998).

Two recent general works are available on political recruitment: Roderic Ai Camp, *Political Recruitment Across Two Centuries, Mexico, 1884–1993* (Austin: University of Texas Press, 1995), which looks at these patterns from the time of Porfirio Díaz to the present, analyzing opposition as well as establishment politicians; and Miguel Centeno, who examines younger, lower-level technocrats in his revealing *Democracy Within Reason, Technocratic Revolution in Mexico,* 2nd edition, (University Park: Pennsylvania State University Press, 1997). For recent trends, see Roderic Ai Camp, "Camarillas in Mexican Politics, the Case of the Salinas Cabinet," *Mexican Studies* 6 (Winter 1990): 85–108; "The Zedillo Cabinet: Continuity, Change, or Revolution?" Western Hemisphere Election Studies Series (Washington, D.C.: CSIS, January 5, 1995); "Technocracy a la Mexicana, Antecedents to Democracy," in *The Politics of Expertise in Latin America,* ed. Miguel Centeno and Patricio Silva (New York: St. Martin's Press, 1997), 196–213; *Mexico's Mandarins: Crafting a Power Elite for the Twenty-First Century* (Berkeley: University of California Press, 2002); and "Political Recruitment, Governance, and Leadership, Has Democracy Made a Difference," in *Pathways to Power, Political Recruitment and Candidate Selection in Latin America* ed. Peter Siavelis and Scott Morgenstern (forthcoming).

One area in domestic politics that has received considerable attention, theoretical and substantive, is the relationship between the government and important interest sectors. For a useful historical view, set earlier in the twentieth century, see Nora Hamilton, *The Limits of State Autonomy, Post Revolutionary Mexico* (Princeton, N.J.: Princeton University Press, 1982). For an interpretation of the changes that took place in the late 1980s, see Howard J. Wiarda, "Mexico: The Unravelling of a Corporatist Regime?" *Journal of Inter-American Studies and World Affairs* 30 (Winter 1988–1989): 1–28. Important new explorations of these and related issues can be found in the Maria Lorena Cook, Keven J. Middlebrook, and Juan Molinar volume mentioned earlier, as well as in three excellent monographs, Diane E. Davis, *Urban Leviathan, Mexico City in the Twentieth Century* (Philadelphia: Temple University Press, 1994); Viviane Brachet-Marquez, *The Dynamics of Domination, State, Class, and Social Reform in Mexico, 1910–1990* (Pittsburgh: University of Pittsburgh Press, 1994); and Strom C. Thacker, *Big Business, the State, and Free Trade: Constructing Coalitions in Mexico* (Cambridge: Cambridge University Press, 2000). An insightful recent analysis is Blanca Heredia's "Clientelism in Flux: Democratization and Interest Intermediation in Contemporary Mexico," paper presented at the National Latin American Studies Association, Guadalajara, 1997.

To understand policymaking generally in Mexico prior to 2000, the best sources include John Bailey's *Governing Mexico;* and Judith A. Teichman, *Policy-making in Mexico, From Boom to Crisis* (Boston: Allen & Unwin, 1988). For specific case studies dealing with the bureaucracy, see Peter Ward, *Welfare Politics in Mexico, Papering over the Cracks* (London: Allen & Unwin, 1986); and Diane Davis, *Urban Leviathan.* For economic policy-making, Jonathan Heath, *Mexico and the Sexenio Curse* (Washington, D.C.: CSIS, 1999); and Eduardo Torres Espinosa, *Bureaucracy and Politics in Mexico* (Brookfield: Ashgate, 1999), are insightful. For decision making in new opposition-controlled settings, but at the state and local levels, see Victoria Rodríguez and Peter Ward, *Policymaking, Politics, and Urban Governance in Chihuahua, the Experience of Recent PANista Governments* (Austin: LBJ School of Public Affairs, University of Texas, 1992); their edited *Opposition Government in Mexico* (Albuquerque: University of New Mexico Press, 1994); and their *New Federalism and State Government in Mexico* (Austin: LBJ School of Public Affairs, University of Texas, 1999). For a national perspective post-2000, see Jeffrey A. Weldon, "State Reform in Mexico: Progress and Prospects," in *Mexican Governance, From Single-Party Rule to Divided Government*, ed. Armand B. Peschard and Sara R. Rioff (Washington, D.C.: CSIS Press, 2005), 27–107.

For specific groups and their relationship to the state, several studies are available. In the context of the relationship to the military, see Roderic Ai

Camp, *Mexico's Military on the Democratic Stage* (Washington, D.C.: CSIS and Praeger, 2005), especially the final chapter for a broad overview from the 1990s to the present; Stephen J. Wager, "The Mexican Army, 1940–1982: The Country Comes First" (Ph.D. diss., Stanford University, 1992), an insightful institutional analysis; Michael J. Dziedzic, "The Essence of Decision in a Hegemonic Regime: The Case of Mexico's Acquisition of a Supersonic Fighter" (Ph.D. diss., University of Texas at Austin, 1986), an excellent case study of Mexico's decision to acquire fighter planes from the United States; Stephen J. Wager, "The Mexican Military Approaches the 21st Century: Coping with a New World Order," *Special Report* (Carlisle, Pa.: Strategic Studies Institute, U.S. Army War College, 1994); and Roderic Ai Camp, "Mexico's Armed Forces, Marching to a Democratic Tune," in *Dilemmas of Political Change in Mexico,* ed. Kevin Middle brook (La Jolla, Calif.: Center for U.S.–Mexican Studies, UCSD, 2004). For difficult to locate data on the armed forces, see George Grayson, *Mexico's Armed Forces, A Factbook* (Washington, D.C.: CSIS, 1999).

The most comprehensive collection on the private sector is Riordan Roett, ed. *Mexico's Private Sector: Recent History, Future Challenges* (Boulder: Lynne Rienner, 1998). For business and politics, the best works on industrial groups are Strom C. Thacker, *Big Business and the State,* and Dale Story, *Industry, the State, and Public Policy in Mexico* (Austin: University of Texas Press, 1986). For the broad relationship between businesspeople and the state, see my *Entrepreneurs and the State in Twentieth Century Mexico* (New York: Oxford University Press, 1989). An excellent case study, having important theoretical implications, is Douglas C. Bennet and Kenneth E. Sharpe, *Transnational Corporations Versus the State, the Political Economy of the Mexican Auto Industry* (Princeton, N.J.: Princeton University Press, 1985). For a small business perspective, see Kenneth C. Shadlen, "Neoliberalism, Corporatism, and Small Business Political Activism in Contemporary Mexico," *Latin American Research Review* 35 (2000): 73–106. The best recent works are those of Yemile Mizrahi, on the relationship between entrepreneurs and the PAN, "A New Conservative Opposition in Mexico: The Politics of Entrepreneurs in Chihuahua (1983–1992)" (Ph.D. diss., University of California at Berkeley, 1994); Carlos Alba Vega, "Los empresarios y el estado durante el Salinismo," *Foro Internacional* 36 (January 1996): 31–79; Matilde Luna, "Entrepreneurial Interests and Political Action in Mexico," in *The Challenges of Institutional Reform in Mexico,* ed. Riordan Roett (Boulder: Lynne Rienner, 1995), 77–94; Ben Ross Schneider, "Why Is Mexican Business So Organized?" *Latin American Research Review* 37, no. 1 (2002), 77–118; and Matilde Luna, "Business and Politics in Mexico," in *Dilemmas of Political Change in Mexico,* ed. Kevin J. Middlebrook (London: Institute of Latin American Studies, University of London, 2004), 332–52.

The most neglected link in this relationship is that between church and state. The most comprehensive work is Roderic Ai Camp, *Crossing Swords: Politics and Religion in Mexico* (New York: Oxford University Press, 1997). For a Mexican view, see Roberto Blancarte, *El poder salinismo e iglesia católica, una nueva convivencia?* (Mexico City: Grijalbo, 1991); and José de Jesús Legorreta Zepeda's insightful collection, *La iglesia católica y la política en el México de hoy* (Mexico: Ibero-American University, 2000). In English, useful descriptions of this relationship are Allan Metz, "Mexican Church–State Relations Under President Carlos Salinas de Gortari," *Journal of Church and State* 34 (Winter 1992): 111–30; Roberto Blancarte, "Religion and Constitutional Change in Mexico, 1988–1992," *Social Compass* 40 (1993): 555–69; Michael Tangeman, *Mexico at the Crossroads, Politics, the Church, and the Poor* (Maryknoll, N.Y.: Orbis, 1995); Paul J. Bonicelli, "Testing the Waters or Opening the Floodgates? Evangelicals, Politics, and the 'New' Mexico," *Journal of Church and State* 39 (Winter 1997): 107–30; and Raúl González Schmal's excellent "The Evolving Relationship Between Church and State," in *Mexican Governance, From a Single-Party Rule to Divided Government*, ed. Armand Peschard and Sara Rioff (Washington, D.C.: CSIS Press, 2005), 230–70.

Labor's relationship to the Mexican government has received more attention than the church or the military. The best general interpretation can be found in Kevin J. Middlebrook, ed., *Unions, Workers, and the State in Mexico* (La Jolla, Calif.: Center for U.S.-Mexican Studies, UCSD, 1991), especially his introductory chapter, "State-Labor Relations in Mexico: The Changing Economic and Political Context," 1–26. A short but helpful overview is also provided in George Grayson, *The Mexican Labor Machine: Power, Politics, and Patronage* (Washington, D.C.: CSIS, 1989). The most significant theoretical examination is by Ruth Berins Collier, *The Contradictory Alliance, State-Labor Relations and Regime Change in Mexico* (Berkeley: International and Area Studies, University of California, 1992). The best case study is Maria Lorena Cook, *Organizing Dissent, Unions, the State, and the Democratic Teachers' Movement in Mexico* (University Park: Pennsylvania State University Press, 1996). For numerous changes in the 1990s and 2000s in a democratic context, see Graciela Bensusán, "A New Scenario for Mexican Trade Unions: Changes in the Structure of Political and Economic Opportunities," in *Dilemmas of Political Change in Mexico*, ed. Kevin J. Middlebrook (London: Institute of Latin American Studies, University of London, 2004), 237–85; and Katrina Burgess, "Mexican Labor at a Crossroads," in *Mexico's Politics and Society in Transition*, ed. Joseph S. Tulchin and Andrew D. Selee (Boulder, Colo.: Lynne Rienner, 2003), 73–108.

The other group whose relationship is analyzed is intellectuals, a more amorphous sector institutionally. Various studies explore the development and contributions of individual intellectual groups, especially writers, but the literature is sparse on the issue of broad intellectual–state relationships. For background, see Roderic Ai Camp, *Intellectuals and the State in Twentieth Century Mexico* (Austin: University of Texas Press, 1985). For recent trends under Fox, Yvon Grenier's "Octavio Paz and the Changing Role of Intellectuals in Mexico," *Discourse* (Spring 2001): 124–143, provides helpful insights. For an important analysis of dissent in Mexico, see Evelyn P. Stevens, *Protest and Response in Mexico* (Cambridge, Mass.: MIT Press, 1974). Dissenting groups, in the form of nongovernmental organizations and popular organizations, are discussed in Joe Foweraker and Ann L. Craig, eds., *Popular Movements and Political Change in Mexico* (Boulder, Colo.: Lynne Rienner, 1990); Douglas A. Chalmers and Kerianne Piester, "Non-governmental Organizations and the Changing Structure of Mexican Politics," in *Changing Structure of Mexico: Political, Social, and Economic Prospects,* ed. Laura Randall (New York: M.E. Sharpe, 1996), 253–61; and Katherine M. Bailey, "Civic NGOs in Mexican Politics: A New Democratizing Force" (Masters thesis, Tulane University, 1998).

Probably no topic on Mexican politics has generated more literature, but few serious, objective analyses, than armed movements. For the EZLN, the most useful works include Thomas Benjamin, *A Rich Land, a Poor People: Politics and Society in Modern Chiapas* (Albuquerque: University of New Mexico Press, 1989); Tom Barry, *Zapata's Revenge: Free Trade and the Farm Crisis in Mexico* (Boston: South End Press, 1995); George A. Collier, "The New Politics of Exclusion: Antecedents to the Rebellion in Mexico," *Dialectical Anthropology* 19 (May 1994): 1–44; and Joseph M. Whitmeyer and Rosemary L. Hopcroft, "Community, Capitalism, and Rebellion in Chiapas," *Sociological Perspective* 39 (Winter 1996): 517–38. John Womack, Jr., has also compiled an excellent reader, *Rebellion in Chiapas* (New York: The New Press, 1999). A sense of the existence and activities of other armed groups, including the ERP, can be obtained from Gustavo Hirales Morán, "Radical Groups in Mexico Today," Policy Papers on the Americas, Center for Strategic and International Studies, Washington, D.C., September 2003.

A group which demands increasing analysis, both at the elite and the mass level, is that of women. Women not only have been essential in the rapid expansion of NGOs, but have increased their presence among the three major parties. The most comprehensive books available to date are Victoria E. Rodríguez, ed., *Women's Participation in Mexican Political Life* (Boulder, Colo.: Lynne Rienner, 1998), and Anna M. Fernández Poncela, ed., *Par-*

ticipación política: las mujeres en México al final del mileneo (Mexico: Colegio de México, 1995). For potential political consequences since 2000, see Roderic Ai Camp and Keith Yanner, "Democracy Across Cultures, Does Gender Make a Difference?" In *Citizenship in Latin America*, ed. Joseph S. Tulchin and Meg Ruthenburg (Boulder, Colo.: Lynne Rienner, 2006); Lisa Baldez, "Elected Bodies: The Gender Quota Law for Legislative Candidates in Mexico," *Legislative Studies Quarterly* 29 May 2004): 231–58; and María del Carmen, "Women and Politics," *Voices of Mexico* 56 (July–September 2001): 7–11. The most comprehensive historical account is Anna M. Fernández Poncela's "La historia de la participación política de las mujeres en México en el último medio siglo," *Boletín Americano* 36, (1996): 111–23. For the importance of feminism generally, see Marta Lamas et al., "Building Bridges: The Growth of Popular Feminism in Mexico," in *The Challenge of Local Feminisms: Women's Movements in Global Perspective* (Boulder, Colo.: Westview, 1995), 324–47. An excellent case study of a feminist public policy issue can be found in Linda S. Stevenson, "Gender Politics in the Mexican Democratization Process: Sex Crimes, Affirmative Action for Women, and the 1997 Elections," paper presented at the David Rockefeller Center for Latin American Studies, Harvard University, Cambridge, 1997. It appeared in Spanish in *Estudios Sociológicos* 17 (May–August 1999), 519–558.

The branches of government and their relationship to the policymaking process have been neglected in the literature on Mexican politics. There is renewed interest in Mexico's legislature, and the most comprehensive studies are Luis Carlos Ugalde, *The Mexican Congress, Old Player, New Power* (Washington, D.C.: CSIS, 2000); Alonso Lujambio *El poder compartido* (Mexico: Oceano, 2000); and Alonso Lujambio, *Federalismo y Congreso en el cambio político de México* (Mexico: UNAM, 1995). Some of the best work on its inner workings are Jeffrey A. Weldon, in his previously cited "State Reform in Mexico: Progress and Prospects," as well as his regular series for CSIS, and the work of Benito Nacif, "Congress Proposes and the President Disposes: The New Relationship Between the Executive and Legislative Branches in Mexico," in *Mexican Governance, From Single-Party Rule to Divided Government* (Washington, D.C.: CSIS Press, 2005), 1–26, and "La no reelección legislativa: disciplina de partido y subordinación al Ejecutivo en la Cámara de Diputados de México," *Diálogo Debate* 1 (July–September 1997): 149–167.

Much new work has appeared on the judicial branch, specifically the Supreme Court, beginning with Pilar Domingo, "Democratization Without Separation of Powers? The Case of the Mexican Supreme Court," paper presented at the Latin American Studies Association, Washington, D.C., 1995, and her "Judicial Independence: The Politics of the Supreme Court of Mexico," *Journal of Latin American Studies* 32 (2000): 705–35; Julio Ríos-Figueroa, "A Minimum Condition for the Judiciary to Become an Effective Power, The Mexican Supreme Court, 1994–2002," paper presented at the Midwest Political Science Association meeting, Chicago, Illinois, April 15–18, 2004; Rosa María Mirón Lince, "El PRI post-hegemónico: liderazgos y decisiones en el Congreso," paper presented at the Latin American Studies Association, Las Vegas, Nevada, October 7–9, 2004; and Jodi Finkel, "Supreme Court Decisions on Electoral Rules After Mexico's Judicial Reform: An Empowered Court," *Journal of Latin American Studies* 35 (2003): 777–99.

Political parties continue to attract attention in the literature, but usually in an electoral context. The most comprehensive, up-to-date survey of the pre-2000 opposition role can be found in the previously mentioned *Opposition Government in Mexico,* edited by Victoria Rodriguez and Peter Ward. For the National Action Party, the best institutional analysis remains Donald Mabry's *Mexico's Acción Nacional: A Catholic Alternative to Revolution* (Syracuse, N.Y.: Syracuse University Press, 1973). Several outstanding works on PAN analyze different perspectives on its evolution during the competitive 1990s and 2000s. They include two major studies: Yemile Mizrahi, *From Martydom to Power, The Partido Acción Nacional in Mexico* (Notre Dame: University of Notre Dame Press, 2003); and David A. Shirk, *Mexico's New Politics, the PAN and Democratic Change* (Boulder, Colo.: Lynne Rienner, 2005). The PRD has not received adequate treatment because of its recent origins. However, for some views of the Democratic Revolutionary Party through its leadership, see Jesús Galindo López, "A Conversation with Cuauhtémoc Cárdenas," *Journal of International Affairs* 43 (Winter 1990): 395–406; and Carlos B. Gil, *Hope and Frustration, Interviews with Leaders of Mexico's Political Opposition* (Wilmington, Del.: Scholarly Resources, 1992). The best analytical work is Kathleen Bruhn, *Taking on Goliath: The Emergence of a New Left Party and the Struggle for Democracy in Mexico* (University Park: Pennsylvania State University Press, 1997). PRI has not been the subject of a serious analysis since the 1980s. A detailed essay that provides recent insights is Nikki Craske's *Corporatism Revisited: Salinas and the Reform of the Popular Sector* (London: Institute of Latin American Studies, 1994). For all three parties, Ann Craig and Wayne Cornelius offer useful conclusions in "House Divided: Parties and Political Reform in Mexico," in *Building Democratic Institutions: Party Systems in Latin America,* ed. Scott Mainwaring and Timothy R. Scully (Stanford: Stanford University Press, 1995), 249–97; and Todd A. Eisenstadt's superb insights into their political behavior in *Courting Democracy in Mexico, Party Strategies and Electoral Institutions* (Cambridge: Cambridge University Press, 2004).

Analyses of elections, election data, and the 1988, 1991, 1994, and 1997 elections specifically abound. Some of the better work in English can be found in Cornelius et al., *Mexico's Alternative Political Futures;* and Edgar W. Butler and Jorge A. Bustamante, *Sucesión Presidencial, the 1988 Mexican Presidential Election* (Boulder, Colo.: Westview Press, 1991), the most detailed examination in English of this benchmark election. A more comprehensive analysis leading up to 1988 is Joseph A. Klesner, "Electoral Reform in an Authoritarian Regime: The Case of Mexico" (Ph.D. diss., MIT, 1988). For a post-1988 analysis, see Keith Yanner, "Democratization in Mexico, 1988–1991" (Ph.D. diss., Washington University, 1992); and Juan Molinar Horcasitas, *El tiempo de la legitimidad, elecciones, autoritarismo y democracia en México* (Mexico City: Cal y Arena, 1991). For the 1991 elections and comparisons between 1988 and 1991, see the excellent work by Jorge Domínguez and James McCann, *Democratizing Mexico: Public Opinion and Electoral Choices* (Baltimore: The Johns Hopkins University Press, 1996); and Joseph Klesner, "Realignment or Dealignment? Consequences of Economic Crisis and Restructuring for the Mexican Party System," in *The Politics of Economic Restructuring,* eds. Cook, Middlebrook, and Molinar, 159–94. For 1994, see Joseph Klesner, "The 1994 Elections, Manifestation of a Divided Society?"; and John Bailey, *The 1994 Mexican Presidential Election Post-Election Report,* Election Studies Series (Washington, D.C.: CSIS, 1994). For 1997, see Armand Peschard-Sverdrup, *The 1997 Mexican Midterm Elections, Post-Election Report,* Western Hemisphere Election Study Series (Washington, D.C.: CSIS, 1997), and Jorge I. Domínguez and Alejandro Poiré, *Toward Mexico's Democratization: Parties, Campaigns, Elections, and Public Opinion* (London: Routledge, 1998). The 2000 election is best described in Joseph Klesner, *The 2000 Mexican Presidential and Congressional Elections: Pre-Election Report* (Washington, D.C.: CSIS, 2000). A comprehensive analysis of why Fox won is provided in Jorge Domínguez and Chappell Lawson, eds., *Mexico's Pivotal 2000 Elections* (Stanford: Stanford University Press, 2003); and Alejandro Moreno, *El votante mexicano: democracia, actitudes políticas y conducta electoral* (Mexico: Fondo de Cultura Económica, 2003).

Political and economic liberalization have received considerable attention since 1987, especially after Salinas's first year in office. A broad, theoretical context can be found in Terry Lynn Karl, "Dilemmas of Democratization in Latin America," *Comparative Politics* 23 (October 1990): 1–21. For highly critical views of Salinas's and Zedillo's political failures, see Andrew Reding's essays, for example, "Mexico Under Salinas: A Facade of Reform,"

World Policy Journal 6 (Fall 1989): 685–729, or "Facing Political Reality in Mexico," *The Washington Quarterly* 20, (1997): 103–16. For more balanced assessments, see John Bailey and Leopoldo Gómez, "The PRI and Liberalization in Mexico," *Journal of International Affairs* 43 (Winter 1990): 291–312; Riordan Roett, ed., *The Politics of Economic Liberalization in Mexico* (Boulder, Colo.: Westview Press, 1992); and Riordan Roett, *The Challenge of Institutional Reform in Mexico* (Boulder: Lynne Rienner, 1995), all of which combine Mexican and North American interpretations. Another helpful interpretation is Robert A. Pastor, "Post-Revolutionary Mexico: the Salinas Opening," *Journal of Inter-American Studies and World Affairs* 32 (Fall 1990): 1–22. For the post-2000 period under Fox, see the previously cited collections by Tulchin and Selee, *Mexico's Politics and Society in Transition*; Crandall, Paz, and Roett, *Mexico's Democracy at Work*, Rubio and Purcell, *Mexico Under Fox*; and Peschard Sverdrup and Sara R. Rioff, *Mexican Governance.* For a brief historical perspective on political modernization, see my "Political Modernization in Mexico, Through a Looking Glass," in *The Evolution of the Mexican Political System,* ed. Jaime Rodríguez (Wilmington, Del.: Scholarly Resources, 1993), 245–64; and Wayne A. Cornelius, "Political Liberalization in an Authoritarian Regime: Mexico, 1976–1985," in *Mexican Politics in Transition,* ed. Judith Gentleman (Boulder, Colo.: Westview Press, 1987), 15–47. The broad consequences of decentralization are evaluated in Victoria Rodríguez, *Decentralization in Mexico* (Boulder, Colo.: Westview, 1997).

The economic side, specifically the potential impact of NAFTA, is analyzed by Sidney Weintraub, ed., *NAFTA's Impact on North American, The First Decade* (Washington, D.C.: CSIS Press, 2004; and Ricardo Grinspun and Maxwell Cameron, eds., *The Political Economy of North American Free Trade* (New York: St. Martin's Press, 1993); and Maria Cook, Kevin Middlebrook, and Juan Molinar, eds., *The Politics of Economic Restructuring.* An insightful comparative approach is offered in Judith Gentleman and Voytek Zubek, "International Integration and Democratic Development: The Cases of Poland and Mexico," *Journal of Inter-American Studies and World Affairs* 34 (Spring 1992): 59–109; and Juan D. Lindau and Timothy Cheek, *Market Economics and Political Change: Comparing China and Mexico.* Privatization is explored by Judith A. Teichman, *Privatization and Political Change in Mexico* (Pittsburgh: University of Pittsburgh Press, 1995); and Jacques Rogozinski, *High Price for Change, Privatization in Mexico* (Washington, D.C.: IADB, 1998).

For the implications of recent changes in U.S.–Mexican relations as they relate to Mexican political development, see Bilateral Commission on the Future of United States–Mexican Relations, *Dimensions of United*

State–Mexican Relations, 5 vols. (La Jolla, Calif.: Center for U.S.–Mexican Studies, UCSD, 1989); and Riordan Roett, ed., *Mexico's External Relations in the 1990s* (Boulder, Calif.: Lynne Rienner, 1991), especially Part 4. Insightful recommendations for the Fox-Bush era are provided in *New Horizons in U.S.–Mexico Relations: Recommendations for Policymakers* (Washington, D.C.: CSIS, 2001); and Pamela Starr, "U.S.-Mexico Relations," *Hemispheric Focus* 12, no. 2 (January, 2004), 6. A broader, general interpretation is available in Tom Barry, Harry Browne, and Beth Sims, *The Great Divide, the Challenge of U.S.–Mexico Relations in the 1990s* (New York: Grove Press, 1994); Jacqueline Mazza, *Don't Disturb the Neighbors: the United States and Democracy in Mexico, 1980–1995* (New York: Routledge, 2001); and Arturo Valenzuela, *The Challenge of Mexico to U.S. Foreign Policy,* Occasional Paper Series, Overseas Development Council, Washington, D.C., June, 1997. For security concerns, see Peter Andreas, *Border Games: Policing the U.S.–Mexico Divide* (Ithaca: Cornell University Press, 2000); John Bailey and Roy Goodson, eds., *Organized Crime and Democratic Governability, Mexico and the U.S.–Mexican Borderlands* (Pittsburgh: University of Pittsburgh Press, 2000); *U.S.-Mexico Border Security and the Evolving Security Relationship, Recommendations for Policymakers* (Washington, D.C.: CSIS, 2004); and David Ronfeldt et al., *The Zapatista Social Netwar in Mexico* (Santa Monica: RAND, 1998).

To understand the economic context, see Sidney Weintraub, *NAFTA's Impact on North America, A Marriage of Convenience: Relations Between Mexico and the United States* (Oxford: Oxford University Press, 1990), and his *NAFTA: What Comes Next?* (Washington, D.C.: CSIS, 1994); as well as George Grayson, *The North American Free Trade Agreement, Regional Community and the New World Order* (Lanham, Md.: University Press of America, 1995). To understand the impact on ordinary Mexicans, see the vivid portrait, in their own words, by Judith Hellman, *Mexican Lives* (New York: New Press, 1994). For the U.S. view of Mexico, see Sergio Aguayo, *Myths and (Mis) Perceptions: Changing U.S. Elite Visions of Mexico* (La Jolla, Calif.: Center for U.S.–Mexican Studies, UCSD, 1998), and *Global Views 2004, Comparing Mexican and American Public Opinion and Foreign Policy* (Chicago: Chicago Council on Foreign Relations, 2004). The most imaginative and speculative interpretation of Mexico's future as part of global economic and noneconomic trends is Michael J. Mazarr, *Mexico 2005: The Challenges of the New Millennium* (Washington, D.C.: CSIS, 1999).

Finally, on the issue of human rights and corruption, Stephen D. Morris, *Corruption and Politics in Contemporary Mexico* (Tuscaloosa: University of Alabama Press, 1991), is the only book-length work to wrestle with this topic in Mexican politics. He has updated his views in Stephen D. Morris, "Political Corruption in Mexico: A Comparative State-Level Analysis," paper presented at the Latin American Studies Association Meeting, Dallas, Texas, March 2003, 13–14. For a comparative exploration, see Roderic Ai Camp, Charley Davis, and Kenneth Coleman, "The Influence of Party Systems on Citizens' Perceptions of Corruption and Electoral Response in Latin America," *Comparative Political Studies* 37, no. 6 (August, 2004): 677–703. To understand the influence of drugs, a good place to begin is Douglas W. Payne, "Drugs into Money into Power," *Freedom Review* 27 (July–August, 1996), 9–104. For the best case study, see Sebastian Rotella, *Twilight on the Line: Underworlds and Politics at the Mexican Border* (New York: Norton, 1997). Human rights continue to be neglected from an analytical point of view, but the recent publications of international and national human rights organizations provide some first-hand data on the Mexican situation. Among the most useful are the Human Rights Watch Americas reports, especially *Human Rights in Mexico, a Policy of Impunity* (June 1990); *Unceasing Abuses, Human Rights in Mexico One Year After the Introduction of Reform* (September 1991); *Implausible Deniability: State Responsibility for Rural Violence in Mexico* (April 1997); and *Systemic Injustice: Torture, "Disappearance," and Extrajudicial Execution in Mexico* (January 1999); Minnesota Advocates for Human Rights, *Harassment of Human Rights Defenders in Mexico* (August 1994), *Stifling Human Rights Advocacy in Mexico* (May 1994), *The Mexican Coordination of National Public Security* (June 1994); Andrew Reding, *Democracy and Human Rights in Mexico* (New York: World Policy Institute, 1995); Inter-American Commission on Human Rights, *Report on the Situation of Human Rights in Mexico* (September 1998); and Bimsa, "Derechos Humanos, Encuesta nacional trimestral de opinión pública," November 2004, 1000 interviews, November 5–10, 2004, +/–3.5 percent margin of error. The most comprehensive, analytical view is Edward L. Cleary, "Human Rights Organizations in Mexico: Growth in Turbulence," *Journal of Church and State* 37, no. 4 (Autumn 1995), 793–812. For regular updates monthly, see *Guión,* a publication of the independent Comisión Mexicana de Defensa y Promoción de los Derechos Humanos.

The Internet has become a useful tool for Mexican research, primarily for documentary and bibliographic searches, but also for articles in the media and leading magazines. For on-line addresses to almost every important Mexican magazine and newspaper, and to all other sources organized by category, see www.lanic.utexas.edu/la/mexico. For relevant material in the United States media, as well as related articles, see the *New York Times,* www.nytimes.com, specifically the Americas directory under contents. By far the most useful governmental documents source is that organized by

David Block of Cornell University, available at www.library.cornell.edu/colldev/adocshome1. The documents are organized by branch of government. For electoral results and parties, see politics directory at lanic site. For government agencies, see www.mexicoonline.com/mexagency. The two best sources for up-to-date articles from the Mexican media are *Reforma*, the influential, independent Mexico City daily, at www.reforma.com.mx and *Proceso*, a muckraking political weekly, at www.proceso.com.mx. Census statistics are available through www.inegi.gob.mx.

Index

A

Abortion, 149
Acción Democrática (AD), 68–69
Acteal, 166
Action of unconstitutionality law, 191
AD. *See* Acción Democrática
Adams family, 117
Advertising, 159, 160, 212, 229
Affirmative action, 96
Age
  political attitudes and, 100–102
  of PRI membership, 237
  voting behavior and, 101, 220, 223, 228, 238
Agrarian reform, 165, 178, 218, 279
Agricultural workers, 274
Aguayo, Sergio, 162
Aguilar Camín, Héctor, 45, 158
Aguilar Zinser, Adolfo, 163, 181
Alamo, 48
Albuquerque, N.M., 29
Alemán, Miguel, 112–13, 125
Alianza Cívica. See Civic Alliance
Almeida, Adalberto, 147
Almond, Gabriel, 56, 82–83, 89, 93
Alvarez, Luis H., 181
Alzate, Fausto, 135n21
Amalistas, 234
Amigos de Fox. *See* Friends of Fox
AMIS. *See* Mexican Insurance Association
Amnesty International, 291
Anahuac University, 127
Annis, Sheldon, 68
Anti-Reelectionist Party, 43
Apple industry, 261
Archbishops, 147
Archdioceses, 145–46
Argentina, 16

Arizona, 48, 257
Assassinations, 6, 141, 181, 248, 294
  of Colosio, 60, 165, 210
  of Madero, 48
  of Obregón, 46
  of Ochoa, 164
Atheism, 82, 90
Attorney General of the Republic, 144, 178, 180, 191, 248, 292
Audiencia, 31
Austerity program, 3, 60, 68, 152, 212, 274, 281, 287
Authentic Party of the Mexican Revolution (PARM), 207
Authoritarianism, 6, 39, 50, 94, 236. *See also* Semi-authoritarianism
  age-related attitudes toward, 100
  in comparative context, 10
  conservatism and, 34
  continuing influence of, 14
  corruption associated with, 250–51
  under Díaz, 41
  under Spanish colonialism, 31, 41
Autonomous Technological Institute of Mexico (ITAM), 115, 127, 157
Avila Camacho, Manuel, 139
Azteca chain, 159
Aztec empire, 27

B

Baby boomers, 220
Baja California, 48, 210, 215, 217, 231, 232
Baldez, Lisa, 96
Banco Unión, 191
Bankers Club, 151
Bank of Mexico, 114, 131, 179

319